Routledge Revivals

God, Literature and Process Thought

Originally published in 2002 *God, Literature and Process Thought* looks at the use of God in writing, as a part of the creative advance, immersed in the processes of reality and affected by events in the world. This edited collection outlines and promotes the novel view that there is much to be gained when those who value the insights of process thought 'encounter' the many and varied writers of literature and literary theory. It also celebrates the notion of *process poesis*, a fresh way of reflecting theologically and philosophically that takes account of literary forms and promises to transform creatively the very structure of process thought today.

God, Literature and Process Thought

by Darren J.N. Middleton

First published in 2002
by Ashgate Publishing

This edition first published in 2018 by Routledge
2 Park Square, Milton Park, Abingdon, Oxon, OX14 4RN
and by Routledge
711 Third Avenue, New York, NY 10017

Routledge is an imprint of the Taylor & Francis Group, an informa business

© 2002 Daniel J.N. Middleton

All rights reserved. No part of this book may be reprinted or reproduced or utilised in any form or by any electronic, mechanical, or other means, now known or hereafter invented, including photocopying and recording, or in any information storage or retrieval system, without permission in writing from the publishers.

Publisher's Note
The publisher has gone to great lengths to ensure the quality of this reprint but points out that some imperfections in the original copies may be apparent.

Disclaimer
The publisher has made every effort to trace copyright holders and welcomes correspondence from those they have been unable to contact.

A Library of Congress record exists under LCCN: 2001045993

ISBN 13: 978-1-138-54189-4 (hbk)
ISBN 13: 978-1-351-00992-8 (ebk)
ISBN 13: 978-1-138-54195-5 (pbk)

God, Literature and Process Thought

Edited by
Darren J.N. Middleton
Texas Christian University, Fort Worth, Texas, USA

Ashgate

For David Jasper, David A. Pailin and Maurice F. Wiles
Teachers and Friends

© Darren J.N. Middleton, 2002

All rights reserved. No part of this publication may be reproduced, stored in a retrieval system, or transmitted in any form or by any means, electronic, mechanical, photocopying, recording, or otherwise without the prior permission of the publisher.

The author has asserted his moral right under the Copyright, Designs and Patents Act, 1988, to be identified as the author of this work.

Published by
Ashgate Publishing Limited
Gower House
Croft Road
Aldershot
Hants GU11 3HR
England

Ashgate Publishing Company
131 Main Street
Burlington, VT 05401-5600 USA

Ashgate website: http://www.ashgate.com

British Library Cataloguing in Publication Data
God, literature and process thought
   1. Theology in literature   2. Process theology
   I. Middleton, Darren, 1966–
230'.046

Library of Congress Cataloging-in-Publication Data
God, literature and process thought / edited by Darren Middleton.
       p.   cm.
Includes bibliographical references and index.
ISBN 0-7546-0545-0
1. Religion and literature.   2. Process theology.
I. Middleton, Darren, 1966–

PN49 .G62 2002
809'.93382--dc21   2001045993

ISBN 0 7546 0545 0

Typeset in Times Roman by N²productions

Contents

Notes on the Contributors	vii
Introduction: Literary Art and Relationality *Darren J.N. Middleton*	1

PART I   PROCESS THOUGHT AND LITERARY THEORY

1 Reading in the Modern Wake *Andrew W. Hass*	13
2 Derrida and Whitehead *Timothy Mooney*	29
3 Concretizing Concrete Experience *Santiago Sia*	47
4 Whitehead's Hermeneutical Cosmology *René P.H. Munnik*	63

PART II   PROCESS THOUGHT AND LITERATURE

5 Suffering and Surrender in the Midst of Divine Persuasion *Aliman Sears*	79
6 Promethean Atheism *Barry L. Whitney*	103
7 Sticky Evil: *Macbeth* and the Karma of the Equivocal *William Desmond*	133
8 Graham Greene's Teilhardian Vision *Darren Middleton*	157
9 Nikos Kazantzakis, Bergson and God *Daniel A. Dombrowski*	173
10 Jacob Boehme and the Romantic Roots of Process Thought *Lewis Owens*	191
11 Denise Levertov's Poetics of Process *Bobby Caudle Rogers*	207

PART III   PROCESS POESIS

12 A Place and a Moment: One Poem about Becoming *Christina K. Hutchins*	229
Bibliography	249
Index	259

Notes on the Contributors

William Desmond is Professor of Philosophy and Director of the International Program of Philosophy in the Higher Institute of Philosophy, Katholieke Universiteit Leuven (Louvain), Belgium. He is the author of many books, including *Ethics and the Between* (SUNY Press, 2001). His *Being and Between* (SUNY Press, 1995) won the Cardinal Mercier Award in 1995, as well as the J.N. Findlay Award of the Metaphysical Society of America for the best book in metaphysics.

Daniel A. Dombrowski is in the Philosophy Department of Seattle University, Seattle, Washington, USA. He is the author of twelve books, including *Kazantzakis and God* (SUNY Press, 1997) and *Rawls and Religion* (SUNY Press, 2001), as well as over a hundred articles in scholarly journals in philosophy and theology.

Andrew W. Hass is Lecturer in Religion and Literature at the Honors College of the University of Houston, Houston, Texas, USA. An editor of the journal *Literature and Theology*, he has published in the specialized area of contemporary critical theory and hermeneutics, and in the general crossover between religion, theology, philosophy and the arts.

Christina K. Hutchins is a PhD candidate in Interdisciplinary Studies at the Graduate Theological Union, adjunct faculty at Pacific School of Religion, Berkeley, and a United Church of Christ (UCC) minister. In addition to recent essays in *Theology and Sexuality, Paideusis* and *Process and Difference* (SUNY Press, 2001), her poems appear widely in literary journals and anthologies, and in *Collecting Light* (Acacia Books, 1999).

Darren J.N. Middleton is Assistant Professor of Literature and Theology at Texas Christian University, Fort Worth, Texas, USA. He has written *Novel Theology: Nikos Kazantzakis's Encounter with Whiteheadian Process Theism* (Mercer University Press, 2000), as well as articles on religion and culture in the Caribbean.

Timothy Mooney is College Lecturer in Philosophy at University College Dublin in Ireland. His interests include phenomenology, deconstruction and process philosophy, and he has published articles in all these areas. He is also co-editor of *The Phenomenology Reader*, to be published by Routledge in 2002.

René P.H. Munnik is Radboud Professor at the University of Twente and Associate Professor in Philosophical Anthropology at Tilburg Unversity, both in the Netherlands. He has published several articles on process philosophy and on the interrelations between religion, natural science and technology.

Lewis Owens received his PhD from Cambridge University for a dissertation on the religious philosophy of the Greek writer Nikos Kazantzakis. He has had articles published on Kazantzakis in various journals and his book, *Creative Destruction: Nikos Kazantzakis and the Literature of Responsibility*, is due for publication in 2002. He currently teaches Religion and Culture in the Department of Theology and Religious Studies, Christ Church University College, Canterbury, England.

Bobby Caudle Rogers is Associate Professor of English at Union University in Jackson, Tennessee, USA. His poetry has appeared in *The Southern Review, The Georgia Review, Shenandoah, Puerto del Sol* and numerous other magazines. His essay on May Sarton was published in *A House of Gathering: Poets on May Sarton's Poetry* (University of Tennessee Press, 1993).

Aliman Sears received an MA in Philosophy from Katholieke Universiteit, Leuven (Louvain), Belgium (1999). He is currently affiliated with Chaminade University in Honolulu, Hawaii, USA, is a member of the Center for Process Studies in Claremont, California, USA, is co-editor of *Bapak's Travel Log: The Comprehensive Version* (Subud Publications International, 2001) and serves as a psychiatric social worker in Honolulu.

Santiago Sia is Professor of Philosophy at Loyola Marymount University, Los Angeles, California, USA. He has taught in universities and colleges in the Philippines, Ireland, England and Belgium. He has published extensively in process philosophy and theology, including *God in Process Thought* (Nijhoff, 1985) and *From Suffering to God* (St Martin's Press/Macmillan, 1994) and is the co-author of a novel, *The Fountain Arethuse* (The Book Guild Ltd., 1997).

Barry L. Whitney is Professor of Religious Studies at the University of Windsor, Ontario, Canada. Author of *Theodicy: An Annotated Bibliography of the Problem of Evil, 1960–1990* (Philosophy Documentation Center, 1998), he is also the editor of *Process Studies*.

Introduction: Literary Art and Relationality

Darren J.N. Middleton

Creative Writers, Process Thinkers: Some Brief Examples

Although it is true to say that the field of literature and theology is growing and becoming more sophisticated and articulate, it is equally correct to say that few scholars working in the particular area of process studies have explored the potentially fruitful exchange between process thought and creative writing. A routine search of the library at the Center for Process Studies in Claremont, California, reveals very little; in fact, only a handful of articles and book chapters exist. Having said this, the researcher who digs beneath the surface of literary art – classic, modern and postmodern – uncovers a treasure trove of items, a fecund series of resources for thinking theologically in a relational world. Consider the English novelist David Lodge. One of Lodge's most engaging characters, Bernard Walsh, is a self-proclaimed agnostic theologian, who has a professional interest in Paradise. But, having come to Hawaii to escort his reluctant father Jack to the deathbed of Jack's estranged sister, he does not, like his fellow tourists, hope for a heavenly holiday. Here is Bernard's opinion of, and challenge to, process theology, culled from Lodge's 1991 novel, *Paradise News*:

> Bernard sat at his desk and took out his notes on a book about process theology he was reviewing for *Eschatological Review*. The God of process theology, he read, is the cosmic lover. '*His transcendence is in His sheer faithfulness to Himself in love, in His inexhaustibility as lover, and in His capacity for endless adaptation to circumstances in which His love may be active.*' Really? Who says? The theologian says. And who cares, apart from other theologians? Not the people choosing their holidays from the travel agent's brochures. Not the drivers of the car transporters. It often seemed to Bernard that the discourse of much modern radical theology was just as implausible and unfounded as the orthodoxy it had displaced, but nobody had noticed because nobody read it except those with a professional stake in its continuation.[1]

In addition to David Lodge, there are other writers who have used the medium of literary art to address or articulate some of the claims associated with process thinkers. One thinks of the American poet Georgia Harkness, and her poem, 'God Suffers', which is taken from her 1935 collection, *Holy Flame*. Here Harkness criticizes the divine *actus impassibilis* of classical Christian theism:

> I cannot think that God could be content
> To view unmoved the toiling and the strain,
> The groaning of the ages, sick and spent,
> The whole creation travailing in pain.
> The suffering God is no vast cosmic force,
> That by some blind, unthinking, loveless power
> Keeps stars and atoms swinging in their course,
> And reckons naught of men in this grim hour.
> Nor is the suffering God a fair ideal
> Engendered in the questioning hearts of men,
> A figment of the mind to help me steel
> My soul to rude realities I ken.
> God suffers with a love that cleanses dross;
> A God like that, I see upon a cross.[2]

Assuredly, Harkness believes that the suffering God saves anything and everything that is worthy of being redeemed, and for our purposes her conviction shows remarkable parallels with an idea first suggested by Alfred North Whitehead: God's consequent nature 'is the judgment of a tenderness which loses nothing that can be saved ... the judgment of a wisdom which uses what in the temporal world is mere wreckage'.[3] Interestingly, Whitehead's process philosophy also appears in D.H. Lawrence's allegedly scandalous novel, *Lady Chatterley's Lover*, when the cripple, Clifford, turns to his wife, Constance Chatterley, and reads from his copy of *Religion in the Making*:

> That evening, Clifford wanted to be nice to her. He was reading one of the latest scientific–religious books: he had a streak of a spurious sort of religion in him, and was egocentrically concerned with the future of his ego. It was like his habit to make conversation with Connie about some book, since the conversation between them had to be made, almost chemically. They had almost chemically to concoct it in their heads.
> 'What do you think of this, by the way?' he said, reaching for his book. 'You'd have no need to cool your ardent body by running out in the rain, if only we have a few more aeons of evolution behind us. Ah, here it is! – "The universe shows us two aspects: on one side it is physically wasting, on the other it is spiritually ascending."'
> Connie listened, expecting more. But Clifford was waiting. She looked at him in surprise.
> 'And if it spiritually ascends,' she said, 'what does it leave below, in the place where its tail used to be?'
> 'Ah!' he said. 'Take the man for what he means. *Ascending* is the opposite of his *wasting*, I presume.'
> 'Spiritually blown out, so to speak!'
> 'No, but seriously, without joking: do you think there is anything in it?'[4]

We know now that Whitehead was not alone in thinking of the evolutionary advance as marked by two antagonistic forces, which can be grasped using the language of 'ascent' and 'descent'. Indeed, Henri Bergson, the Nobel laureate, also promoted the notion that life is a tussle between two impulses, one which propels us upward, the *élan vital*, and one which tries to push us downward, matter.[5]

Now, Bergson's evolutionary vitalism makes him one of the founding fathers of process philosophy, and one of his supporters was the Irish dramatist Bernard Shaw, whose *Man and Superman* is a literary meditation on the struggles of humankind vis-à-vis the so-called 'Life Force', or Bergson's *élan vital*:

> Don Juan: In the Heaven I seek, no other joy! But there is the work of helping Life in its struggle upward. Think of how it wastes and scatters itself, how it raises up obstacles to itself and destroys itself in its ignorance and blindness. It needs a brain, this irresistible force, lest in its ignorance it should resist itself.[6]

Besides Shaw, the Cretan man-of-letters Nikos Kazantzakis, whom Bergson taught in 1908, published a lyrical essay in 1927, *The Saviors of God: Spiritual Exercises*, and most reader-critics of Kazantzakis's work view this text as a versification of Bergsonian transformism:

> In the temporary living organism these two things collide: (a) the ascent toward composition, toward life, toward immortality; (b) the descent toward decomposition, toward matter, toward death. Both streams well up from the depths of primordial essence. Life startles us at first; it seems somewhat contrary to nature, somewhat like a transitory counteraction to the dark eternal fountains; but deeper down we feel that Life is itself without beginning, an indestructible force of the Universe. Otherwise, from where did that superhuman strength come which hurls us from the unborn to the born and gives us – plants, animals, men – courage for the struggle? But both opposing forces are holy. It is our duty, therefore, to grasp that vision which can embrace and harmonize these two enormous, timeless, and indestructible forces, and with this vision to modulate our action.[7]

Bergson's ideas had an enormous impact on Kazantzakis and Shaw, and they also found a home among many philosophers and theologians, especially the Jesuit thinker Pierre Teilhard de Chardin, who counts as yet another architect of the process system of thinking theologically. Teilhard's own version of process theology, which is sometimes described as 'pan-Christism', treats the universe as a forward movement, leading inexorably to a final consummation, the fullness (*pleroma*) of the Mystical Body of Christ. At least two Roman Catholic creative writers, the English novelist Graham Greene and the American essayist Annie Dillard, have made use of Teilhard's ideas in their work. In Greene's *A Burnt-Out Case*, for instance, Querry, a famous builder of churches and a collector of women, escapes the relentless attention of the European media and flees to a leprosy clinic in a deserted African village, but even here he is hard pressed to avoid giving an account of himself. In one particularly telling scene, Doctor Colin tries to engage Querry on the subject of religion, without much success, but it is Doctor Colin's own beliefs, his 'very small hope', that perhaps represents Greene's finest fictional elaboration on Teilhardian themes:

> 'I want to be on the side of change,' the doctor said. 'If I had been born an amoeba who could think, I would have dreamt of the day of the primates. I would have wanted anything I did to contribute to that day. Evolution, as far as we can tell, has lodged itself finally in the brains of man. The ant, the fish, even the ape has gone as far as it can go, but in our brain evolution is moving – my God – at what a speed! I forgot how many hundreds of millions of years passed between the dinosaurs and the primates, but in our own lifetime we have seen the change from Diesel to jet, the splitting of the atom, the cure of leprosy.'
> 'Is change so good?'
> 'We can't avoid it. We are riding a great ninth evolutionary wave. Even the Christian

myth is part of the wave, and perhaps, who knows, it may be the most valuable part. Suppose love were to evolve as rapidly in our brains as technical skill has done. In isolated cases it may have done, in the saints ... if the man really existed, in Christ.'

'You can really comfort yourself with all that?' Querry asked. 'It sounds like the old song of progress.'

'The nineteenth century wasn't as far wrong as we like to believe. We have become cynical about progress because of the terrible things we have seen men do during the last forty years. All the same, through trial and error the amœba did become the ape. There were blind starts and wrong turnings even then, I suppose. Evolution today can produce Hitlers as well as St. John of the Cross. I have a small hope, that's all, a very small hope, that someone they call Christ was the fertile element, looking for a crack in the wall to plant its seed. I think of Christ as an amœba who took the right turning. I want to be on the side of the progress which survives. I'm no friend of pterodactyls.'[8]

A writer who for many years has pestered God with her questions regarding evil and the human condition, Annie Dillard recently authored *For the Time Being*, a book addressing the life and work of Teilhard de Chardin, particularly his strong belief that Christ's mystical body is evolving within evolution. While Dillard acknowledges that Teilhard produced a 'peculiarly disagreeable lexicon', a glossary of concepts that found little favour with the Roman Curia, and which frequently frustrates students of twentieth-century philosophical theology, she resolutely insists that his theology of evolution repays the closest attention.[9] An unfinished universe lies before us, Dillard opines, following Teilhard, and the lure of the Cosmic Christ involves a call 'to build and divinize the world, to aid God in redemption', to accelerate evolution in its push towards the Omega point.[10] 'God decants the universe of time in a stream,' she claims, 'and our best hope is, by our own awareness, to step into the stream and serve, empty as flumes, to keep it moving.'[11]

No account of those scholars who suppose that God moves through time is complete without mention of Charles Hartshorne, whose 'dipolar panentheism' has received warm and enthusiastic support from many thinkers in the last three decades. Significantly, Hartshorne has himself addressed the relationship between theology and fiction. In a brief article, 'Some Theological Mistakes and Their Effects on Modern Literature', Hartshorne traces the concept of determinism – the conceptual target of many process thinkers – as an implied metaphysic in the literary art of Thomas Love Peacock, Robinson Jeffers, William Wordsworth, Robert Frost, Thomas Hardy, Wallace Stevens, and a number of others.[12] His reason for approaching literature in this way is so that he can highlight the logical pitfalls in a deterministic way of looking at our world.

Although writing at different times and for different reasons the aforementioned process thinkers and creative writers nonetheless appear united, at least for the most part, by their fascination – one might call it an obsession – with the conviction that God is actually a part of the creative advance, actively immersed and supremely involved in the processes of reality, and affected by events in the world. Citing these brief examples serves as an introduction to the general aim of *God, Literature and Process Thought*, which is to explore and evaluate what happens when intellectuals associated with process thought 'encounter' literary theorists and writers of imaginative fiction. It is to the substance of this present volume of essays that I must now turn.

Reading for/as Process

In the last two decades, scholars have written some important books and a substantial number of essays on process thought and science, economics, spirituality, psychology, and theology, Christian as well as Jewish, but a book devoted to the alliance between process thought and literature has not been written or published. *God, Literature and Process Thought* seeks to correct this oversight. It does this by providing, in one volume, an instructive tool for studying a variety of process thinkers in conversation with numerous literary theorists and artists. Our book is divided into three parts. In Part I, four scholars reflect on the dynamic interplay that occurs when process thought and literary theory are brought together in a creative nexus of sorts. In Part II, seven writers attempt to serve as fair-minded arbiters of a lively exchange between various process thinkers (Whitehead, Bergson, Teilhard and Hartshorne) and numerous creative writers (Aeschylus, Blake, Byron, Coleridge, Goethe, Greene, Joyce, Kazantzakis, Levertov, Schelling and Shakespeare). Finally, in Part III, one writer with training in process theology offers her own poetic reflections on the processes of reality, thereby suggesting that our anthology is capable of embodying the very thing it celebrates: *process poesis*.

Andrew W. Hass opens the part devoted to process thought and literary theory with a view of reading based on a notion of process, a notion informed in particular by twentieth-century thinkers Wolfgang Iser, Whitehead and Martin Heidegger. According to Hass, Iser's reader-response approach, which demands a performative role from the reader, is emblematic of a shift from discovering what might be given behind a text, to creating meaning through interaction with the text. This shift finds philosophical support in Whitehead's ontological notion of a 'production of novel togetherness' and in Heidegger's later notion of language which 'grants an abode for the being', whereby reading now helps constitute the being of the reader. This theory of reading is then explored practically in a brief passage from James Joyce's *Finnegans Wake*, in which, through textual extravagance, a theological understanding of 'Other' emerges, allowing for a bearing witness both to the loss of hermeneutical innocence and to the new, ethical possibilities which the process of reading opens up before this Other.

Recent literary theory takes its lead from the work of Jacques Derrida, the French poststructuralist thinker, and so, following Hass, Timothy Mooney addresses the resemblances between Whitehead and Derrida, focusing on the thorny question of essentialism. Derrida's work has often been understood in terms of transcendental philosophy, and Mooney acknowledges that this is indeed one of its aspects. Derrida's deconstruction of the essence–accident opposition, however, is also informed by ideas in evolutionary biology and systems-theory, this strand having been brought out in recent studies by Henry Staten and Christopher Johnson. Mooney argues that when we look at the later work of Whitehead it is possible to discern remarkable similarities between Whitehead and Derrida. After all, Whitehead's philosophy is also an evolutionary one, as Mooney shows, which rejects the idea of fixed and fully determined essences. A greater emphasis is certainly laid on order by Whitehead, especially in his accounts of eternal objects and God, but, from Mooney's perspective, these aspects of his thought are both carefully qualified and eminently open to revision.

Revising and transforming process philosophy stands at the centre of Santiago Sia's essay, which issues a clarion call to process thinkers: consider and comprehend the voice(s) of those who write stories, plays and poems, because they have mastered the art of concretizing their experience, something process thinkers often promise to do, but very often seem unable to accomplish. Contemporary process thought has of course emphasized the contributions of Whitehead and Hartshorne in providing an alternative conceptuality in understanding and articulating our experience of reality. These contributions, which have led to the formation of a metaphysical scheme, seem, at least to Sia, to be rooted both in a particular understanding of the role of reason and in the attempt to meet the challenge of the times. What is also called for, however, but relatively ignored by process thinkers, is the task of preserving 'the concreteness of experience' rather than merely analysing it. Thus Sia's essay argues that process thought, following its own methodology, can benefit from 'listening to poets and literary writers'. Drawing on Whitehead's references to literature in his writing, Sia develops Whitehead's insight that 'literature preserves the wisdom of the human race' and that 'it is the storehouse of that crude evidence on which philosophy should base its discussion'. In developing this insight, Sia critiques Plato's criticisms of poetry and, from a process perspective, enters into a dialogue with contemporary European philosophers regarding the alliance between literature and philosophy. René P.H. Munnik is one such European philosopher, and his essay closes the first part of the present volume, relating Whitehead's concept of a dynamic world to theories about textual expression and interpretation. Offering Whiteheadian readings of concepts such as 'effective history', 'polysemia', 'impossibility of reconstructive interpretation' and 'understanding as a process of fusion of horizons' (Hans-Georg Gadamer), Munnik argues that Whitehead's process cosmology is 'hermeneutical' in the strict sense of the word.

Aliman Sears's process theological reflections on M.S. Sia's novel, *The Fountain Arethuse*, opens the second part of our anthology, and his work is the first of seven different essays addressing and assessing the relationship between particular process thinkers and specific creative writers. Set in the university town of Leuven in Belgium, *The Fountain Arethuse* deals with the concreteness of life and the challenges it offers. Among other concerns, the experience of pain and suffering occupies a prominent role in the narrative and, as Sears points out, the novel's main characters display various responses to their experience of suffering. In the eyes of a young literature instructor, for example, the death of a loved one results in enmity towards an allegedly uncaring God. Furthermore, a philosopher researching the problem of evil suffers anxiety over the connection between his intellectual work and suffering people in the world. Sears explores the underlying process theodicy in *The Fountain Arethuse* through an analysis of, and reflections on, its plot, its characters and its dialogues. Sears also shows the connections between process themes in this novel and the theodicy developed in the authors' other book, *From Suffering to God*, and he compares their position with other process theodices, particularly those developed by David Ray Griffin and Barry L. Whitney. Throughout his essay, Sears indicates how the authors of *The Fountain Arethuse* conceive the relationship between literary expression and philosophical reasoning, and he offers his own assessment of their approach to the problem of evil by discussing ways in which literature may expand philosophical reflection.[13]

Barry L. Whitney's essay continues the theodicy theme, using ancient literature as a key to unlock the door to a new understanding of the problem of evil. In Whitney's view, the Greek myth of Prometheus, given its classic form by Aeschylus in *Prometheus Bound*, has been far more influential in western culture than has been recognized. The early church theologians were influenced by Hellenistic culture and so conceived the Christian God in terms of Greek thought, an imaginative blend of Aristotle's God and Zeus – omnipotent, impassible, cruel and condemning. With the ushering in of the modern age after the Renaissance and the Enlightenment, the Promethean myth, which pits Prometheus's rebellion in the name of freedom against a callous Zeus, gained new prominence, especially in the thought of major atheists. The irony in contemporary atheism, and in the problem of suffering by which atheists challenge belief in God, is that the God defended by Christian theologians and rejected by atheists is not an adequate vision of the Christian God. For Whitney, process philosophers and theologians present a much more viable understanding of God, and thereby undercut the basis for modern atheism and dissolve the traditional formulation of the problem of evil.

'Sticky evil' clings to Shakespeare's *Macbeth*, according to William Desmond, and his essay explores the meaning of this phrase using categories of process. Sticky evil refers to evil's indelible character. It is represented in the image of Lady Macbeth trying to wash Duncan's blood from her hands: 'Out damned spot, out I say!' And she cannot wash off the blood; it is sticky, not only in a physical sense, but in a metaphysical sense. The evil congeals. In Desmond's eyes, *Macbeth* is redolent with this sticky evil, this thickness of darkness itself. What sense of process is here at work? In answering this question, Desmond speaks of 'the karma of equivocity'. His view is that process is itself equivocal, not univocal, and always ambiguous between good and evil. Evil is no mere deprivation, but is parasitical on this equivocal process. In short, *Macbeth* is the play of equivocal process: nothing is, but what is not. Desmond argues for a karma in this equivocal process. There is a doom in the process which is set in motion by the equivocal mixing of human powers and powers other than human. Can this karma of the equivocal be called a fate? How is the relation of human powers and this doom reflected in the stickiness of evil? Do we have philosophical categories to handle sticky evil and the karma of the equivocal process? Is process philosophy adequate? For Desmond, these questions, particularly the last one, come together to form one overall question: can a philosophy primarily interested in categories that help determine explanation illuminate what seems to exceed all univocal determination?

Like the essays offered by most of the other contributors in this second part, Darren Middleton's work connects the problem of suffering to the problem of God. However, unlike the other essayists, he introduces the provocative notion that evil lurks within the heart of deity. Using Graham Greene's novel *The Honorary Consul*, he gives an account of Greene's interest in Teilhard de Chardin's Catholic process thought, and especially Teilhard's belief that there is a continual evolution within Godself. Middleton focuses on Greene's main protagonist, Father Rivas, and his belief that God possesses a 'day-time face' and a 'night-time face'. According to Father Rivas, God requires our assistance in order to evolve from God's 'night-side' to God's 'day-side'. Significantly, Teilhard speaks of God or Christ evolving towards absolute light and goodness, and that God needs us to advance the evolutionary process. Through an examination of Greene's original typescripts of *The Honorary Consul*, Middleton shows that Greene's process vision is expressed in a literary and poetic form; through fiction, that is, Greene can be seen to foster a process spirituality of creativity, where all women and men co-create the world with God.

A strikingly similar process spirituality of creativity lies at the centre of Nikos Kazantzakis's literary *œuvre*, and Daniel A. Dombrowski's essay attempts to show how and why this is so. He begins by tracing the life and writings of this impressive Greek poet, essayist and novelist, paying particular attention to the influence of the process philosopher Henri Bergson on his concept of God. The 'Cry of God' serves as a call forward to new possibilities, some of which may strike us as terrifying. Some key process concepts in Kazantzakis are treated in this essay, including transubstantiation (*metousiosis* or *metabole*), the 'new middle ages', as well as Kazantzakis's dipolar theism and his mysticism, and Dombrowski ends with a consideration of Kazantzakis's method and of his views regarding panexperientialism and death.

While Lewis Owens refers to the work of Henri Bergson and Nikos Kazantzakis in his own essay, his primary focus is Jacob Boehme and the Romantic roots of process thought. For Owens, the core tenets of process thought – terms such as creativity, becoming, process and time – had their genesis in the notion of a self-manifesting deity espoused by the mystic Jacob Boehme, who is justifiably seen by Hartshorne as the founder of dipolar theology. Owens shows how Boehme's thought greatly influenced the later thought of the Romantic Schelling as well as the religious philosophy of Bergson and Berdayaev, all of whom are seen by Hartshorne as members of the distinguished family of process philosophers. Furthermore, Boehme's influence also affects the Romantic verse of Blake, Wordsworth and Coleridge, which suggests that such poetic literature remains a most authentic channel for expressing the dynamism of process thought.

Poetry stands out as the mainstay of Bobby Caudle Rogers's essay, which uses Henri Bergson's evolutionary vitalism as a lens through which to view Denise Levertov's verse. Like all lyric poetry, the lines in Levertov's later poems seek to raise themselves from the page in a struggle towards transcendence. And according to Rogers, this struggle becomes unself-consciously theological by the time of her 1994 book, *Oblique Prayers*. Her imagery is famously small and mundane, like that of her most significant poetic forebear, the High Modernist William Carlos Williams. 'God's in the dust,' she writes, '/not sifted//out from confusion'. Hers is a poetry of moments, a poetry of the small, luminous surprise. From Rogers's perspective, Bergson's notions of time, past and change form a useful means to approach Levertov's world of continuous utterance and refinement, her beatitudes of dust. Rogers's essay ends the second of our three parts, and it serves as important prolegomenon to our third part, which features Christina K. Hutchins's original poem about becoming, an example of versifying relationality, because this final component of our anthology also uses Levertov as a source for thinking as well as for writing.

The fruit of many conversations and exchanges over the last three years, *God, Literature and Process Thought* outlines and promotes the novel view that there is much to be gained when those who value the insights of process thought 'encounter' the many and varied writers of literature and literary theory, and vice versa, and it celebrates *process poesis*, a fresh way of reflecting theologically and philosophically that takes account of literary forms, and which promises to transform creatively the very structure of process thought today.

Without a doubt, a book covering this range of topics and issues, written by contributors from around the globe, is utterly reliant on the industriousness and kindness of many, worthy souls. Allow me to close by naming just a few. First, as editor, I would like to take this opportunity to express my deep appreciation to all the essayists in this volume, for believing the time is right to offer our anthology, and for sustaining an important dialogue through the past few years. Second, I want to record my indebtedness to the editorial, administrative and marketing staff at Ashgate Publishing in Aldershot, Hampshire, England. Third, I am most grateful to two former students and dear friends, Austin C. Dickson and Gretchen S. Koch, who scrutinized, evaluated and corrected important aspects of the present volume in its manuscript phase. Making certain deadlines would have been impossible without your assiduousness. Fourth, my wife Betsy, while away from our home in Fort Worth in pursuit of a doctorate at Duke University, has been my most ardent ally throughout the long months it has taken me to assemble, edit and deliver this book. And finally, I offer this volume to my former teachers: David Pailin (BA, Manchester), Maurice F. Wiles (MPhil, Oxford) and David Jasper (PhD, Glasgow), and as I do I recognize that without their innovative work, in philosophical theology, Christian doctrine and literature and religion respectively, I would not be what I am today. All three men have bestowed incalculable riches upon me, and I offer this modest token in return.

Notes

1. David Lodge, *Paradise News* (London: Secker and Warburg, 1991), 36.
2. Georgia Harkness, *Holy Flame* (New York: Bruce Humphries, Inc., 1935), 308.
3. Alfred North Whitehead, *Process and Reality: An Essay in Cosmology*, corrected edition, edited by David Ray Griffin and Donald W. Sherburne (New York: The Free Press, 1978), 346.
4. D.H. Lawrence, *Lady Chatterley's Lover*, with an introduction and notes by John Lyon (London: Penguin Books, 1990), 243. In his notes to *Lady Chatterley's Lover*, Lyon tells us that the passages subsequently cited in the sixteenth chapter of the novel are near-perfect quotations from Alfred North Whitehead's *Religion in the Making*. See 331.
5. Henri Bergson, *Creative Evolution*, authorized translation by Arthur Mitchell (New York: Henry Holt and Company, 1911), 11, 249–50.
6. Bernard Shaw, *Man and Superman: A Comedy and a Philosophy* (London: Penguin Books, 1987), 141.
7. Nikos Kazantzakis, *The Saviors of God: Spiritual Exercises*, translated and with an introduction by Kimon Friar (New York: Simon and Schuster, 1960), 43–4.
8. Graham Greene, *A Burnt-Out Case* (New York: Bantam Books, Inc., 1962), 121–2.
9. Annie Dillard, *For the Time Being* (New York: Alfred A. Knopf, 1999), 102.
10. Ibid., 127.
11. Ibid., 175.
12. Charles Hartshorne, 'Some Theological Mistakes and Their Effects on Modern Literature', *Journal of Speculative Philosophy* 1.1 (1987): 55–72.
13. To avoid any confusion here, or in Chapter five, the editor wishes to point out that Marian and Santiago Sia also publish under the name 'M.S. Sia', which means that both texts, Sia,

M.S., *The Fountain Arethuse: a Novel Set in the University Town of Leuven* (Lewes, UK: The Book Guild Publishers, 1997); Sia, Marian F. and Santiago Sia, *From Suffering to God: Exploring our Images of God in the Light of Suffering* (New York: St Martin's Press/ Basingstoke UK: Macmillan, 1994) are best understood as co-authored texts.

I
PROCESS THOUGHT AND LITERARY THEORY

Chapter 1

Reading in the Modern Wake

Andrew W. Hass

Introduction

One way the present world might be characterized is as one in which reading has lost its innocence. This is not to say that, at some stage in the past, there was no sense of misreading, or of reading poorly. We know that even for the ancient Greeks there was a 'right' way and a 'wrong' way to approach a text, and certainly Christian theologians from the Patristics to, and culminating in, the Reformers had astute and sometimes unforgiving principles about reading that goes astray. It is not a naïve assumption that all able readers are naturally impeccable readers which has been lost, for there has never been any notion of a flawless act of reading. It is rather an assumption of what reading can and ought to achieve which has been lost. And since what one can and ought to achieve was largely something *given* by the text, and this given was taken for granted, we can deem belief in such a given 'innocent', insofar as premodern readers did not set out to do harm or injury to that given, as the etymology of 'innocent' suggests. One simply had to find it, and by the most appropriate and accurate means possible. But such a given has come under great attack since the turn of our modern times. One might even say, as a mark of the postmodern era, it has been effectively killed off. We no longer assume a given brought to us by the text, other than the givenness of the text itself. This death of the given leaves all readers in a position of liability, for the act of reading implicates the reader as much as it does the text in the resultant 'meaning', whether that meaning now be innocuous or nocuous, naïve or knowing.

What we are speaking of here is, of course, a classic hermeneutical issue: how does meaning or significance emerge from a text? Does it come about through an excavation of the text, carried out by a competent reader using the correct critical tools? Or is it brought to the text by the reader, and manifested through the response of the reader? Is there perhaps a joint participation between text and reader, where both sides carry responsibility for what is meaningfully produced? We can say that the trajectory of critical approach to texts in the past century has moved from one where meaning is discovered to one where meaning is generated. The notion that something resides beyond, behind or prior to the text has given way to the notion that meaning arises only when reader confronts text. This shift in the locality of meaning has thus shifted the idea of agency: the text becomes less an agent for something outside of itself, and the reader less an agent for attaining this something through a proper analysis or proper critical posture. What is *given* is simply text and reader; what results from their coming together is now of critical importance. This shift raises important questions. If reading, having eaten from the tree of hermeneutical knowledge, is now expelled from a paradise of given certainties, where is it left to wander? What are readers to make of themselves, upon the loss of fixed and stable meaning?

Iser and Process

Rather than reading as excavation or discovery, we might talk of reading as *process*. Of course, we would hardly be the first to do this. Wolfgang Iser, one of the more notable of 'reader-response' theorists, has been using such a term since the early 1970s.[1] For Iser, reading becomes an event through which the reader participates not just in the construction of textual meaning, but in those processes which allow one to experience everyday reality. Here, reading, and the reality which reading facilitates, do not depend on givens, but rather on what is *not* given, on the indeterminacy or 'blanks' within a text. The reader's own perceptions fill in these blanks and, in turn, construe or actualize meaning. The process of reading, then, demands from the reader something other than a mere utilization of correct critical tools governed by 'authorial prescription'.

As Iser sees it, the process of reading (fiction in particular) demands a performative role, a role which is as much philosophic as it is creative: philosophic, because it accounts for the reality structures in all our experience of the objective world, not simply in our experience with a written text; and creative, because the reader becomes a co-actor within the play of the text, helping determine the 'outcome' of its story.[2] Anthony Thiselton, who treats Iser in relation to theological issues, traces the philosophical side of this role back to Husserl.[3] We might trace the creative side back to any number of Romantic theorists, as Iser himself grants.[4] What is significant to both sides is that, once a metaphysical breach has been made, once, that is, the text is no longer *representative*, representing something behind or previous to itself – a fixed reality or truth, a meaning, an author, an intention[5] – and once the reader shares in the *responsibility* of this text, reading can no longer be simply a technique, a set of rules to be followed, a skill to be mastered. Reading must in some sense help constitute the *being* of the reader.

Philosophically, it is not surprising that any theory of reading which begins this side of the text, that is, with the reader, should find its roots in phenomenology. For such a theory binds itself to things at hand, or, as the case may be, *not* at hand, which the reader's consciousness must deal with in immediacy. The mediation required when extratextual elements are presupposed does not operate here. A phenomenology of reading begins with the text as it is encountered; it does not rely on transcendent features to make themselves known, or to be made known and brought to light. Such a responsive understanding will always lead in a twofold direction: towards an ontology, and towards some notion of process, towards a *being* and a *becoming*. For reading as response must take into account both that which is being responded to and the nature of the response in the individual who is responding. In Kantian terms, these are not regulative issues, but constitutive issues. They help determine the very nature of what it means to *be* a reader. They help determine the *coming into existence* of meaning. And they help determine the very *act* of reading as an open, dynamic, fluid experience, a moment of creativity, equal in potential to the creativity which brought about the text in the first place. In Iser's terms, the acting reader, as a given being, gives of him- or herself and, in turn, brings forth 'something that in itself is not given'.[6]

This process of ontology and creativity, of being and becoming through the act of reading, does not owe its philosophical heritage only to a Husserlian phenomenology. Nor are Iser's notions the only way to manifest theoretically this process. Heraclitus, through to Schleiermacher, Hegel and, more recently, Bergson, Whitehead and Heidegger, could all be called upon in some way to support a theory of reading as process. And literary critics from Stanley Fish to Jonathan Culler, Umberto Eco, Norman Holland and David Bleich offer their own manifestations, drawing from such extended fields as language theory, semiotics, psychoanalysis and sociopolitics.[7] What we find, since Schleiermacher's hermeneutics of the early nineteenth century, and very much since Wittgenstein's philosophical turn to language of the early twentieth century, is that engagement with a text involves issues that hitherto belonged only in the philosopher's realm or in the creative artist's realm. Now neither of these realms can be divorced from the act of reading; indeed, the act becomes a multifaceted exercise with the profoundest of implications. Postmodernism, for whatever else it claims to be, can at the very least be seen as a movement that has made a point of highlighting these implications. And thus its fixation with 'textuality'. Postmodernism has also, in the process, conflated the realms of philosophy and art, so that being and becoming, existence and the bringing to existence are, necessarily, inextricable with one another. This conflation, especially as it relates to the act of reading, can be seen in two of the philosophical figures mentioned in connection with this century, one who is generally not claimed by postmodernists, Alfred North Whitehead,[8] and one who most certainly is, Martin Heidegger.

Whitehead's Process

Whitehead's theories, especially as found within the seminal Gifford Lectures later published as *Process and Reality*, have been given much attention since the 1970s by theologians.[9] But they have received little attention from literary theorists or philosophers interested in hermeneutics. This is perhaps because Whitehead's concerns were with finding links between philosophy and modern science (the subtitle of his major work is 'An Essay in Cosmology') and to this end he developed a technical vocabulary that seemed to rely on the metaphysical and rationalistic assumptions central to a foundationalism which modern, and indeed postmodern, literary and hermeneutical theory rigorously question.[10] As a consequence, Whitehead's name has seldom appeared in texts dealing with theories of reading. Is this justified? We would need to devote an entire and inevitably lengthy discussion to Whitehead's philosophy in order to answer thoroughly this question. But a brief look at Whitehead's ontology does suggest that something can be gained from the Whiteheadian model.

Whitehead's notion of process goes beyond a simple understanding of a series of events being continually played out. He has formulated his notion into a distinct principle: 'The *how* an actual entity *becomes* constitutes *what* that actual entity *is*; so that the two descriptions of an actual entity are not independent. Its "being" is constituted by its "becoming". This is the "principle of process"'.[11] This principle works alongside a certain mode of perception of reality, whereby 'the contemporary world is consciously prehended as a continuum of extensive relations'.[12] Within this continuum, 'every "being" is a potential for a "becoming"',[13] so that, extending Heraclitus, 'no thinker thinks twice', and indeed, 'no subject experiences twice'.[14] Ontologically, reality, made up of actual entities or 'occasions', is a series of givens. But these givens are not static entities; they are self-creative, arising from their own potentiality, while at the same time dependent on all other given occasions for their being and coming into being and allowing others to come into being. In this modified monism, creativity plays a central part. For the givenness of any being carries with it both the *potential* for creating itself anew in relation to other beings, and the *realization* of this potential, so that 'givenness' is actually a combination of the old and the new, what Whitehead calls a *synthetic givenness*.[15] This synthesis becomes a unifying principle of creativity, bringing the novelty of an individual entity together with the multiplicity of all other entities, a 'production of novel togetherness'.[16] Under such production, being and becoming merge; being is always already in the process of becoming. Ongoing creativity, in other words, is part of what it means to *be*.

Bracketing off other aspects of Whitehead's theories, with their concomitant technicalities, and utilizing just this creative ontology, we might describe the process of reading then as a 'production of novel togetherness'. If a text is approached under the assumption that there are no prior *givens* standing behind it, what is then initially given is only the text itself, in all its variety, and the individual as potential reader of that text. Similar to Iser's understanding, the act of reading synthesizes the individuality of the reader with the multiplicity of the text, from which arises something new in both the text and the reader. This newness, once it has arisen, does not reach a state of completion and remain there, but is continually remade as the reader continues to defer to the text, or rereads the text, or refers to other texts. Thus the given text, as it is being read, is always in a state of becoming, while the reader, as he or she reads, is also partly recreating him- or herself *vis-à-vis* the text. We might say the text comes together as a coherent whole only when the reader engages in an active relation with it, for it is the reader who provides the integrative links to make the text's various parts cohere: who, that is, realizes the text's potential for meaning. Such a provision Whitehead terms 'feelings' or, more technically, 'prehension' (and when something is excluded in the linkage, 'negative prehension').[17]

Iser speaks of 'actualizing' and 'concretizing' dimensions of potential meaning.[18] We might simply call this the ability to 'come away with something' from the text, whether with 'meaning' in its traditional sense, or with some kind of provocation. Whatever the case, this something will always be new or novel – a created thing – for the synthesis of the individual with the multiple potentials of the text will be unique in every encounter. The reader never 'experiences twice', and thus the results of reading are continually regenerated. But the reader must also be changed in order to experience differently each time. The reading process also alters the reader, creating not only a new perspective on the text, but a new *being* with which to approach the text at all. As an active participant in the generation of meaning, the being itself becomes modified, because part of what a text here *means* is now the reader's facility to prehend and integrate. This modification is possible because being is defined in terms of *relation*, and not in terms of static essence. The *how* this meaning/being *becomes* constitutes the *what* this meaning/being *is*.

Now all we have done is impose a truncated philosophical model (an ontology, more accurately) upon a theory of reading. As yet we have done little to substantiate this practically. Below we will try to justify some of our claims by looking at a specific, and decidedly exaggerated, work of fiction. The point to be seen now is that a process of reading is conceivable whereby text and reader are so mutually dependent that the philosophical notions of existence (text/reader) conflate with the aesthetic notions of bringing into existence (meaning).[19]

Heidegger under Process

The chief problem of Whitehead's philosophy for hermeneutics, and hence for a theory of reading, is its inadequate theory of language. Any theory of reading must take into account how language works, and how its inner structures relate to the individual. It must rely on some understanding not only of the mechanics of a linguistic system, but equally, if not more importantly, of how those mechanics come to be appropriated in the speaker or reader. We have seen how a phenomenology is important in this equation, for it allows for the presentation of things as they appear in the immediacy of consciousness. But this equation also requires some sense of the individual consciousness and its existence itself; it requires, that is, an *existential* understanding. This is consistent with all modern hermeneutics since Schleiermacher, who was the first to impress the subjective side of reading on any theory of interpretation.

Martin Heidegger, in reacting to the shortcomings he saw in Husserl's phenomenology, was the first to push the notion of consciousness to its most ontologically basic level, seeking out the 'Being of beings' in light of the context which any being finds itself in, a context which the earlier Heidegger sees as hermeneutically understood and which the later Heidegger sees as more specifically tied to language. And this is in large part why theories of reading have only fully developed since Heidegger: they do not all depend on Heidegger's specific existential programme, but they most all depend on the *contextualizing* of the individual Being which that programme opened up. Whitehead's organic philosophy makes no provision for existentiality in the thinking, feeling or 'prehending' subject — subjective consciousness is derivative and not ontologically basic to the being of an actual entity — and thus language for Whitehead is not a matter of consciousness.[20] Language becomes rather an example of 'symbolic reference', a reference which a subject draws through a vague, not quite unconscious, but certainly unreflective ability to correlate two differing perceptions. This ability is neither existential, nor purely phenomenological, nor in any way self-critical, but simply happens as an experience (Whitehead never tells us why).[21] Though the two sides to be correlated may be contextualized (taken out of the past and placed into the present, as Whitehead might say), the mode by which they are contextualized, or this ability to correlate them, never is, and it is this latter contextualization which has become so crucial to theories of reading. Thus Whitehead's ontological process falls short of the provisions modern hermeneutics of reading have deemed necessary.

By *contextualization* we do not refer to the traditional notion of a *Sitz im Leben*, where historical, biographical and cultural concerns determine analysis. We refer rather to the contextualization or entextualization of Being itself within the structures of language, or, what will amount to the same thing, within the structures of thought. Heidegger has done more than anyone else to expose and develop this contextualization. In his early magnum opus, *Sein und Zeit* (1927), he set out to describe Being as it is contextualized against the horizon of temporality, or time. This contextualized Being, or *Dasein*, has as part of its existential structure the dimension of understanding, by which it is both constituted and opened up towards its own future possibility. *Dasein's* understanding is not of a 'what', but of 'Being as existing', which must include not only Being as such but 'potentiality-for-Being', or 'Being-possible'.[22] Here Heidegger's concept is similar to Whitehead's merging of being and becoming. But, as Heidegger describes, this constitutive understanding is necessarily tied to interpretation, where he defines interpretation as 'the working-out of possibilities projected in understanding'.[23]

Moreover, this interpretation does not arrive out of nowhere; it is based on presuppositional qualities in *Dasein*, what Heidegger calls fore-having (*Vorhabe*), fore-sight (*Vorsicht*) and fore-conception (*Vorgriff*). These fore-structures are fundamental for any knowing, but they involve *Dasein* in a vicious hermeneutical circle, since to have understood anything at all one will have already understood what is to be interpreted. Such a circle means that *Dasein* is *by nature* hermeneutical, with no possibility of escape, since the very structure of its Being, understanding, depends on an interpretive predisposition. But escape is not what concerns Heidegger. The circle is precisely what allows the possibility of knowing. As Heidegger explains: 'The "circle" in understanding belongs to the structure of meaning, and the latter phenomenon is rooted in the existential constitution of *Dasein* – that is, in the understanding which interprets. An entity for which, as Being-in-the-world, its Being is itself an issue, has, ontologically, a circular structure.'[24] The circle is not therefore vicious and to be avoided. It cannot be avoided. In Heidegger's now famous words: 'What is decisive is not to get out of the circle but to come into it in the right way.'[25]

What is this 'right way'? For the early Heidegger it is the realization of the basic conditions for interpretation and knowing, specifically, the conditions of contextualization that constitute Being and that make Being 'itself an issue', conditions which Whitehead's model fails to realize (especially the latter condition). For the later Heidegger, the right way comes to focus more and more on language. Some have criticized the apparent disjunction between the earlier and later Heidegger as a move away from the rigorous grounds of philosophy to the more woolly grounds of poetry. For Heidegger this move was no disjunction, but a natural and necessary move away from traditional metaphysics, to which even his *Dasein* was falling prey, and a move towards a more originary form of Being's coming into the open – originary not in the sense of a grounded a priori, but of a ground-breaking event.[26] This event is the event of language.

'In his Hölderlin lectures from the 1930s', writes Gerald Bruns, 'Heidegger says that, contrary to the metaphysical tradition, language is not to be understood as any sort of linguistic or conceptual system; rather, it is an event in which all that is is summoned for the first time into openness of being; and this event is what Heidegger calls poetry (*Dichtung*, not *Poesie*).'[27] This *Dichtung* brings to light in the purest manner the essence of Being, or the truth of a thing. 'Language speaks', he claims, and in doing so it calls forth the presence of a thing within the world, bringing it from concealment to unconcealment. Reflection on language is reflection on truth – 'truth' for Heidegger is the Greek *aletheia*, literally 'not being concealed'[28] – and so the truth of Being emerges in and through language, or, in Being's most unconcealed form, in and through *Dichtung*, poetry, the work of art.

We can see the continuing existential concern in Heidegger's turn to language, and why it would be so influential for reading. Engaging with language is not, under this way of thinking, an innocent or in any way neutral activity. It engages one's whole Being. Even more, it allows Being to come fully into the open. For Heidegger, a person speaks or listens to language 'in such a way that this speaking [or listening] takes place as that which grants an abode for the being of mortals'.[29] Language is not to be taken for granted, but in fact does the granting itself, providing the space in which the truth of Being is manifested and made known. Here we see once again the confluence of philosophy and art, the bringing together of *what* a thing is with *how* that thing comes into being. For Heidegger, whether in his earlier or later thought, the *what* and the *how* cannot be divorced, since the *what* is constituted in the *how*, or the *how* is contextualized within the *what*, and both are caught inexorably within a hermetically (or hermeneutically) sealed circle. That language or *Dichtung* becomes both the opening into this circle and its sealant, that a work of art has the potential to furnish grounds for existence – these developments allow us to extend further our notion of reading as a process.

If we borrowed from Whitehead the idea of a 'production of novel togetherness', we could advance this idea by allying it to Heidegger's sense of language and art: reading is also 'that which grants an abode for the being' of a reader. An individual reader first confronts the multiplicity of a text. The mutual integration of the reader and the text alters both participants, producing something new. This synthesis is not of a Hegelian kind, where one side (thesis) and its opposite (antithesis) are subsumed into a new entity. It is rather a granting or an event which bestows a dwelling place for the two sides. Here 'to dwell' would mean both to exist and to bring into existence, to be and to become, to reside and to build. As Heidegger states, in expanding Hölderlin's phrase 'poetically man dwells': 'poetry first causes dwelling to be dwelling. Poetry is what really lets us dwell. But through what do we attain to a dwelling place? Through building. Poetic creation, which lets us dwell, is a kind of building.'[30] As this building is constituted by language, we could say that reading is a kind of building, in both the nominal and verbal senses of this word, that in reading we create a building for our Being, and in the process, we build ourselves into something we were not previously. This is certainly a process, for it entails a continual process of contextualization, or of entextualization, of building up a text from a text, of building up a Being from beings, so that the reader is never fully outside the text, and the text never fully outside the reader, the two dwelling together in the act of reading itself. The novel togetherness furnishes the existential abode, and it is only in and through such a building that we then 'walk away with something' from the experience.

Using certain understandings of Whitehead and Heidegger, we can see how a theory of reading need not then depend on *givens* standing behind a text or language, but can build on the *givens* of text and reader alone to make something which is both wholly new and irrevocably contextualized. This theory now demands a reckoning. We have assumed and left out much in our brief and selective rendering of theorists so far. How should the resulting notion of reading play itself out practically? Can reading possibly live up to the far-reaching theories we have just imposed on it?

Joyce in Process

The radical nature of the demands – that reading through hermeneutical closure open up the true nature of existence – requires a radical text to exemplify the point clearly and decisively. Ironically, however, the most radical text for this purpose is anything but clear and decisive. It is perhaps the most unclear, most indecisive, and to many minds the least accessible text which yet is granted literary importance. This text, of course, is James Joyce's *Finnegans Wake*.

Joyce's final *tour de force* has confounded more than its share of readers and theorists since its publication as a full book in 1939. Yet it has also gained increasing interest as theories of reading have developed, especially since the poststructuralist turn in the 1960s. From Eco's 'process of unlimited semiotics' to Derrida's incisive deconstructive word play, *Finnegans Wake* has received the attentions of those concerned with the unruly, refractory nature of texts and language.[31] But it is not merely for the endless punning and word play, nor for the apparent linguistic anarchy, that this text deserves our attention now, but for its impact on, or substantiation of, reading as a process. It may seem odd that this text should substantiate any reading, since it is probably the least read of all the supposedly 'great texts' of literature. If it deserves our attention, we will have to account for the fact that it receives so little attention from general readership, or at least explain why it has tended to dissuade more readers than persuade.

Initially, we might say that most readers still, out of an inveterate and culturally driven habit, approach a text as if to come away with something pre-given by the text: a story, a plot, a definable meaning, a moral, a sense of history, the author's own thoughts and so on. We all do this unthinkingly, for our assumptions about texts are still generally met; we can most often find what we have been told to look for when we read, whether that be a story, a plot, a meaning, a discernible narrative, or some other such feature. Virtually all readers would have approached this essay with such assumptions and, whether or not they agree with its conclusions, will have had those basic assumptions met in some way (to disagree vehemently with this essay will have confirmed those assumptions). But *Finnegans Wake* will not let one do this, will not, that is, meet any of the traditional assumptions about what to expect from a text. The reason it is so seldom read, the reason so few readers endure to the end, is that most readers do not, to return to Heidegger's phrase, 'come into it in the right way'. To approach the text as if something should be *found* will only lead to disappointment. Nothing is to be found. But much is to be *made*, by which we mean much is waiting to come to light in the interaction with the text's inexhaustible possibilities. If a reader embarks upon the text with the assumptions we have been trying to lay out here – that reading is a mutual excursion, an event that takes place between text and reader, each one building up the other, so that in novel production a space for both is provided, a new space made up of old remnants, of unavoidable presuppositions that are reconstituted – then *Finnegans Wake* comes alive. If one expects to discover a fixed meaning, one will be interminably frustrated, and no text is so merciless with its frustration as this one. But if one expects to generate meaning, fluid meaning, one will be endlessly engaged, and no text is so open to such engendering, cooperative engagement as this one. It can be a reader's Nemesis or a reader's Muse, depending on what is taken for granted.

Let us take a portion of the text:

> With however what sublation of compensation in the radification of interpretation by the byeboys? Being they. Mr G.B.W. Ashburners, S. Bruno's Toboggan Drive, Mr Faixgood, Bellchimbers, Carolan Crescent, Mr I.I. Chattaway, Hilly Gape, Poplar Park, Mr Q.P. Dieudonney, The View, Gazey Peer, Mr T.T. Erchdeakin, Multiple Lodge, Jiff Exby Rode, Mr W.K. Ferris-Fender, Fert Fort, Woovil Doon Botham ontowhom adding the tout that pumped the stout that linked the lank that cold the sandy that nextdoored the rotter that rooked the rhymer that lapped at the hoose that Joax pilled.
> They had heard or had heard said or had heard said written.
> Fidelisat.[32]

At first glance, the passage seems to make no sense whatsoever. Perhaps even at a second or third glance. Having been pulled from its context, without any indication of what precedes or follows it, we might give it the benefit of the doubt, and say that sense could only be had if and when it was recontextualized into the larger passage or chapter from which it was taken. But contextualization of this kind would offer us little help, as that which immediately surrounds it appears equally nonsensical or enigmatic. About all we could say with any certainty at the outset was that what we had just read was written in some form of the English language (although the last word might confuse us even on this point).

What then do we make of this passage? This is an apt question, for we indeed are left with something to *make*, having been given very little of the customary features of textual significance. Does this give us licence to make just anything, to contort and manipulate the words to say and mean anything we like? This may be the charge of some, having lost all bearings for usual meaning-production or referentiality. But we have not lost *all* bearings. The text clearly signals some bearings, albeit unorthodox ones. As we reread the passage, certain familiar bearings begin to emerge, and prohibit us from going simply anywhere we fancy. To go anywhere we fancy requires bearings of some kind anyway – we cannot fancy from a vacuum, as Heidegger has taught us – and so, were we to integrate in any way with the passage, our fancy would have to be guided to some degree by what it was encountering in the text. As a measure of valuable reading, let us try to maximize this degree.

Our initial readings might have brought to the fore some vague connections with several discernible features: a list of unknown gentlemen, a child's nursery rhyme, the interpretation or witness of some event, and a Latin word or phrase having something to do with 'fidelity' or 'being faithful'. These all provide bearings, though for each reader the bearings will be placed differently, or lead in different directions. Certain words or phrases will also trigger other words or notions not necessarily connected with these initial bearings, but calling for connection in some way nevertheless. One example, which in fact does conceivably connect with the final Latin phrase, may be the religious allusions in the names and addresses: 'S. Bruno's' (St. Bruno, it can be surmised), 'Dieudonney' (pronounced the same as that which would translate in French 'God-given'), and 'Erchdeakin' (for archdeacon). The allusions do not supply a logic to give them cohesion or sense, but they do infuse the passage in a suggestive way. They provide the reader with possibilities.

Let us try to realize some of the possibilities afforded by the text. The passage begins with four Latinate words ending in '-ation'. The first of these captures the eye by its rarity – 'sublation'. The dictionaries tell us it is a word connected with the field of logic, and denotes a denial, contradiction or negation. Something in the passage, we might guess, stands to be undermined. For those schooled in philosophy, sublation would trigger something yet further, Hegel's *Aufhebung*, usually translated as 'sublation' in English. In Hegel's dialectic, *Aufhebung* refers to both the cancelling and the preservation of the two opposing sides in a synthesis. If we take the first 'of' as an objective preposition, it is 'compensation' that seems to be sublated. The third Latinate word, 'radification', is a pun on the words 'ratification' and, it would appear, 'radical'. The ratification, or confirmation of something, is radical. This something is the fourth word, 'interpretation'. Rendered together, then, the first sentence might read: interpretation's radical confirmation possesses a sublation of compensation. Or an interpretation cannot really confirm anything, since the compensation granted between interpreter and event is always sublated. Preserved or destroyed? we might ask, recalling Hegel. The sentence appears to ask the same question: 'with what sublation?'

Construing the possibilities in this manner, a self-reflexivity emerges in the passage, for it seems to be telling us that interpretation, even of its own self, is a flexible and uncertain business, which we have both just confirmed and denied (sublated) by interpreting it as such – confirmed by rendering it in only one of a myriad of ways, denied by rendering it to confirm what we have just claimed for it, which seems contradictory. Our rendering seems to have caught us in a closed circle, for what we claim the text may claim – interpretation is an open event – is on the one hand based clearly on what we have brought to the text, the preceding arguments of this essay, yet on the other hand is possible only because the text seems to go out of its way to furnish this interpretive leeway. Which side is dictating this leeway, ourselves with our theories, or the text, with its radical openness? Caught in the circle of our language, which dictates either side, it is neither, and yet both.

But there is more to the passage. The interpretation *in* the passage is 'by the byeboys'. Whoever the ones interpreting are, they are in effect called incidental figures, by the by. 'They being?', we might commonly ask. But the text states the matter, 'Being they', as if in response to our unstated question. The statement that should be a question reduces us to the supposedly incidental things at hand. This curtailed statement should put us immediately in mind of Heidegger's *Dasein*, or Being-there. Could the six listed names that follow, along with their addresses, in any way reflect the Being and the abode of Being that Heidegger eventually claimed for language? But the 'they' are not 'there'. These beings are clearly exaggerated fictional names with exaggerated fictional addresses. And they themselves are followed by an even more preposterous accumulation of figures – 'tout', 'stout', 'lank', 'sandy', 'rotter', 'rhymer' and 'Joax' – all of whom purportedly stand as interpreters or witnesses to some event. To claim a Heideggerian reading of these names seems the height of preposterousness.

But let us not judge too hastily. What is happening with these 'Being they'? The more formal names are not 'there' as persons in our real world, surely, but they are 'there' in the text, in their respective abodes. Added to them are figures in an accumulative rhyme, modelled on the nursery rhyme 'The House that Jack Built'. The rhyme works by building up successive causations, so that the object of one clause becomes the subject of the succeeding relative clause, whose object becomes the subject of the next clause, and so on. The effect of this build-up in the original rhyme is to give an unwavering sense of teleology, whose source is reliably the same each time, 'the house that Jack built'. The abode is always fixed. But in this passage, the source is altered, 'the hoose that Joax built', and what results from it is a jumbled uncertainty. Here the abode is hardly fixed. One could say it is sublated, denied its original form, and yet oddly preserved in the scheme of the rhyme. But it goes beyond even a Hegelian sense, for the altered abode invites the reader in to make something of the dwelling. So again, we could read the text as reflecting the reading or interpretative process itself. A textual space is provided, but not one we would expect. We find a 'Multiple Lodge', in which manifold possibilities present themselves. Our reading becomes a building-up of successive encounters with the text's features, much as the scheme of the nursery rhyme builds up.

But here our source is never fixed, and creatively alters each time. Were we to take the whole of *Finnegans Wake* into view, we would find Joyce himself doing this throughout: The 'House that Jack Built' model occurs several times, each with a different result: 'the garden Gough gave', 'the hoax that joke bilked', for example.[33] In the first of these occurrences early in Chapter One, the source turns out to be 'the ensuance of existentiality'.[34] If we restricted ourselves to our passage above, we could have no idea of Joyce's more profound intentions for this scheme. But, authorial intention aside, we might have been able to arrive at a similar sense of existentiality, for we could say the 'Being they' has called us into the shifting abode of the text, in which, dwelling, we are called to make the 'beings' become something new, to complete the half-finished building, so to speak, and provide a place for our own Being to reside. This we have done by completing the building according to our notion of reading as process, which creates a highly self-reflexive building. But our interpretation bears witness to the text's own interpretation of itself, whose incidental figures 'radify' an interpretation always open, and open especially to sublation.

'Bearing witness' then becomes crucial not only to this passage but to reading as a whole. What is being witnessed? Isolating the passage as we have, we are not given any details as to what event or story the 'by the byeboys' are standing as witnesses for. But it is not *what* the event is, but *how* it is witnessed which is of the greater importance. 'They had heard or had heard said or had heard said written.' Their witness never gets outside language or the text. We could certainly isolate this sentence and take it as a great poststructuralist credo. But if reading is the event we are bearing witness for, we could also take it as an indication of reading's process. For in reading we are bearing a witness of the text, whose own bearings witness to our understanding, so that we can bear witness *to* and *for*, or *on behalf of*, the text.

This process is a reciprocation between text and reader, a novel togetherness, which constitutes interpretation. We bear witness of the text by the text, a circularity indeed, but one which affords us the greatest creativity of our language and, in the process, the space to bear witness to our Being constituted by that language.

Yet if bearing witness is more than mere solipsism, if it is offering confirmation or testimony to an event on someone's or something's behalf, involving an 'other' to oneself, how trustworthy is a witness based on textual circularity and sublation? How faithful to the event can it be? The final word of our passage seems at first to undermine any faith or trust. 'Fidelisat' is not a Latin word, but a misspelling of the Latin 'fidelitas' meaning 'faithfulness' or 'fidelity'. Like the ending of the rhyme, the alteration seems to undercut the reliability of witness. And yet we could also read the neologism, as others have,[35] as a possible running together of the Latin phrase 'fideli sat', translated as '[it is] sufficient for the faithful one'. The adjective 'sat' ('enough', 'adequate', 'sufficient') would become significant. The witness or interpretation may not return one to the original event or a *given* behind the text, but it *suffices*. It is enough for validating the truth, for uncovering or granting the place from which existence can find its ground. For this ground is only ever textual, founded as it is upon language, through which, if we remain in Heidegger's wake, existence has its being.

In *Finnegans Wake*, then, we are given the fullest scope for reading as an ever-developing process. As Iser has stated in writing on Joyce's earlier novel *Ulysses*, and yet with even more relevance for its successor, 'we are confronted with the processing of reality rather than with its representation'.[36] Thus the old conventions of reading – seeking out what an author might have meant, seeking out what might be represented – must give way in Joyce to a new approach which 'serves to elucidate the processes by means of which everyday life is made accessible to experience',[37] or by which Being becomes Being. This is no easy task, as the reading of *Finnegans Wake* will attest. And its implications are great, begging extended examination and appraisal. But one effect is certain: under such a process, the reader is much more liable or responsible for what he or she comes away with, a fact which can be both more enlivening and more disturbing.

An 'Other' Process

As most theorists of reading will admit, modern theories of reading inevitably lead to an ethics of reading. Who is the reader liable or responsible *to*? We have mentioned that reading is a bearing of witness which involves an 'other'. Who or what is this 'other'? And do we stand in judgment before it? Such questions cannot ultimately be avoided. If we return to *Finnegans Wake* we may find a clue as to how such an ethics might be situated. We have suggested that the 'The House That Jack Built' nursery rhyme acts as an exemplar for the way reading, and indeed understanding, takes place: an accumulation of facts, events or encounters trace themselves back to a certain source, 'the house that Jack built'. In *Finnegans Wake*, this source is never the original. It is always something new. The scheme is present, but the 'house' is forever rebuilt, becoming such diverse structures as 'the ensuance of existentiality' and 'the hoax'.

In the middle of the book, the rhyme's scheme traces back to a source that is particularly significant:

> Eat early earthapples. Coax Cobra to chatters. Hail, Heva, we hear! This is the glider that gladdened the girl that list to the wind that lifted the leaves that folded the fruit that hung on the tree that grew in the garden Gough gave.[38]

The central metaphor of the entire novel, the Fall, is found here, as the 'house' becomes the 'garden Gough gave', Eden. The original Judaeo-Christian source of humanity, then, comes into play (alongside the earlier 'existentiality'), but the true source, God, is not named, or is renamed 'Gough', as if to sublate once again any sense of a Source or God-given original. Is it all merely a 'hoax' then? We began by saying that reading had lost its innocence. Reading has eaten the fruit by which it falters into knowledge, and is cast out of its original abode, never to return to its source. It is left to wander the world over, in hopes perhaps to regain or rebuild that abode in some form elsewhere, but with the knowledge of good and evil now informing and altering every step. This biblical paradigm, so crucial to *Finnegans Wake*, is also at work behind poststructuralist theory, as someone like Derrida speaks of 'the fall' of language and, increasingly, of the ethics in tracing the 'other' whose original source cannot be retrieved by language. This Other is ultimately theological in nature if reading is an issue of sources ('In the beginning was the Word'). But it is still theological if reading is a process whose sources are forever renewed.

The inability to locate the origins of textual significance upon a fixed or permanent – that is, metaphysical – site, and yet the ability to produce, or reproduce, textual significance by virtue of a self-imposing – that is existential – engagement brings us into a certain and inevitable theological dynamic. For this creative elusivity, this shifting origin which demands a continually new origination, this ungraspable meaning through which meaning is generated, ultimately concerns that about which we cannot speak, the Unnameable Other of a particular and long-established Judaeo-Christian theological and mystical tradition. Within this dynamic, language functions as a totally inadequate instrument for determining the divine Other, and yet, paradoxically, is also completely necessary for keeping the Other 'other'. Or, as Meister Eckhart might have rendered it, language is what allows us to 'ask God to free us of "God" ', that is of the limiting conceptions of the divine that fixate both God and ourselves.[39] Language provides for this peculiar liberation (from ourselves as much as from any form of physical or metaphysical idolatry) through a complex of linguistic, semantic, logical and conceptual differentials, enmeshed in a manner which necessarily entails slippage but which, in addition, calls for the regenerative input that keeps us responding and responsible to the Other as divinely other. Caught within this complex is the word 'God' itself, which Joyce, like the Hebraic Tetragrammaton, avoids directly, recasting it into 'Gough' in the instance of his Edenic play. This kind of textual regeneration finds expression in all Joyce's refabrications of the 'The House That Jack Built' scheme,[40] which refuse closure, and open the reader up to his or her own regenerative plurality of meaning. It is within such a 'housing', then, that one encounters the Totally Other: an Other who is not the giver or the given behind the text, but is that which allows anything to be given at all, including the very complex of language, and an Other who thus can ultimately be determined only by a resounding silence within that language.

So it is this Other that we 'bear witness' to in the process of our reading. And not just in the textual excesses of a work like *Finnegans Wake*. One might say that the reason the Bible has remained so paramount, not only within theological traditions, but within literary and literary critical (hermeneutical) traditions as well, is that it invites this very process of reading. To be sure, it has lent itself to an ethics of the kind which easily solidifies into a dogmatism, a legality, an ideology or a fundamentalism. But this happens more often as a result of the Bible not being *read*, of the Bible rather being dispensed or appropriated under a predetermining rubric which makes of the text a proprietary instrument or, worse, a nostrum. But when the Bible is read as a text in process, a text which, by its very nature, and in the engagement with it, ruptures and opens up upon itself, and sometimes in spite of itself, then its reading becomes truly transformational, as the reader's own being is ruptured and opened to new possibilities before the Other. This approach leads to a very different kind of ethics, whose prescriptive nature becomes a renewable provision and sufficiency – a 'seeing in advance', as it were, the delimitations (and our ethics are always in some manner delimiting notions or actions) which require a creative, regenerative responsibility and fidelity, a 'Fidelisat' – a sufficiency for the one faithful to the witness. The exact boundaries of this sufficiency are of course what need to be rigorously determined by each specific situation, and this is no straightforward process, imposing upon us our greatest challenge in the cultural and moral tumult of our turn-of-the-century times. But if our loss of hermeneutical innocence is the measure of these times, then our fidelity must be, if nothing else, to a reading that does not return us to a closed garden, but keeps us tilling the open ground from which we have been taken, that ground of all our textual terraces which makes up our language, our thought and our being.

Notes

1. See, for example, Wolfgang Iser's essay 'Indeterminacy and the Reader's Response in Prose Fiction', first published in *Aspects of Narrative*, edited by J. Hillis Miller (New York: Columbia University Press, 1971), 1–45, and reprinted in Wolfgang Iser, *Prospecting* (Baltimore MD: Johns Hopkins University Press, 1989), 3–30. In speaking of the 'reality' experienced by a reader within a text, he writes: 'Reality, then, is a process of realization necessitating the reader's involvement, because only the reader can bring it about' (*Prospecting*, 26).
2. 'The play of the text is therefore a performance for an assumed audience, and as such it is not just a game as played in ordinary life, but it is actually a staged play enacted for the reader, who is given a role enabling him or her to act out the scenario presented.' See Wolfgang Iser, 'The Play of the Text', in *Languages of the Unsayable*, edited by Sanford Budick and Wolfgang Iser (Stanford, CA: Stanford University Press, 1987), 336. (Also reprinted in *Prospecting*, 258.)
3. Anthony C. Thiselton, *New Horizons in Hermeneutics* (Grand Rapids, MI: Zondervan, 1992), 516.
4. Wolfgang Iser, 'Ulysses and the Reader', *Prospecting*, 131.
5. Representation, of course, is aligned to the whole notion of *referentiality*, which has been the key issue for so many theories of language, and which is often used in place of the

notion of a 'given', whether the reference is to a physical object in the world, or to a fixed meaning, and so on. We have used the word 'given' instead of 'reference' because it better carries the idea of metaphysical priority. What we are more concerned with is not whether words have reference to something else, but the nature of that reference and something else – is it prior to and fixed, or concurrent and flexible?

6. Wolfgang Iser, 'Representation: A Performative Act', *Prospecting*, 248.
7. See Thiselton, *New Horizons in Hermeneutics*, 524–50; also Raman Selden, *The Theory of Criticism* (New York: Longman, 1988), 186–221.
8. David Ray Griffin is a notable exception to Whitehead's omission from postmodern discussions. See his notion of *constructive postmodern thought* in his *Founders of Constructive Postmodern Philosophy: Peirce, James, Bergson, Whitehead, and Hartshorne* (Albany, NY: State University of New York Press, 1993).
9. The work of John Cobb, Jr. in particular gave rise to an entire theological subspecies: 'process theology'.
10. Even though, it must be admitted, both Dilthey and Husserl attempted to make a foundational science out of hermeneutics and phenomenology respectively.
11. Alfred North Whitehead, *Process and Reality: An Essay in Cosmology*, corrected edition, edited by David Ray Griffin and Donald W. Sherburne (New York: The Free Press, 1978), 23.
12. Ibid., 61.
13. Ibid., 65.
14. Ibid., 29.
15. Ibid., 44–5. Whitehead's use of the term 'synthetic' here is not to be confused with Kant's use of the term. For Kant, 'synthesis' was a function of the mind's coming to understanding within a speculative or critical framework, or what he called 'the mere result of the power of imagination' (*Critique of Pure Reason*, translated by Norman Kemp Smith [London: Macmillan, 1990], 112). Whitehead, who repudiated speculative philosophy, and Kantian doctrine in particular (Preface to *Process and Reality*, xiii), champions an organic philosophy in which subjective consciousness is derivative and not primary (*Process and Reality*, 161–2). The 'synthesis' within any givenness, then, is part of the holistic reality of things, subjective only by virtue of the fact 'that the whole universe consists of elements disclosed in the analysis of the experiences of subjects' as actual entities (166). The synthesis is thus not epistemological, but ontological. See below for its relation to Hegel's understanding of synthesis.
16. Whitehead, *Process and Reality*, 21.
17. See ibid., 219ff.
18. Thiselton, *New Horizons in Hermeneutics*, 517.
19. Under such a mutual dependence, the term 'text' cannot of course be limited simply to written words on a page, for this would imply that one's existence is in some measure dependent upon literacy, upon the ability to read within a chosen language. The term thus has to be broadened to include any set of symbols, schema or semiotic codes which can be conceived as carriers or potentialities of meaning, including visual images, communal rituals, bodily gestures and so on. The term 'textuality' has been employed for this very purpose within contemporary theory.
20. Whitehead, *Process and Reality*, 160–62.
21. See ibid., 180–83. Whitehead tells us that a correlation is established between two species of perceived things when 'one species has some "ground" in common with a perceptum of another species' (180). He does not explicate what constitutes this 'ground' or how the correlation is established, issues which a theory of language, or any hermeneutics for that matter, precisely seeks to resolve. One can take the work of Paul Ricoeur as a prime example.

22. Martin Heidegger, *Being and Time*, translated by John Macquarrie and Edward Robinson (Oxford: Basil Blackwell, 1962), 183.
23. Ibid., 189.
24. Ibid., 195.
25. Ibid., 195.
26. In the 1950s, Heidegger affirmed the continuity between *Sein und Zeit* and what was to follow later: 'What mattered to me then and still does is to bring out the Being of beings – though no longer in the manner of metaphysics': from *On the Way to Language* (New York: Harper and Row, 1971), as quoted by Thiselton, *New Horizons in Hermeneutics*, 106.
27. Gerald L. Bruns, *Hermeneutics Ancient and Modern* (New Haven, CT: Yale University Press, 1992), 232.
28. See specifically *Being and Time*, 56–7 and 261–6; and later, 'The Origin of the Work of Art', in Martin Heidegger, *Poetry, Language and Thought*, translated by Albert Hofstadter (New York: Harper and Row, 1971), 51ff.
29. Martin Heidegger, 'Language', in *Poetry, Language and Thought*, 192.
30. Martin Heidegger, ' "... *Poetically Man Dwells* ..." ', in *Poetry, Language and Thought*, 215.
31. Umberto Eco, *Limits of Interpretation* (Bloomington, IN: Indiana University Press, 1990), 137–51; Jacques Derrida, 'Two Words for Joyce', in *Post-Structuralist Joyce: Essays from the French*, edited by Derek Attridge and Daniel Ferrer (Cambridge: Cambridge University Press, 1984), 145–59.
32. James Joyce, *Finnegans Wake*, with an introduction by Seamus Deane (London: Penguin, 1992), 369.
33. Ibid., 271, 511.
34. Ibid., 18.
35. Brendan O Hehir and John M. Dillon, *A Classical Lexicon for Finnegans Wake* (Berkeley, CA: University of California Press, 1977), 338.
36. Iser, 'Ulysses and the Reader', 135.
37. Ibid., 137.
38. Joyce, *Finnegans Wake*, 271.
39. Meister Eckhart, *Selected Writings*, edited and translated by Oliver Davies (London: Penguin, 1994), 205.
40. Even as that scheme has apparent roots in a Hebrew chant, 'Had Gadyo', first found in a 1590 edition of the *Haggadah*: *The Oxford Dictionary of Nursery Rhymes*, edited by Iona and Peter Opie (London: Oxford University Press, 1975), 231.

Chapter 2

Derrida and Whitehead

Timothy Mooney

Introduction

A rejection of the notion of substance, an emphasis on intraworldly experience and an incorporation of ideas from modern biology are just three of the distinctive features of Alfred North Whitehead's process metaphysics or philosophy of organism. The last two features give his scheme a heavily naturalistic tinge, despite his positing of eternal objects or universal forms of definiteness, which – together with subjective aims or final causes – are instantiated in a divinity prior to worldly realization.[1] Such naturalism might seem largely to preclude a comparison with the work of Jacques Derrida, with other differences between the two being left aside. Derrida began his career as a student of phenomenology and structuralism, and by far the greater number of his philosophical writings have been devoted to thinkers who are explicitly post-Kantian. Yet this does not mean that he is a transcendental philosopher who abandons experience and the empirical world in favour of language and consciousness.

In this chapter I argue that Derrida's work, which has been shown to be heavily informed by systems theory and evolutionary biology, is not in fact shut off from the extraconscious and extralinguistic dimensions of actuality. I also suggest that his deconstructive approach is strikingly similar to Whitehead's in rejecting essentialism, namely, the idea of fixed and determined essences that underlie accidental properties and changes. From a Derridean perspective, one might even see Whitehead's alternative as insufficiently radical, since it seems to posit not just eternal objects and God, but a cosmology in which the most fundamental beings or 'actual entities' undergo no essential changes or mutations in their respective histories. It is arguable, however, that the latter conclusion would only be consequent on a restrictive interpretation of the pathways of process possible in Whitehead's metaphysics.

In the first part of this chapter I will outline briefly Whitehead's account of essentialism and his proposed alternative. In the second I will turn to Derrida's outline of 'the centre' and ensuing deconstruction. Here I contend that his conceptions of *différance* and iteration have an applicability beyond language and consciousness, drawing on recent studies to illustrate this. In the final section, I note that Whitehead's cosmology can be modified to meet the likely deconstructive objections, in that it need not involve eternal objects or God, and I maintain that his subjective aims do not preclude essential changes or evolutionary mutations on the part of actual entities.

Whitehead's Critique of Essentialism

Throughout his later career, Whitehead is adamant that the concepts of independent and substantial existence are two of the greatest errors that have infected the philosophical tradition. He already finds the genesis of these notions in the Ionian thinkers, who wanted to find some fundamental stratum that underlies and composes nature. Their various answers, he claims, were all couched in terms of stuff or matter or material which is *simply located* in space and time. That is to say, regions of space and periods of time were taken as having no essential reference to other regions and periods. In Whitehead's account, this primitive conception of a separable and simply located substratum has hindered philosophy and science ever since, inasmuch as it initiated the tendency to see the fundamental existents in just this fashion.

Whitehead argues that Plato compounded the error of independent existence. The theory of immutable forms existing over and above the physical world denigrates flux or process, for the things that flow are regarded as limited or imperfect, excluded from what they are not. And if the opposites 'static' and 'fluent' are taken to characterize separately diverse actualities, the attempt to explain their interplay will involve contradiction at every single step.[2] Although Aristotle opposed this bifurcation of reality, continues Whitehead, it was in his thought that the ideas of underlying and independent existents came to be comprehensively married. This marriage was accomplished through his subject–predicate logic – which simplifies the polyadic relations holding in reality into two terms – and through his correlative definition of primary substance as that which is neither predicated of nor present in a subject.[3]

If we ask for a full description of such a primary substance or individual fact, observes Whitehead, we are given an answer in terms of the various qualities or characteristics which, when taken together, are held to constitute the real thing in question. Such an answer may be pragmatically necessary in everyday life, but as a statement about the nature of things, it must be regarded as seriously inadequate:

> Each substantial thing is thus conceived as complete in itself, without any reference to any other substantial thing. Such an account ... renders the interconnected world of real individuals unintelligible. The universe is shivered into a multitude of disconnected substantial things, each thing in its own way exemplifying its private bundle of abstract characters which have found a common home in its own substantial individuality. But substantial thing cannot call unto substantial thing. A substantial thing may acquire a quality, a credit, but real landed estate, never. In this way Aristotle's doctrines of Predication and of Primary Substance have issued into a doctrine of the conjunction of attributes and of the disjunction of primary substances. All modern epistemologies, all modern cosmologies, wrestle with this problem. There is, for their doctrine, a mysterious reality in the background, intrinsically unknowable by any direct intercourse. In the foreground of direct enjoyment, there is the play and interplay of various qualities diversifying the surface of the substantial unity of the solitary individual in question.[4]

In Whitehead's view, the foregoing account is essentialist in that the primary substance remains fundamentally unchanged through its life-span. The problem is not with the word 'substance', but rather with the concept of a continuous stuff which endures without differentiation. Inasmuch as it may indeed undergo alterations with regard to its accidental qualities and relations, the substance remains 'numerically self-identical in its character of one actual entity throughout its accidental adventures'.[5]

This concept was carried to its logical conclusion by Descartes, who claimed that the substantial individual requires nothing but itself in order to exist and sundered the material from the mental, thus making a virtue of incoherence. And here too, states Whitehead, in rather Procrustean fashion, is to be found the starting-point of the systems of Berkeley, Hume and Kant. As the development of the Ionian idea of a separable substratum, Aristotle's conception has formed the basis of scientific materialism.[6] For Whitehead, however, this notion of static substance has been broken down by recent advances in physics, that is, by the work of Planck and Einstein and their successors. Physics can now be seen as the study of smaller organisms and biology of the larger ones, with both disciplines pointing towards a new cosmology which will stress process, transition and relativity instead of stasis and solitude.[7] It is in *Process and Reality* that Whitehead sets out such a new cosmology.

In this scheme, eternal objects or universal forms of definiteness are second in importance to actual entities or actual occasions and only exist through the latter, which include amongst their number God. Each actual entity is a process and a result, and though Whitehead always insists that beings cannot be sundered from their processes of becoming, every actual entity that has become passes from a 'satisfied' subject to a 'perishing' superject. It comes to provide determinations for those becoming actual entities which will succeed it.[8] Actual entities can only become – and become just what they are – by appropriating determinations from previous ones, so that these acts of appropriation, entitled 'prehensions' or 'concrete facts of relatedness' have an essential and not an accidental character. What is abandoned here, stresses Whitehead, is any idea of an isolated and unchanging subject of change.[9]

The macroscopic world of stones, animals and humans is composed of ordered groups or 'societies' of these basic actual entities, and to emphasize the priority of the category of relation over that of substance, Whitehead argues that the analysis of actual entities into prehensions is the exhibition of their most concrete elements.[10] Every prehension involves a subject or prehending actual entity, an object or actual entity being prehended, and a subjective form, the particular way the subject prehends the object. It can be noted that this overall account is panpsychist in that every actual entity possesses both a physical and a mental pole, though the second is derivative of the first and is negligible in the simplest actual entities.[11] Hence the distinctions drawn, not just between positive prehensions (also called 'feelings') and negative prehensions, but between those feelings which are physical and those which are conceptual.

A physical feeling is the most elementary prehension, and involves its subject preliminarily encountering one of its object's simple or complex forms of definiteness (the initial datum) and then grasping that form concretely (the objective datum). Since the form of definiteness was itself grasped in a certain way by the object, the present subject feels in a certain conformity with the former. Put another way, the way it feels its objective datum will be marked by the way in which its object once felt that datum. In this way the prehending subject is passive or receptive as well as being active or perceptive. Also there is a minimal continuity of subjective form between actual entities, the one being reproduced in the other.[12] But if physical feelings grasp concrete slices of relevant objects for their subjects, conceptual feelings do not. Here there is no progression from the initial to the objective datum. A conceptual feeling is the feeling of an eternal object in its individual essence, abstracted from the actual entity in which it is realized, so that this concrete entity is not felt at all.[13]

Following Leibniz, Whitehead describes conceptual prehension in terms of appetition, which is the creative principle of unrest in all things that tends towards the realization of the possible. Every physical feeling brings with it an appetite for its continuance or change in the future, and thus gives rise to a conceptual feeling. To give an example from the macroscopic world, self-preservation involves the appetite for continuance, whereas thirst involves an appetite for change, namely its quenching. In both cases, appetition enables the passage beyond immediate experience as an unrealized possibility is conceptually grasped and pursued. Thus a conceptual feeling is the entertainment by a subject – in however elementary a manner – of a possible form of definiteness that this same subject may assume at some stage in the future. It is the valuation of an abstract possibility as opposed to the concrete feeling of an actual fact.[14]

Negative prehensions feel neither concrete actual entities nor abstract eternal objects. Rather they 'eliminate from feeling'. But a negative prehension does constitute a bond with these entities, however negligible it may be. Because it is a definite act of excluding them from positive inclusion in its subject, a negative prehension must have a certain minimal 'awareness' of them as unsuitable or irrelevant. For the same reason a negative prehension always has a subjective form, no matter how faint or trivial, for it can only reject some possibility of inclusion in a particular way. For Whitehead, a prehending subject retains the imprint of what it might have been. What it has avoided can still be an important component of its make-up.[15]

In the Whiteheadian scheme, the positive and negative prehensions in a process of becoming, from the earlier and simpler to the later and more complex, are guided by a certain plan aimed at a certain end, and this he terms the 'subjective aim' of the actual entity. Operating in and through conceptual feelings, the subjective aim determines – at least from the subject's perspective – the subjective forms of all those prehensions that follow on from the first simple physical feeling or feelings that initiated that same subject's act of becoming. For this reason the subjective aim is the 'final cause' of the process of becoming.[16] It is not hard to discern a resemblance between the subjective aim of an actual entity and the entelechy of the monad in Leibniz. Though Whitehead is once again careful to reject any subject–predicate or substance–attribute schema:

> The term 'subject' has been retained because in this sense it is familiar in philosophy. But it is misleading. The term 'superject' would be better. The subject–superject is the purpose of the process originating the feelings. The feelings are inseparable from the end at which they aim; and this end is the feeler. The feelings aim at the feeler, as their final cause. The feelings are what they are in order that their subject may be what it is ... If the subject–predicate form of statement be taken as metaphysically ultimate, it is then impossible to express this doctrine of feelings and their superject. It is better to say that the feelings *aim at* their subject, than to say that they *are aimed at* their subject. For the latter mode of expression removes the subject from the scope of the feeling and assigns it to an external agency. Thus

the feeling would be wrongly abstracted from its own final cause. This final cause is an inherent element in the feeling, constituting the unity of that feeling.[17]

The subjective aim is, thus, concerned with an actual entity as it will be in its final form. Though it can be emphasized that it does not determine completely the process of becoming, because it will be recalled in its physical feelings at least the developing subject or superject has to feel with a certain conformity to its objects.

As the final product of these 'superjective' and 'objective' determinations, an actual entity is in each case an instance of creativity, a passage into novelty whose character transcends all other existents to a greater or lesser degree. The point is that it is not the undifferentiated reproduction of some fixed or self-identical essence. On this account, nature is never the same twice, always passing beyond itself.[18] Through its component actual entities, then, the universe as a whole is a creative advance into novelty, from the higher organisms down to what has traditionally been seen as dead matter, so that evolution is not merely a biological phenomenon. The various forms of order, which prevail amongst societies of actual entities, define a particular 'cosmic epoch'. But in the future new types of order may come to prevail, constituting further cosmic epochs in the ever evolving process that is reality.[19]

Whitehead attributes the stability of the creative process, not just to the realized past, but also to God, who is a dipolar actual entity and the equiprimordial accompaniment of creativity and the world. In God's 'primordial nature' God conceptually prehends the totality of unrealized eternal objects and embodies their ideal order in so doing. For this reason, adds Whitehead, the initial phase of every other actual entity's subjective aim is an endowment, which it 'inherits from the inevitable ordering of things, conceptually realized in the mind of God ... the initial stage of the aim is rooted in the nature of God, and its completion depends on the self-causation of the subject–superject'.[20] Whitehead goes on to remark that in the later self-causative stage the becoming entity will transcend all other existing actual entities, God included.[21]

The second aspect of the divinity is God's 'consequent nature', which is God's physical prehension of every other actual entity as it becomes or realizes itself. God grasps the actual entity in its original vibrancy and preserves its modes of feeling in Godself. In this way God evolves with the spatiotemporal world and is implicated in its incompleteness. This implies that both God and the spatiotemporal world are in the grip of the creative advance, with each being a source of novelty for the other; the first originates novelty in the world through its primordial nature, the second a consequent novelty in the divinity through its concrete becomings. In this account, claims Whitehead, God is not an adjunct introduced to save metaphysical principles from collapse, for God serves instead as their chief exemplification.[22]

Derrida's Deconstruction of the Centre

Derrida's account of the philosophical tradition does not begin with the Ionians, yet quickly comes to manifest a close resemblance to Whitehead's critique of independent, substantial existence. Influenced by the Nietzschean attack on Platonic metaphysics, Derrida claims that philosophy in general is born from a desire for presence, for some ultimate actuality or form which can be intellectually intuited beyond time and change.[23] He goes on to claim that this fundamental desire itself ensues from what could be broadly described as a fear of the outside, in which the outside denotes everything that lies beyond oneself or one's comprehension. It is broadly the domain of the world, of the mediate, the contingent, the variable and the uncertain. The fear of the outside, then, is the fear of everything that is unknown or uncanny or uncontrolled.[24]

For Derrida, the fear of the outside and correlative desire for presence manifest themselves in all theories of a centre, that is, of an underlying ground and indestructible point of orientation. In 'Structure, Sign, and Play in the Discourse of the Human Sciences' (1966), he states that this notion can even be found in some theories that seem to emphasize structurality and relatedness rather than substantial independence. He contends that from the very beginning of philosophy:

> The function of this center was not only to orient, balance, and organize the structure – one cannot in fact conceive of an unorganized structure – but above all to make sure that the organizing principle of the structure would limit what we might call the *play* of the structure ... it has always been thought that the center, which is by definition unique, constituted that very thing within a structure, which, whilst governing the structure, escapes structurality. This is why classical thought concerning structure could say that the center is, paradoxically, *within* the structure and *outside* it... The concept of centered structure – although it represents coherence itself, the condition of the *episteme* as philosophy or science – is contradictorily coherent. And as always, coherence in contradiction expresses the force of a desire. The concept of centered structure is in fact the concept of a play based on a fundamental ground, a play constituted on the basis of a fundamental immobility and a reassuring certitude, which itself is beyond the reach of play.[25]

The notion of a centre beyond the reach of play, states Derrida, is at one with the notion of being as presence, with the concepts and names given to the centre serving as subdeterminations of presence. Foremost in the Classical period are Plato's ideas and Aristotle's forms, the highest of the latter being the intelligible and self-absorbed prime mover.[26] Foremost in modernity are the Cartesian Cogito and the 'living present' of consciousness in Husserl. Both are posited as the ground of truth and evidence, though Descartes will ultimately guarantee the veracity of worldly ideas by appealing to a divine mind.[27] But in every single case, whether ancient or modern, the centre is once again taken as transcending empirical facticity and contingency.

Derrida maintains that the various appeals to a centre or core of presence have produced a series of 'violent hierarchies' in the western tradition whereby one term of a binary opposition or conceptual couple is taken as pre-eminent and essential, and the other as accidental and inferior. Soul has been privileged over body, the intelligible over the sensible and the living sounds of speech over the frozen marks of writing.[28] As Henry Staten has stressed, essence and accident are in fact the most general rubrics under which to range all other instances of opposition and subordination: 'all concepts in general of opposition between positive value and privation, inside and outside, purity and contamination, ideal or logical and empirical, a priori and contingent'.[29]

The strategy of deconstruction is to unravel these violent hierarchies, and hence Derrida's positing of an original '*différance*' or an 'arche-writing'. Derrida seems to say that a differential relation within and between every entity or a function infects it from its very beginning with a non-present heterogeneity, which is incapable of complete interiorization or sublation. Something can only present itself, according to Derrida, if it is an element in a system, and this involves other non-present elements, with all the elements being spaced out in the manner of a text or weave and nothing being simply present or closed or hermetically self-contained. As in Whitehead's system, unity implies relatedness in both a positive and a negative sense, with each entity or function being both open and closed to other ones in all its phases.[30]

I cannot enter into a detailed discussion of *différance* within the confines of this chapter, but it is to be noted that it first emerges in Derrida's account of Husserl's living present. Husserl realized that self-awareness has a synthetic character, such that the awareness of the present moment (primal impression) must pre-reflexively carry a memory of the preceding moment (retention), and anticipate the succeeding one (protention). His 'living present' is nothing other than this triform intentional structure. But whereas Husserl holds out for the possibility of transparent self-awareness, Derrida points out that the retended moment upon which consciousness must reflect is already a modification of what was once a primal impression but is now absent. Consciousness involves an inevitable delay which precludes it from transparently knowing itself.[31]

Derrida goes on to maintain that consciousness is incapable of mastering meaning, which it deploys through language. Following Saussure, he contends that linguistic terms are not just differentially constituted, but also open to change. Through repetition or iteration in different contexts, they can take on ideal meanings over and above their existing ones, and this power of mutating proliferation is an ineradicable part of their structure. A term or phrase can become detached, not only from the subject that utters and inscribes it, but also from the wider text of which it is a part. It can be grafted onto other texts in other contexts that may alter radically the originally intended meaning. Since the iterable medium may alter the message, what is said or written may always become radically different from what one meant in saying or writing.[32]

Derrida's interpretations of Saussure and Husserl are suggestive of a textual idealism, which confines itself to a language or consciousness, for he has remarked that everything is produced textually, through *différance*, and that 'there is nothing outside the text'.[33] Yet he has been quick to argue that *différance* is just one necessary condition of possibility of an entity or function, not a sufficient one. And the 'I-think' of consciousness is not a substantial or transcendental given, but a property that emerges from the living body and physical nature.[34] Furthermore, it can be stressed that his notion of textuality as *différance* or arche-writing is taken to embrace, not just natural language, but also 'action, movement, thought, reflection, unconsciousness, experience, affectivity and so on'.[35]

This general application can also be discerned when Derrida states that 'writing' appears irreducible in current scientific fields, most notably in biology. In the genetic codes that go towards making them what they are, he observes, living organisms bear the trace of an indefinite chain of ancestors. The same coding points to organisms and determinations which are not yet present and can thus be understood as a particular type of inscription. In Derrida's view, this is why 'the contemporary biologist speaks of writing and *pro-gramme* in relation to the most elementary processes of information within the living cell'.³⁶ But what is most noteworthy from the perspective of the present study is that not only the concept of *différance*, but also those of iteration and mutation will be given a general extension in deconstructive thinking.³⁷

I noted above that Derrida rejects any notion of a centre which would organize a structure but remain beyond the play of that structure. Yet it is not clear that the positing of *différance* of itself amounts to a rejection of essentialism. One might characterize a centre as a complex code, which is differentially constituted while still holding on to an idea of monoform finality, that is, of a single end or goal the process of development towards which is determined by this centre. The process might go off course and the centre as synthetic complex be destroyed, but such events would be regarded as external accidents that occasionally impinge on what would otherwise be an absolutely invariant process towards a set end. As Christopher Johnson argues, this classically metaphysical finalism goes back to Aristotle and is refined by Hegel:

> All objects, says Aristotle, have their own proper form, progressively realized during their respective histories: the end is contained in the beginning, the alpha is the omega. Any interference with this natural history Aristotle considers to be the violent or unnatural infraction of some external agency. This vitalist basis of the teleological argument has a particularly strong legacy in Western metaphysics. Hegel, for example, uses the metaphor of the seed to explain the unfolding of the concept... Hegel's metaphor of the seed, in accordance with the scientific culture of his time, avoids the pitfall of preformationism (the future configuration of the tree is not contained in miniature in the seed, but is 'enveloped in a spiritual manner'). Despite this, the basic premise of purposeful, predetermined development, by analogy with vital processes, remains. Indeed, in the Hegelian system the accidents or *peripeteia* envisaged by Aristotle as unnatural perturbations can be reabsorbed (recuperated, reappropriated) through the play of the dialectic, the more general evolution towards the Absolute remaining untouched.³⁸

Derrida agrees with all this, holding that 'force and potentiality, *dynamics*, have always been thought... within the horizon of an eschatology or a teleology that refers, according to a circle, to an archeology', with potentiality being 'the systematic predetermining of becoming as production and development'.³⁹ And he is clearly unhappy, notes Johnson, with any variant of this classical finalism. Derrida objects to the positing of fully determining forms that would stifle force or, more precisely, enclose progression towards the future within themselves. What is required instead, he maintains, is an 'economy' of force and form that will counter these simple oppositions.⁴⁰ He does sketch just such an account, and it is here that Johnson finds affinities between his work and concepts from general systems theory. It will therefore be helpful to consider the latter before turning to Derrida's exposition.

In systems theory, a code or programme is the memory of its structure or system, and it does have a goal-seeking or *teleonomic* function in that it seeks to conserve and perpetuate that system.⁴¹ But since it needs a channel or medium of transmission within the world, a code is liable to random interference, that is, to *noise*. And on this theory there is never a channel of information without some noise. But because of a looseness in its connections, the system can absorb and integrate a considerable degree of noise, surviving the changes the latter wreaks while still progressing towards its overall goal. The capacity of the system to go towards a final state in different ways or from alternative pathways is entitled *equifinality* by Ludwig von Bertalanffy, the founder of general systems theory.[42] The manner in which a code is realized through its system, therefore, is not strictly set or predetermined.

Johnson remarks that the looseness of connections allows for survival because fixed or finalized connections would result in 'a kind of paralysis: the system would be unable to adapt to a changing environment, it would have no reserves of alternatives to draw upon'.[43] An even more interesting plank of systems theory, however, is the idea that in certain circumstances the output of the system can return in part to alter its input. To put it more precisely, some of the alternative pathways taken by the coded system in response to the random influx of external changes can actually alter its code or programme through a process of feedback. In its attempts to conserve the system, the code can itself be subjected to alteration: it can be 're-programmed', as it were, for another end or goal. This process of divergence in which similar initial conditions lead to different end-states in different circumstances is termed *multifinality* and is not more amenable to calculation than the events which are its catalysts.[44]

Thus a system is seen as exposed to alteration in its total constitution, from the whole and the parts right through to the code or programme. And Johnson notes that a living organism can be seen as an open system par excellence in that it 'survives only through a relation of export and import of energy and information with its environment'.[45] Certainly, another end with which the organism may be 're-programmed' will usually just involve a slight divergence from the original one and not upset the organism's relative stability. But it is a divergence nonetheless, and its possibility precludes a singular or monoform finalism. Also multifinality, as a preclusion of finalism or vitalism, rules essentialism – the demarcation of fixed essences on the one hand from superficial accidents on the other – out of court, which can be illustrated when we consider biological evolution as an instantiation of multifinalism.[46]

As Henry Staten observes, there was a recognition in Darwinian evolutionary theory that slight divergences within a species only have an 'accidental' character insofar as they are subspecies or varieties, which are based on individual differences. But if successive individuals accumulate these individual differences, they can, in time, add up by non-specific gradations to distinct species, the conceptual insight of Darwinism being that accidental varieties are already incipient species. The minute change from one gradation to the next, notes Staten, 'contains an increment of essential or specific change: the transition to a new category has already begun in the slightest individual variation'.[47] Each 'essence' with its tiny variations is in Staten's words a *transitive essence*, a term within an identity continuum that has 'no distinct or unique essence boundary to separate it from the immediately surrounding terms'.[48] It is transitive in being itself part of the way towards the essence of something distinct from it.

What we can now provide, following on Staten and Johnson, is an outline of the way aspects of Derrida's own account converge strikingly with some of the major concepts current in general systems theory and biology. For Derrida, the centre or code or programme of a system also has a teleonomic role, broadly orienting the structure as well as organizing and balancing it.[49] Being inscribed in a worldly and open structure, however, the stabilizing centre or code may itself be subject to random interference or perturbation as it is iterated. 'The procedures of "routing" and of distribution, the paths of transmission,' claims Derrida, 'concern the very support of the messages sufficiently not to be without effect on the content.'[50]

Derrida embraces equifinalism in that his unhappiness with the 'systematic predetermining of becoming' by a teleological mechanism carries over into a rejection of the conception of an interior design. This would be 'simply anterior to a work which would supposedly be the expression of it'.[51] The development of a structure, he contends, cannot be enclosed by its centre or code any more than by its present context, with neither centre nor context constituting an 'absolute anchorage'.[52] And precisely because there is no such determining centre, it is impossible to specify the particular routes that the structure will pursue so as to maintain its stability once 'otherness introduces determination and puts the system in circulation'.[53]

One might already suspect that Derrida is open to this conclusion when he affirms a 'play in the machine', a looseness in each structure's components. But it can also be shown that he subscribes to the idea of multifinality. He suggests that the *telos* of every structure must be comprehended in the most indeterminate form consistent with its retention, and that the affirmation of play implies '*genetic* indetermination'.[54] And he expounds his own thesis of the mutability of a code or centre as follows:

> As the heterogeneity and absolute exteriority of the seed, seminal différance does constitute itself into a programme, but it is a programme which cannot be formalized. For reasons that *can* be formalized. The infinity of its code, its rupture, does not take a form saturated with self-presence in the encyclopedic circle. It is attached, so to speak, to the incessant falling of a *supplement to the code*... That the sense of this coupling by the *is* should be one of fulfilment, a fulfilling productivity that comes not just to repeat but to complete nature through writing, would mean that nature is somehow incomplete, that it lacks something needed for it to be what it is, that it has to be supplemented. Which can be done by nature alone, since nature is all... The accident or the throw of the dice that 'opens' such a text does not contradict the rigorous necessity of its formal assemblage. The game here is the unity of chance and rule, of the programme and its leftovers or extras.[55]

Put another way, the seminal *différance* in a centre or code or the looseness that it shares with its structure allows for its reinscription, that is, for the supplementary recombination or reprogramming initiated by the influx of the random. The alterations wrought in a code are related to the alternative paths taken by its structure, with such deviation of itself alone having the capacity to change the course of what might first appear to be 'an imperturbable destination and an inflexible order'.[56] There is thus a continual interrelation of and competition between force and form or randomness and code, so that the new continually occurs through a code's worldly iteration.[57]

New Pathways of Process

It is now clear that what unites Whitehead's metaphysics and Derrida's deconstructive strategy is their explicit rejection of fixed, predetermining essence. The one rejects the concept of unchanging subjects of change, and the other that of an immutable centre standing outside what it governs. Yet the proponent of deconstruction might ask whether Whitehead has comprehensively rejected the concept of a centre and the essentialism that has traditionally gone with it. In this regard we can anticipate some likely objections from this perspective, objections which are not unique to this approach and which in some cases have been made by critics who argue that Whitehead violates his own dictum that metaphysical principles should admit of no exception.

Difficulties already emerge in Whitehead's accounts of eternal objects and of God's primordial nature. To claim that there is a totality of unrealized eternal objects which can be conceptually entertained in their individual essences is to claim some being for bare universals which, dependent though they may be on God, are nonetheless sundered in the first instance from the world of process. In affirming the separate existence of these abstract entities, notes Donald Sherburne, Whitehead slips into the Platonic sundering of being and becoming he decries elsewhere.[58] Since God prehends every abstract or concrete eternal object through God's primordial and consequent aspects, furthermore, God is accorded a range of experience which is radically different from that accorded to the passing actual entities which constitute the realm of becoming.

This range of experience is particularly problematic with regard to God's physical prehensions. A worldly actual entity refers mediately to other places and times through prehensions of proximate predecessors which have provided data for it, data which relate in turn to still more previous actual entities. Yet God somehow has the capacity of immediately prehending worldly entities as they become. In Derrida's language, He takes a place outside the text, outside the empirical weave of prehensive relations in which data can only be supplied by perishing superjects. Since God is unchanging in one of God's aspects and constantly becoming in the other, the question arises – a question first articulated by A.H. Johnson – as to how worldly actual entities can ever prehend God from their own standpoints.[59] In deconstructive terminology once again, God is a centre beyond the play in which each thing becomes an object for other subjects.

From a Derridean perspective, the other thesis, which is that the first stage of a subjective aim is an endowment received from God, would disjoin force from the form, making an actual entity's final cause come from outside into an antecedent world that initially provides data for physical prehension alone. But even if this particular difficulty could be resolved, the Derridean might further claim that the very idea of a subjective aim which operates through conceptual feelings and guides both positive and negative prehensions reintroduces essentialism. The becoming subject admittedly has to feel with a certain conformity to its objects, receiving determinations from them, but this might only occur when these determinations accord completely with the subjective aim, having survived the filtering process of negative prehensions.

On this account, the actual entity's process of becoming would be an example of monoform finality, of an absolutely invariant process towards a set end. This interpretation appears to find a considerable degree of textual support when we look at Whitehead's characterization of societies as against actual entities:

> The society, as such, must involve antecedents and subsequents. In other words, a society must exhibit the peculiar quality of endurance. The real actual things that endure are all societies. They are not actual occasions. It is the mistake that has thwarted European

metaphysics from the time of the Greeks, namely, to confuse societies with the completely real things which are the actual occasions. A society has an essential character, whereby it is the society that it is, and it also has accidental qualities which vary as circumstances alter. Thus a society, as a complete existence and as retaining the same metaphysical status, enjoys a history expressing its changing relations to changing circumstances. But an actual occasion has no such history. It never changes. It only becomes and perishes.[60]

What seems to distinguish the more fundamental actual entity, then, is the absence of change or alteration in its process of becoming. Such change might be seen, to repeat Johnson's words, as 'the violent or unnatural infraction of some external agency'. Whitehead himself appears to adopt this position conclusively when he speaks of every becoming actual entity as 'internally determined but externally free'.[61]

If these objections are the ones most likely to be made from a deconstructive perspective, it remains to be seen whether Whitehead's system can be defended against them. It may be possible to qualify or modify or even abandon some of his theses without jettisoning the system as a whole. There is no doubt that Whitehead himself comprehends his metaphysics in fallibilistic terms. Speculative philosophy, he remarks, is nothing but the *endeavour* to frame a scheme in which every item of our experience will be capable of interpretation, and in philosophical discussion 'the merest hint of dogmatic certainty as to finality of statement is an exhibition of folly'.[62]

Two ways in which the metaphysics of process can be modified involve the abandonment of both unrealized eternal objects or bare individual essences and of the divinity. Those forms of definiteness which will be empirically realized – and are thus possible – could be taken as emergent from the world itself, making eternity no more than an abstraction. Such an account of emergence – which cannot be reproduced in this short essay – has been sketched by Lewis S. Ford.[63] And if actual and possible forms of definiteness can be explained in immanent terms, the same may be true of their ordering, so that in these respects it is not necessary to posit the primordial nature of God in the first place. In this naturalistic account, ideal order might be understood as a regulative idea to which empirical forms merely approximate.

The consequent nature of God might be more easily rejected as metaphysically superfluous, since it does not appear to function as a ground. Detailed discussion of this point must also be passed over for reasons of space. But it can be noted that Whitehead admits to the difficulty of how actual entities in the world could ever prehend a divinity that does not provide data through perishing, stating that this is a genuine problem which he never attempts to solve.[64] There remains, however, the final function attributed to God in God's primordial nature, namely, that of endowing every other actual entity with the initial stage of its subjective aim.

Donald Sherburne has contended that the past of the empirical world is in fact adequate to perform this function. It is quite possible, on his view, to draw a distinction between an actual entity in the immediate past that is dominant for one which is currently becoming, and a group of past actual entities which only exercise an oblique influence on the latter. Through its prehension the dominant entity can supply the subjective aim for the new process of becoming, so that form or teleonomic finality will not be sundered from bare physical force.[65] One may add that this (much less Platonic) account brings the processes of becoming in actual entities closer to the forms of reproduction found in much larger organisms or living societies.

It is interesting to note that in *Adventures of Ideas*, Whitehead himself comes to emphasize that an actual entity does not arise 'out of a passive situation which is a mere welter of many data', and affirms 'a continuity between the subjective form of the immediate past occasion and the subjective form of its primary prehension in the origination of the new occasion'.[66] And Nancy Frankenberry and Lewis Ford cite his additional references to an initial situation that includes 'a factor of activity which is the reason for the origin of that occasion of experience'. This situation 'with its creativity can be termed the initial phase of the new occasion' and 'can equally well be termed the "actual world" relative to that occasion'.[67] These remarks can cohere with the position articulated in the earlier *Process and Reality* while still suggesting an openness to the alternative forwarded by Sherburne.

I noted above that a Derridean might nonetheless see a Whiteheadian naturalism as susceptible to the charge of essentialism if it retains the notion of a subjective aim utilizing negative prehensions, denies change in an actual entity's process of becoming, and takes this process as internally determined but externally free. In these concluding paragraphs, I will argue that Whitehead can meet these charges. What can first be stated is that his account of negative prehensions does not in itself imply monoform finality and thus exclude evolutionary change or mutation. Apart from cases of irrelevance, an actual entity may only eliminate a predecessor from feeling where the latter threatens to seriously unseat or destroy the new process. The actual entity's subjective aim may only be *broadly* teleonomic, admitting into feeling other entities, which will change the manner in which it realizes itself or even modify the relevant aim itself. To paraphrase Derrida, the entity would be both open and closed at the same time.

But the Derridean might retort that it is just these possibilities of equifinality and multifinality which Whitehead has excluded in denying change and affirming internal determination. Yet, if one looks again at the difference drawn between actual entities and societies, one can contend that change in this context has been equated with *accidental* change, that is, with 'accidental qualities which vary as circumstances alter'.[68] I would like to suggest that it is this form of change alone that Whitehead refuses to attribute to actual entities. On this interpretation, an actual entity can be taken as undergoing essential change in its process of becoming, with each positive prehension contributing to its ultimate determination. This would square with his insistence that we abandon any conception of unchanging subjects of change.

Whitehead does allow an actual entity a modicum of looseness or flexibility. More precisely, he admits to the possibility of equifinality in that the internal determination of an actual entity can be attained in various ways. In the flux that is its process of becoming, he remarks, 'every instance of internal determination assumes *that* flux up to *that* point. There is no reason why there could be no alternative flux exhibiting that principle of internal determination'.[69] But it can again be asked whether this has banished essentialism, since the principle of internal determination still remains and could be read as an explicit adherence to monoform finality.

But here, as elsewhere, Whitehead's position is more nuanced than appears at first glance. He does hold that an actual entity is internally determined in its process of becoming, but does not take its final determination as fixed from the outset:

The concrescence of each individual actual entity is internally determined and is externally free. This category can be condensed into the formula, that in each concrescence whatever is determinable is determined, but that there is always a remainder for the decision of the subject–superject of that concrescence. This subject–superject is the universe in that synthesis, and beyond it there is nonentity. This final decision is the reaction of the unity of the whole to its own internal determination. This reaction is the final modification of emotion, appreciation, and purpose. But the decision of the whole arises out of the determination of the parts, so as to be strictly relevant to it.[70]

The crucial point is that the internal determination of the actual entity is not just that of its initial subjective aim – vital though that may be – but also of its parts, parts which involved the prehensive internalization of aspects of other entities and which have made their own contribution to the end-state, a final modification of *purpose* amongst other things. This thesis, in which internal determination is not to be taken as the rigid outcome of an initial and invariant aim, is confirmed when Whitehead says that efficient causation is operative in more than one phase of an aim, and that 'an originality in the temporal world is conditioned, though not determined, by an initial subjective aim'.[71]

If my presentation of Whitehead's view holds up it therefore constitutes – at the very least in naturalistic form – a thoroughgoing critique of essentialism, which is not susceptible to the likely Derridean critique. But I would like to conclude by stating that I have been one-sided in only considering how Whitehead might be attacked from a deconstructive perspective. I have not broached the question of how a Whiteheadian might criticize Derrida. One possible line of objection is that Derrida characterizes evolutionary change in efficient terms only, as the passive receptivity by a structure of external information which ultimately imposes changes on that structure's teleonomic code. Whitehead is adamant that novelty must additionally be explained in self-creative terms, with an actual entity in its final, reactive phase 'putting the decisive stamp of creative emphasis upon the determinations of efficient cause'.[72] Yet the viability of this, as of other objections, is the preserve of a separate study.

Notes

1. Alfred North Whitehead, *Process and Reality: An Essay in Cosmology*, corrected edition, edited by David Ray Griffin and Donald W. Sherburne (New York: The Free Press, 1978), 31–2.
2. Whitehead, *Process and Reality*, 209, 346–7.
3. Ibid., 13, 50, 137, 209.
4. Alfred North Whitehead, *Adventures of Ideas* (New York: The Free Press, 1967), 132–3. This work is an elaboration of the theory of reality already set out in *Process and Reality*. So far as I am aware, none of Whitehead's later works depart from this theory in any significant way.
5. Whitehead, *Process and Reality*, 78.
6. Ibid., 6, 78.
7. Ibid., 78–9.
8. Ibid., 23, 29, 40, 45.
9. Ibid., 19, 20, 22, 29.

10. Ibid., 23, 61–2, 99–103, 110.
11. Ibid., 23, 239, 248. In Whitehead's account, the mental pole of an actual entity need not involve sense-perception or consciousness. These functions are only found in higher-level organisms and should be regarded as complex outgrowths of more basic prehensive activities. If there are no factors in human experience which are not also found in the lower and less specialized levels of nature, he argues, then any assertion that human experience is a fact within nature is mere bluff, and we should admit at least a provisional dualism. See his *Adventures of Ideas*, 184–5.
12. Whitehead, *Process and Reality*, 113–14, 231–8; Whitehead, *Adventures of Ideas*, 183–4.
13. Whitehead, *Process and Reality*, 232, 240, 243, 290.
14. Ibid., 32–3, 69, 247–8, 276. Whitehead's account of conceptual prehension seems to be modelled on the idea of appetition as it is summarily presented in the *Monadology*, sections 15, 19, 22. These sections have been shown in their relation to Leibniz's other writings by Nicholas Rescher in *G.W. Leibniz's Monadology: An Edition for Students* (London: Routledge, 1991), 79–98, *passim*.
15. Whitehead, *Process and Reality*, 23, 41–2, 226–7.
16. Ibid., 69, 85, 277.
17. Ibid., 222.
18. Ibid., 31, 213, 222, 289.
19. Ibid., 91, 95, 151, 288.
20. Ibid., 244.
21. Ibid., 222.
22. Ibid., 343, 345–6, 348–9.
23. Jacques Derrida, *Writing and Difference*, translated by Alan Bass (Chicago: University of Chicago Press, 1978), 194; Jacques Derrida, *Of Grammatology*, translated by Gayatri Spivak (Baltimore, MD: John Hopkins University Press, 1976), 70–71.
24. Jacques Derrida, *The Ear of the Other: Otobiography, Transference, Translation: Texts and Discussions with Jacques Derrida*, translated by P. Kamuf and A. Ronell (Lincoln, NE: University of Nebraska Press, 1988), 115–16. See also Jacques Derrida, *Dissemination*, translated by Barbara Johnson (Chicago: University of Chicago Press, 1981), 128.
25. Derrida, *Writing and Difference*, 278–9.
26. Jacques Derrida, *Margins of Philosophy*, translated by Alan Bass (Chicago: University of Chicago Press, 1982), 52–3, 157–8.
27. Derrida, *Of Grammatology*, 97–8; Derrida, *Margins of Philosophy*, 158, 172. See also Jacques Derrida, *Speech and Phenomena and Other Essays on Husserl's Theory of Signs*, translated by David Allison (Evanston, IL: Northwestern University Press, 1973), 6, 52–4.
28. Jacques Derrida, *Positions*, translated by Alan Bass (Chicago: University of Chicago Press, 1981), 29, 41–2. Extended critiques of intellectual intuition and simple presence go back at least as far as Kant, Schelling and Hegel, and Derrida is well aware of this. But if such forms of intellection and immediacy are explicitly rejected in their texts, he counters, they may still serve as core values which implicitly orient these works – Hegelian dialectics, for example, seeks to overcome differences and contradictions and culminate in a self-present absolute beyond representational thinking. See *Positions*, 43–4, 96. Such recurrent values are in Derrida's view responsible for the regressive elements in great texts.
29. Henry Staten, *Wittgenstein and Derrida* (Lincoln, NE: University of Nebraska Press, 1984), 17–18.
30. Derrida, *Margins of Philosophy*, 13–14; Derrida, *Positions*, 26–7.
31. Derrida, *Speech and Phenomena*, 64–9, 85–6.
32. Derrida, *Margins of Philosophy*, 315–18, 326–9.

33. Derrida, *Positions*, 26–7; Derrida, *Of Grammatology*, 163.
34. Derrida, *Of Grammatology*, 47, 165; Derrida, *Positions*, 49, 81–2, 88.
35. Derrida, *Of Grammatology*, 8–9. Derrida will later add: 'The phrase which for some has become a sort of slogan, in general so badly understood, of deconstruction ("there is nothing outside the text"), means nothing else: there is nothing outside context. In this form, which says exactly the same thing, the formula would doubtless have been less shocking. I am not certain that it would have provided more to think about ... What I call "text" implies all the structures called "real," "economic," "historical," socio-institutional, in short: all possible referents. Another way of recalling once again that "there is nothing outside the text." That does not mean that all referents are suspended, denied, or enclosed in a book, as people have claimed, or have been naïve enough to believe and to have accused me of believing. But it does mean that every referent, all reality has the structure of a différantial [*sic*] trace, and that one cannot refer to this "real" except in an interpretative experience. The latter neither yields meaning nor assumes it except in a movement of différantial referring. That's all' (Jacques Derrida, *Limited Inc*, translated by Jeffrey Mehlmann and Samuel Weber and edited by Gerald Graff, Evanston, IL: Northwestern University Press, 1988, 136, 148, translation slightly emended). It should of course be noted that there is quite a difference between stating that there is nothing outside a text and nothing outside a context, so Derrida's accusation of naïvety is hardly appropriate in this instance at least.
36. Derrida, *Of Grammatology*, 9, 70.
37. In the natural world as well as in conventional discourses or texts, stresses Derrida, every term or atomic element is already a germ which can only advance through an endless process of dissemination, another word for the productive division, grafting and proliferation that is iteration. See Derrida, *Dissemination*, 304.
38. Christopher Johnson, *System and Writing in the Philosophy of Jacques Derrida* (Cambridge: Cambridge University Press, 1993), 156. See also Aristotle's *On the Parts of Animals*, 641b20–642a5 in *De Partibus Animalium I and De Generatione Animalium I*, translated by D.M. Balme (Oxford: Clarendon Press, 1972) 9, and *Hegel's Lectures on the Philosophy of Religion*, volume 1, translated by E.B. Speirs and J.B. Sanderson (London: Routledge and Kegan Paul, 1962), 61.
39. Derrida, *Margins of Philosophy*, 60; Derrida, *Of Grammatology*, 187; Derrida, *Positions*, 96.
40. Derrida, *Writing and Difference*, 19–20, 26–7. See also Derrida, *Limited Inc*, 149.
41. Johnson, *System and Writing*, 147–8, 172. In his *General Systems Theory: Foundation, Development, Applications* (London: Penguin Press, 1971), 76–7, Ludwig von Bertalanffy argues that a teleonomy does not have to be understood as a *vis a fronte* mysteriously attracting a system, but as a causal *vires a tergo*. This is not a restatement of classical causality in that the relevant *vires a tergo* need not be single or unilinear.
42. Bertalanffy, *General Systems Theory*, 39, cited in Johnson, *System and Writing*, 146.
43. Johnson, *System and Writing*, 178.
44. Ibid., 148, 178; Bertalanffy, *General Systems Theory*, 37–9.
45. Johnson, *System and Writing*, 144.
46. Ibid., 148.
47. Staten, *Wittgenstein and Derrida*, 96–7. In the same place Staten cites Darwin: 'Certainly no clear line of demarcation has as yet been drawn between species and sub-species – that is, the forms which in the opinion of some naturalists come very near to, but do not quite arrive at, the rank of species: or again, between sub-species and well-marked varieties, or between lesser varieties and individual differences. These differences blend into each other by an insensible series, and a series impresses the mind with the idea of an actual passage. Hence I look at individual differences, though of small interest to the

systematist, as of the highest importance for us, as being the first steps toward such slight varieties as are barely thought worth recording in works of natural history. And I look at varieties which are in any degree more distinct and permanent, as steps toward more strongly-marked and permanent varieties; and at the latter, as leading to sub-species, and then to species ... From these remarks it will be seen that I look at the term species as one arbitrarily given, for the sake of convenience, to a set of individuals closely resembling each other, and that it does not differ essentially from the term variety, which is given to less distinct and more fluctuating forms. The term variety, again, in comparison with mere individual differences, is also applied arbitrarily, for convenience's sake'. (Charles Darwin, *The Origin of Species*, edited by L. Harrison Matthews, London: Everyman, 1971, 59–60.)

48. Staten, *Wittgenstein and Derrida*, 97.
49. Derrida, *Writing and Difference*, 408; Derrida, *The Ear of the Other*, 29.
50. Jacques Derrida, *The Post Card: From Socrates to Freud and Beyond*, translated by Alan Bass (Chicago: University of Chicago Press, 1987), 104. See also Jacques Derrida, 'My Chances/Mes Chances: A Rendezvous with Some Epicurean Stereophonies', translated by Irene Harvey and Avital Ronell in *Taking Chances: Derrida, Psychoanalysis, and Literature*, edited by Joseph Smith and William Kerrigan (Baltimore, MD: Johns Hopkins University Press, 1984), 2.
51. Derrida, *Of Grammatology*, 187; Derrida, *Writing and Difference*, 11.
52. Derrida, *Limited Inc*, 9, 12.
53. Derrida, *Writing and Difference*, 289; Derrida, *Dissemination*, 163. See also 202, 304; and *Writing and Difference*, 289.
54. Jacques Derrida, 'Discussion following "Structure, Sign, and Play"', in *The Languages of Criticism and the Sciences of Man: The Structuralist Controversy*, edited by Richard Macksey and Eugenio Donato (Baltimore, MD: Johns Hopkins University Press, 1970), 265–72. See also Derrida, *Writing and Difference*, 26, 126–7, 292.
55. Derrida, *Dissemination*, 52–4, cited in Johnson, *System and Writing*, 168 (translation slightly emended).
56. Derrida, 'My Chances', 7.
57. With respect to human existence, Christopher Johnson has contended that biological evolution is to all intents complete, with development only continuing in the cultural and technological spheres (*System and Writing*, 170–71). Yet our biological make-up can hardly be sundered completely from our cultural and technological condition. Derrida refers sympathetically to André Leroi-Gourhan's contention that 'A toothless humanity that would exist in a prone position using what limbs it had left to push buttons with, is not completely inconceivable' (*La geste et la parole, Tome I*, Paris: Albin Michel, 1964, 183, cited in Derrida, *Of Grammatology*, 85).
58. Donald Sherburne, 'Whitehead without God', in *Process Philosophy and Christian Thought*, edited by D. Brown, R.E. James Jr. and G. Reeves (Indianapolis, IN: Bobbs-Merrill, 1971), 325–6.
59. A.H. Johnson, 'Some Conversations with Whitehead Concerning God and Creativity', in *Explorations in Whitehead's Philosophy*, edited by Lewis S. Ford and George L. Kline (New York: Fordham University Press, 1983), 9–10.
60. Whitehead, *Adventures of Ideas*, 204.
61. Whitehead, *Process and Reality*, 27, 46.
62. Ibid., xiv, 3.
63. Lewis S. Ford, 'The Creation of "Eternal Objects"', *The Modern Schoolman* 71.3 (1994): 191–222.
64. Johnson, 'Some Conversations with Whitehead Concerning God and Creativity', 10. It should be observed that God's consequent nature would have a grounding function if the

preservation of the ways in which actual entities feel as they become were somehow passed on to the initial phases of the subjective aims of subsequent actual entities. But, so far as I am aware, these initial phases are taken to ensue from his primordial nature alone.

65. Brown *et al.*, *Process Philosophy and Christian Thought*, 328.
66. Whitehead, *Adventures of Ideas*, 179, 183.
67. Ibid., 179. See Nancy Frankenberry, 'The Power of the Past', *Process Studies* 13.2 (1983): 133. See also Lewis S. Ford, 'Creativity in a Future Key', in *New Essays in Metaphysics*, edited by Robert C. Neville (Albany, NY: State University of New York Press, 1987), 182–3.
68. Whitehead, *Adventures of Ideas*, 204.
69. Whitehead, *Process and Reality*, 46–7.
70. Ibid., 27–8.
71. Ibid., 47, 108.
72. Ibid., 47.

Chapter 3

Concretizing Concrete Experience

Santiago Sia

Introduction

Contemporary process thought has emphasized the contributions of Alfred North Whitehead and Charles Hartshorne in providing an alternative conceptuality in understanding and articulating our experience of reality. These contributions, rooted in a metaphysical scheme, seem to disclose a certain understanding of the role of philosophy and to illustrate an attempt to meet the challenge of the times. It is therefore understandable that, given this direction in its development, process thought would be regarded as particularly attuned to some of the concerns in theology and receptive to a dialogue with Buddhist thought, contemporary science, feminism, environmental concerns, and other areas. Process thought is indeed a fertile field in which one can conduct a dialogue. Even more significantly, it provides a vision or a framework, including the formulation of a new language, to articulate that vision.[1] Process thinkers seem to have heeded Whitehead's call that we should 're-create and re-enact a vision of the world, including those elements of reverence and order without which society lapses into riot, and penetrated through and through with unflinching rationality'.[2]

The development of a conceptuality requires sustained and concentrated thinking. Neglecting this demand leads to superficiality and narrowness. It is therefore to be expected that process thinkers would engage in abstract thinking in their attempts to further Whitehead's and Hartshorne's legacy and would respond to contemporary issues to show the relevance and the appropriateness of their insights. To use Whitehead's well-known metaphor of the flight of an aeroplane to describe speculative philosophy, the thrust of process thought has been mainly with the flight itself and with the landing.

It would of course be a mistake to claim that there has been a neglect of the first stage of the flight of the aeroplane.[3] In fact, some analysis of experience and its role in providing data for speculative thinking has concerned process thinkers. But it seems that, while process thinkers have always stressed the concreteness of experience, the methodology followed has always run the risk of losing the very concreteness of experience. This comes as no surprise insofar as the development of process thought has been at the philosophical level ('philosophical' understood both in the strict as well as in the broad sense), a level that cannot be forsaken without damaging the credibility and the forcefulness of its metaphysical vision.

It would, however, be equally damaging were process thought, in its important task of strengthening its conceptual framework and showing its relevance, to forget the need to preserve the very concreteness of experience. There is after all a difference between analysing 'concrete experience' or applying the process metaphysical scheme to 'other concrete experiences', and appreciating experience 'in its very concreteness'. Admittedly, the last task would seem to take us back rather than forward. To be engaged in preserving the concreteness of experience would hardly be called 'development' since it would be pre-philosophical. And any exploration at the pre-philosophical stage is always subject to vagueness, subjectiveness and inconsistency – features which undermine the development of a conceptuality. Despite these dangers, however, I would argue that the very methodology of process thought demands that time and effort be spent too at the initial stage of the flight of the aeroplane. Or, as Edmund Husserl puts it, we also need to go back to the things 'before science and philosophy'. We should heed Hartshorne's call to pay attention to the 'pre-theological' experiences or Hans-Georg Gadamer's suggestion to explore the life-world 'without either metaphysical preconceptions or transcendental pretensions'.

Turning to the Concrete

In this context of turning to the more concrete expressions of our experiences of reality, Whitehead himself has some interesting observations. He regards, among others, literature (and poetry in particular) as such a concrete expression and a source for philosophical thinking. Here Whitehead manifests a closeness, even if rather implicit, not only with the rich European literary–philosophical tradition, but also with certain concerns of contemporary European philosophers.[4] There is an interesting passage which provides some insight into Whitehead's understanding of the relationship between poetry and philosophy. In his *Modes of Thought*, he writes: 'Philosophy is akin to poetry. Philosophy is the endeavour to find a conventional phraseology for the vivid suggestiveness of the poet. It is the endeavour to reduce Milton's 'Lycidas' to prose, and thereby to produce a verbal symbolism manageable for use in other connections of thought'.[5] And in another work, *Adventures of Ideas*, he acknowledges that what philosophy does is to build on what is a strong foundation, explaining that philosophy expresses 'flashes of insight beyond meaning already stabilized in etymology and grammar'.[6]

Despite the famous wish of Plato to banish poets from the Republic and the ancient quarrel between poets and philosophers, there has always been a close, if at times tense, relationship between the art of poetry and the act of philosophizing. Western philosophical tradition, at least in its dominant form, may not be as keen, compared to the Asian philosophical heritage for instance, on regarding literature in general and poetry in particular as a rich source of philosophical insight. In fact, many would maintain a certain distinction, with clearly described features, between what is literary and what is philosophical. There is in certain quarters of European philosophy, which insists on criticism, depth and comprehensiveness, a rather negative attitude towards poetry. Martin Heidegger in his essay 'What are Poets For?' bemoans the fact that philosophers consider a dialogue with poetry as 'a helpless aberration into fantasy'.⁷ This rather negative attitude can be traced back to Plato, the great European philosopher. As Whitehead puts it, the emergence of the critical discontent with the poets is exemplified by Plato.⁸

Nonetheless, there has also been an acknowledgment by some European philosophers that Plato's understanding of poetry *vis-à-vis* philosophical thinking was too restricted. Much poetry contains a great many philosophical insights, and some philosophical writings, insofar as these are the works of well-respected philosophers, are in genres which are more literary. (One can readily recall the writings of many of the existentialist thinkers.) Romanticism, which upholds spontaneity, emotion and individuality, arose in reaction to the perceived inadequacy of the kind of theoretical reason upheld by the Hegelian system. The Romantics felt that poetry provides the most adequate path to truth. In the essay cited above, Heidegger maintains that the course of the history of Being will lead thinking into a dialogue with poetry. Gadamer's *Literature and Philosophy in Dialogue*, promotes that exchange of views between literary writers and philosophers.

The relationship between literature (particularly poetry) and philosophy appears to be an issue in contemporary European philosophical debates, especially in the context of philosophical hermeneutics. Paul Ricoeur's conviction that there is always a Being-demanding-to-be-said (*un être-à-dire*) which precedes our actual saying prods him on to the poetic uses of language. Towards the end of *Being and Time*, Heidegger had stated that the propositional form in which he had been writing was not really adequate to capture his thought. (It is an observation reminiscent of Søren Kierkegaard who refers to a mode of communication in which the writer uses all the artistic means at his disposal to awaken the reader to what can only be indicated, not stated.) The later Heidegger becomes more specific. Preoccupied with language as the 'house of Being', he pointed to the inextricable connection between our conception of the world and our language: Language alone brings beings as beings into the open for the first time. Maintaining that poetic language is the purest form of language speaking, he considers that in poetic language, language speaks itself (*Die Sprache spricht*) and unfolds its true essence. The essence of poetry is 'the founding of truth' (as Heidegger understood it). He had confidence in poetic language's ability to evoke the nature of things whereas he had grave reservations about the form of writing that he had himself adopted. In fact, he regarded the poet, whose 'projective saying' enables new aspects of Being to reveal themselves, as the true philosopher.⁹

Given the claim made by process thinkers that concrete experience serves as the basis of the process scheme of things and the interest of process thought in Europe to contextualize its development in the European scene, surely an important area that needs to be explored further by European process thought is the relationship between poetry (and literature in general) and philosophical reflection.¹⁰ Hartshorne had carried out such an inquiry regarding the role of religious texts and practices in his development of philosophical theology. It seems that the current interest in philosophical hermeneutics can provide the scene for investigating and developing further Whitehead's thoughts on literature and poetry and in relating his contributions to what European philosophers are debating.

Literature and Philosophy: a Whiteheadian Nexus

In this section, I should like to suggest how the dialogue between literature and philosophy can be grounded in Whitehead's thought. In doing so I also hope to indicate why the methodological task of preserving the concreteness of experience, specifically in literature, is an important one for process thought.

Whitehead regards the word 'experience' as 'one of the most deceitful in philosophy'.[11] Nonetheless, he maintains that what philosophy describes or discloses through the system of general ideas is 'our experience'. This means that for him the primary datum for philosophical analysis is none other than subjective experiencing. This 'subjectivist bias' is for Whitehead an ontological principle (referred to as 'the reformed subjectivist principle'). As he puts it, 'apart from the experiences of subjects there is nothing, nothing, nothing, bare nothingness'.[12] Insofar as it is an ontological principle, experiencing is not, as is commonly understood, limited to human experiencing. Whitehead rejects any sharp distinction between humans and other beings, living and non-living. To make such a sharp distinction, according to him, is too vague and hazardous.[13] He therefore universalizes experience, extending it to all realms of reality.

What makes human experience distinctive is that it includes thinking. But it does not constitute the generic nature of human existence since humans live even when asleep and are unconscious. Whitehead regards thinking as derived from sensation; however, not in the sense in which that is interpreted by the sensationalist theory of the empiricists, who maintain that perception is the conscious entertainment of definite and clear-cut 'sensa'.[14] According to Whitehead, experience cannot be identified with clear, distinct and conscious entertainment of sensation, explaining that the unborn child, the baby in its cradle, or one in the state of sleep, and so on have a vast background of feeling which is neither conscious nor definite. 'Clear, conscious discrimination is an accident of human existence. It makes us human. But it does not make us exist. It is of the essence of our humanity. But it is an accident of our existence.'[15] On the other hand, the structure of human experience discloses the structure of reality itself. As he puts it, 'We construct the world in terms of the types of activities disclosed in our intimate experience.'[16] One can find therefore in descriptions of human experience what Whitehead refers to as factors which also enter into the descriptions of less specialized natural occurrence.[17]

Whitehead describes every occasion of experience, human or otherwise, as dipolar; that is to say, it has an aspect of subjectivity and another aspect of objectivity, of process and permanence. 'It is mental experience integrated with physical experience. Mental experience is the converse of bodily experience.'[18] His reformed subjectivist principle is thus a claim that the final fact is a subject experiencing objects which in turn are determined subjects. Subject and object are thus regarded as interlinked in the same final fact. This claim amounts to a rejection of the extreme realist position of the sensationalist principle of the empiricist tradition which holds that 'the primary activity in the act of experience is the bare subjective entertainment of the datum, devoid of any subjective form of reception'.[19] As Whitehead explains it, experience is not purely a private qualification of the mind. He adds that, 'if experience be not based upon an objective content, there can be no escape from a solipsist subjectivism'.[20] Accordingly, he affirms that 'the world within experience is identical with the world beyond experience'[21] and that what René Descartes discovered on the side of subjectivism 'requires balancing by an "objectivist" principle as to the datum for experience'.[22]

Whitehead describes two modes of experience, independent but each contributing its share of components into one concrete moment of human experience.[23] He calls the clear, conscious, sensory mode 'perception in the mode of presentational immediacy'. But this mode of experience is based upon and derived from a more elemental form of experience, which is vague and unconscious and which he calls 'perception in the mode of causal efficacy'.[24] The mode of causal efficacy, which Whitehead describes as heavy and primitive, dominates primitive living organisms.[25] He explains that, in human experience, this elemental form of perception is exhibited by the 'witness of the body': 'it is this witness that makes the body the starting point for our knowledge of the circumambient world'.[26] Senses are specializations of the witness of the body: 'we see with our eyes, we do not see our eyes' while our body is 'that portion of nature with which each moment of human experience intimately cooperates'.[27] For this reason Whitehead maintains that it is difficult to determine accurately the definite boundary of one's body and that it is very vaguely distinguishable from external nature.[28] He regards the body as united with the environment as well as with the soul.[29] Causation then, as far as Whitehead is concerned, is not an a priori category within the mind alone, as in Immanuel Kant, but an element in experience.[30] As he puts it, 'The notion of causation arose because mankind lives amid experiences in the mode of causal efficacy.'[31] Thus the elemental form of perception is causation, it being an element of the very structure of reality.

Whitehead defines the mode of presentational immediacy as 'our immediate perception of the contemporary external world, appearing as an element constitutive of our own experience'.[32] It expresses how contemporary events are relevant to each other while preserving a mutual independence.[33] In this mode contemporary things are 'objectively' in our experience. No actual thing is objectified as such but only an abstraction. Among these abstract entities are those called sense-data; for example, colours, sounds, tastes, touches and bodily feelings.[34] Compared to the mode of causal efficacy, presentational immediacy leads to knowledge that is vivid, precise and barren. It is also to a large extent controllable at will; that is to say, that one moment of experience, through various modifications, can predetermine to a considerable extent the other characteristics of the presentational immediacy in succeeding moments of experience.[35]

The fusing of these two modes into one perception is called by Whitehead 'symbolic reference'. He explains that in symbolic reference 'the various actualities disclosed respectively by the two modes are either identified, or are at least correlated together as interrelated elements in our environment', the result being 'what the actual world is for us, as that datum in our experience productive of feelings, emotions, actions, and finally as the topic for conscious recognition when our mentality intervenes with its conceptual analysis'.[36] This linking of the two modes, which leads to human symbolism, shows that there are common structural elements since they are perceptions of the same world. However, there are gaps, which means that their fusion is indeterminate. Whitehead adds that 'intellectual criticism founded on subsequent experience can enlarge and purify the primitive naïve symbolic transference'.[37] He contrasts symbolic reference with 'direct recognition' insofar as the latter is 'conscious recognition of a percept in a pure mode, devoid of symbolic reference'.[38] As a matter of fact, however, there is no complete ideal purity of either perceptive experience without any symbolic reference.[39] Error may arise in symbolic reference inasmuch as direct recognition may disagree in its report of the actual world. In symbolic reference mental analysis is rather at a minimum. On the other hand, it compensates for this in its imaginative freedom.

Symbolic reference precedes conceptual analysis, but the two promote each other. One may be inclined to associate symbolic reference with mental activity, but Whitehead holds that it is a matter of pure convention as to which of our experiential activities we term mental and which physical since, as we have already noted, for Whitehead there is no proper line to be drawn between the physical and the mental constitution of experience. Moreover, much of our perception is subtly enhanced by a concurrent conceptual analysis. There is no conscious knowledge without the intervention of mentality in the form of conceptual analysis.[40] Symbolic reference is a datum for thought in its analysis of experience. Our conceptual scheme of the universe should generally and logically be coherent with it and should correspond to the ultimate facts of the pure perceptive modes. But when this does not happen, we then should revise our conceptual scheme to retain the general trust in the symbolic reference, while accepting as mistaken definite details of that reference.[41]

Whitehead also defines symbolic reference as 'the organic functioning whereby there is transition from the symbol to the meaning', when some components of experience, that is symbols, elicit consciousness, beliefs, emotions and usages, respecting other components of its experience, that is meaning. It is 'the active synthetic element contributed by the nature of the percipient'.[42] Symbolic reference is, as Whitehead defines it in another context, 'the interpretative element in human experience'.[43] In this sense, symbolic reference is related to language. In language we have a fundamental type of symbolism: 'The word is a symbol, and its meaning is constituted by the ideas, images and emotions, which it raises in the mind of the hearers.'[44] But in addition to the bare meaning, words and phrases carry with them an inclusive suggestiveness and an emotional efficacy associated with the way they had been used in history.[45] Whitehead expresses this point clearly: 'a word has a symbolic association with its own history, its other meanings and with its general status in current literature. Thus a word gathers emotional signification from its emotional history in the past; and this is transferred symbolically to its meaning in present use'.[46] He maintains that the whole basis of the art of literature is 'that emotions and feelings directly excited by the words should fitly intensify our emotions and feelings arising from contemplation of the meaning'.[47]

Given the above consideration by Whitehead on experience and our expression of that experience, what Whitehead has to say on literature is particularly relevant: 'It is in literature that the concrete outlook of humanity receives its expression. Accordingly it is to literature that we must look, particularly in its more concrete forms, namely in poetry and in drama, if we hope to discover the inward thoughts of a generation.'[48] We have already noted that he holds that the ultimate appeal is to experience, and now he adds his reason why he puts much stress on the evidence of poetry: 'My point is, that in our sense-experience we know away from and beyond our own personality, whereas the subjectivist holds that in such experience we merely know about our own personality.'[49] Whitehead points out that one function of great literature is to evoke a vivid feeling of what lies beyond words.[50] Literature manages to combine what Whitehead considers to be a curious mixture of 'tacitly presupposing analysis, and conversely of returning to emphasize explicitly the fundamental emotional importance of our naïve general intuitions'.[51]

It is interesting to compare Whitehead's observations with Goethe's comments on poetry. Goethe holds that it is reality that provides, as it were, 'the points to be expressed'.[52] According to him, reality is the kernel. It also supplies the motive. And Goethe's advice to the poet is: 'Only have the courage to give yourself up to your impressions, allow yourself to be delighted, moved, elevated; nay, instructed and inspired for something great: but do not imagine all is vanity, if it is not abstract thought and idea.'[53] As he reflects on his own role as poet, Goethe has this to say:

> It was in short not in my line, as a poet, to strive to embody anything *abstract*. I received in my mind impressions, and those of a sensuous, animated, charming, varied, hundred-fold kind – just a lively imagination presented them; and I had, as a poet, nothing more to do than to round off and elaborate artistically such views and impressions, and by means of a lively representation so to bring them forward that others might receive the same impression in hearing or reading my representation of them.[54]

In a different context, the novelist–philosopher Iris Murdoch makes a similar observation regarding literary modes of expressing our concrete experiences. She points out that literary modes are an everyday occurrence: they are very natural to us, very close to ordinary life and to the way we live as reflective beings. She remarks that we are beings who constantly use words, employing language to make interesting what is originally dull or incoherent. Thus we are immersed in a literary atmosphere, where we live and breathe literature. We all are, as she describes us, 'literary artists'. Literature or art of any sort results because of 'the desire to defeat the formlessness of the world and cheer oneself up by constructing forms out of what might otherwise seem a mass of senseless rubble'.[55]

For Whitehead, literature is a way of capturing the concreteness of experience. In addition, the poetic rendering of our concrete experience, according to him, reminds us that 'the element of value, of being valuable, of having value, of being an end in itself, of being something which is for its own sake, must not be omitted in any account of an event as the most concrete actual something'.[56] By 'value' he understands the intrinsic reality of an event. It is an element that permeates through and through the poetic view of nature. He illustrates this point by referring to the nature-poetry of the Romantic poets, which he regards as a protest not only on behalf of the organic view of nature, but also against the exclusion of value in the description of reality. As he puts it rather succinctly, 'the romantic reaction was a protest on behalf of value'.[57]

Whitehead furthermore notes the significance of literature in its description of nature. Citing the works of Wordsworth, he compares the poet's view of nature with the strained and paradoxical view which modern science offers to us: 'Wordsworth, to the height of genius, expresses the concrete facts of our apprehension, facts which are distorted on the scientific analysis. Is it not possible that the standardized concepts of science are only valid within narrow limitations, perhaps too narrow for science itself?'[58] Whitehead bemoans the overemphasis on the intellectual, an attitude that he considers prevalent in the learned world. Such an attitude, he claims, 'sterilizes imaginative thought, and thereby blocks progress'.[59] Similarly, W.B. Yeats remarks in a rather forceful fashion: 'By reason and logic we die hourly, by imagination we live.'[60] Whitehead reminds us that all productive thought has resulted from and developed because of the poetic insight of artists, or by the imaginative elaboration of schemes of thought capable of utilization as logical premises,[61] while philosophical thought has created for itself difficulties by dealing exclusively in very abstract notions.[62] In this connection, what Whitehead has to say about the advance of ideas is particularly significant:

> Now, so far as concerns beliefs of a general character, it is much easier for them to destroy emotion than to generate it. In any survey of the adventure of ideas nothing is more surprising than the ineffectiveness of novel general ideas to acquire for themselves an appropriate emotional pattern of any intensity. Profound flashes of insight remain ineffective for centuries, not because they are unknown, but by reason of dominant interests which inhibit reaction to that type of generality.[63]

On the other hand, Whitehead points out that 'the language of literature breaks down precisely at the task of expressing in explicit form the larger generalities – the very generalities which metaphysics seeks to express'.[64] One then needs to go further than literary language to philosophical language which uses reason. Whitehead regards reason as a factor in experience, one that directs and criticizes the urge towards the attainment of an end which has been realized in imagination but not in fact.[65] He adds that 'the essence of Reason in its lowliest forms is its judgments upon flashes of novelty, of novelty in immediate realization and of novelty which is relevant to appetition but not yet to action'.[66] Explaining further his point, he states:

> In its lowliest form, Reason provides the emphasis on the conceptual clutch after some refreshing novelty. It is then Reason devoid of constructive range of abstract thought. It operates merely as the simple direct judgment lifting a conceptual flash into an effective appetition, and an effective appetition into a realized fact.[67]

Whitehead assigns to reason, and thus to philosophy, the task of understanding and purging the symbols on which humanity depends.[68]

As we have already noted in our discussion of the modes of perception, Whitehead maintains that consciousness itself does not initiate the process of knowledge. Rather, we find ourselves already engaged in it, 'immersed in satisfactions and dissatisfactions, and actively modifying, either by intensification, or by attenuation, or by the introduction of novel purposes' and that 'after instinct and intellectual ferment have done their work, there is a decision which determines the mode of coalescence of instinct with intelligence'.[69] Here reason acts as 'a modifying agency on the intellectual ferment so as to produce a self-determined issue from the given conditions'.[70] Reason has a tremendous effect in selecting, emphasizing and disintegrating data.[71] In this sense one can say, according to Whitehead, that thought is mainly concerned with the justification or the modification of a pre-existing situation.[72] While all knowledge is conscious discrimination of objects experienced, this conscious discrimination – to return to the point discussed earlier – is 'nothing more than an additional factor in the subjective form of the interplay of subject with object... All knowledge is derived from, and verified by, direct intuitive observation'.[73]

Whitehead also insists that it is the business of rational thought (which brings us to the issue regarding methodology in process thought) to describe the more concrete fact from which abstract thought has been derived.[74] Literature, which conveys meanings through rich and concrete images, powerful metaphors and engaging analogies, is a fertile field for philosophical reflections, which with the aid of reason make such literary language more explicit. Philosophy attempts to disclose a complete matter of fact in all its dimensions. Philosophy, at least for Whitehead, is intended to regain an undivided world, to think together all aspects of reality. Its aim is to disclose 'a complete fact' in all its scientific, aesthetic, moral and religious aspects. His well-known definition of speculative philosophy is 'the endeavour to frame a coherent, logical, necessary system of general ideas in terms of which every element of our experience can be interpreted'.[75] Whitehead states that the rationalists failed to disclose a complete fact because of their chief error of overstatement.[76] They overstated abstraction and landed in a dogmatic fallacy. Understanding as a function of philosophy 'to harmonise, refashion, and justify divergent intuitions as to the nature of things', Whitehead then argues that philosophy must 'insist on the scrutiny of the ultimate ideas, and on the retention of the whole of the evidence in shaping our cosmological scheme. Its business is to render explicit, and – so far as may be – efficient, a process which otherwise is unconsciously performed without rational tests'.[77] Philosophy makes the content of the human mind manageable by adding meaning to fragmentary details, by disclosing disjunctions and conjunctions, consistencies and inconsistencies.[78] Moreover, Whitehead regards philosophical reflections as ongoing. Philosophy is an 'endeavour', an 'essay': an adventurous attempt or search. As Whitehead puts it, 'Philosophy is the search for premises. It is not deduction.'[79] It is not surprising, then, that he describes philosophy as 'descriptive generalization' inasmuch as it should describe, rather than explain, reality.[80] He is critical of traditional philosophy which explained things and whose preoccupation was with the principles which constitute the concrete things, thereby ignoring the very concreteness of reality.[81] Whitehead also uses the term 'imaginative generalization' to refer to philosophy,[82] highlighting the point that by an imaginative leap the philosopher attempts to capture those aspects of reality which logical technicalities cannot reach.[83]

The following passage summarizes Whitehead's conception of the philosophical task in the context of what has been said so far:

Philosophy is the critic of abstractions. Its function is the double one, first of harmonising them by assigning to them their right relative status as abstractions, and secondly of completing them by direct comparison with more concrete intuitions of the universe, and thereby promoting the formation of more complete schemes of thought. It is in respect to this comparison that the testimony of great poets is of such importance. Their survival is evidence that they express deep intuitions of mankind penetrating into what is universal in concrete fact. Philosophy is not one among the sciences with its own little scheme of abstractions which it works away at perfecting and improving. It is the survey of sciences, with the special objects of their harmony, and of their completion. It brings to this task not only the evidence of the separate sciences, but also its own appeal to concrete experience. It confronts the sciences with concrete fact.[84]

In our philosophical discussion about our experience of reality, Whitehead reminds us of three ideas we need to keep in mind: '(i) our direct intuitions which we enjoy prior to all verbalization; (ii) our literary modes of verbal expression of such intuitions, together with the dialectic deductions from such verbal formulae; (iii) the set of purely deductive sciences, which have been developed so that the network of possible relations with which they deal are familiar in civilized consciousness'.[85] He warns us that the chief danger in philosophy is dialectic deductions from inadequate formulae which exclude direct intuitions, such as those found in literature.[86]

Two Suggestions for Process Thought

If the above observations are indeed based on and reflect Whitehead's concerns, two areas in methodology seem to suggest themselves for further development in process thought, particularly in the European context:

First is the construction of a process methodology which is more consistent with its claims regarding the role of concrete experience – more inclusive of poetic and other literary insights as the foundation for more abstract reflection. I am not advocating the kind of methodology associated with Kierkegaard's 'subjective truth of human life or existence', the pursuit of which calls for a radical break with cognitive or theoretical reason. Nor do I have in mind the juxtapositioning of the two fields in the way of Dilthey – although the context was the human and natural sciences – who, while appreciating both the need for rationality, objectivity and rigour and the fullness of human life, advocated a doctrine of knowledge which separates *Erklären* and *Verstehen*. Husserl rightly rejects this dualism of explanation and understanding, maintaining that it is the task of genuine philosophy to bridge that gap. Nor is this methodology being suggested a matter of simply quoting from poetry to illustrate or expand a philosophical point. Rather, what seems to be called for is genuinely 'listening' to what poets say, in the way described by Heidegger in his 'What are Poets For?'[87] It is a method which gives poets 'their own space', *pace* Plato, not only in the Republic but also in the philosophical arena. Whitehead acknowledges that 'literature preserves the wisdom of the human race'[88] and that it is 'the storehouse of that crude evidence on which philosophy should base its discussion'.[89] It is a method that demands listening to the poets and other literary writers, inquiring as to the meaning of their words, reflecting critically on the lines of the poem or the texts and developing further, even correcting, their insights. Undoubtedly, there is the issue of which poems and which texts can be used. But that problem arises, because of the demands of selectivity, no matter in what context we turn to our sources for our philosophical reflection.

Second is the use of more literary modes of communicating process insights to complement, rather than replace, the strictly philosophical writings which advance Whiteheadian and Hartshornean scholarship. Philosophy is explanatory of abstraction, not of concreteness.[90] Whitehead's insistence that fresh insights should not be burdened by the baggage of connotations led to his introduction of an original glossary. While this has the distinct advantage of achieving a clarity and preserving a novelty which would not be possible with the use of a more traditional vocabulary, it has nevertheless not only created obstacles to a more extensive dialogue with non-Whiteheadian philosophers, but it has also prevented others from profiting from the richness of process thought. The method of sharing the results of the process journey in the aeroplane is important. I am not referring here to 'popularizing' process thought, with the connotation of 'watering down' its insights. Rather, I am talking of the need to disseminate process insights more widely. W.B. Yeats's remark that we should 'think like wise men, but communicate in the language of the people' is particularly apt. The European philosophical tradition has always made use of, among others, various literary forms: poetry, novels, plays, dialogues and so on, to reach the minds – and hearts – of the public. It is a tradition that process thought could well participate in and benefit from.[91]

Notes

1. In previous work I have indicated how the metaphysical vision of Whitehead and Hartshorne has enabled many of us to articulate our religious experiences. The argumentation in the present essay complements the one made in the earlier work. See Santiago Sia, 'Process Thought as Conceptual Framework', *Process Studies* 19.4 (1990): 248–55.
2. Alfred North Whitehead, *Adventures of Ideas* (New York: The Free Press, 1967), 126.
3. One has only to note the different entries under the heading 'Literature and Process Thought' in the bibliography compiled by the library of the Center for Process Studies in Claremont, California, USA.
4. Parts of this chapter are based on a discussion paper presented at the European Society for Process Thought Conference held at Kortrijk, Belgium and Lille, France.
5. Alfred North Whitehead, *Modes of Thought* (Cambridge: Cambridge University Press, 1938), 49–50.
6. Whitehead, *Adventures of Ideas*, 291.
7. Martin Heidegger does warn that scholars of literary history consider the dialogue to be 'an unscientific violation of what such scholarship takes to be the facts'. See Heidegger, *Poetry, Language, Thought*, translated by Albert Hofstadter (New York: Harper and Row, 1971), 96. For a helpful anthology on this topic, see Hazard Adams, editor, *Critical Theory Since Plato* (New York: Harcourt Brace Jovanovich Publishers, 1971).
8. Whitehead, *Adventures of Ideas*, 12.
9. See, among his other writings, *On the Way to Language*, translated by Peter D. Hertz (New York: Harper and Row, 1971). Heidegger maintains that the purity of poetic language is such that it is not important to know anything about the poet or the origins of the poetic work. Poetic language which reveals the essence of being, and not ordinary language, is the truly original manifestation of human language. Reference to Heidegger here is not meant to signify an agreement with his methodology as will be evident in what follows in the main text. While Heidegger's dissatisfaction with philosophical discourse leads him to poetic language, what I am claiming is that poetry and other literary forms are a valuable *source* for philosophical thinking.
10. This observation is meant to complement the work that is being done to relate Whitehead and Charles Hartshorne to main European thinkers such as Kant and Hegel and to the other issues of interest to Continental philosophy. Jan Van der Veken provides a useful survey in his 'Process Thought from a European Perspective', *Process Studies* 19.4 (1990), 240–47.
11. Alfred North Whitehead, *Symbolism: Its Meaning and Effect* (Cambridge: Cambridge University Press, 1928), 19.
12. Alfred North Whitehead, *Process and Reality: An Essay in Cosmology*, corrected edition,

edited by David Ray Griffin and Donald W. Sherburne (New York: The Free Press, 1978), 167.
13. Alfred North Whitehead, *Science in the Modern World* (Cambridge: Cambridge University Press, 1926), 79; also his *The Function of Reason* (Oxford: Oxford University Press, 1929), 5.
14. Whitehead, *Adventures of Ideas*, 228.
15. Whitehead, *Modes of Thought*, 116. In *Function of Reason*, 62, Whitehead explains, 'The equating of experience with clarity of knowledge is against the evidence. In our own lives, and at any one moment, there is a focus of attention, a few items in clarity of awareness, but interconnected vaguely and yet insistently with other items in dim apprehension, and this dimness shading off imperceptibly into undiscriminated feeling. Further, the clarity cannot be segregated from the vagueness. The togetherness of the things that are clear refuses to yield its secret to clear analytic intuition. The whole forms a system, but when we set out to describe the system direct intuitions play us false. Our conscious awareness is fluctuating, flitting, and not under control. It lacks penetration. The penetration of intuition follows upon the expectation of thought. This is the secret of attention.'
16. Whitehead, *Modes of Thought*, 115.
17. Whitehead, *Adventures of Ideas*, 237.
18. Whitehead, *Function of Reason*, 25–6.
19. Whitehead, *Process and Reality*, 157.
20. Ibid., 152.
21. Whitehead, *Adventures of Ideas*, 293. On page 268 and the following pages, Whitehead discusses the dichotomy within the objective content of an occasion of experience in terms of 'appearance and reality'.
22. Whitehead, *Process and Reality*, 160. The following passage is a particularly helpful summation by Whitehead: 'An occasion of experience is an activity, analysable into modes of functioning which jointly constitute its process of becoming. Each mode is analysable into the total experience as active subject, and into the thing or object with which the special activity is concerned. This thing is a datum, that is to say, is describable without reference to its entertainment in that occasion. An object is anything performing this function of a datum provoking some special activity of the occasion in question. Thus subject and object are relative terms. An occasion is a subject in respect to its special activity concerning an object; and anything is an object in respect to its provocation of some special activity within a subject. Such a mode of activity is termed a "prehension". Thus prehension involves three factors. There is the occasion of experience within which the prehension is a detail of activity; there is the datum whose relevance provokes the origination of this prehension; this datum is the prehended object; there is the subjective form, which is the affective tone determining the effectiveness of that prehension in that occasion of experience. How the experience constitutes itself depends on its complex of subjective forms' (226).
23. In *Symbolism*, Whitehead actually mentions three modes, the third being 'the mode of conceptual analysis' (20).
24. Whitehead, *Function of Reason*, 78–9.
25. Whitehead, *Symbolism*, 52.
26. Whitehead, *Process and Reality*, 112.
27. Whitehead, *Modes of Thought*, 115.
28. Ibid., 114.
29. Ibid., 161.
30. Whitehead, *Process and Reality*, 166–7.
31. Ibid., 175. The term that Whitehead uses to describe this is 'prehension'. See *Process and Reality*, 19.

32. By 'presentational immediacy' Whitehead explains that he means what is usually termed 'sense perception', but not as having exactly the same connotations as that term. See *Symbolism*, 25. He maintains that 'presentational immediacy is only of importance in high-grade organisms, and is a physical fact which may, or may not, enter into consciousness. Such entry will depend on attention and on the activity of conceptual functioning, whereby physical experience and conceptual imagination are fused into knowledge', and that 'the reason why low-grade purely physical organisms cannot make mistakes is not primarily their absence of thought, but their absence of presentational immediacy' (19, 24). Also, for most events, he presumes that their intrinsic experience of presentational immediacy is so embryonic as to be negligible. 'This perceptive mode is important only for a small minority of elaborate organisms' (29).
33. Whitehead, *Symbolism*, 19. He cites the main facts about presentational immediacy to be: '(i) that the sense-data involved depend on the percipient organisms and its spatial relations to the perceived organisms, (ii) that the contemporary world is exhibited as extended and as a plenum of organisms, (iii) that presentational immediacy is an important factor in the experience of only a few high-grade organisms, and that for the others it is embryonic or entirely negligible' (26).
34. Ibid., 30.
35. Whitehead provides a useful summary with the following passage: '... the intervention of any sense-datum in the actual world cannot be expressed in any simple way, such as mere qualification of a region of space, or alternatively as the mere qualification of a state of mind. The sense-data, required for immediate sense-perception, enter into experience in virtue of the efficacy of the environment. This environment includes the bodily organs. For example, in the case of hearing sound the physical waves have entered the ears, and the agitations of the nerves have excited the brain. The sound is then heard as coming from a certain region in the external world. Thus perception in the mode of causal efficacy discloses that the data in the mode of sense-perception are provided by it. This is the reason why there are such given elements. Every such datum constitutes a link between the two perceptive modes. Each such link, or datum, has a complex ingression into experience, requiring a reference to the two perceptive modes. These sense-data can be conceived as constituting the character of a many-termed relationship between the organisms of the past environment and those of the contemporary world' (ibid., 62–3).
36. Ibid., 21.
37. Ibid., 35.
38. Ibid., 22.
39. Ibid., 64.
40. Ibid., 23.
41. Ibid., 64.
42. Ibid., 9.
43. Whitehead, *Process and Reality*, 173.
44. Whitehead, *Symbolism*, 2.
45. Ibid., 79.
46. Ibid., 99. In *Adventures of Ideas*, Whitehead actually points out that there is no 'mere knowledge' since knowledge is always accompanied by emotion and purpose (5).
47. Whitehead, *Symbolism*, 98–9. There is a certain vagueness in symbolism. Compared to direct experience which is infallible in that what one has experienced has been experienced, symbolism is very fallible 'in the sense that it may induce actions, feelings, emotions, and beliefs about things which are mere notions without that exemplification in the world which the symbolism leads us to presuppose' (7).
48. Whitehead, *Science and the Modern World*, 106.
49. Ibid., 125.

50. Whitehead, *Modes of Thought*, 7.
51. Ibid., 6.
52. This text is included in Adams, *Critical Theory Since Plato*, 514.
53. Ibid., 514.
54. Ibid., 515.
55. Iris Murdoch, *Existentialists and Mystics: Writings on Philosophy and Literature* (London: Chatto and Windus, 1997), 6. Murdoch maintains that, despite the fact that philosophy and literature are so different, they are both truth-seeking and truth-revealing activities. They are cognitive activities, explanations. She adds that 'how far re-shaping involves offence against truth is a problem any artist must face' (10). Writing in *Modes of Thought*, Whitehead claims that philosophic truth is to be sought in the presuppositions of language rather than in its express statements. He maintains that this is why philosophy is akin to poetry in that both of them seek to express that ultimate good sense which we term civilization. 'In each case there is reference to form beyond the direct meaning of words. Poetry allies itself to metre, philosophy to mathematical pattern' (viii).
56. Whitehead, *Science and the Modern World*, 131.
57. Ibid., 132.
58. Ibid., 118.
59. Whitehead, *Modes of Thought*, 59.
60. Quoted in J.M. Cocking, *Imagination: a Study in the History of Ideas* (London: Routledge, 1991), viii.
61. Whitehead, *Process and Reality*, 9.
62. Ibid., 18.
63. Whitehead, *Adventures of Ideas*, 220.
64. Whitehead, *Process and Reality*, 11.
65. Whitehead, *Function of Reason*, 5.
66. Ibid., 15.
67. Ibid., 18.
68. Whitehead, *Symbolism*, 8.
69. Whitehead, *Adventures of Ideas*, 58.
70. Ibid., 58.
71. Ibid., 127.
72. Ibid., 140.
73. Ibid., 227.
74. Ibid., 239.
75. Ibid., 285; Whitehead, *Process and Reality*, 3.
76. Whitehead, *Process and Reality*, 11.
77. Whitehead, *Science and the Modern World*, ix.
78. Whitehead, *Modes of Thought*, 67.
79. Ibid., 105.
80. Whitehead, *Process and Reality*, 15–16.
81. Whitehead, *Adventures of Ideas*, 143.
82. Whitehead, *Process and Reality*, 7.
83. Ibid., 6.
84. Whitehead, *Science and the Modern World*, 122.
85. Whitehead, *Adventures of Ideas*, 177.
86. Ibid., 177–8.
87. We have tried to implement this suggestion in a recent book: M.F. Sia and S. Sia, *From Suffering to God: Exploring Our Images of God in the Light of Suffering* (New York: Macmillan/St Martin's Press, 1994). Theodore Walker's review in *Process Studies* 28.1–2 (1999), 147–8, refers specifically to the methodology followed in this book.

88. Whitehead, *Adventures of Ideas*, 247.
89. Ibid., 291.
90. Whitehead, *Process and Reality*, 20.
91. In the novel, *The Fountain Arethuse* (Lewes, UK: The Book Guild, 1997), we made use of process insights in developing both the plot and the dialogues. It deals with, among other things, 'the concreteness of life' and the choices one has to make in life. See W. Beardslee's review of it in *Creative Transformation* 7.1 (Fall 1997), 23 and that of Theodore Walker in *Process Studies* 28.1–2 (1999), 148–9. Finally, see Aliman Sears's essay in the present volume.

Chapter 4

Whitehead's Hermeneutical Cosmology

René P.H. Munnik

In the course of modern western philosophy, hermeneutics can be considered as a main topic in contemporary fundamental ontology. As a particular human activity, hermeneutics is the art of interpretation of signs, texts and dreams; its goal is to elucidate the obscured meanings they are supposed to convey. The Greek priests, practising their *hermeneutikè technè* in order to explain the oracles or the signs in the sky, were by no means the first exponents of this proficiency. It is as old as humankind. And perhaps it is of all times; that depends on how Whiteheadian one is and how radical one takes the notion of interpretation. In the Christian era, when the organization of life centred upon the Holy Scripture and its authoritative explications, the study for their correct interpretation became of vital interest. So, while the quest for correct understanding gained cultural and intellectual importance, its attention was mainly confined to the interpretation of texts. It became a theological–philological discipline. Johann Conrad Dannhauer's *Hermeneutica sacra*, a book about the method and the rules to be obeyed for correct text interpretation, is the first work in modernity which contains the term 'hermeneutics' in its title.[1] But it is only one exponent of the long intellectual tradition of the *subtilitas explicandi*.

However, interpretation is not confined to the Bible and not even to texts; it applies to all human expressions, which need clarification to be understood. According to Wilhelm Dilthey, understanding (*Verstehen*) and hermeneutic explication (*Auslegung*) of the expressions of human life are the defining characteristics of a whole class of sciences, the humanities or 'human sciences' (*Geisteswissenschaften*). This realm includes the study of history, national economy, jurisprudence, political science, religion, literature and poetry, plastic arts and music, philosophical systems and world views, and, finally, psychology. 'All these sciences consider the same great fact: mankind'.[2] Dilthey's interest was not primarily directed to the specific methods of these human sciences, but rather to their scientific status as such. In his *Aufbau der geschichtlichen Welt in den Geisteswissenschaften*, containing his 'Project for a Critique of Historical Reason', Dilthey investigated the demarcations between natural science and the human sciences, and undertook an analysis of the notions of 'understanding' and 'explication' as well as of the conditions of their possibility. The latter should serve as the epistemological legitimation of the human sciences in the same way as Immanuel Kant's *Critique of Pure Reason* has done for natural science.

Dilthey's point of view concerning the demarcation of natural sciences and human sciences is well illustrated by his statement, 'We explain nature, but we understand the [*Seelenleben*] inner life', thereby emphasizing a sharp distinction between nature and the inner life.[3] For him, 'nature' is covered by a Newtonian/Kantian conception of it, and the only way to conceive ('explain') it adequately is by natural science. The 'inner life', on the other hand, is *not*, at least not in his later works, a psychological category. It is human life as a historical category which expresses itself in instances of 'objective spirit' such as art, religion, legal systems, literature, traditions, lifestyles and so on. Only the meanings of these expressions can be understood, and the human sciences are the sciences for their adequate interpretations.

According to Dilthey the difference between natural sciences and human sciences is not constituted by the fact that there are two types of things, physical things and 'expressions', but by the fact that these two types of inquiry fashion their objects in a different way. In human life, on a pre-reflective level, the physical aspect and the mental aspect – the inner life – appear undivided in the immediate impressions. But as different objects of natural sciences and human sciences respectively, they are 'legitimately fashioned abstractions'.[4] And both are 'objects, created by the faculty of knowledge, in order to reconstruct the impressions'.[5] In the effort of understanding originates a 'spiritual object' (*geistiges Objekt*), which is the experienced, but not sensually perceived, meaning. In the effort of physical explanation originate physical objects. In the human sciences, the physical aspect of things is forced back into the role of bare conditions and means of expression. In natural science, our direct impressions of nature are drawn back behind the abstract conceptualizations of it, in terms of space, time, mass, velocity and so on. Nature, thus conceived as the object of natural science, is foreign to the inner life: *So ist die Natur uns fremd*.[6] Nevertheless, Dilthey held that natural science is the only adequate way of conceiving nature, and so he arrived at the conclusion: 'There is no understanding of this world [nature] and we can assign value, meaning and sense to it only by analogy with ourselves.'[7]

But what renders the human sciences possible as a scientific enterprise? Dilthey believed that life itself contains the categories for its own adequate interpretation. They belong essentially to human life, which expresses itself in history and is capable of understanding these expressions. Human life must be considered as the threefold notion of *life–expression–understanding*. And this universal nature of mankind serves as the a priori condition for the possibility of the human sciences: life understands life, and it does so exclusively via the interpretation of its own expressions. As for Dilthey, this thesis had a strong anti-metaphysical bearing. It implies that the questions for the meaning of life and self-understanding of humankind cannot be settled from some viewpoint *sub specie aeternitatis* or a direct inspection into the nature of things. They can only be answered via the circuitous route of the interpretation of specific historical and contingent expressions of life. Even the self-understanding of the individual is not an instance of the immediate autopresence of the subject with itself, as René Descartes' *res cogitans*, but it results from an interpretative *soliloquium*: a dialogue of the subject with itself. In a sense, Dilthey assigned to the human sciences the important role of being instruments for the self-reflection of humankind. This, together with the fact that Dilthey was mainly concerned with the a priori conditions of understanding and not with the specific methods for interpretation, makes his hermeneutics 'philosophical'.

A more radical concept of understanding and interpretation is found in Friedrich Nietzsche's works, and it marks a stage in the transition from philosophical hermeneutics to hermeneutic philosophy. For example, aphorism 374 of *The Gay Science* is about 'our novel infinitude' and states that human existence (*Dasein*) is essentially finite (perspectival) and interpreting in character. But the acknowledgment of this finitude implies the recognition of a novel infinity of the world. 'The world has become infinite once again: as far as we cannot dismiss the possibility that it contains an infinitude of interpretations.'[8] Nietzsche contests the claims of classical metaphysics: an uninterpreted world is an unknown world. He conceived reality as a reservoir of possible interpretations and the act of interpretation as eliciting or 'bringing into light' some meaning while others remain in darkness. There are no facts, there are only interpretations; there is also no Archimedean viewpoint, no direct access to the 'things in themselves' in order to examine the truth value of different interpretations.

It is this radical conception of hermeneutic understanding and interpretation which is at work in Martin Heidegger's remark that possibility stands higher than actuality.[9] His conception of truth as *alètheia* literally means dis-closure or uncovering of meaning. In *Being and Time*, Heidegger investigates the meaning of being (*Sinn von Sein*) in terms of an analysis of human existence (*Dasein*), defined as that being which 'in its very being, is concerned about this being itself'.[10] In this analysis the term 'hermeneutics' primarily points to the ontological constitution of *Dasein* itself and only in a derivative sense to the human sciences. Thus hermeneutics has become another word for (fundamental) ontology, for being is conceived as possibility, interpretability. Moreover, human existence turns out to be radically historical, because wherever and whenever it finds itself, it is thrown into a historical context in which reality is already interpreted for it on a pre-ontological level. No one is ever occupied with the task of getting acquainted with reality from an absolute zero. On the other hand, it is not only thrown into or subjected to the interpretations which it finds; it actively projects or discloses novel meanings.

A key issue for Heidegger is that every interpretation has the modality of a possibility, and the chief danger is in the forgetting that it *is* a possibility. The result of a petrified tradition of interpretation is unthoughtfully conceived as an indisputable self-evidency. It may make reality 'manageable' for current modes of thought, but it is in fact a form of forgetfulness of being itself. Heidegger's 'destruction' of the history of ontology is a strategy used to soak off congealed notions about the ultimate nature of things in order to find an openness for the temporality of being and the temporariness of all our interpretations of it. It is a search for truth, not in the sense of a correspondence with the things in themselves, but in the sense of an uncovering of possible meanings. Heidegger's treatment of technology as 'nothing technological' but as a dangerous mode of disclosing should be considered from this perspective, as well as his rather eccentric conception of what it means to conceive a 'thing as a thing', his notoriously violent interpretations of philosophic texts and his abundant construction of neologisms. It also accounts for the important role he assigns to poetry; for poetry is the laboratory of uncovering new meanings, of bringing things into a new light as yet unseen. In short, of the encounter with truth: *Dichterisch wohnet der Mensch* ('poetically man dwells').

According to Heidegger interpretation is not the reconstruction of the original meaning of fixed expressions like texts, but it is the *venture* of opening or uncovering possible – temporary – meanings. It is the human mode of finite, mortal being in and for which Being as such discloses itself as possibility. Heidegger radicalizes and broadens philosophical hermeneutics into hermeneutic philosophy. Philosophy is hermeneutical, because it consists in the reflective coexecution of the (self-) interpretation which *Dasein* always already *is*. In subsequent sections, I will argue that there are some close affinities between his position and Whitehead's philosophy of process. However, there are also divergences, one of which is that Heidegger confines himself exclusively to human existence or *Dasein* as the exemplary instance of being. He considers nature in terms of entities whose character is not that of *Dasein*, which are interpretable but do not enjoy any meaning for themselves or, as Whitehead would say, whose actuality is supposed to be vacuous.[11]

Whitehead's Cosmology as a Hermeneutics of Nature

Let us, for a moment, return to Dilthey's position, which implies that there can be no hermeneutical understanding of nature. Dilthey himself recognized the fact that both physical objects and the 'spiritual objects' of understanding are legitimately fashioned abstractions. But how about the physical aspect of life in concrete experience preceding the abstraction? As an example, in my direct impression of a certain landscape, it is not at all conceptualized in terms of space, time, mass and velocity. Its disclosure is an element in life itself (*Lebensbezug*).[12] But it is still a physical existent, and it is full of meaning. The aesthetic values it expresses, however dim and unverbalizable they may be, have fascinated artists for centuries. So we should keep in mind that the disjunction of nature and meaning only appears at a certain level of abstraction. Dilthey takes the abstractness of the human sciences for granted, because his concern was to argue for their scientific status.

Whitehead's concern is quite another. For him 'it must be one of the motives of a complete cosmology to construct a system of ideas, which brings the aesthetic, moral, and religious interests into relation with those concepts of the world which have their origin in natural science'.[13] But the objects of these interests, such as beauty and goodness, as well as the historical objectifications of these interests themselves in art, moral and religious systems, belong to the subject-matter of the human sciences. So Whitehead's philosophical motive is integration rather than demarcation. However, the bringing-into-relation by the system of general ideas needs an ontological justification; the system can only legitimately bring into relation what in concrete reality is in fact related. The primary philosophical issue is not to construct a system, but to conceive a complete fact – or, rather, since such an apprehension can never be finally attained, to stick to the project of a critique of abstractions.

Dilthey never conceived his philosophical hermeneutics as such a critique. Rather, he sought the scientific status of the human sciences in the 'legitimately fashioned abstractions'. So, when Dilthey criticized metaphysics, he may have been right in respect to some strains of classical metaphysics, but he would have been in no position to challenge Whitehead's concept of speculative philosophy. The critic of abstractions cannot reasonably be criticized from an abstract standpoint. Whitehead would agree with Dilthey that in pre-reflective experience the physical and mental aspects ('poles') appear undivided, and that on this level nature is apprehended *with* its aesthetic values. He would certainly not agree with Dilthey that this apprehension would solely be the result of some analogy on behalf of ourselves and that it would not have any ground in the expressiveness of nature itself. In Whitehead's opinion, Dilthey commits the fallacy of misplaced concreteness, because he renders the perspective of classical mechanics the honour of being the standard of the philosophical concept of nature. Dilthey's acknowledgment that 'physical science is an abstraction' remains a confession of philosophic failure.[14] An adequate account of nature should imply at least a final cause. There is hardly a text of Whitehead's to be found in which he does not emphasize this idea. In *Process and Reality* this becomes clear in the first few chapters. All reality is analysed in terms of internally related actual entities, which, according to the ontological principle, are the only reasons.[15]

Moreover, the becoming of actual entities is guided by a subjective aim, which, according to the eighth categoreal obligation, 'is at intensity of feeling'.[16] As for Whitehead, the key notion for understanding nature is that the energetic activity considered in physics is the emotional intensity entertained in life.[17] 'We shall never elaborate an explanatory metaphysics unless we abolish the notion of valueless, vacuous existence,' says Whitehead, since a dead nature can give no reasons.[18] To deny this is a form of obscurantism.[19] Whitehead conceives all reality, including nature, in terms of actual entities which have a self-interest in the way of feeling and aim.[20] And if it is true that 'the zero of intensiveness means the collapse of actuality', then this aim for intensity, 'importance', or aesthetic value, is what in classical metaphysics would be called a *conatus essendi* – an urge for being.[21] Like Heidegger's *Dasein*, every actual entity is a being, which in its very being, is concerned about this being itself.

According to Whitehead, a metaphysical account of nature implies a hermeneutical interpretation of natural phenomena; the creative advance is the outcome of processes or strategies in which this aim for intensity is expressed. This interpretation, which promotes the art of life, seeks to understand reason as a fact in the world.[22] Many examples can be given here. He considers natural laws as contingent habits of nature, in which a particular mode of self expression is realized, that will eventually fade into unimportance as new interests will dominate.[23] These laws are historical, and they persist as long as they contribute to the achievement of aesthetic value. Referring to the principle of (conceptual) reversion that is essential for aesthetic experience, Whitehead states that the physical quantities are aggregates of physical vibrations, and physical vibrations are the expression among the abstractions of physical science of the fundamental principle of aesthetic experience.[24] This practising of the art of life in terms of the achievement of aesthetic value is also found in the strategies for dealing with the disharmony in the world in order to avoid 'aesthetic destruction' on the level of physical purposes included in all actual entities.[25]

Whitehead's cosmology endeavours to understand nature as exhibiting the art of life. This understanding is what makes his cosmology 'hermeneutical'. But there is a more fundamental level where the theme of hermeneutics comes in. It is in the kind of self-interest or self-occupation at the base of the 'practising' of this art of life itself, that is, of being actual. The abolishment of vacuous actuality makes nature understandable for the philosopher, but it also forces one to consider any actuality in terms of self-enjoyment. The question is: can this self-enjoyment be considered an interpretative act? If this is so, then Whitehead offers a genuine hermeneutical ontology.

Whitehead's Hermeneutical Ontology

Can actual entities be considered as interpretative acts, and if so, in what sense? If one considers 'understanding' and 'interpretation' in terms of an intellectual endeavour to clarify obscured meanings of expressions, then most actual entities will not do the job. But it is not necessary to hold that understanding and interpretation should result in a clarifying exposition. Even Dilthey, in his short note on 'musical understanding', believed that any enjoyment of music involves hermeneutical understanding.[26] A piece of instrumental, absolute music is a togetherness in experience (*Lebenszusammenhang*) in the form of a temporal succession of notes, rhythms and contrasts which come and go. These are not determined by any necessity, but only by their relevance so as to realize an aesthetic value (*Realisation eines aesthetischen Wertes*) within this togetherness.[27] No intellectual effort can retrieve these expressions from their obscurity; their interpretation is unsolvable as a discursive accomplishment.[28] However, they are understandable as expressions of (the depths of) life. They are understood by being appreciated in the experience of the hearer with the specific tonality or the 'whatness' of the aesthetic values, which the musical piece expresses, thus telling tales about the unseen.

It is on this level of aesthetic feeling that we should consider the sort of understanding and interpretation that is proper to actual entities. It is also on this level that there are remarkable parallels between Whitehead's and Dilthey's thought. As I indicate, Dilthey's conception of interpretation is dominated by the threefold notion of *life–expression–understanding*. Whitehead's account of interpretation is also dominated by a threefold notion: the Category of the Ultimate involving *creativity–many–one*. In fact, Whitehead conceives 'interpretation' in terms of *composition* – of *many* expressions concrescing into *one* final 'understanding' – rather than in terms of an explanatory exposition. But let us take a closer look. There are two levels on which understanding and composition meet.

The first level, indicated in *Modes of Thought*, concerns the compository character of the things given for understanding, which 'always involves the notion of composition'.[29] In this way there can be understanding of a composite thing in terms of its interrelated components, and there can be understanding of a thing as a component within a larger whole. These two modes, internal and external understanding, presuppose each other, but at least a complete external understanding is never finally attainable: 'We can never understand a composition in its full concrete effectiveness for all possibilities of environment.'[30] Of course, this problem is close to Dilthey's 'aporia of understanding' and Hans-Georg Gadamer's considerations concerning the hermeneutical circle, which implies that the understanding of part of a text or any composite work presupposes the understanding of the whole, and vice versa.[31] For Gadamer, this means that the process of understanding must necessarily start from anticipatory presuppositions and prejudices about the meaning of the whole – a limiting horizon – and that it can never achieve a final revelation of the meaning that it seeks; understanding is a provisional enterprise. For Whitehead, this problem is not at all confined to texts, because it poses itself in every instance of understanding within a world of internally related existents.

There is, however, a more fundamental level on which 'composition' and 'understanding' meet. On this level it is not the *object* of understanding that is conceived in terms of a composition, but it is the *act* of understanding which is conceived as compositary; to understand is to compose. In *Adventures of Ideas*, Whitehead argues against sensationalist epistemology. Sensationalism affirms that the final content of experience is construed as an 'interpretation' of the original sense-impressions, impressions that make us 'accept' a world of substantial objects. But no material for this 'interpretation' is provided by the sense data themselves, and so it stays conjectural from an empiricist point of view.[32] Whitehead argues that this indispensable element of interpretation is always provided by the immanence of the past in the 'interpreting occasion', by means of its non-sensuous perceptions.[33] He writes: 'The percipient directly integrates antecedent real functionings of that object in antecedent occasions of the soul's life. The so-called "interpretation" is the conflation of real history, and is not a top-dressing of conjecture.'[34] Although Whitehead does not intend to give an exhaustive description of the notion of interpretation here, I contend that the account of 'interpretation' as the 'conflation of real history' is of fundamental significance.

Whitehead interprets experience as the self-enjoyment of being one among many, and of being one arising out of the composition of many.[35] This composition is always expressible in terms of the composite constitutions of the individual occasions.[36] But what does the individual occasion compose? It brings together in complex unity its actual world or causal past, given for it as a disjunctive multitude of *expressions*. He states, 'expression is the gift from the world as many to the world as one'.[37] Indeed, the satisfaction or final fully determinate feeling of each past actual occasion is preserved as an element in the givenness of the world.[38] This determinate feeling of the given actual occasions is objectively immortal as a qualification of the creativity for every successor. In this sense, every actual occasion *expresses* itself as an inscription in the creativity for all its successors. Every actual occasion yet to become is a concrescence of prehensions, that is, a concrescence of the receptions of these expressions.[39]

Therefore, novel feelings emerge issuing in a new expression, inscribed in creativity to be carried as a datum for its successors. It is the nature of a feeling to pass into expression.[40] There is an act of interpretation, consisting in the process in which a multitude of given fixed expressions becomes the one novel expression with a definite attitude or response towards the given expressions, and which adds itself to that multitude. This is just a 'hermeneutical' rendering of the Category of the Ultimate. Each actual entity is an act of interpretation in the way of a composition of fixed expressions. Its 'becoming' is its functioning as an act of interpretation; its subjective immediacy is its 'understanding' of the world for and of itself in terms of feeling and emotion; its objective immortality is its functioning as a superject or fixed expression implying its interpretability for its successors.

There is nothing mysterious about this process. In every account of the historical reality or creative advance in which fixed expressions ('the dead') are appropriated in novel understanding ('by the living'), one will find an analogous rendering of the facts:[41] for example, in the becoming of texts and their effective history. Every text, considered as a complex fixed expression, has its effective history (*Wirkungsgeschichte*) or 'objective immortality' constituting its inevitable 'givenness' as well as its interpretability for its successors. And every text, even if not intended as an interpretative exposition of others, nevertheless interprets these texts given for it by being its own novel composition arising out of the inheritances of the past. For example, there can be important theological texts which do not mention the Apostle Paul, Augustine or Aquinas, but there can be no *relevant* theological text that does not respond implicitly or explicitly, consciously or unconsciously, to the *texts* of the Apostle Paul, Augustine, Aquinas and countless others. A definite attitude towards these 'given' texts implies an interpretative appropriation of them. A text which does not in any way respond to what is given for it remains, if possible at all, a trivial incident. A text containing a relevant response may be individually unimportant if it simply co-responds to a vast tradition of interpretation, and it may be important if it throws a new light on the old words. Such an important text is like the literary texts of Goethe and Shakespeare:

> They deal with what all men know, and they make it new. They do not bring to the world a new formula nor do they discover new facts, but in expressing their apprehensions of the world, they leave behind an element of novelty – a new expression forever evoking its proper response.[42]

Whitehead states that this example from literature is taken merely for the sake of easy intelligibility, since the kind of process which it exemplifies is not at all restricted to the 'regional ontology' of literature; it applies to fundamental ontology as a description of actuality as such.

So the question is not *whether* Whitehead offers a hermeneutical ontology, but rather, *what* concept of hermeneutics is involved in it. Here we come to the radical notion of interpretation and understanding as found in Heidegger, and once again the idea of interpretation as composition forces itself upon us. If we assert that interpretation in the Whiteheadian sense means the becoming of a novel expression in terms of a composition of the many expressions which it finds, it may be asked if there can be any interpretation that simply reproduces the 'original meaning' or aesthetic value expressed in its world. The answer must be that even on the level of low-grade actualities there cannot be such a complete reproduction, because this would violate the irreversibility of time:

> Apart from inhibitions or additions, weakenings or intensifications, due to the history of its production, the subjective form of a physical feeling is re-enaction of the subjective form of the feeling felt. Thus the cause passes on its feeling to be reproduced by the new subject as its own, and yet as inseparable from the cause. But the re-enaction is not perfect.[43]

However, this sheer impossibility of a total reproductive appropriation of the cause's feeling in the new subject 'as its own' is not the only issue, because the new subject does not even aim at such a reproduction. It aims at 'interestingness' and importance.[44] In a sense, Whitehead's account of the interpretative process or concrescence is the reverse of what one will find in reconstructive hermeneutics. Reconstructive hermeneutics *starts* with the affirmation of the obscurity or non-obviousness of the expressions that it seeks to interpret, and it *aims* at clarifying by recovering its 'original meaning'. Dilthey's *Nacherleben*, or conformal experiencing, exemplifies this idea. For Whitehead, on the other hand, the interpretative process starts with '*sympathy*, that is, feeling the feeling *in* another and feeling conformally *with* another'.⁴⁵ But these conformal feelings belong to the initial phase of not yet integrated feelings, and it is in the process of integration or composition that the initial conformations are transformed into contrasts. The novel occasion does not aim at conformation. It starts from a situation of unintegrated conformations and it aims at novelty and aesthetic intensity. Its actual world is given as a multiplicity of expressions or 'beings' in the sense of 'potentialities for being elements in a real concrescence',⁴⁶ and in the concrescence the potential unity of these many beings acquire the real unity of a novel expression. In other words, its actual world is given as a reservoir of potential meanings for the concrescing actuality, and its process of actualization consists in 'eliciting' or 'bringing into light' some complex meaning or aesthetic value which it expresses. The actual world for an actual occasion is essentially 'polysemic', and the interpretative process is more concerned to attain interestingness than to attain truth. Of course, I am referring to Whitehead's dictum that it is more important that a proposition be interesting than that it be true.⁴⁷ I will return to the relation of actual occasions and propositions in the last section.

It is important to observe that Whitehead considers truth to consist in a truth-relation of correspondence. That is clearly not Heidegger's concept of truth as *alètheia*. According to Heidegger, 'interestingness' as the uncovering of possible new meanings as yet concealed *is* the encounter with truth itself. If we realize this difference in concepts of truth, then Whitehead's insistence on 'interestingness' is an insistence on the radical concept of interpretation: the creative advance into novelty is the *venture* of opening or uncovering new meanings or aesthetic intensities. Where such uncovering succeeds in attaining importance, its expression becomes a 'sacrament', eliciting the intuition which interprets it.⁴⁸ This is nothing else than its initiation of its own effective history. At the same time, this adventurous creative advance is through and through historical. What, within some context or some era, has gained importance, may turn into triviality within a future context, as it becomes an element in compositions which involve its contamination. It suffers the iterability of every strongly incarnated meaning.⁴⁹ It has been revealed once as appealing, but it is always in danger of losing its appeal, as it is disseminated into the future. It is temporary and it has the status of a possibility, as Heidegger would say.

Whitehead's Poetical Universe

So far I have been considering Whitehead's metaphysics as a hermeneutical ontology: to be actual means to be an interpretative/expressive act. The aim of this interpretation is not to reproduce the meaning or subjective form of the expressions which are interpreted, but to introduce aesthetically intensive novelty into the world. It is essentially creative. Moreover, to be creative in terms of interpretation and expression means to be poetical in a very strict sense. After all, *poièsis* means to create rather than to write poetry. The human literary art of poetry can be considered as a 'morbid overgrowth of functions which lie deep in nature'.⁵⁰ Of course, in most actualities – the ones that do not individually contribute to novelty – this poetical character is almost negligible. But it gains importance in those actualities which significantly exemplify the adventurous art of life; they 'dwell poetically'. What constitutes their genius? It is their poetical ability to make 'good metaphors'. To demonstrate, we have to take into account Whitehead's theory of propositions.

Whitehead considers propositions to be 'a manner of germaneness of a certain set of eternal objects to a certain set of actual entities'.[51] The set of eternal objects – or pure potentials – is the predicate, and the set of given actual entities is the logical subject. Since an actual entity is bipolar, it synthesizes physical as well as conceptual prehensions, and any incomplete phase of its concrescence is 'impure' and has the unity of a proposition.[52] An 'incomplete' actual entity is itself a matter of fact in potential determination.[53] Propositions can be 'true' (conformal) or 'false' (non-conformal), but their truth or falsehood is of minor importance compared to their function as a proposal for feeling. Consider, for example, a non-conformal proposition. It is false, but it tells a tale that might be told about its logical subject. And when it is admitted into feeling:

> A novelty has emerged into creation. The novelty may promote or destroy order; it may be good or bad. But it is new, a new type of individual, and not merely a new intensity of individual feeling. That member of the locus has introduced a new form into the actual world; or, at least, an old form in a new function.[54]

So the untrue proposition is the instrument of novelty in the making. In fact, it is a metaphor.

According to Aristotle, a proposition has literal sense when a genus is predicated of its species,[55] whereas metaphor is the application of an alien name by transference either from genus to species, from species to genus, from species to species, or by analogy.[56] This distinction between literal and metaphorical expressions largely corresponds to Whitehead's distinction between conformal and non-conformal propositions. But what, according to Aristotle, is the function of metaphor? In *Rhetoric* he writes:

> We will begin by remarking that we all naturally find it agreeable to get hold of new ideas easily: words express ideas, and therefore those words are the most agreeable that enable us to get hold of new ideas. Now strange words simply puzzle us; ordinary words convey only what we know already; it is from metaphor that we can best get hold of something fresh. When the poet calls old age a 'withered stalk', he conveys a new idea, a new fact, to us by means of the general notion of 'lost bloom', which is common to both things.[57]

Metaphor does exactly what an actual entity does; it introduces novelty in the world. It interprets what is given in terms of a non-conformal or contrasting proposal to prehend a given thing from a new perspective, thereby introducing a novel understanding, a novel meaning or aesthetic value. The actuality which entertains it will become a fixed expression, a new fact in the world. If it is important, it may play the role of the commencement of a new tradition. And within this tradition it may lose its appealing character as a metaphor. It becomes worn-out metaphor, a matter of course, a commonplace, an old story. At that point it will be in need of novel metaphors to vivify it. It needs new poets.

The evolutionary process is significantly advanced by those actualities that exemplify this art of life, namely, to make good metaphors. According to Aristotle, good metaphors must be fitting, which means that they must not be far-fetched or they will be difficult to grasp. Nor can they be obvious, or they will have no effect, in which case they will be deprived of liveliness.[58] To Aristotle, metaphors must be drawn 'from things that are related to the original thing, and yet not obviously so related'.[59] To create them implies an 'intuitive perception of the similarity in dissimilars'.[60] Whitehead would say that it implies an eye for the 'relevance' of unrealized potentials as to the 'original thing' as well as for 'balance', which is the adjustment of identities and diversities, as a prerequisite for intensity.[61]

Aristotle affirms that this art of introducing novelty cannot be educated. He says that 'the greatest thing by far is to be a master of metaphor. It is the one thing that cannot be learnt from others; and it is also a sign of genius'.[62] Whitehead would agree with this, since originality cannot be inherited from tradition. And for the same reason he would *not* agree with Aristotle's conviction that it can only come through natural talent or long practice.[63] As for Whitehead it requires an element of immediate inspiration, *praemotio*, or initial aim, derived from God, which determines the initial relevance of eternal objects as to any given state of affairs.[64] Without God there would not be any difference between 'better' or 'worse' alternatives in whatever impasse; there could not be any degree in relevance of novelty, and the art of making good metaphors would be degraded into a restless tangle of arbitrary transferences which in the end comes to nothing.

Whitehead calls God the 'poet of the world'.[65] But from the point of view which I have developed, it may be more appropriate to call God the *Muse*, animating the *autopoièsis* that constitutes the world. And like all poetry, the world and every worldly creature misses its final goal unless it be acknowledged and appreciated by an ideal interpreter. The tragedy of an advancing world is that no worldly interpreter can do total justice as to the expressions which it finds. God is not only the primordial Muse, expressing Godself by exciting the poetic enthusiasm – literally as *en-theousiasmos*, 'being lured' or even 'being existed' (Jean-François Lyotard) or as the initial provocation for its autonomous originality – of the creatures. In addition, God is the consequent ideal interpreter, transferring and inscribing all creatures for what they can be in God's own everlasting autobiography. Whitehead's hermeneutical ontology is encompassed by a hermeneutical onto-theology in which God is not comprehended as the *focus imaginarius* of a religious interpretation of reality. God is the one we have to refer to if we want to have some grasp of what should amount to 'expression' and 'interpretation'.

Notes

1. Johann Conrad Dannhauer, *Hermeneutica sacra sive methodus exponendarum sacrarum literarum* (Strassbourg, 1654).
2. Wilhelm Dilthey, *Gesammelte Schriften*, volume 7 (Stuttgart and Göttingen: Verlag Teubner/Vandenhoeck & Ruprecht, 1968), 79 (my translation).
3. Wilhelm Dilthey, *Gesammelte Schriften*, volume 5 (Stuttgart and Göttingen: Verlag Teubner/Vandenhoeck & Ruprecht, 1968), 144 (my translation).
4. Dilthey, *Gesammelte Schriften*, volume 7, 81.
5. Ibid., 85.

6. Ibid., 90.
7. Ibid., 92.
8. Friedrich Nietzsche, *Nietzsche Werke. Kritische Gesamtausgabe*, volume V_2 (Berlin and New York: Walter de Gruyter, 1973), 309 (my translation).
9. Martin Heidegger, *Sein und Zeit* (Tübingen: Max Niemeyer Verlag, 1986), 38.
10. Ibid., 12 (my translation).
11. Ibid., 44.
12. Dilthey, *Gesammelte Schriften*, volume 7, 229-30.
13. Alfred North Whitehead, *Process and Reality: An Essay in Cosmology*, corrected edition, edited by David Ray Griffin and Donald W. Sherburne (New York: The Free Press, 1978), xii.
14. Alfred North Whitehead, *Adventures of Ideas* (New York: The Free Press, 1967), 186.
15. Whitehead, *Process and Reality*, 24.
16. Ibid., 27.
17. Alfred North Whitehead, *Modes of Thought* (Cambridge: Cambridge University Press, 1938), 168.
18. Alfred North Whitehead, *The Function of Reason* (Oxford: Oxford University Press, 1929), 30; and Whitehead, *Modes of Thought*, 135.
19. Whitehead, *The Function of Reason*, 43-4.
20. Alfred North Whitehead, *Religion in the Making* (New York: Meridian, 1974), 97; and Whitehead, *Modes of Thought*, 167.
21. Whitehead, *Religion in the Making*, 100.
22. Whitehead, *The Function of Reason*, 8, 10.
23. Whitehead, *Modes of Thought*, 155.
24. Whitehead, *Religion in the Making*, 112; and Whitehead, *Process and Reality*, 277.
25. Whitehead, *Adventures of Ideas*, 260; and Whitehead, *Process and Reality*, 276.
26. Dilthey, *Gesammelte Schriften*, volume 7, 220-24.
27. Ibid., 221.
28. Ibid., 224-5.
29. Whitehead, *Modes of Thought*, 45.
30. Ibid., 60.
31. Dilthey, *Gesammelte Schriften*, volume 5, 334.
32. Whitehead, *Adventures of Ideas*, 180.
33. Ibid., 218.
34. Ibid., 263.
35. Whitehead, *Process and Reality*, 145.
36. Ibid., 147.
37. Whitehead, *Modes of Thought*, 20.
38. Whitehead, *Process and Reality*, 220.
39. Whitehead, *Modes of Thought*, 23.
40. Ibid., 26.
41. Whitehead, *Process and Reality*, xiii.
42. Whitehead, *Religion in the Making*, 131.
43. Whitehead, *Process and Reality*, 237.
44. Whitehead, *Modes of Thought*, 12.
45. Whitehead, *Process and Reality*, 162.
46. Ibid., 22.
47. Whitehead, *Adventures of Ideas*, 244; and Whitehead, *Process and Reality*, 259.
48. Whitehead, *Religion in the Making*, 128.
49. For the notion of iterability or 'deforming repetition', see Jacques Derrida, *Marges de la philosophie* (Paris: les Éditions de Minuit, 1972), 365-93.

50. Whitehead, *Adventures of Ideas*, 271.
51. Whitehead, *Process and Reality*, 188.
52. Ibid., 188.
53. Ibid., 22.
54. Ibid., 187.
55. Aristotle, *The Complete Works of Aristotle*, edited by Jonathan Barnes, Bollingen Series LXXI_2, (Princeton, NJ: Princeton University Press, 1984), volume 1, 207.
56. Aristotle, *The Complete Works of Aristotle*, edited by Jonathan Barnes, Bollingen Series LXXI_2, (Princeton, NJ: Princeton University Press, 1984), volume 2, 2332.
57. Aristotle, *Complete Works*, volume 2, 2250–51.
58. Ibid., 2251.
59. Ibid., 2253.
60. Ibid., 2335.
61. Whitehead, *Process and Reality*, 32, 278.
62. Aristotle, *Complete Works*, volume 2, 2334–5.
63. Ibid., 2250.
64. Whitehead, *Process and Reality*, 244. The concept of *praemotio* comes from the Catholic doctrine of grace. It is the divine initiative preceding every autonomous act of the creature, and it has some similarities with Whitehead's concept of 'initial aim'.
65. Whitehead, *Process and Reality*, 346.

II
PROCESS THOUGHT AND LITERATURE

Chapter 5

Suffering and Surrender in the Midst of Divine Persuasion

Aliman Sears

We take it in stride when we hear Lady Macbeth proclaim that while giving suck to an infant she may, 'while it was smiling in my face, Have pluck'd my nipple from his boneless gums, And dash'd the brains out', but such depravity is real: in the United States about 600 children are killed each year by their mothers.[1] Evil seems to be ubiquitous. And evidence for the human propensity toward evil is overabundant, as are accounts of evil (murder) in the animal world.[2] If a caring God exists, why is there so much evil and suffering in the world? Furthermore, do human beings have a responsibility to abate evil? If so, what is the nature of evil and how may evil be nullified?

In this chapter we will examine how we might transpose our traditional thinking and *dissolve* the 'problem of evil' instead of trying to *solve* the problem of evil along traditional lines. We will examine an underlying theme in Marian and Santiago Sia's recent novel *The Fountain Arethuse* (hereafter: *Arethuse*), and see that this theme is a transformed version of the traditional approach to the problem of evil. Instead of dealing with the question of the existence of divinity, the Sias ask, 'What kind of God can we continue to believe in, given the presence of so much undeserved suffering?'[3] It turns out that the kind of God we can continue to believe in bodes well with the religious comportment of 'surrender', and that this comportment is the path that leads towards dissolving the problem of evil.

The basis for the Sias' novel is the Whiteheadian/Hartshornean approach to philosophy and theology, called 'process philosophy' or 'process theology'. Before writing the novel *Arethuse* the Sias had written an academic book, *From Suffering to God: Exploring our Images of God in the Light of Suffering*, and this earlier text explores some of the very same questions raised in *Arethuse*, but from a more scholarly point of view.[4] In addition to examining the problem of evil in general, this chapter will trace common themes in the two books and explicate the underlying theodicy in *Arethuse*. I will also show the connections between *Arethuse* and the Hartshornean idea of God and divine power. In Charles Hartshorne's conceptual scheme, God is not the sole cause of creaturely actions and is therefore not solely responsible for evil. As the writings of Alfred North Whitehead and Hartshorne show, this implies nothing less than a reconception of divine power as traditionally conceived. This reconception leads to different approaches (I will explicate three such approaches) to the problem of evil, and it also leads to a revised interpretation of our relation to divinity. Since God does not control human actions, it follows that humans have the responsibility to 'surrender', so as to bring God's power into the world and thus help abate evil in the world.

The Recovery of Reason

Present-day thinking about theology and religion distances humanity from its own spiritual roots. Thus, before we examine the above issues in detail, let us first turn our attention to the need today to recover the use of reason in the portrayal of divinity, with the hope that it may become clear that the domain of theological investigation is important for all persons; theistic, agnostic and atheistic.

Modern thinking deprecates the power of reason. In this age of Nietzsche, Heidegger *et al.*, deconstructive postmodernism indicts theologians and philosophers of religion with practising ontotheology, and with presuming that reason can yield truth. Pope John Paul II laments that 'There is the distrust of reason found in much contemporary philosophy, which has largely abandoned metaphysical study of the ultimate human questions in order to concentrate upon problems which are more detailed and restricted, at times even purely formal.'[5] Abandonment of the ultimate questions happens not because of the unintelligibility of the thinking underlying theology or metaphysics, but because of the inability of the modernistic, narrow, scientifically oriented conception of reason that is currently in vogue. Talking about God entails opening up this narrow notion of reason and letting reason regain its ancient ground of 'robustness'. This is a recovery of the reason used by Plato, Socrates and Aristotle; the reason that starts in wonder and is open to all human experience and activity, the reason imbued with a teleological ethos, the reason of thinking and of feeling. Whitehead laments that 'Philosophy has been haunted by the unfortunate notion that its method is dogmatically to indicate premises which are severely clear, distinct, and certain; and to erect upon those premises a deductive system of thought.'[6] Modernistic reason has narrowed the domain of philosophical and theological thinking.

In contrast, the expanded reason of *constructive postmodernism* can widen the domain again. Against *deconstructive postmodernism*, a construction of world-views and knowledge is still needed today, but the reconstruction should be launched from a broader platform than tradition allowed in the past. The new reconstruction should take into account the whole of human experience. The question is: can we account for *all* human experience in a coherent way? This widening of parameters is called *constructive postmodernism*, and it cuts across traditional battle lines (of, for example, empiricism/rationalism and realism/idealism). The path of investigation is shaped from a wider platform: the investigation of reality is shaped by literature and the arts as well as science and theology – all realms are respected. Constructive postmodernism is a creative synthesis of pre-modern, modern and postmodern intuitions.[7] An important part of these intuitions is our felt, prethematic or prereflective experiences in the world.[8] Constructive postmodernism expands the domain of investigation by giving credence to feeling and action in the world as well as to thinking.

In terms of theology, this expanded view may show us that nearly everyone already has an image or idea of God, and that we already use reason to deal with that image, and finally that it is thus possible to change that image. Regarding religionists, even those who appeal to Mystery about perplexing theological matters at a minimum prereflectively believe in contending with the divine in a logically coherent manner (that is, even negative theology has a logic). Regarding those with an atheistic mindset, the word 'God' has meaning for atheists, because an atheist must have a definite idea of what he or she rejects.[9] This assumed definition of God, naturally, profoundly shapes a person's stance towards divinity and spirituality. Childish or incoherent notions of divinity often breed atheism. If we already have an idea of God, it is possible to refine and evolve that idea.

Recovering the power of reason may let us participate in the spiritual dimension of human existence which we prethematically feel is part of us. It is important to recover reason and engage in this constructive postmodern search for intelligibility because people in general already have the resources to engage in a deeper spiritual existence, but traditional viewpoints currently distance people from that awareness. Holding the narrow materialistic or sensationistic world-view, or even a traditional theistic world-view, may further today's nihilistic attitude wherein notions of religion and spirituality are either absent or only theoretically operative in our day-to-day lives. And so, by re-examining traditional theism in the light of the Whiteheadian/ Hartshornean reconception of divine power, a shift in human awareness towards a deeper spirituality may occur; religious persons may see and feel more deeply the basis of their spirituality and shift into an ecumenical realm characterized by an appreciation of the mystical dimension. In turn, the agnostic and even atheistic worlds may shift towards the process theistic point of view wherein spirituality may come alive. It is this process theistic point of view that we examine through a consideration of *Arethuse* and *From Suffering to God*.

Arethuse and *From Suffering to God*

Arethuse and *From Suffering to God* both sprang from within the philosophical and theological horizon offered by the Whiteheadian/Hartshornean synthesis of premodern, modern and postmodern intuitions. Both books attempt to communicate that reason can be used in the search for God by reconstructing a world-view from a multifaceted theme: the Whiteheadian/Hartshornean 'event ontology'. They seek to communicate issues related to process metaphysics and process theology: *Arethuse* in a literary mode, and *From Suffering to God* in an academic mode. Santiago Sia has stressed that it is important to develop a methodology followed in process thought that takes seriously the role of concrete experience in thinking, and is inclusive of literary and poetic insights as a basis for abstract thinking.[10] Recovering the use of literary and poetic insights is part of the purpose of *Arethuse*. Sia has likewise stressed the importance of making process ideas more readily available through using literary modes of presentation.[11] At the same time, *From Suffering to God* argues for the need to develop those insights philosophically.

From Suffering to God makes connections between literature, theology and philosophy. It points out that conventional religious attitudes – the traditional concept of God and the traditional formulation of the problem of evil – lead directly to atheism for many people today, but that, if those attitudes are shifted, belief and faith may emerge instead of atheism. Using the thinking of Hartshorne, the book outlines the role of human reason in thinking about God, and explores notions of God as Co-Sufferer and as Liberator. It takes as its starting point the observation that some people live in bleak situations but continue to believe in 'the God of Life', to use a phrase coined by Gustavo Gutiérrez, noted Latin American liberation theologian. Rather than suffering being a route to atheism, knowledge of God can deepen or even arise in the midst of suffering. According to the authors, 'Whereas atheism, given the presence of considerable misery and evil in the world, protests against belief in God, [our] aim is to give due regard to the experiences of many people who continue to believe in God despite suffering, impoverishment and oppression. But unlike traditional theism, this work starts not with a developed concept of God but with reflections on the experience of suffering and asks what it can disclose about God.'[12] Therefore, although the book addresses the problems of suffering and evil, it is not a theodicy in the traditional sense of a purely logical vindication of belief in God.

Arethuse grew spontaneously from the soil of these issues, and was written after the Sias completed writing *From Suffering to God*. Set in the university town of Leuven, Belgium (where the Sias actually wrote *From Suffering to God*), *Arethuse* offers original responses to perplexities faced by people in the throes of everyday life. Fictitious scholars from around the world, thrown into the hub of university life in Leuven, grapple with their lives and with their disciplines. We see how philosophical assumptions shape the decisions and attitudes of the characters: the senseless death of Sean O'Shea, the husband of a young literature lecturer (Aisling O'Shea) from Ireland, results in Aisling's enmity for an uncaring God. How can God let this happen? Moreover, Richard Gutiérrez, an American philosophy instructor desperately seeking tenure, arrives in Leuven and questions the relationship between his intellectual commitment to Thomistic philosophy and his lived experience of the everyday world: what relevance does an academic inquiry into *the problem of evil* have for real people undergoing real suffering? Finally, an eminent Polish philosopher, Piotr Malachowski, turns to process philosophy as he tries to come to grips with the abominations suffered by his family in the Nazi camps of World War II: given the depravity of the Nazis and the suffering of his parents in the camps, how can we countenance the reality of a caring God?

With this said, we may now explore the underlying process theodicy in *Arethuse* through an analysis of, and reflections on, some of the events and characters.

Is God to Blame?

Aisling O'Shea, the young English literature lecturer from Ireland, has received a grant to study 'postmodernism and literature' at the Mercier University in Leuven, Belgium. Accompanying her is her six-year-old son, Philip. Aisling is carrying the burden of raising Philip alone. Her husband, Sean, was a fellow teacher at Aisling's university in Dublin. The two met while doing their graduate work and, as they delved deeper into literature, she English and he the Classics, their relationship deepened.

They were married and enjoyed a full life in Dublin until, when Philip was just a year old, Sean was senselessly killed by a drunk driver. This crushed Aisling – her world had utterly collapsed and she almost gave up.

At one point in the novel Aisling is recalling an event that took place five years before her arrival in Leuven when she, Sean, and the one-year-old Philip had just returned to Dublin from a leisure-filled vacation in southern Spain. As soon as they arrived back home in Dublin, they received a phone call saying a friend's one-year-old child had been in an accident and was in a critical condition at a local hospital. Sean immediately dropped everything and went to the hospital to console the parents, Patrick and Eileen, in their difficult time. This is an example of a practical response to human suffering: rather than going to the hospital and trying to explain anything or provide answers for the parents, Sean simply sits in solidarity with them, thus sharing their burden. Meanwhile, Aisling stayed at home unpacking suitcases and caring for the baby:

> It was almost 11.00 o'clock in the evening when Aisling heard a car pull up on the driveway. While waiting for Sean she had unpacked their suitcases, fed the baby and put him back to sleep. She had been restless throughout. Bad news like that always unsettled her. She breathed a sigh of relief. 'Thank God, he's back,' she muttered.
>
> The doorbell rang. Did he forget his keys? She wondered. Sean was so anxious to be of some comfort to their friends in their moment of pain he must have forgotten them. She hurried down the stairs... She opened the door.
>
> It was the Gardaí.
>
> 'Mrs Aisling O'Shea? I'm afraid that we have some very bad news for you. Can we come in?' The two Gardaí removed their caps and followed Aisling, who had gone pale...
>
> There had been an accident, the Gardaí explained... Sean did not have a chance. He died instantly, while the other driver managed to pull himself out of the wreck.[13]

The Gardaí reported that Sean had spent a few hours sharing in the suffering and difficulty with Patrick and Eileen. Simply his presence, rather than any words, provided tremendous comfort for the parents.

After the Gardaí left that night, Aisling went through stages of bewilderment, denial and finally anger. In her bewilderment she sobbed uncontrollably in the midst of a vacuous feeling. She dragged herself around the house throughout this agony, going from room to room fleeing the complete emptiness pressing in upon her. When she finally realized it was not a nightmare her denial turned into a seething anger – anger at God:

> She could feel her muscles tense up. She was clenching her fists, as she wanted to strike hard, really hard, at whoever was responsible for this. Not just the driver, but whoever allowed that situation to happen. Blast any community that does not prevent such things! Curse those barmen who keep selling drinks to those who are already too drunk to decide for themselves. Where are those parents who did not instill responsibility into this driver, even if they had to *beat* it into him? The pain he was causing her was unforgivable. Curse ...
>
> '*God, why did you let this happen?*' Aisling cried out. 'We had always been taught to love you and trust in your goodness. This is not good, this is wrong. Then why, with all your power, did you not prevent the accident? Just a few minutes more and Sean would have missed the other driver.' She was angry with God, angry because, unlike Sean who had tried to take care of Philip, God was not caring enough for the likes of Sean and her. God seemed

in fact to be toying with them, giving them a happy life, only to snatch it away now. 'God, how can you do this? Why do you do this?' ... *What kind of God was this?*[14]

The bewildered Aisling was in pain partly as a result of her notion of an all-perfect, all-powerful, and all-controlling God, a belief from her childhood. In *From Suffering to God*, the Sias delineate some of the theological background involved in this traditional conception of God's power, and in juxtaposition offer a Hartshornean or process view. On this view, God does not fully control the actions of creatures because creatures enjoy true freedom, therefore the blame does not rest solely with God as Aisling imagines. When Aisling asked, *What kind of God was this?* she was asking a crucial question. Since our ideas of God can only be humanly constructed notions, if our experience contradicts our notion of God, we have to question and challenge that received or traditional idea of God. I suspect atheists become who they are because they reject an inadequately cultivated concept of God, not because they disbelieve in God *per se*.[15]

Rather than blaming God for injustices, we should look to ourselves and our societies, for we are truly free creatures. To be truly free entails accountability; if we are accountable because we are truly free then we cannot blame God. Hartshorne says, 'The creatures must determine something of their own actions, and to this extent the supreme capacity to influence others cannot be power unilaterally to determine the details of reality.'[16] God and creatures co-create in a social manner, with God leading the way.[17] On this scenario, Sean and the people around him (the drunk driver, the bartenders, the parents of the drunk driver and so on) are all partly responsible for his death; God is not the sole cause. On Hartshorne's view, God sets the limits of the universe by way of the natural laws and this only means that the arena creatures have to operate in is advantageous and ordered in the long run rather than risky and chaotic – but some risks are necessarily involved.[18] 'God provides creatures with such guidance or inspiration as will optimise the ratio of opportunities and risks ... while setting the best or optimal limits to freedom.'[19] Given this view, Aisling is wrong in blaming God.

Instead of claiming that God causes evil, Hartshorne asserts that the root of evil in the world is the clash of decisions made by free creatures, and this is bound up with Hartshorne's conviction regarding the nature of *creativity*. Creativity pervades all of reality. It is the basic notion in Hartshorne's interpretation of causality. All processes atomic, biological, social and so on, are creative in some sense. Creativity lies in the nature of all things that they may enter into a complex and creative unity with other things.[20] On Hartshorne's view, elements from the past enter into the constitution of the entity being shaped in the present, and these acts contour or condition the present, but they do not *determine* the present because any coming together always involves some creativity:

> Causes, including God as Supreme Cause, never determine the effect in all its details. While a cause is necessary in the sense that there can be no effect without a cause, it does not follow that the event will take place in precisely the way it is predicted, even when all the necessary causes are present. All one can say is that it may take place. There will be *an* effect but it will not be a fully determinate effect. Because every effect has a creative aspect it is never literally anticipated.[21]

Today's scientists, especially given the findings in particle physics, are also encountering this statistical notion of causality, even in terms of the actual laws of physics themselves.[22] Because of (among other things to be discussed) this unknown element of creativity and the harmonization or lack of it that result from free choices, evil sometimes occurs. The night Sean died he and others made certain free decisions about driving a car. There are virtually hundreds of small decisions made at the time of driving and at other times that ultimately effect the probability of a person getting into an accident or not: for example, route taken, speed, physical condition of one's body, physical upkeep of the car, as well as various decisions by other persons, such as decisions made by the drunk driver, his friends at the pub, the employees of the pub, the police and the societal stance regarding drunk driving. Hartshorne stresses also that chance plays a role in the probabilistic notion of causes, because the degree to which free decisions harmonize is partly given by chance. God persuades entities along the most harmonious path, but God does not eliminate freedom or chance in the process: 'Through the laws of nature God puts restrictions within which the lesser agents can effectively work out the details of their existence. These limits ensure that universal creativity does not end in universal chaos and frustration. But because of chance, there will still be elements of chaos and frustration; but they remain subordinate to the general order and harmony.'[23] The root of all tragedy in the world, then, is the clash of free creaturely creativity.[24]

Some classical theists, however, vehemently retain the notion of a traditionally omnipotent God and are uncomfortable with the scenario of co-decision or co-creation between God and humans. But by maintaining the idea of an utterly omnipotent God, theists fuel an atheistic argument that God as creator and administrator of everything is thus responsible for everything in the world. The traditional view that God imposes an omnipotent will on the world, and that the will of creatures carries little weight, spawns the atheistic conclusion that because evil exists a good God cannot exist. Hartshorne says:

> Sometimes I think this should be shouted from the housetops: the most famous, and probably the most influential, atheistic argument implies a misconception of the idea of divine power, a misconception that does not exalt God but really degrades Him to the level of a tyrant unwilling or unable to inspire and permit in others any genuine decision-making.[25]

The questions for classical theism are: What problems could God *possibly have*, being supremely and eternally secure, with participating in co-creation with truly free creatures? Is it possible to have an unequivocally meaningful universe without creatures who make unequivocally free decisions? Hartshorne thinks not. The radical absurdity of such a meaningless universe came crashing down on Aisling the night of Sean's death because, in her case, the absurdity stemmed from her notion of an omnipotent and all-controlling God. Hartshorne maintains, 'No worse falsehood was ever perpetrated than the traditional concept of omnipotence. It is a piece of unconscious blasphemy, condemning God to a dead world, probably not distinguishable from no world at all.'[26] Aisling was *literally feeling* this absurd, dead world, and was suffering from that feeling.

God as *Actually* Caring

Another aspect of Aisling's suffering over the death of her husband is that she had difficulty finding solace in God given her assumption that God is perfect and impassible and therefore cannot sympathize with creatures. If God is all-controlling and removed from our personal situation, and makes decisions by an unknown logic about what happens in the world, one possible reaction is Aisling's reaction: feelings of profound abandonment. Classical theism holds that God is perfect and impassible, therefore God cannot feel passion, disappointment or sorrow. Anselm wanted to deny any passion in God, yet concomitantly he wanted to sustain the notion of a compassionate God. To solve this dilemma, Anselm held that 'God is compassionate in terms of our experience, but not so in terms of God's being. While we experience the effect of God's compassion, God does not.'[27] The questions here become: Is such one-way help possible? If God does not *actually* care and feel for us in our suffering, then where is our comfort? It seems that classical theism demands that humans somehow ignore the normal biological and psychological necessities of human existence.

Tradition reports that John Wesley's dying words were, 'The best of all is this, that God is with us.' If God is truly 'with us' God would be compassionate with us and share in our sorrows. In Chapter three of *From Suffering to God*, the Sias consider another aspect of the process theistic notion of God: a God 'with us' is, in some sense, a Co-sufferer. They explore this idea by using the analogy of a practical response to human suffering, namely, the comforting of victims by joining in immediate and unconditional solidarity with them. In *Arethuse*, this response is well illustrated. Sean does this by immediately going to the hospital to console his friends Patrick and Eileen in their moment of need, even though his personal situation requires his presence at home. The burden of the suffering parents is greatly eased even though Sean spends little time actually *talking* to Patrick and Eileen. The parents share their fears by telling Sean some of the details of the accident their son was in, and Sean simply listens, taking on the burden, and sits quietly in solidarity with them for several hours. This is co-suffering. The knowledge and the feeling that other people *truly care* about us in moments of suffering can intensely ease our burden: given our psychological make-up, this may be the only way that any entity (including God) can help ease suffering. In times of crisis, barriers between people fall and real sharing takes place, with therapeutic results. If God does not suffer with us in solidarity and, as Anselm claims, is only *apparently* and not really moved by our plight, it is hard to see how such a being can ease our suffering. Something is amiss with Anselm's God if that God only causes us to feel that God is compassionate, while the reality is that God is not compassionate.

Surrender and God's Persuasive Power

Sean's death tore Aisling apart and left her abandoned and without hope, but eventually she was able to surrender that hopelessness and move on. Prior to that point, however, the nights were long and lonely and the days filled with hardship. She was mistaken for an unmarried mother; she experienced people's prejudice and hate towards her, and she suffered the humiliation of single men taking her for 'a poor weak thing' that sorely needed the protection of stalwart men like themselves. All this made her bitter, but 'She knew that simply fighting back in rage and bitterness was not going to end the misery and frustration that she was experiencing. She was being hurt by others, and she was helping them hurt her even more by being bitter and angry ... She was contributing to the seeming absurdity of life.'[28] The God she was taught to believe in, one who oversees and controls everything, was no longer a God she could believe in. In a dialogue with Richard Gutiérrez, the American philosopher on a sabbatical in Leuven, Aisling admits that she lost her faith: 'It was the very idea of paying homage to a God who couldn't care less about me. Why should I care about *that* God?'[29] Unknown to Aisling, her loss of faith in *that* God was the first step towards her 'surrendering' and eventual ability to move ahead with her life in the midst of a new faith. We will return to Aisling's situation after we elucidate our particular notion of surrender.

What is meant by surrender? Process thinking posits that God acts from within creatures and provides for each entity a persuasive lure of feeling that leads the creatures in the most harmonious direction contingent upon their particular present and past situation. Religion or spirituality then must be about feeling this divine lure in ourselves. The idea of 'surrender' as a religious comportment centres upon the fact that reality is too complex to fathom with our discursive reasoning process. William James quips that moralists often prescribe intense use of the will in observance of religious or ethical law, but that it 'only makes them two-fold more the children of hell they were before'.[30] Continually trying to second guess something as complex as human existence may lead to severe frustration. Instead, James recommends self-surrender, and by this he means giving up an attitude of responsibility, and taking on an attitude of indifference; by doing so the very things that one thought one was surrendering are in fact gained. Although I have the greatest respect for James, nevertheless surrender as he describes it may be further nuanced because surrender as a spiritual comportment is different from apathy, renunciation, or passivity. If one merely resigns effort because the path is too difficult, or if one's surrendering is contingent upon receiving some grace or guidance, then the self is still at the centre of awareness. Being concerned about the self, naturally, is *antithetical* to self-surrender. Surrender requires thrusting oneself into the middle, into that 'no-man's land' of both doing and not doing, of both activity and passivity.[31]

In a manner of speaking, one must surrender without attempting to surrender. 'Surrender' as used here is a perplexing concept, more akin to concepts found in eastern religion and philosophy. Again, surrender does not mean abdication, disempowerment or resignation, but quite the contrary. Surrender is the capacity to set aside worries, immediate goals and desires, to make room for action in the moment. Surrender means letting go and not acting – but it also means struggling with what Whitehead would likely call 'the remainder of things'. In surrendering one waits for the myriad of circumstances to arrange themselves so that with one small adjustment the whole falls into place. Three examples are helpful here: in order for an athlete to win a contest, surrendering the goal of winning may empower him/her to perform at the maximum capacity and with spontaneity: surrendering enables the mind and body to be free so as to render the crucial act at the crucial moment. Second, a business owner should surrender the immediate success of his/her business so as to operate impartially within the folds of novelty and spontaneity. This surrender is the essence of negotiating risk in the business world. Third, some martial artists are able to 'become' their opponent: through surrendering their own will they feel the prereflective will of their opponent, thereby feeling the mode of attack at the same time that their opponent feels that they should initiate an attack. This then enables them to meet the attack and foil it spontaneously. In all three of these examples the person does not simply give up – they surrender. In fact, surrender somehow *intensifies* the quest or the activity.

Surrender as a comportment is found in traditions such as Quietism and Taoism. Regarding the latter, 'Tao' signifies 'Way' or 'Path'. Taoism is characterized by opposites in harmonious interaction, and one such pair of opposites forms the concept of doing and not-doing, or 'non-action'. *Wu-wei* in Chinese means 'non-action' or 'non-doing'. However, it does not mean total passivity or inactivity. A person implementing the *wu-wei* in his/her life surrenders and simplifies, and relies on proper timing to resolve the situation into a harmonious resolution. In Taoism *wu-wei* is regarded as the secret to a happy and harmonious life, for through non-action all things can be accomplished:

> Learning consists in daily accumulating;
> The practice of Tao consists in daily diminishing.
> Keep on diminishing and diminishing,
> Until you reach the state of No-Ado [non-action].
> No-Ado, and yet nothing is left undone.[32]

Accumulation and learning are certainly necessary for human lives, but at some point we must surrender that learning and 'unlearn' so as to foster spontaneity, non-interference and the capacity to let things take their natural course when necessary. To apprehend the 'vague beyond' one must shake free from learning.[33]

But non-doing, and non-interference, like surrender, do not mean removing oneself from the world of daily action and living (as for example an ascetic or hermit often does), rather it means acting from within a stance of being guided. Lao Tzu says 'Keep on diminishing and diminishing', which implies that one has in fact learned about things in the past, enabling diminishment now to occur. Thus non-doing happens from *within* learning and doing. Lest we think that this diminishing results in an abandonment of our duties, he immediately states the other side of the opposition, 'yet nothing is left undone'. When one attains the state of non-doing then life has been simplified so that there is the time, the awareness and the mindfulness to bring to fruition all relevant questions and tasks one is faced with.[34] Through surrender it is possible to discern, via human feeling, the most intense and harmonious path for one's daily life, and since that path is through the lived world, which includes others and the physical environment, this intensity and harmony is not solely personal, rather it permeates the *Lebenswelt*. Sean was being guided away from the accident that eventually took his life: had he surrendered enough to heed that guidance, perhaps he would not have been in the wrong place at the wrong time.

Surrendering is a form of struggle, struggling in the middle while concomitantly letting go of the outcome of the struggle. Aisling's surrender was her struggle with the dissonance produced in her by challenging experiences she faced in relation to Sean's death, and by the ramifications of those experiences in relation to her religious beliefs. In Aisling's case, when she was finally able to surrender the bitterness and sadness caused by Sean's death and by other people's prejudice towards her, she was liberated and felt she also had to surrender her paradoxical notion of an all-controlling God. When one examines human experience in the midst of suffering, three alternatives may emerge: acceptance that God somehow causes unjust suffering, or atheism, or revision of the concept of God.[35] Notice that Aisling asked why she should care about *that* God. She surrendered her externally based faith in that God, the all-controlling God of religious tradition. It is vital to note that she did not become an atheist, or an agnostic; rather, she occupied those in-between spaces of the middle – between theism, atheism and agnosticism. After Sean's death she still had faith, but faith in *what*? An awareness emerged from within her prereflective faith as she discovered a God who has the power of 'persuasion'. Aisling's faith deepened in the midst of her suffering through her surrender.

How did this happen? Aisling tells Richard that her infant son Philip showed her the meaning of persuasive power. Aisling had two gifts: an underlying prereflective faith and Philip. These gifts brought about a beneficial change in her attitude from remorse and bitterness about Sean's death to courage and acceptance. Richard asked her about the change in her attitude from bitterness to courage and acceptance:

> 'And what brought about the change?'
> 'Philip.'
> 'Philip? You mean he suddenly spoke and told you to shape up?'
> 'Yes!' ...
> '[Philip] got up and spoke in a loud voice. No, seriously, it was not as spectacular as that. But have you ever thought of the power of the helplessness of a baby? ... In your [philosophy] books that's probably a contradiction... I always tell the students during one of my lectures that I would bet that no matter how interesting somebody's lecture may be, if somebody brought a helpless baby into the lecture hall, everyone's attention would be directed to that cooing baby. There's power in that. It's a different kind of power. It doesn't dominate, it attracts. It doesn't threaten, it influences.'
> 'You must forgive me, but I don't see the connection between that and God.'
> 'I don't blame you. [Coming to this realization] took me a long time... The whole thing made me wonder what made me blame God. Well, I had been taught that God could do everything. So God could have prevented the accident. But the accident still happened. But what if God were like the helpless infant, like Philip a few years ago?'
> 'God, a helpless infant? And to think that I've been defending God's almighty power in my research!'
> 'But it doesn't make God any less powerful. Only that it's a different kind of power.'[36]

Aisling explains that she had been blaming God for Sean's death, but the fault was with the drunk driver and the causal chain of human decisions and actions. God does not solely control everything, and thus is not solely responsible for everything. She realized that as a mother she had certain responsibilities towards her infant, and that she, not God, was liable for fulfilling those responsibilities. A question then arose in Richard's mind regarding the efficacy of this kind of persuading power:

> 'And how does that tie in with the way you describe power?'

> 'That God, because God has chosen to share the responsibility, appeals to us to exercise that responsibility. God doesn't force us. Just as a helpless baby does not and cannot. But when a baby looks up to you, you know through those teary eyes or smiling face, the baby is exerting an influence on you.'
> 'Doesn't that make God weak?'
> 'Is someone weak who enables you to do something? Is a teacher less powerful for inspiring others to accomplish more? Is a poet or an artist any less effective than a tyrant? Is a Muse irrelevant?'[37]

Richard questions this notion of power, and thinks that persuasive power may be weak, but Whitehead and Hartshorne hold that it is the most effective power in the universe. On a personal level our actions are based on persuasive power in that our mind mainly *persuades* our body to act. On a social level, a CEO, a politician or an administrator cannot *efficiently* cause much of anything; it is only through persuasive power and thus the *free decisions of the ones being persuaded* that the politician is successful. Thus persuasive power is wider in scope than direct efficient power. Because God works through the fabric of reality in a ubiquitous manner (throughout all space and time), God's persuasive power is not a limited form of power extant in, for example, creatures such as ourselves with bodies living in three dimensional space for a few million years. God's persuasive power is far beyond this. God persuaded the evolution of all matter and energy from a chaotic state at the beginning of the universe into the order and harmony that has resulted in the natural world and intelligent beings such as ourselves. This is immense power, exerted over an immense period of time, with results that some call surprising and others call miraculous. Creation is so marvellous and complex that we have been trying to discern the nature of that order and harmony for millennia, and no doubt will continue trying to do so (this is the very quest of philosophy, science and religion). Richard arrived on the scene approximately 15 billion years late with a tiny sphere of influence, a small amount of persuasive and efficient causal power (the latter is due mainly to his two hands and two legs that enable him to manipulate his immediate physical surroundings) and he thinks the persuasive power of God may be weak! It is these very categories that are giving Richard trouble in his research about the problem of evil. Because he is thinking in classical terms Richard is running directly into a dead end when confronted by the traditional idea of God's power and how it relates to suffering in the concrete world.

Persuasive Power: Malachowski Opens a Space

In a dialogue between Richard and Professor Malachowski, Richard makes explicit the implicit difficulties with his own approach to the problem of evil. In addition, the content of the dialogue itself points to a more robust approach to the problem of evil, an approach that is pursued in the academic book *From Suffering to God*.

For the past three years Richard has been working on a book (his first) dealing with the problem of evil, and has made little progress in the preceding year. He is under pressure and is suffering from anxiety in the attempt to finally finish the book, because its completion is important as he is applying for tenure at his university in the

United States. He is hoping for inspiration while at Mercier University in Leuven so he can finish writing the last chapter. Richard is discussing the problem regarding his research with the Polish professor Piotr Malachowski, who started on a philosophical and theological search for meaning after the death of his family in the German concentration camps. Professor Malachowski traversed philosophy and theology, and after many years was led to the process philosophical point of view where he hopes to find a way to make sense of appalling suffering and evil. The underlying feeling is that Richard is frustrated because his solution to the problem of evil, using the traditional Thomistic approach, does not speak to the experience of the suffering people he has encountered in his daily life.

Richard's approach to the problem of evil is along discursive lines, and may be characterized as the traditional or 'generic' problem of evil.[38] Below, we see Richard alluding to those who see the problem of evil as a logical puzzle, and he is referring to this approach. Richard himself takes this generic approach but is becoming suspicious of his own thinking.

By using a synoptic Whiteheadian view, Professor Malachowski is able to help Richard pin down the reasons why he has become uncomfortable with his approach and why his research is not proceeding. Similarly to Sean taking on the burden and co-suffering in silence with his friends at the hospital, Professor Malachowski does not lecture Richard or give him ready-made solutions to his problem. A dialectic, familiar to those with experience in clinical psychology, occurs in this dialogue wherein the older more experienced Professor Malachowski opens intellectual and interpersonal 'space' for Richard's frustrations. In a sense Malachowski 'lures' Richard into discovering the solutions himself. I will first briefly explicate this five-step dialectical process (A to E below) and then follow with an example from the dialogue.

(A) Richard shares. Richard has a problem that is weighing on his feelings, and he shares his burden with Professor Malachowski.

(B) Professor Malachowski feels and intensifies Richard's problem. Because Malachowski is aware on a deeper level, and aided by the synoptic view of process thought, he is able to feel the source of Richard's frustration. However, the professor does not move to 'solve' the problem, but instead *reshapes* the problem and thematizes it for Richard. This enables Richard to see and feel the nature of the problem more clearly so that Richard's own consciousness can attack the problem directly. The claim here is that this approach actually enables Richard to be more aware of his own thoughts and feelings.

(C) Professor Malachowski opens himself to genuine listening. He opens up to Richard by engaging in real listening. He encourages Richard to talk by stepping back and leaving the space and freedom for Richard to say whatever he needs to. Put another way, Professor Malachowski truly cares.

(D) Richard begins to answer his own questions. Because of this help, Richard is able to bring to light some aspects of solutions to his problem. Where do these aspects come from? They come from Richard, because the source of questions also harbours the answers to those questions: 'a question bears with it an implicit answer, no matter how vague it may be when the question is asked. For if the questioner had no knowledge at all of the answer, he or she would not have been able to raise the question in the first place'.[39] Questions and problems crop up against a background of

implicit knowledge and the task of the helper or teacher is to lure the questioner or student into bringing that implicit knowledge to the foreground themselves.
(E) Malachowski points the way forward. Finally, and only in the end, Malachowski uses ideas from process thought to show Richard that possibilities exist for thinking along more fruitful and fundamental lines.

Let us see how these five factors are at play in a dialogue from *Arethuse*. The passages are lettered (A to E, keyed to the elements above) in the dialogue so as to differentiate the elements more easily:

> *(A)* Richard disclosed the difficulty he was experiencing in completing his work. Somehow there was an important factor missing in his scholarly research, he confided to Dr. Malachowski. 'I feel that I'm working on a solution without knowing what the real problem is,' remarked Richard...
> *(B)(C)* 'That sounds strange. We philosophers are supposed to be able not only to evaluate the merits of each argument but also to clarify the issues.' The professor looked Richard in the eye. 'You are talking about the proper starting point for our philosophizing, aren't you?'
> *(A)* 'Possibly. But I don't just mean articulating what the philosophical issues in a problem are.' Richard tucked his left hand under his right elbow. 'Take human suffering, for instance. A very concrete reality if there ever was one. I've worked on this topic for some time now and yet when I am faced with the challenge of talking to someone who's just lost a loved one, or an individual who has just been through a disaster, I'm lost for words. Surely we philosophers should be able to say something meaningful in situations like that.'...
> *(B)(C)* 'But do you expect philosophy to say something meaningful in this situation?'[40]

Malachowski is opening the problem up for Richard and bringing out elements of Richard's own feelings and thoughts about the problem of evil, while Malachowski temporarily sets aside his own concerns and ideas. In the novel we already know that Malachowski *does* believe that philosophy should say something meaningful about human suffering. This is clear because the genesis of Malachowski's philosophizing lies in trying to find meaning in the suffering and death of his parents in the Nazi camps; his quest is not a purely intellectual one but also an existential one.[41] But instead of immediately using his own experience and arguing that philosophy should say something meaningful about human suffering, Malachowski surrenders his own point of view by asking Richard if *he* (Richard) thinks philosophy should say something meaningful regarding the problem of suffering.

Next, continuing the dialectical exchange, Richard states that philosophy should say something meaningful about human suffering, and cautiously shares his worries with the professor that philosophy focuses too much on knowledge and too little on human experience. Again, Malachowski makes an effort to stimulate Richard's thinking:

> *(B)(C)* 'But do you expect philosophy to say something meaningful in this situation [regarding suffering]?'
> *(A)* 'Yes, since the study of philosophy is meant to provide us with wisdom. But I sometimes get the impression that what we philosophers have become concerned with is knowledge and more knowledge.' Richard paused, not knowing how his remarks would be accepted.

(C) 'Go ahead, I'm listening,' the older professor, who took a sip from his glass of Beaujolais, was encouraging.
(D) 'We sometimes blame the sciences for accumulating all this information and math for juggling with figures and becoming too abstract in the whole process. And yet aren't we doing the same thing? I know of some philosophers who regard the problem of evil, for instance, as an intellectual puzzle. They get a lot of kicks from solving problems which are of their own making. In the end one could ask what that has to do with life.'
(B) 'Wait now. Are you talking about the problem of suffering or of philosophy as a problem?... Are these not separate issues?'
(D) 'That is precisely *the* problem. We philosophers are so fond of being clear about the issues that we start classifying reality.'
(B) 'But how can you expect to address the issues adequately if you have not clarified them? That *is* important, as you know.'
(D) 'True, but sometimes we do lose the real issue as we dissect, as it were, what we perceive to be the problem. I remember my Asian colleague once quoting Mencius, who said that what one dislikes in clever men is their tortuosity.'[42]

It seems as if Richard is telling (or enlightening) Professor Malachowski that philosophy is too abstract, too classificatory and so on, but it is important to realize Malachowski already believes this. Richard is coming to grips with the facts that philosophers are too fond of classification and abstraction, and that they lose sight of the real issues through dissection, but this deeper awareness is being lured out of Richard via the conversation. With the next comment, however, for the first time Malachowski uses process philosophy and hints at a possible solution to Richard's problem. He says that both formal analysis *and* speculative delight are required in contemplating the major questions. The implication is that Richard has to widen his viewpoint considerably instead of conceiving philosophy as either formal or informal, creative or analytic. Richard has to surrender his dichotomous attitude about what philosophy is, and occupy the arduous middle between speculation and scholarship. Malachowski says:

(E) '... there is something in Whitehead's *Adventures of Ideas* that I was reading just this morning... He was alerting us to what is lost from speculation by scholarship. He says, in speculation there is delight and discourse while in scholarship there is concentration and thoroughness. Of course, Whitehead claims that for progress both are necessary.'
(D) 'I believe we have lost the "feel" of the problem because of all our disputations ...'
(B) 'But that's not the domain of philosophy, at least as commonly understood.'
(D) 'Exactly, we have left out an important aspect of the problem in our philosophizing.'
(C) 'And what is that?' quizzed the professor.
(D) 'The element of life. The importance of experience. The necessary connection between our thinking and our living.'
(C) 'And how does that relate to the problem of suffering you mentioned earlier on?'
(D) 'That we need a different way of describing the problem. Philosophy shouldn't attempt a solution until it has done justice to the reality of suffering. [But] It's much too abstract to do that. At least the way philosophical thinking has become.'[43]

Recall the events just before the car accident that ended Sean's life: Sean's practical response to the suffering of his friends at the hospital was to shoulder their burden in silence, and similarly here we see Malachowski take on Richard's problems by being 'silent', by opening an interpersonal space for Richard; Malachowski provides a lure. This opening of space is akin to Malachowski exercising persuasive power. Richard now knows he must reconnect to concrete experience to do justice to the reality of human suffering. Richard seems to feel this because he says, 'we need a different way of describing the problem', but he cannot actually surrender his classical approach just yet. Richard is still stuck at the level of the logical analysis of the 'generic problem of evil'.[44]

Different Approaches to the Problem

It is useful at this stage to make a distinction between three approaches to the question of evil and divinity. These three approaches are (1) a traditional theodicy or logical defence, (2) what I call a 'robust theodicy', and (3) what I call a *theopraxical* approach.

The popular and traditional approach to the problem (the approach alluded to as purely formal and insufficient even by the present Pope) is a theodicy or logical defence. This is a purely theoretical logical defence wherein the theist defends against the atheistic charge that the proposition 'God is omnipotent and all-good' is logically inconsistent with the proposition 'evil exists'. Leibniz coined the term 'theodicy' (with his book entitled *Théodicée*, from the Greek *theo-dike*). *Dike* signifies 'order' or 'right' and thus one way to think of what a theodicy does is that it attempts to make God right or make God conform to an order. In the spirit of ensuring order, the important point for a traditional theodicy is that the argument make logical sense, and little weight is given to the plausibility or ramifications of the argument. Many theists, for example Alvin Plantinga,[45] argue that it is wholly sufficient to provide a defence of this sort.

But our friend Richard in *Arethuse* is beginning to have misgivings about such an approach and is leaning towards a fuller point of view that may be characterized as a 'robust theodicy'. Examples of such theodicies are the works of, among others, Hartshorne, David Ray Griffin and Barry L. Whitney.[46] Today's world needs a full or robust theodicy that is more holistic in scope as opposed to past eras where a logical vindication of God was sufficient because belief in God was widespread. Griffin points out that in the past the traditional idea of God was not called into question even in the face of the evils of the world because belief was woven into the fabric of society. But today biblical criticism has changed our stance towards the authority of the Bible, and thus abstract approaches to the issue of evil and suffering are inadequate.[47] Griffin also says, 'In our situation, the theologian needs [using Hartshorne's phrase] a "global argument", the purpose of which is to show that a theistic interpretation can illuminate the totality of our experience, including the experience of evil, better than nontheistic interpretations.'[48] Process theodicy involves reconceiving the notion of God's power, but this reformulation is not undertaken solely as an answer to the problem of evil, rather for a broad range of reasons that have to do with reconceiving our entire world-view in a constructively postmodern way: God's power is reconceived so as to explain coherently the relation of religion to the evolutionary origin of our world, to explain contradictions in scripture, to explain miracles (some of these may be better explained as paranormal or psi events) and to explain the diversity of religions.⁴⁹ Part of this theistic reformulation involves acknowledging new findings in physics and the other sciences. In a holistic way, the robust theodicy is supplied with substance from other fronts also undergoing constructive reformulation.

We find a differently situated approach in *From Suffering to God* and in *Arethuse*. The element of *praxis* becomes important. This third approach I call a *theopraxical* approach. It is not enough to produce a logical vindication, or even an expanded or more holistic theoretical framework. An important ramification of establishing that holistic theoretical framework is the realization that the question of God and of evil is partly an empirical question because God acts through empirical reality. The 'argument' regarding God and evil also extends into the realm of *praxis* or worldly action. Co-suffering and surrender (as a religious comportment) are important behaviours in addressing the evils and problems in the world.

From Suffering to God focuses less on the theist–atheist debate (that is, the question of God's existence or non-existence) and more on the human *practical response* to suffering. Because the *theopraxical* approach is not burdened by the elements of the theist–atheist debate, it can address the issues of God and evil in a more comprehensive way. For example, *From Suffering to God* starts with the practical response of *believers* to the problem of suffering and then explores theological and philosophical issues implicit in those *already theistically oriented* responses. This stance permits the Sias to move farther into the issues and effectively suggest that since *all* free creatures participate in creating evil in the world in some sense, even if they are not explicitly aware of it,⁵⁰ it is therefore the duty of all free creatures to *alleviate* the suffering of others.⁵¹ The *theopraxical* approach acknowledges that an important part of dealing with the problem of evil involves personal action in the world.

The idea of praxis comes across clearly in *Arethuse* with the attitude of Dr Fuentes, the liberation theologian from the Philippines. Instead of questioning the existence of God, he questions the traditional idea of God and moves directly into the ramifications or implications as regards acting in the world. Dr Fuentes is a seminary professor of philosophy sent to Leuven by his bishop for a sabbatical, and he personifies the approach towards the problem of evil taken in *From Suffering to God* and in many liberation theologies. Going back to the dialogue in *Arethuse*, Richard and Dr Malachowski are joined by Dr Fuentes. After Malachowski has summarized what he and Richard had discussed regarding the problem of suffering, Dr Fuentes directly responds, and he cuts across the traditional lines of the debate:

> 'Who was it who said – I think it was Heidegger – philosophers are reducing reality to a mentally fabricated axiomatic project. I can understand your situation.' Dr. Fuentes, who was about ten years older than Richard, looked at him. 'Although my difficulty with the way philosophy generally handles the problem of evil is that it is seen too much as a theodicy. Too much attention is given to the challenge of atheism. Don't you agree?' He turned his head in the direction of Dr. Malachowski, who nodded. 'And so we are expected to provide a coherent and credible resolution of how God can be defended as almighty *and* all-good when there is so much evil and suffering around us... *The important question is not theodicy but idolatry.*'⁵²

Dr Fuentes has a different approach to the problem of evil, one forged in the hot furnace of experiences under an oppressive political regime. He is not concerned with fighting against atheism and with defending God's almighty power in the face of atheistic arguments. He notes that such an approach is indeed an important aspect of the problem, but what is more important is that people are suffering and being told, ludicrously, that it is 'in God's controlled and controlling plan' for them to suffer horribly. They are told by the church that their suffering is God's punishment. Worse, they are told that human beings simply cannot know why God is choosing to cause their babies to be born tubercular and their young children to starve to death, while God chooses health and happiness for those in the more economically developed nations. But Dr Fuentes does not believe God is choosing this, and is concerned that the government (and even the churches) are perpetrating a horrific evil themselves by handing down a notion of God that is idolatrous. Dr Fuentes says, 'The danger for us is that in our attempts to defend God, as it were, we could be perpetuating idols.'[53] He claims that the main question surrounding the problem of evil is not whether God exists, but 'What kind of God can we continue to believe in, given the presence of so much undeserved suffering?'[54]

In addition, Professor Malachowski is concerned about praxis or dealing with the real world. He has been asking the same questions about the nature of God because of his experience with the concentration camps of World War II. The genesis of his philosophical search was the reality of the human suffering in the concentration camp, and his philosophizing is kept alive by his physical visits to the camp. As mentioned above, he had the opportunity to further his career at a distinguished university, but refused the appointment because it entailed leaving Poland. The camp at Majdanek was the source of his philosophizing:

> Truth stared him in the face as he meditated on the events which led to the death of his parents. As he wandered about the camp, a routine that he religiously followed, looking in distress at the piles of shoes of the former inmates, as he dodged the wire fence that had trapped his parents and several others in a pitiful existence, as he imagined the bitterness and the frustration that reduced humans to mere skeletons, he often asked why, why did such evil things happen? Why was suffering perpetrated by evil people?[55]

Some sufferers feel abandoned by God, but many feel their faith deepened. Why is their faith deepened? Malachowski searched theology, then philosophy, and ended up seriously questioning the traditional notion of God. The idea of a God who had to be defended in the face of suffering may not be a God worthy of worship. A good question is, What kind of God is God? The answer, implicit in the Sias' novel but explicit in their scholarly book, is that the process notion of God is a persuasive God who truly co-creates with creatures. And further, God needs no defence because truly free creatures make decisions that sometimes result in evil, and God never coerces creatures.[56]

Nature Alive: towards a Different Conception of God

The different approaches to the problem of evil and God entail a novel concept of God. If *theo-dike* signifies the attempt to make God right or make God conform to an order, then the 'robust theodicy' and the *theopraxical* approaches above are both truer to 'theodicy' or *Théodicée* than a traditional theodicy, because both approaches necessitate modifying the inherited concept of God. Ideas of God, whether they be directly received in a revelatory sense, or wrought by the hands of theologians and philosophers, are humanly constructed notions.[57] Thus it makes sense that, if our inherited notion of divinity is paradoxical when confronted with manifest experience (such as the experience of evil), we amend that notion of divinity.

As mentioned earlier, most persons have a prereflective idea of God. There seems to be good reason to turn to this prereflective idea because God need not be conceptualized in the traditional manner as an utterly spiritual, transcendent, omnipotent, omniscient being in a separate heavenly reality fully controlling the material world. There is hope for those of us who have an intuitive inkling about the religious life, but are confused about the traditional idea of God. The process idea of God, as set forth by Whitehead and Hartshorne (and others), is examined in the Sias' novel and scholarly book. The books delineate an alternative notion of God that squares with human intuition. On this view, God is a persuasive force congenial in reality rather than a controlling being external to reality.

Today, given the microscope, biology, mathematics, quantum physics and so on, we know that in principle there is little difference between plant life, animal life and human life. 'All life is either unicellular or multi-cellular, and a cell is a living individual which in a certain measure determines its own activities in response to stimuli from without.'[58] Further, entering the realm of matter, given the findings of twentieth-century science, the concept of dead, inert matter does not do justice to new scientific discoveries. Thus the first step to a new conception of God is to realize that not only humans, animals and plants are alive, but also, in a sense, all of nature is 'alive'. All of reality, in a sense, experiences. 'An occasion of experience which includes a human mentality is an extreme instance, at one end of the scale, of those happenings which constitute nature.'[59] For the most part, the world consists of primitive experience or aboriginal consciousness, or *life*. Scientists tell us that plant life (for example, algae) developed from inorganic matter some three billion years ago. It stretches credulity to believe that some sort of enigmatic or mystical transformation suddenly took place in history that resulted in life or animate matter – the appeal to Ockham's razor results rather in the belief that the conditions for life and consciousness are congenial in reality in the first place: nature is alive. Even among physicists, there is wide agreement that there must be some kind of 'primitive choice' at the quantum levels of reality.[60]

Considering that all of nature is alive allows us to extend the notion of sentience upwards, to the world and the universe as a whole, and this leads to a new concept of God. On the physical level, the British chemist James E. Lovelock and the American biologist Lynn Margulis formulated the 'Gaia hypothesis' wherein the Earth's matter, air, oceans and land surface form a complex system which can be seen as a single living organism. This might be a wild hypothesis to some, but it helps us expand our thinking about the nature of our world. Expanding this 'Gaia' notion upwards and fitting it into a more philosophical framework leads to the Platonic or Plotinian *World Soul*. Again generalizing up from this hypothesis we arrive at the whole cosmos as a single, feeling reality, or God. Consider Hartshorne's analogy where the soul is to the body as God is to the world:

> The body is a *society* of billions of cells, each a highly organized society of molecules and particles or wavicles. At a given moment each of us, as a conscious individual, is a single reality; but our body is no such single reality. Each white blood corpuscle is a tiny animal... Similarly, God's cosmic body is a society of individuals, not a single individual. The world as an integrated individual is not a 'world' as this term is normally and properly used, but 'God'. God, the World Soul, is the *individual integrity* of 'the world', which otherwise is just the myriad of creatures.[61]

If we accept Hartshorne's analogy, then we may feel God's cosmic body because we are a part of it. This is not a Hegelian move, or a bringing of God into presence. The move here is more fundamental than these because it calls into question the very assumptions upon which we build our world-view in this scientific epoch. In this epoch we think in dualistic terms that engender a schism between nature and life, between humanity and God, between mind and matter. Hartshorne and Whitehead aim to close the ontological, epistemological and psychological gaps between humanity and God. But Hartshorne does not unite them with a *pantheism*. It is our habitual thinking which declares that God is either utterly external to the universe or utterly immanent. Rather, Hartshorne's position is one of *panentheism*, which is midway between the traditional view of God being the wholly independent and universal cause of the universe and the traditional pantheistic view wherein God simply *is* the universe. On Hartshorne's view God is inclusive of the world, but not solely inclusive of the world – God is also something more: a unifying factor. This is similar to the way that the human soul is inclusive of the body – yet the soul is also something more: a unifying factor. When we escape the confines of traditional thinking and instead think about God and creatures bound together in co-creation, the problem of evil and responsibility gets transformed – possibly *dissolved*.

Conclusion

As Richard said, there is a necessary connection between our thinking and our living. One of the keys to escaping the confines of the philosophy and the theology of our epoch, and thus dodging at least the brunt of the blow of the *problem of evil*, is to expand our world-view and conceive of God as acting persuasively from within in a co-creative process, and realizing that the problem of evil does not involve exonerating God but rather re-examining God and the nature of God's power in relation to ourselves.

Breaking out of the strictures of thinking and moving into the frontiers of incorporating feeling and intuition into a world-view does not mean abandoning rationality. On the contrary, it means regaining the original ground of reason in all its 'robustness'. Overcoming the schism between the so-called 'material' and so-called 'spiritual realms' means seeing the connections between literature, philosophy, the sciences and theology. Mending the material/spiritual schism in awareness means realizing that the ground of literature, philosophy, the sciences and theology is the same ground. We surrender and try to feel our way forward along that ground because the infinite complexities of the universe cannot be univocalized with our minds. Instead of trying to *solve* the problem of evil as Richard does, Aisling reaches into the *immanent beyond* and *dissolves* the problem by actualizing her prereflective faith that the universe somehow makes sense. Aisling is not duped into abandoning spirituality simply because the image of God she learned about as a child turns out to be inadequate. Instead, she moves forward in a theopraxical sense into a deeper spiritual life.

Richard, Aisling, Malachowski and Fuentes faced the perplexities of everyday life, and did so with the help of God as the source of order leading them away from evil and suffering. Therefore wherever they met evil and suffering in their co-creation, they were not heeding the ever-present divine guidance – they were not surrendering to God. Evil is ubiquitous, yet it need not be. Opening ourselves via surrender to the divine lure, feeling and acting upon the will of God is, indeed, the fundamental human inquiry and can only be answered with the quest that comprises an entire human life from birth to death. Surrendering to a God who lures creatures, even in the midst of suffering, and occupying that seemingly impossible 'middle' space between activity and passivity, is the way to actualize a co-creation that brings God's harmonious atemporal vision into the temporal world. This is the path to overcoming evil. This is the crux of the process theodicy, as well as the hope of those who ask, as does Dr Fuentes, 'What kind of God can we continue to believe in, given the presence of so much undeserved suffering?'

Leuven, Belgium – 1999

Notes

1. Lyall Watson, *Dark Nature: A Natural History of Evil* (London: Hodder & Stoughton, 1995), 175. Also see William Shakespeare, *Macbeth* (I, vii, 56–8).
2. For example, see Frans De Waal, *Peacemaking Among Primates* (Cambridge, MA: Harvard University Press, 1989). Also see Jane Goodall, *The Chimpanzees of Gombe* (Cambridge, MA: Harvard University Press, 1986).
3. Marian Sia and Santiago Sia, *The Fountain Arethuse: A Novel set in the University Town of Leuven* (Lewes, UK: The Book Guild Ltd., 1997), 107.
4. For reviews, see Theodore Walker, 'Reviews of *From Suffering to God*, and *The Fountain Arethuse*', *Process Studies* 28.1–2 (1999): 147–9.
5. Pope John Paul II, Encyclical Letter number 20: *FIDES ET RATIO, of the Supreme Pontiff John Paul II to the Bishops of the Catholic Church on the Relationship Between Faith and Reason*, September 1998, 56.
6. Alfred North Whitehead, *Process and Reality: An Essay in Cosmology*, corrected edition, edited by David R. Griffin and Donald W. Sherburne (New York: The Free Press, 1978), 8.
7. David Ray Griffin (ed.), *The Reenchantment of Science: Postmodern Proposals* (Albany, NY: State University of New York Press, 1988), xi.
8. Causality is a felt, prereflective experience. All persons feel the present as causally

influenced by past events. Even those sceptics that verbally deny causation cannot efface the prereflective belief in real causation. See John B. Cobb Jr. and David Ray Griffin, *Process Theology: An Introductory Exposition* (Philadelphia: The Westminster Press, 1976), 31.
9. Marian Sia and Santiago Sia, *From Suffering to God: Exploring our Images of God in the Light of Suffering* (London: The Macmillan Press, Ltd., 1994), 1.
10. Santiago Sia, 'Concretising Concrete Experience: A Discussion Paper on a Possible Task for Process Thought in Europe', Paper presented at a conference on 'The Future of Process Thought in Europe', Lille, France, 1 April 1997, 4. Also see Santiago Sia, 'Process Thought as Conceptual Framework', *Process Studies* 19.4 (1990): 248–55.
11. On this score see some of the early and entertaining essays by Whitehead such as Alfred North Whitehead, 'The Clerk of the Weather', *Cambridge Review* 7, 10 February 1886, no page numbers available; also Alfred North Whitehead, 'Davy Jones', *Cambridge Review* 7, 12 May 1886, 311–12.
12. Sia and Sia, *From Suffering to God*, 10.
13. Sia and Sia, *The Fountain Arethuse*, 46–7.
14. Ibid., 52.
15. Sia and Sia, *From Suffering to God*, 1–2.
16. Ibid., 129–30.
17. Note that 'co-creation' is not an omnipotent God sharing power with creatures. An omnipotent God sharing power may be called 'traditional free will theism' and is a position that opposes process theism. For (at least) 10 problems with traditional free will theism, see David Ray Griffin, *Evil Revisited: Responses and Reconsiderations* (Albany, NY: State University of New York Press, 1991), 16–22.
18. See Charles Hartshorne, 'A New Look at the Problem of Evil', in *Current Philosophical Issues: Essays in Honor of Curt John Ducasse*, edited by F.C. Dommeyer (Springfield, IL: Charles C. Thomas, 1966), 209–10.
19. Sia and Sia, *From Suffering to God*, 131.
20. Whitehead, *Process and Reality*, 21.
21. Sia and Sia, *From Suffering to God*, 135.
22. See an essay by a widely respected physicist regarding the postulation that physical laws evolve: Walter Thirring, 'Do the laws of nature evolve?', in *What is Life? The Next Fifty Years*, edited by Michael P. Murphy and Luke A.J. O'Neil (Cambridge: Cambridge University Press, 1995), 131.
23. Sia and Sia, *From Suffering to God*, 133.
24. Because of their particular approach, some process theologians (particularly Hartshorne), have been cited with overlooking heinous or monstrous evil. For an attempt to address this issue, see the declaration of 'Demonic Evil' in Griffin, *Evil Revisited*, 31–40, wherein the demonic is defined as creativity that diverges strongly from the divine creative aims in a violently destructive manner.
25. Charles Hartshorne, 'Can We Understand God?', *Louvain Studies* 7.2 (1978): 75–84.
26. Charles Hartshorne, *Omnipotence and Other Theological Mistakes* (Albany, NY: State University of New York Press, 1984), 17–18.
27. Sia and Sia, *From Suffering to God*, 61.
28. Sia and Sia, *The Fountain Arethuse*, 276.
29. Ibid., 277.
30. William James, *The Varieties of Religious Experience: A Study in Human Nature*, with an introduction by Martin E. Marty (New York: Penguin Books, 1985), 110.
31. There are overtones here of William Desmond's philosophy of 'the between'. Desmond articulates a fourfold sense of being: univocal, equivocal, dialectical and metaxological being. On pain of oversimplification, we note that the univocal sense of being puts

emphasis on simple sameness and sweeping unity; the equivocal breaks out of this unity to do justice to diversities which cannot be mediated; the dialectical tries to mediate equivocity and overcome the equivocal difference, but sometimes dialectic may be too self-involved because its mediation reorganizes and fundamentally changes what it reconciles. Thus the metaxological sense of being avoids the reduction of a dialectical subordination: it lets the other three senses of being, even if they repudiate one another, live in a dynamic interrelationship. There is no closure here, nor is there simply a free play of capacities. The metaxological between is complex and full of harmonies and tensions, as is our notion of 'surrender'. Surrender is in-between activity/passivity, in-between light/dark, and not quite grey either. Regarding this fourfold sense of being, see William Desmond, *Desire, Dialectic and Otherness: An Essay on Origins* (New Haven, CT: Yale University Press, 1987).

32. Lao Tzu, *Tao Te Ching*, translated by John C.H. Wu and edited by Paul K.T. Sih (New York: St John's University Press, 1961), 69.
33. Alfred North Whitehead, *Modes of Thought* (Cambridge: Cambridge University Press, 1938), 8.
34. Yet, at the same time, surrendering is not something one 'does' or 'accomplishes'. For example, '*hsü*' in Chinese Taoism means 'emptiness' or 'purity' wherein one becomes at peace with the Tao: in tranquillity the self is transcended. Contemplative Taoists attain *hsü* by stilling their thought processes and passions, and some practise for many years, but they are denounced by other Taoists as attempting to strive for something that is beyond human possibility. Rather, the latter Taoists hold, if one attains *hsü* it 'simply happens'. We may say it happens because the effort to attain it was actually an obstacle to the attainment. Negotiating the obstacle is surrender.
35. Regarding the debate over this issue, see Chapters one and four in Sia and Sia, *From Suffering to God*; also see Hartshorne, 'Can We Understand God?'
36. Sia and Sia, *The Fountain Arethuse*, 277–8.
37. Ibid., 278–9.
38. This problem results from maintaining simultaneously that (1) God is omnipotent; (2) God is omnibeneficent; and (3) evil exists. These three assertions taken together, unqualified or undenied, must necessarily result in a logical contradiction.
39. Sia and Sia, *From Suffering to God*, 19.
40. Sia and Sia, *The Fountain Arethuse*, 104.
41. For example, instead of accepting teaching positions at more prestigious universities, Professor Malachowski chooses to stay in Lublin, Poland, because the Majdanek camp is physically close to his university. The actual camp is the situation that stimulates his philosophizing and the font that feeds his craving for answers.
42. Sia and Sia, *The Fountain Arethuse*, 104–5.
43. Ibid., 105–6.
44. See David Basinger and Randall Basinger, 'The Problem with the "Problem of Evil"', *Religious Studies* 30.1 (1994): 89–97, wherein it is suggested that the 'generic' approach to the problem of evil is becoming an unfruitful polemic that allows both theists and atheists to hide in the shadows of ambiguous argumentation. The generic or purely logical defence should be surpassed for a more substantial debate.
45. For example, see Alvin Plantinga, 'Reply to the Basingers on Divine Omnipotence', *Process Studies* 11.1 (1981): 25–9, *passim*; and Alvin Plantinga, *God, Freedom and Evil* (London: George Allen & Unwin Ltd, 1975), 7–73.
46. For example, see David Ray Griffin, *God, Power, and Evil: A Process Theodicy* (Philadelphia: Westminster Press, 1976), and David Ray Griffin, *Evil Revisited*. Also see Barry L. Whitney, *Evil and the Process God*, Toronto Studies in Theology, volume 19 (New York: The Edwin Mellen Press, 1985).

47. Griffin, *God, Power, and Evil*, 256.
48. Ibid., 256.
49. Ibid., 3-4.
50. An important element of western religious clemency entails asking forgiveness for 'sins of omission' and sins caused without the knowledge of the person (for example, see the Roman Catholic Act of Contrition). This element fits well with Hartshorne's view that the clash of free creativities sometimes produces evil effects unknown to the creatures.
51. For arguments regarding our duty to alleviate the suffering of others, see Sia and Sia, *From Suffering to God*, Chapter seven.
52. Sia and Sia, *The Fountain Arethuse*, 106 (emphasis mine).
53. Ibid., 107-8.
54. Ibid., 107.
55. Ibid., 183.
56. A technical digression may be helpful here. In Whitney, *Evil and the Process God*, it is suggested that the Hartshornian position that God acts solely persuasively needs more clarification because Hartshorne can be interpreted as holding that God must act coercively in certain cases such as imposition of physical law. Thus Whitney raises the issue of whether God's power may be a mixture of persuasion and coercion (99-114). He suggests in a preliminary way that God's lure may be persuasively effective to a degree that is directly correlated to the creature's openness to it; the more open we are the more persuasive (and thus coercive) God is (12 and 130). This is intriguing, and I further suggest that radical openness to the lure means not more coercion but more freedom, and that rejection of the divine lure leads to coercion and 'purification'. In other words, being consistently radically open to the divine lure means that eventually more order and harmony is prehended from the past, and this means a richer initial aim (thus more viable choices in self-constitution) and thus more freedom. On the other hand, a radical rejection of the lure means eventually more chaotic data are extant in the past, and thus are inherited from the past, and this results in a 'purification' of the past in present behaviour (something akin to a spiritual/psychological crisis or the mystic 'Dark Night'). The past comes back to haunt (parallel to eastern notions of karma). Regarding the continuous rejection of the lure and thus the inheritance of more and more chaotic data, initial aims would be meagre and thus the degree of coercion high: that is, the entity has little choice in the attempt to maintain complexity of experience or order of experience.
57. Hartshorne holds that divine revelation cannot be directly received in an infallible manner, which implies that revelation is partly human construction. See Hartshorne, *Omnipotence and Other Theological Mistakes*, 37.
58. Charles Hartshorne, *Creative Synthesis and Philosophic Method* (London: SCM Press Ltd., 1970), 49.
59. Alfred North Whitehead, *Adventures of Ideas* (New York: The Free Press, 1967), 184.
60. Psychicalism (or panpsychism, or panexperientialism, or the event ontology of process thinking) is being considered today in relation to a reformulation of the fundamental principles of nature, particularly in the field of particle physics. See the works of David Bohm in David Ray Griffin, editor, *Physics and the Ultimate Significance of Time: Bohm, Prigogine, and Process Philosophy* (Albany, NY: State University of New York Press, 1986); also see Griffin, *The Reenchantment of Science*, and Roger Penrose, *Shadows of the Mind: A Search for the Missing Science of Consciousness* (London: Vintage Press, 1995), 393-421.
61. Hartshorne, *Omnipotence and Other Theological Mistakes*, 59.

Chapter 6

Promethean Atheism

Barry L. Whitney

Introductory Remarks

The ancient Greek myth of Prometheus, first presented in a written version in Hesiod's *Theogony* and *Works and Days* (sixth century BCE), and later by Aeschylus in *Prometheus Bound*, (fifth century BCE), has had a long and interesting history in the western world.[1] It is by far less known but, in my view, has been more subtly influential, than Sophocles's *Oedipus Rex* (fifth century BCE), despite the latter's prominence in Freudian psychoanalysis.

Aeschylus produced *Prometheus Bound* in Athens in 465 BCE as part of a trilogy that is lost, except for the masterful first play and fragments of the second.[2] In brief, the play depicts the suffering of Prometheus, strapped and nailed to a rock by agents of Zeus, as punishment for stealing fire and other essentials to ensure the survival of humanity. Prometheus performed this theft in defiance of Zeus's disdain for the human species. Zeus had previously usurped control of Olympus from his father, Uranus, who had been aided by the other gods and titans, except for Prometheus and fellow titan, Oceanus, both of whom had remained loyal to Zeus. In Aeschylus's play, Prometheus remains on stage the entire time, an impressive, larger-than-life figure who stands bound to a rock, alone, except for the chorus and three visitors: first, Oceanus, representing the traditional religion of the audience, as do his daughters, the chorus, both of whom seek to convince Prometheus to concede to Zeus's demand that he reveal the secret knowledge of Zeus's fate and to plead for Zeus's remission of his punishment; then Io, the only human being in the play, who has been transformed by Zeus (or by Zeus's wife Hera, perhaps) into a cow and who wanders about in a daze, Zeus having wooed and impregnated her; and finally Hermes, who is sent by Zeus to threaten Prometheus into revealing the secret knowledge and recognizing Zeus's authority.

There are many interrelated and important themes embedded in the Promethean myth. My intention, however, is to focus on two of the most important: Prometheus's rebellion against Zeus and his suffering at the hands of Zeus. Both have been influential in the post-mediaeval 'modern' world with respect to the growing rejection of church (and political) authority and in the consequent rise of atheism. More subtly perhaps, these Promethean themes have been one of the bases also for the renewed and hotly debated discussions of 'theodicy'[3] in which sceptical opponents challenge traditional theism as rendering genuine freedom meaningless – despite theists' protests to the contrary – since human freedom seems inconsistent with the traditional conception of God who alone (again, despite protests by theological defenders of traditional theism to the contrary) is, like Zeus, responsible for causing or permitting evil and suffering.

Survival, Defiance and the Fall

Before discussing these themes in detail, it is appropriate to note some of the related themes in order to glean something of their contributions to the main themes that occupy us here. Hesiod (and Aesop, in his *Fables*, both sixth century BCE), for example, emphasized the familiar theme of Prometheus as creator, a theme which likely was popular among the general populace in ancient Greece. Hesiod's *Theogony* describes Prometheus's creative act of moulding humankind from clay and instilling in this creation the breath of the goddess Athene. Hesiod describes Prometheus also as the friend of humankind, bringing to us the gift of fire which symbolizes the very basis of human society and civilization. The story in Hesiod tells us that Prometheus had deceived Zeus by offering him an insulting apportionment of a sacrificed oxen, to which Zeus had responded by punishing him: Prometheus was 'bound by Zeus / In cruel chains, unbreakable, chained round / A pillar, and Zeus roused and set on him / An eagle with long wings, which came and ate / His deathless liver.'[4] After an intolerably long period of suffering, Hercules is to come to kill the eagle and free Prometheus. Zeus further punishes humanity by having Hephasitos (symbolizing Fire) create Pandora, whose infamous box unleashed a host of sufferings and ills.

In the skillful hands of the master Athenian playwright, Aeschylus, the figure of Prometheus is given a far more extended development, including an intriguing esoteric layer of meaning in which the actors become metaphors for the soul's transmigration through the physical, intellectual and spiritual worlds – a view which represents the forbidden knowledge taught to initiates in the Eleusinian mystery cult of which Aeschylus most likely was a member.[5] The brothers of Prometheus described in Hesiod's version – Atlas, Menoitios and Epimetheus – have no role in Aeschylus's tragedy, nor does the Pandora story, which Aeschylus likely perceived as trivial misogyny, unworthy of high drama.

Among other themes in Aeschylus's version is his emphasis, as in Hesiod, on Prometheus's role as the empathetic, philanthropic benefactor of humanity, having stolen fire from the Olympian gods and bestowed it and other essential gifts upon human beings. Yet the motive for this theft is not the same in Aeschylus as in Hesiod: for the latter, Prometheus himself was implicated in (and perhaps the occasion for) Zeus's displeasure with humanity, while for Aeschylus, Zeus's hatred for mortal humanity clearly preceded Prometheus's defiant act. Indeed, for Aeschylus, Zeus is far more obdurate and antagonistic towards human beings than is the Zeus in Hesiod and Aesop.

In Aeschylus, moreover, Prometheus is not only humanity's benefactor, but a heroic and defiant rebel who stood resolutely and bravely alone against Zeus's callous use of his newly acquired divine authority. Prometheus becomes a larger-than-life symbol of nobility and courage, set against Zeus's cruelty and tyranny. Aeschylus emphasizes Zeus's lack of concern for humankind and his desire 'to destroy the entire human race and to plant a new one in place of it'. It is the hero of humanity, Prometheus, who resists Zeus's disdain and cruelty, and who represents and saves mortal humanity from Zeus's (unexplained) desire to 'utterly destroy' us and send us all to death in Hades.[6] For this, Aeschylus celebrates Prometheus as the advocate for humankind and – more importantly for our discussion here – he sets up an irreconcilable conflict between Zeus and Prometheus which sets the stage for the later atheistic uses of this myth. Prometheus remains inspirationally steadfast in his defiance and rebellion against Zeus's tyranny, refusing to succumb to the torture, and refusing to acknowledge Zeus's authority or to reveal the secret knowledge he has of Zeus's future demise.

There is another dimension of this theme of secret or forbidden knowledge, a dimension which has an important and particular relevance for the discussion in this chapter. The theme of forbidden knowledge is displayed not only in the esoteric revelation of the secret knowledge of the Eleusinian cult, but also as the more general prohibition of knowledge forbidden by the gods and, I would note, the consequences of seeking or obtaining such knowledge. The fact that Aeschylus's Prometheus defied Zeus by revealing the forbidden knowledge of survival to humanity (represented by fire) in order to ensure humanity's survival rendered Prometheus a hero in high relief, while Zeus was shown to be, and condemned as, a despised villain. As noted above, without the gifts Prometheus provided for human beings, our mortal species would not have survived. Prometheus, indeed, gave us much more than fire: his gifts included all the essentials for human life and laid the groundwork for the basis of human civilization: the healing arts, remedies to ward off diseases, the art of divination, oracles, omens, metals, intelligence and reason, language and mathematics and so on.[7]

It is appropriate, at this point, to note that these substantial themes in Aeschylus's Promethean drama – particularly, for our purposes here, the heroic defiance and rebellion against a cruel and unjust Zeus – have important similarities with biblical themes, as well as major differences. In the Book of Genesis, for example, Adam and Eve were forbidden to taste of the fruit of the Tree of the Knowledge of Good and Evil. In the centre of the Garden of Eden, God had placed two trees: the Tree of Life and the Tree of the Knowledge of Good and Evil. Regarding the latter, God had prohibited Adam and Eve to eat its fruit (Genesis 2:15–17) but, tempted by the serpent, who assured Eve that eating the forbidden fruit not only would cause her no harm, but would open her eyes so that she would 'be like God' (Genesis 3:4–5), Eve succumbed to this lie and to the temptation to acquire the forbidden knowledge. Adam (perhaps out of love for Eve or perhaps to share in Eve's supposed new-found knowledge and not wanting to be left behind!) likewise ate the fruit. The results of their disobedience were catastrophic: Adam and Eve indeed were awakened to forbidden knowledge, knowing good and evil, but, to their dismay, they did not become 'like God' but were punished for their 'origin sin', as was Prometheus for his disobedience. Similarly, the punishments in both accounts seem unusually cruel and uncompromising: for Adam and Eve it was banishment from the garden and the curse of hardships, which humans from that moment were forced to endure in relationships, daily work and child bearing (Genesis 3:16–19).

One noteworthy point here, as we compare the Genesis account with the Promethean myth, is to understand that, while in the Promethean myth rebellion and disobedience resulted in the very survival of humanity, the biblical account led to the 'fall' of humanity into a lifetime of sin and suffering for Adam and Eve and their progeny. While both accounts show how defiant acts against God or Zeus lead to great suffering (fire, despite its essential role for human survival, is also dangerous), the positive aspect of both rests in the assurance of our survival as a species. This Aeschyelan theme is suggested by Milton in his epic, *Paradise Lost* (1667), which elaborated upon the Adam and Eve story and interpreted the 'fall' as a victory. It was the defiant act and subsequent 'fall' of Adam and Eve which enabled humanity to escape from an original state of innocence, seen by Milton as equivalent to ignorance, and which enabled them and their progeny to advance towards a fuller knowledge and wisdom.[8] Yet, of course, this knowledge, despite its benefits, was gained at the price of losing blissful innocence. As in the Promethean myth, the Genesis story, in Milton's controversial interpretation, involves the paradox of a 'fall' into sin, but also its benefits.[9] And there is another paradox, suggested by Chaucer's Wife of Bath's Prologue (in *Canterbury Tales*, 1388): human beings have an innate passion for knowledge, and this passion increases when there are things which have been prohibited: 'Forbede us thyng, and that desiren we' (we desire what is forbidden).[10]

This paradox and other questions have long puzzled theologians about the Genesis account of the 'fall'. Why, for example, would God have planted this forbidden fruit tree in the midst of the garden when, given the propensity of humanity to crave that which is forbidden, disobedience seemed inevitable? Was not, then, the placing of this temptation before Adam and Eve an act of cruelty, similar to the cruelty displayed by Zeus towards humanity and its titan benefactor? Or was the prohibition, perhaps, intended as a just test of humanity's obedience and faith, a faith in God rather than in human self-sufficiency? Whatever the explanation, what is relevant here (see below) is that the Zeus-figure in the Promethean myth was later merged with the God in the Bible, leading to a theological conceptualization of the Christian God that emphasized those passages (largely Old Testament) in which God appeared as a cruel and wrathful Zeus, destroying cities and punishing his 'chosen' people – despite other depictions of the God of the Bible as a loving creator of all things as goods, and as a God who constantly blesses and is involved in the lives of his 'chosen people' as those with whom a covenant was made to carry the message of salvation.

Another example of legendary defiance, although not of disobedience, against God's prohibitive imposition of limits on human knowledge suggests a morally justifiable motive for God's actions, partially exonerating God from later atheistic accusations of divine cruelty. The Book of Job presents the story of a 'blameless and upright' man (Job 1:1) who suffers unusually harsh and unjust cruelty at the hands of Satan.[11] The story's author assures us that God remains Lord over all creation, but has permitted Satan's torture of Job (Job 1:6–12) as a test of Job's faith. The author likely seeks to show that God's justice can be exonerated despite the manner in which creation had been ordered, that is, where good and evil are not compensated in direct proportion to our deeds.[12] Satan wreaks havoc on Job, taking away everything but his life: his wife, his children, his possessions, his health, his reputation and his dignity. And yet, despite the counsel of his four friends, three of whom misleadingly insist that his suffering is God's punishment for his unacknowledged sinfulness, Job persistently maintains his innocence and, in utter despair, demands an explanation from God (Job 10:1–2). After a long and deafening silence following Job's further demands for an audience with God, God finally responds to Job, and in the voice of a whirlwind answers not with the desired and anticipated explanation for Job's suffering but with a stern admonishment of Job for seeking and demanding knowledge which is incomprehensible to Job and, for this or other reasons, is forbidden (Job 38:2–3). Wisdom, it is clear to Job, lies solely in God, not in human understanding (Job 28:28).

As with God's warning to Job, so it is with Milton's Adam in *Paradise Lost*. Here it is Adam who is subjected to the warning from the Archangel Raphael against seeking to know too much of Heaven: 'Blest pair; and O yet happiest if ye seek / No happier state, and know to know no more'; 'Heaven is for thee too high / To know what passes there; be lowly wise: / Think only of what concerns thee and thy being; / Dream not of other worlds.'[13] And it is likewise in Dante's *The Divine Comedy* (1321) wherein a departed soul, Peter Damien, warns Dante/the pilgrim, who has travelled through Hell and Purgatory to approach the highest Heavens, that the knowledge he has gained is forbidden to mortals: 'The truth you fathom lies so deep / in the abyss of the eternal law, / it is cut off from every creature's sight. / And tell the mortal world when you return / what I told you, so that no man presume / to try to reach a goal as high as this.'[14]

Similar warnings appear in many biblical passages, other than those noted above in Genesis and Job. And yet, paradoxically, there are many passages in which knowledge of God, forbidden and inaccessible to most, is revealed to certain prophets who then are encouraged to reveal that knowledge to the people, mostly in the form of warnings about their sinful ways and the punishment to come if they do not repent. Among the examples of this kind of revelation are the visions of God and/or heaven given to Isaiah (Isaiah 6:1–13), Moses (Exodus 3, 19), Jeremiah (Jeremiah 23:18, 22) and Ezekiel (Ezekiel 1:4–28), visions which established their authority to speak on God's behalf. Paul's ministry similarly was ordained (Acts 9:3–9, 26:12–18), yet in a passage wherein he speaks in the third person about being 'caught up into Paradise', there is paradox in the fact that he then claims that he 'heard inexpressible words, which it is not lawful for man to utter' (2 Corinthians 12:1–5). Other biblical passages similarly warn about disclosing certain aspects of forbidden knowledge (Genesis 11:6–7; John 1:18; Colossians 1:15; 1 Timothy 1:17, 6:16; Exodus 33:20).[15] Perhaps the paradox is resolved in Jesus' announcement to his disciples that he has come to reveal knowledge of God and salvation hitherto forbidden and inaccessible (John 1:18, 14:8–11). The knowledge Jesus revealed, however, was by no means all knowledge of heaven and earth, but rather knowledge which was essential for salvation. Some knowledge (see below) is far too dangerous and otherwise inappropriate for us to possess.

While any adequate interpretation of this intriguing theme of forbidden knowledge in biblical texts is obviously too complex to attempt here, and even more so if we were to attempt a meaningful and thorough comparison of these texts with similar themes in the Promethean (and other ancient Greek texts), what I suggest we take notice of here is the differences between the nature of Zeus in Aeschylus's Prometheus myth and the nature of Yahweh, the biblical God, in the Job and Genesis accounts, and in the other passages noted above. In the Promethean myth the divine prohibition against forbidden knowledge is occasioned by Zeus's disdain for humanity. By contrast, the God of the Bible – despite what may appear to be a similarly unjust cruelty towards Adam and Eve, and Job – is understood by its writers and later theologians as acting always and consistently in love and justice towards humanity. God, after all, is the loving Creator of everything that exists, and who has created humanity in the very 'image and likeness' of the Creator (Genesis 1:26). Surely, then, while it would be inconceivable that such a God would seek to harm us, we lack full understanding, nonetheless, of God's reasons for placing limits on knowledge. We can suggest, of course, various explanations for God's prohibitions against seeking certain aspects of knowledge: such knowledge may be beyond our comprehension, thereby rendering the point of prohibition mute; or perhaps God has revealed what is otherwise inaccessible knowledge only to those whom God has chosen to speak on behalf of the divine will for his 'chosen people'. Or perhaps God has imposed limits to protect us from knowledge which is far too dangerous and threatening for us to know or experience, given our limited and fragile natures and the state of our spiritual maturity.

Philosopher Nicholas Rescher has suggested much the same with respect to scientific knowledge, namely, that we must maintain a 'fog of uncertainty' about certain things since, otherwise, we would be unable to protect ourselves from various dangers: the unmasking of our illusions, for example, or knowing too much about the true nature of reality, or about ourselves, or about our future, or gaining knowledge that would threaten the future of our species, as may be the case with uncontrolled genetic engineering (DNA manipulation, cloning and so on), or the biochemical warfare research about which the implications are uncertain.[16] Such considerations, particularly as demonstrated in literature (Melville, Camus, Dickinson, Milton, Dante, Marlowe, Goethe and so on), have been elaborated in an informative book by Roger Shattuck: it is, as he demonstrates in these authors, dangerous to know too much or too little about something (as philosophers Francis Bacon and Immanuel Kant had pointed out). For in either case, we lose perspective of the thing known or observed.[17] In considering, then, God's reasons for prohibiting aspects of knowledge, we can now understand more clearly, I think, why God's imposition of limits is necessary, as is God's subsequent permission of the human suffering which ensues when limits are violated. Such a God is not to be confused, accordingly, with the cruel tyrant of Prometheus, for Zeus has neither created nor sustains humanity but, rather, has imposed arbitrary limits on humanity to ensure our demise, denying us the essential gifts stolen by Prometheus, gifts which have been forbidden not for noble purposes – to protect us, or as gifts for those chosen for the task of dispensing divine knowledge for the good of humanity, and so on – but, rather, to ensure our annihilation. Thus, while Zeus and the biblical God have apparent similarities, there seem to me more significant and important differences.

History, however, has witnessed the blending of the two visions of God. As Christianity grew in Hellenistic culture, its understanding of God was influenced by and interpreted in terms of this culture, including the Hellenic god popularly represented by Zeus, and the attributes of the God of Plato (in Augustine's writings) and of Aristotle (in Aquinas's writings), the latter defining God as an impersonal but absolutely powerful force, the 'Unmoved Mover', the 'Uncaused Cause', the 'First Cause', or 'Final Cause' (*telos*) upon which all worldly events depend. The contention of process theologians is that this misrepresentation of the Christian God is responsible, or at least largely so, for an unsolvable problem of evil and, I would add, it is largely responsible for the rise of atheism during the past three or four hundred years.[18] After more than a thousand-year reign, during which time a uniform faith and obedience to God were maintained as standard Christian teachings and attitudes – and during which time worldly (secular and 'pagan') knowledge, human creativity and concern for the worldly life (as opposed to concern for spiritual life) were frowned upon – the revival of ancient Greek thought and, with it, a worldly humanistic philosophy and a renewed interest in natural science occurred in the Renaissance, accelerated in the Enlightenment's Age of Reason, and continuing to extend its powerful influence in the modern world. Not only was the Promethean myth rediscovered in the midst of this developing 'modern' world, but Prometheus became the symbol of its defiance and of the atheistic rebellion against the perceived tyranny of the Christian God, a God whose traditionally ascribed attributes seemed inconsistent with human suffering and as threatening to human freedom and dignity.

I shall return to this specific point later, but wish to turn, first, to examine more closely some relevant passages in *Prometheus Bound* in order to provide a more detailed account of the differences between Zeus and the God of the Bible, Yahweh, thereby explaining more clearly the atheistic rebellion which has emerged in the modern world. Suffering at the hands of Zeus, and the Platonic–Aristototelian conception of God as an impersonal, impassible, immutable, uncaring and unilateral power, has been merged into Christianity's understanding of God. Hellenistic thought, while conquered politically, nonetheless has infiltrated the theology and religious culture of its conqueror.

Zeus, Yahweh and the Problem of Evil

The cruel tyranny of Zeus is revealed in the extraordinarily harsh punishments he executed on Prometheus in both Hesiod's and Aeschylus's versions. This cruelty is amplified in the latter's influential presentation as the playwright informs us of Zeus's unexplained disdain for humanity, his abuse of Io, his terrible vengeance against the fellow gods and titans who had rebelled against him, and, of course, his overreactive and extremely cruel punishment of Prometheus. References to the tyranny, callousness and cruelty of Zeus are sprinkled liberally throughout the text of *Prometheus Bound*, beginning in the unforgettable first scene. Here, the impressive yet agonizing figure of Prometheus is dragged onto the stage and nailed and bound to a rock in an isolated and dismal mountain crag (in Hesiod, Prometheus was merely bound to a column). Hephaistos (Fire) works with Kratos (Might) and Bia (Violence), to bind and nail Prometheus to the rock, instructing us as he does that 'the heart of Zeus is inexorable'. Zeus's callousness toward his fellow gods and titans, against humanity and against Prometheus is continually emphasized by Aeschylus: 'of woebegone morals he made no account, but desired to destroy the entire race and to plant a new one in place of it'. Prometheus complains throughout the play about the 'capriciousness' and 'cruel threats' of Zeus, his 'harsh' punishment and his 'keeping justice to himself', that He is 'the tyrant of the gods' who causes unjust and cruel 'agonies' and so on. Notably, none of the characters in the play disputes this view of Zeus.[19]

By contrast, Job, the Bible's main protagonist against the perceived injustice of God (Yahweh) has a much different focus. God is not presented as an unjust and cruel Zeus, but rather as a just and loving Creator, who cares for the creation despite its sinful and rebellious nature which has led to its just suffering. Rather than cursing God, as Aeschylus's Prometheus had cursed Zeus – 'I care less than naught for Zeus' – Job's response to the unfair punishment he has received supposedly at the hands of God gives rise to declarations of his love and worship of God, as he remains steadfast in his trust of God's justice, despite his despair and frustration throughout the ordeal in not being able to comprehend why God has permitted such suffering.[20] In the end, God is not overthrown, as was Zeus, according to Prometheus's secret knowledge of Zeus's demise but, rather, God's benevolent rule is reaffirmed and acknowledged by Job as such: 'I have uttered [complaints about] what I did not understand / Things too wonderful for me, which I did not know… Therefore, I abhor myself / And repent in dust and ashes' (Job 42:3–6).

While the problem of comprehending and reconciling God's goodness in permitting (or, in some cases, apparently causing) human suffering is not answered in the Book of Job, there are several partial answers scattered throughout the biblical texts: suffering, for example, is attributed not merely to divine punishment, but to God's warning, or as educational discipline, or a test of faith, or as the means by which to bring about spiritual development and maturity, and so on. Biblical writers, to be sure, were not concerned to provide a systematic solution to the problem of God and suffering, a theological justification to exonerate God for causing or permitting human suffering; they accepted suffering as part of God's incomprehensible will and recognized that evil was to be overcome by penance and atonement to a good and just God. Evil was seen as resulting from human free will and, more increasingly after the Babylonian exile (sixth century BCE) to the corrupted yet free agency of fallen angels who tempted humanity to use its freedom for acts and decisions which produced evil ends. Such evil powers were to be resisted, as was so clearly demonstrated in the spiritual warfare ministry conducted by Jesus.

It is relevant to note here that in post-biblical, historical theological discussions of the problem of evil, two main approaches can be distinguished: the existential (or personal), which focuses on the aforementioned biblical strategy of resistance to and coping with evil, and the rational, which seeks an intellectually viable and comprehensive understanding about the relationship between God and suffering. Both approaches begin and end in faith, but the latter moves beyond faith by seeking a rational comprehension, as far as such is possible, that will supplement the faith. This, indeed, is the very nature and task of 'theology' – as distinguished from 'philosophy of religion' or 'philosophy' – both of which focus on rational arguments and empirical evidence, and exclude the faith assumptions of 'theology'. Three main theological solutions (theodicies) have been proposed: (a) the traditional Augustinian (which has dominated Christian thought since its origins in the early fifth century); (b) Alfred North Whitehead's process theodicy (which was unsystematically proposed in his writings from the 1920s to the 1940s, and elaborated (although, again, unsystematically) by Charles Hartshorne from the 1950s to the end of the 1990s; and (c) John Hick's so-called 'Irenaean' or 'soul-making' theodicy, initiated in the 1960s (but with roots in the nineteenth-century theologian, Freidrich Schleiermacher, and in the second-century Greek Church Father, Irenaeus). These theodicies all seek to comprehend how, despite causing or permitting evil, God (*theos*) is just (*dike*) – as faith assures us God is – despite human suffering.[21]

In what follows, my argument is that process theodicy, more convincingly than traditional theodicy (and Hick's revisions of such), conceptualizes God in a way that avoids the Zeus-like characteristics wrongly attributed to the God of traditional Christianity and of western atheism. These characteristics, which define God as 'impassible' (unaffected by the world or its creatures), unilaterally 'omnipotent' (all-powerful, literally conceived, and as such predetermining), 'omniscient' (all-knowing, eternally and timelessly), 'immutable' (unchanging, and hence unresponsive to the contingencies of the world and its creatures) and so on – have rendered the theodicy issue virtually unsolvable and, consequently, have been a major reason for the rise of contemporary atheism. Process theists argue that not only the 'traditional' (Augustinian, Thomistic, Early Protestant) theodicies have misrepresented – or, at the very least, have not been able to present without incredible complexity and paradoxical tension – the true nature of God, but so likewise has Hick's 'modern' Irenaean alternative which, while proposed as a radical alternative to traditional theism and theodicy, remains very traditional in its conception of God as all-powerful.[22] These traditional theodicies, then, continue to promote the historical conceptualization of God which seems far too Hellenistic and far too similar to the cruel and unjust sovereignty of the Zeus-figure against whom Prometheus contended. In short, process theologians claim that traditional theism has suffered from an overdose of Greek metaphysics and from the tyranny of Prometheus's nemesis, the cruel, unjust and powerful Zeus.

Promethean Atheism

My contention here is that the traditional conception of God led inevitably to the problem of evil; it led also to the rise of modern atheism for which the problem of human freedom, dignity and suffering at the hands of God had become central issues. When the Zeus-like image of God was taken into the early Christian Church, the ground had become fertile for scepticism and atheism. The arrival of a full-fledged secular atheism, however, had to remain dormant during the thousand-year reign of the Age of Faith (c. fourth to fourteenth centuries). Before this, the Promethean theme of rebellion and defiance against Zeus's authority continued in writings and reflections in the Greek and Roman era. In general, it seems that the Greeks largely idealized Prometheus's revolt against divine tyranny, while the Romans largely deplored this revolt as a symbolic rebellion against Roman central authority.[23] Juvenal (55–140 CE) and Lucian of Samosata (c.120–180 CE, who wrote in Greek), for example, wrote gruelling satires of the Promethean myth.

But soon the Roman Empire would fall and become Christian (fourth century), and by the time of Augustine (354–430), the Christian Church, following the Roman lead, had managed to suppress Greek myths and philosophies, though ironically, the influence of Hellenistic thought on the developing Christian theological conception of God had been significant, especially since the Augustinian synthesis of Greek and Christian ideas. It was only after the ensuing millennium reign of Christianity that the Renaissance and Enlightenment ushered in a growing discontent with Church authority and its theology, concurrent with a renewed interest in and awareness of the apparent conflict between human freedom and belief in the God of Christendom, an awareness reflected and symbolized most influentially, perhaps, in the Promethean myth. The Faustian myth, of course, also was exploited (by Marlowe and Goethe) to express the new human attitude of freedom from the Church and the political authority of monarchs, as was the rise of the new sciences (and its empiricist method, sanctioned by the Empiricist philosophers), initiated by the Copernicus revolution (fifteenth century) and the shocking assault on freedom and Church authority by Luther (sixteenth century) and Calvin (seventeenth century), founders of the Protestant Reformation.

Freedom had become an increasingly central humanistic issue, no longer debated solely within the once-safe confines of Christianity (until Luther's rejection of free will). In this context, perhaps no theme exemplified by the Promethean myth has been more prevalent and influential than the theme of Promethean atheism and rebellion against the perceived tyranny of the gods – the God of Christianity – and the institutional religion which sanctioned such a conception of God. Prometheus was no longer seen merely as a Titan-god of ancient Greek mythology and drama, but had become the archetypical human, expressing humanity's best, most noble, heroic qualities, a symbol of human potential, freedom and progress.

This view of Prometheus had become one of the most powerful symbols that expressed the awakening of western Christendom from its mediaeval slumber. This awakening, as noted, witnessed the revival of a humanism which exalted human freedom and creativity and, as such, directed the focus of attention away from God and the spiritual world to the world of natural science and its pinnacle, humanity and human reason. Following this renaissance of new thought, or rather, as a natural progression of it, history witnessed the Enlightenment's empiricism, rationalism and the naturalistic methods and assumptions of the new sciences, which sought truth without appeal to supernaturalism or divine revelation – a method forged mainly by Bacon and Galileo, the latter being credited for successfully promoting the new Copernican world-view, and both of whom generally have been considered founders of modern science. Both also had a decisive role to play in the separation of the study and purpose of religion and science, a separation which continues to this day.

The Enlightenment's world-view culminated in Newton's laws of motion and gravity by which he proposed a 'clockwork', 'mechanical' universe ruled by natural laws, rather than by divine fiat. In short, Newton's cosmology challenged the traditional wisdom concerning the very nature of the cosmos and God's place in it. The discovery of new worlds (both extraterrestrially and in the world itself) enlarged human horizons and curiosity, and the printing presses led to a literacy unheard of in previous generations. Significant also were discoveries in the physical sciences: physics, anatomy, geology, and Darwinian biological evolution, and so on. These discoveries gave further impetus to the growing scepticism about religious supernaturalism, replacing it, first, with a natural religion, deism (wherein God was defined solely as Creator and, as such, became increasingly remote and irrelevant), and then, as the result of a growing scepticism and agnosticism, with atheism.

Numerous influential writers exemplified this new atheism, but it was Voltaire's *Pandore* (1740), perhaps, which was largely responsible for promoting the Promethean myth into public prominence. Prometheus was displayed as the benevolent creator of humanity, while Zeus/Jupiter/the Christian God were depicted as the cruel tyrant who causes the evil and suffering in the world. Napoleon's scientist during his Egyptian campaign, the Marquis Pierre de La Place (eighteenth century), to note one further prominent example, all but deified human intellect and rationality while rejecting traditional religious beliefs as failing to meet the criteria of scientific and philosophical rationality – a view currently held by philosophical and scientific logical positivists and empiricists who limit knowledge to that which is gained by the scientific method. Such (arbitrary) limitations on what constitutes knowledge have dominated modern thinking, but have not gone unchallenged. Postmodern philosophy of science, represented by Thomas Kuhn, Paul Feyerabend and many others challenged the empiricist assumptions. Whitehead had challenged them decades earlier in a vast and complex metaphysical system. A mathematical physicist and philosopher, Whitehead argued against the naturalistic and empiricist assumptions and methods, claiming correctly that they beg the question as to what constitutes legitimate knowledge. Whitehead's process metaphysics acknowledges a far more fundamental, pre-conscious, non-sensuous experience, which includes religious knowing, not verifiable by the limitations of the scientific method.

While the earliest versions of the Promethean myth (in ancient and modern times) did not express atheism – expressing, rather, rebellion against the tyrannical reign of Zeus – a strong atheistic interpretation, as noted above, developed in the modern era (from the eighteenth century and, perhaps, before this) as the Promethean rebellion against Zeus became a major rallying point for the growing ranks of sceptics and atheists who interpreted the myth as symbolic of their rejection of the God of classical western theism. The Promethean myth, far more clearly than Marlowe's or Goethe's presentations of the Faustian myth, I suggest, embodied and symbolized the atheistic call for rebellion in the name of human freedom against the cruelty of a Zeus-like God. To a remarkable degree, the Promethean myth has played a significant role in the thought of many of the most influential sceptics and atheists during the past two or three hundred years.

It may be no exaggeration, moreover, to argue that Christian theology – paradoxically, tragically, ironically – inundated as it was with Aristotelian and Zeus-like images of God, must assume its (significant) share of the blame for the rise of the modern atheistic protest against such a God. Christian theism has incorporated into its conception of God, as noted above, attributes of a Zeus-like tyrant, focusing more on God's impersonal distance from creation, and on divine power, than on benevolence and personal care. The rather distant Yahweh who, despite being personalized in Jesus, was taken into the Church's theology as a God who seemed more Aristotelian than personal. Such a God is defined as 'impassible' (unaffected by the world and its creatures); 'immutable' (an unchanging 'perfection'); 'impersonal'; unilaterally 'omnipotent' (so that nothing happens except by the deliberation of God's own will, either permitting it to be done, or doing it directly); 'omniscient' (including a foreknowledge such that 'there can be no increase in the content of God's knowing'); absolute – a conception (as noted above) that was worked out most significantly by Augustine among the early Church Fathers and later adapted by Aquinas in his 'mediaeval synthesis' of Aristotelian and Christian thought.

Process theologians contend that this synthesis not only contributed in no small measure to the theodicy problem, but laid the groundwork also for the modern atheism which extolls human freedom over divine control as an 'either/or' dilemma: either human freedom or belief in God.[24] Traditional theologians defended their conceptualization of God within a paradox of complex argumentation, while insisting also (with the exception of Luther and Calvin and their early followers) that human beings were free and morally responsible agents. The apparent contradiction in holding these views simultaneously has been a thorn in the side of Christian theology since the Enlightenment, and had been the focus of many disputes from the very beginnings of Christian theological history. While these challenges to the Augustinian resolution (Manicheans, Donatists, Pelagians, Semi-Pelagians, Arians and so on) had been defeated historically, the Protestant Reformation carried the arguments much further in its denial not only of Church authority (arguing for the authority of Scripture alone) but in its shocking rejection of the genuineness of human freedom and its role in the process of salvation. This radical theology served to reinforce the strong determinism implicit, but denied by theologians in the Catholic Church, in the traditional understanding of God's sovereign providence. As such, Luther's protests gave atheistic sceptics further grounds and incentive for the rejection of such a God in the name of human freedom, the quality so highly valued in the post-mediaeval world.

Both Catholics and Protestants claimed Augustine as their inspiration: Protestants exploited the complexities of the free will/divine grace paradox, arguing from certain passages in Augustine, for example, that only Adam and Eve had been free, since their progeny had inherited a 'fallen' nature, the 'original sin' caused by the Adamic 'fall' into disobedience and sin, resulting in the state of *non posse non peccare* ('not able not to sin'). We can do nothing good without God's enabling grace, which itself is unmerited and predetermined unilaterally by God. No human act is free since nothing can occur without God's permission and, as Augustine had stated, this permission is in fact God's causative determination of the act: 'For it could not be done did He not permit it – and of course His permission is not unwilling, but willing' and 'if He wills it, it must necessarily be accomplished'. Augustine's God 'sets in motion even in the innermost hearts of men the movement of their will, so that He does through their agency whatever he wishes to perform through them'.[25]

Defending human freedom *vis-à-vis* God's power and foreknowledge in view of such 'hard' passages in Augustine has been a formidable task for traditional theologians and post-Reformation Catholic theologians. The authoritative voice of Aquinas (thirteenth century) had been no more successful, however, than Augustine's proposed resolution of the problem. Indeed, it can be argued that Aquinas's writings, while far more systematically presented, are far more complex and forbidding than Augustine's, and few Protestant theologians or sceptics have been willing to venture into the nuanced and technical reasoning of Aquinas and his followers in order properly to refute the claims presented there. Aquinas offered various and complex arguments, expanding upon Augustine and others, for a reconciliation of human freedom and divine grace. Among these is his controversial distinction between the 'primary cause' of every event (God) and the 'secondary cause' (the creature), an argument Luther dismissed summarily.[26] The difficulty in accepting Aquinas's arguments as conclusive and convincing, however, can be seen in the debate between the 'Thomists' and the 'Molinists', the latter employing a controversial concept of *scientia media* ('middle knowledge') to justify, more clearly than had Aquinas in their view, the compatibility of the traditionally conceived God and human freedom. In recent years, there has been a great flurry of discussion about the merits and demerits of the concept of 'middle knowledge'. The fact, moreover, that the Catholic

Church has not pronounced an official verdict on this dispute bears testimony to the complexity and inconclusiveness of the issues involved.

From the perspective of process theologians, of course, neither the Thomist nor the Molinist solutions have developed a coherent and convincing understanding of how free will is coherent with the traditional doctrine of God. The problem, for process theologians, is that the traditional conception of God is invalid, and this renders human freedom virtually inconceivable, except to proclaim verbally that free will is genuine; that is, concluding without justification that free will has been reconciled with God's traditionally conceived attributes.[27] One problem for traditional theists has been to show how one and the same act can be decided 'necessarily' and entirely by God, while at the same time allegedly it is decided by creatures 'contingently'. Hartshorne exploits this problem as follows: 'in spite of what Thomists say, it is impossible that our act should be both free and yet a logical consequence of a divine action which "infallibly" [eternally and necessarily] produces its effects. Power to cause someone to perform by his own choice an act precisely defined by the cause is meaningless'. Any attempt to defend genuine human freedom *vis-à-vis* such a God is ' "meaningless" and beyond intelligible account'.[28] Luther and other early Protestant reformers had argued a somewhat similar case but, rather than seeking to defend the compatibility of human freedom and the traditional doctrine of God, they rejected human free will as incompatible with such a God.

It is not an exaggeration to suggest, once again, that such controversy within Christianity has been a breeding ground for the atheistic protest against traditional theism, especially since it seemed to deny genuine human freedom. For this and a host of other concerns about the conception of God in traditional theology, process theists – following Whitehead and, more especially, Hartshorne's exhaustive development and defence of the Whiteheadian vision of God – have undertaken a radical revision of the conception of God in traditional theism and, in doing so, have shown not only how a more adequate conception of God is coherent with human freedom, but how this, in turn, confronts sceptics and atheists with a conception of God which is not susceptible to their past criticisms of traditional theism. In short, process theism has deconstructed the foundation of contemporary atheism, showing that atheism is based on an invalid and inadequate conception of God. No longer is there a forced option to choose between human freedom or belief in God. Process theism proposes a 'both/ and' position.

Commentators, friend and foe alike, have continually pointed out the undeniable taint of a strongly deterministic strain in the traditional conception of God, despite Augustine's and Aquinas's insistence to the contrary and their defence of genuine human free will. The issue, as I see it, is no longer the atheistic challenge against belief in God's existence, but whether traditional theology has conceptualized the most adequate and valid understanding of God. In one sense, the issue may be mute for theologians, since we must and do assume the genuineness of human freedom, despite the failure of theological studies to comprehend and demonstrate more fully and convincingly how such freedom can be reconciled with the God conceptualized by traditional theologians. Theologians, I am suggesting, must presume human freedom is genuine, in spite of the early Protestant reformers' rejection of free will, since, if this were not the case, there would have been no point in God's creation of creatures who could have contributed nothing to God. This would have reduced God to the sole, unilateral determiner of all events – all goods and evils – a concept which contradicts not just human freedom but God's goodness and love, given the Holocaust and the horrendous evils humanity has endured. Further, without genuine freedom, both Jesus's ministry and the biblical prophets' numerous calls to repentance from sin and evil would be reduced to meaninglessness chatter. Augustine and Aquinas, among others, have acknowledged this need to assume free will.

Nonetheless, when theologians venture outside the confines of theology to confront sceptics and atheists, we must do more than presume the genuineness of human freedom. We must make the most coherent and convincing argument possible for such freedom and, correspondingly, promote an understanding of God which clearly and convincingly (more so than in traditional theism) is coherent with this freedom. It is this very task that process theologians have undertaken. History has shown us that the humanistic atheism which has emerged in western culture rejects the existence of the classical western understanding of God as an omnipotent, predetermining ruling Caesar, a Zeus-like tyrant against whom human freedom and dignity would indeed be threatened. Whitehead, however, rightly condemned the traditional doctrine as making God a 'tyrant', a 'dictator', a 'despot', 'the one supreme reality omnipotently disposing a wholly derivative world', 'the supreme agency of compulsion'.[29] Whitehead explains further in the following, now famous, passage:

> When the Western world accepted Christianity, Caesar conquered, and the received texts of Western theology were edited by his lawyers... The brief Galilean vision of humility flickered throughout the ages, uncertainly. In the official formulation of the religion, it has assumed the trivial form of the mere attribution of the Jews that they cherished a misconception of their Messiah. But the deeper idolatry, of the fashioning of God in the image of the Egyptian, Persian, and Roman imperial rulers, was retained. The Church gave unto God the attributes which belonged to Caesar.[30]

Process theologians make similar claims:

> Is it not ... the case, that the conviction that God is [solely] immutable is part of the Hellenistic rather than the biblical heritage? And, while it was taken up into Christianity by Scholasticism, is it not a fair question to ask whether this aspect of the Hellenization of the Gospels did not itself violate the biblical vision of a personal God ... and what sense can we make of a person, either human or divine, who is so unrelated as to be unaffected by others?[31]

The God of Traditional Theology and the Rise of Promethean Atheism

The battle lines have been drawn. Galileo's new geocentric cosmology focused attention on the earth and humanity: the 'heavens' were no longer understood as a spiritual realm; God became more and more impersonal and distant with the rise of deism and the rejection of traditional supernatural religion; humanists put their faith in human reason and focused on humanity, the natural world and especially on human freedom which was no longer restricted by the traditional church or monarchy; the Enlightenment increasingly separated the realms of religious and scientific inquiry.

All of this and more seemed to force a choice between the new Enlightenment paradigm and the traditional religious paradigm. Scientific humanism rejected belief in God as antagonistic to the reality and sufficiency of human reason and freedom. Traditional theism appealed to the mystery of revelation, no longer accepted by humanists, and to its complex and virtually incomprehensible scholastic arguments for a paradoxical relationship between divine grace and human nature, between God's foreknowledge and predestination power with genuine human freedom. From the perspective of process theists, as noted, the tragic – indeed, ironic – problem has been that atheists and traditional theists assume the same misconception of the attributes of God. I wish to document this point by the witness of influential sceptics in literary and philosophical fields, and, if space permitted, could expand this testimony immeasurably with further representatives in these fields, as well as in scientific, psychological and many other fields besides. All of these testimonies witness the rejection of the traditional conception of God as a threat to human freedom and dignity. Prometheus, implicitly, or just as often explicitly, is cited as the symbol of this rejection of God, identified with the cruel Zeus.

Johann W. Goethe (1749–1832), for example, extolled and popularized not only the legendary figure of Faust for which he is best known, but also the larger-than-life figure of Prometheus, who, with Faust, symbolized humanity's struggle against the powerful forces that affect us: God, nature and past authority. Goethe did not complete his full-scale dramatic production of *Prometheus* (only a fragment remains) but he did publish a short, 57 line poem, 'Prometheus' (1773), which clearly shows his dissatisfaction with traditional Christian belief:

> I know of no poorer thing
> Under the sun than you gods!
> And the breath of prayers,
> And you would starve
> If children and beggars
> were not fools full of hope...
> I, know you?
> When did you ever allay
> The agony that weighed me down?
> Did you ever dry
> My terrified tears?
> Was I not forged into mankind
> By almighty Time?
> Here I sit, forming man
> In my image, ...
> A race to resemble me:
> To suffer, to weep,
> To enjoy, to be glad –
> And never to heed you,
> Like me![32]

Other prominent examples include the Romantic poets, particularly Lord Byron (1788–1824) and Percy Bysshe Shelley (1792–1822) who, in the name of human freedom and dignity, promoted Prometheus as a symbol of noble rebellion and polemic against Christianity's capricious God. For Byron (especially his *Prometheus* fragment of 1816), Prometheus became a symbol of divinity and endurance who calls upon humanity to defy its 'funeral destiny' by turning our fate into a victory.[33]

Byron's friend, Shelley, the most political of the Romantic poets and perhaps the strongest antagonist towards belief in a personal God, states in his epic poem, *Prometheus Unbound* (1820), the following: 'Prometheus is, as it were, the type of the highest perfection of moral and intellectual nature, impelled by the purest and the truest of motives to the best and noblest ends.' Zeus, by contrast, is the 'almighty tyrant', identified explicitly by Shelley with the Christian God. In his *Notes* regarding his first major poem, *Queen Mab* (1813), furthermore, Shelley rejects such a God, replacing it with the familiar Romantic alternative, a 'pervading Spirit coeternal with the universe'. Shelley's atheistic disdain for classical Christian theism runs throughout his work. He has no patience with a personal God or a God who directs us with 'a peculiar providence'.[34] As Shelley and Byron fought for political freedom in Italy and Greece, their writings against traditional Christianity recommended a similar defiance of tyranny. As the tyrant God of Christianity is overthrown, they believed, so likewise will earthly tyrants be overthrown.

Further examples of atheistic protest against the God of traditional theism include the philosopher Ludwig Feuerbach (1804–72) who, upon the publication of his influential book, *The Essence of Christianity* (1841), was often referred to as the 'new Prometheus'. He promoted 'the humanization of God' and sought to transform and dissolve theology into anthropology. In an earlier book, *Thoughts on Death and Immortality* (1830), he had denied both immortality and a personal God, views which had an impact on the highly influential thinkers, Nietzsche, Marx and Freud, all of whom followed Feuerbach's lead in condemning religion as an illusion, and his belief that God is merely a projection of human qualities and needs. Karl Marx (1818–83), for example, extolled Prometheus as 'the noblest of saints and martyrs in the calendar of philosophy' for his defiance of Zeus who, Marx held, is reflected in the Christian God and who by his remoteness and control has alienated humankind. The preface to Marx's doctoral dissertation (University of Jena, 1841) contains the aforementioned citation, as well as the following remark: 'Philosophy makes no secret of it. The confession of Prometheus' "In simple words, I hate the gods," is its own confession, its own aphorism against all heavenly or earthly gods who do not acknowledge human self-consciousness as the highest divinity. It will have none other besides.'[35]

The influence of Friedrich Nietzsche (1844–1900) remains immense. His madman, in *The Gay Science* (1882–86), announced the death of God, the ominous ring of which still reverberates in society. Nietzsche tirelessly promoted the Promethean 'will to power', in explicit opposition to the God of traditional Christianity theism which, in Nietzsche's view, fostered dehumanizing attitudes of resignation and submission to authority. In *Beyond Good and Evil* (1886), Nietzsche warred against Christian morality, condemning it as 'self-mutilation' and 'slave morality'. In *The Birth of Tragedy* (1872), he emphasized the world-affirming world-view of the Greeks, praising Aeschylus in particular. Nietzsche's *Twilight of the Gods* (1888) and *The AntiChrist* (1888), two late short books, spoke of the 'sick house and dungeon atmosphere' of Christianity as a religion of pity, weakness and loss of freedom and power. Nietzsche's comparison of Prometheus and Adam in *The Birth of Tragedy* asserted that, while Adam's sin was contemptuous disobedience, Prometheus's sin was in fact a courageous rebellion.[36]

Jean-Paul Sartre (1905–80), the uncompromising atheist, is difficult to interpret with respect to his affirmation of human freedom, on the one hand, and its relationship to his denial of God, on the other. Yet, minimally, we can affirm that Sartre's basic conviction that humanity is free by nature, indeed 'condemned to be free', implied that no God could interfere with this freedom. Albert Camus (1913–60) likewise rebelled against classical theism, especially its conception of divine omnipotence. Camus rejected such a God as indifferent to human suffering, and called on humanity to replace God by taking on responsibility for our own histories by confronting the absurdities of life – exemplified best, perhaps, in Camus' hero, Sisyphus.[37]

Sigmund Freud's (1856–1939) influential psychology reduced religion to sexual needs and immature illusions, and the wish for security. His presentation of an authoritarian father-figure in the image of Zeus implied a God who was the object of need and hatred. Religion, Freud claimed – reminiscent of Marx's view of religion as 'opium for the masses' – functions as a narcotic, as an antidote to humanity's helplessness against inner and outer threats. Freud had little tolerance for traditional religious belief, seeing it as neurotic and a dangerous hindrance both to society and to human maturity. Hans Küng's interpretation of Freud's views is insightful: 'What Feuerbach wanted from the philosophical standpoint and Marx from the political–social, Freud sought from the standpoint of depth psychology: emancipation, comprehensive liberation, more humanity on the part of man. It meant in particular opposition to tutelage, domination, oppression by religion, Church, and God himself.'[38] While it was Sophocles's Oedipus that Freud chose as his symbol for overcoming illusions and the establishment of self-autonomy, his writings on Prometheus, although considerably fewer, were related to this theme: Prometheus stands up, in the name of freedom, as did Oedipus, against the primordial father, the son asserting his autonomy. Such psychological theories, though later modified by Carl Jung (1875–1961) and others, have been powerfully influential in their antagonism towards traditional religion and its concept of God. Jung is much more sympathetic towards religion than Freud, yet he promotes, not Christianity, but a universal spirituality which has given him status as the psychological guru of New Age religion. His view of Christianity is clearly presented in his *Answer to Job* (1969). Here he speaks of the need to seek a better understanding of deity than the 'immoral', 'divine savagery and ruthlessness' displayed by Yahweh.[39]

Process Theology's Rejection of the God Atheists Reject

My argument is that Whiteheadian–Hartshornean process theism provides a more systematic, coherent and cogent vision of God than does the traditional conception of God. Process theism is a radically revised interpretation of the attributes of God and of God's relationship to creation, an interpretation which has immense implications for Christian thought and its struggle with contemporary atheism, despite resistance and misunderstanding still by the majority of traditional theists, Catholic and Protestant alike. In short, process theism undercuts the very foundation of modern Promethean-inspired atheism. Likewise, process theism 'dissolves' the traditional problem of evil, reducing it to a 'pseudo-problem' created out of a 'mass of undigested notions too vague or self-inconsistent to permit any useful application to rational argument'.[40] Process theism reveals the fundamental, indeed, ironic, flaw of Promethean atheism, namely, that the God atheists reject (and traditional theists defend) is a misrepresentation of God. God is not the all-determining power, nor the cruel and remote Zeus. God does not negate or threaten genuine creaturely freedom but, as Hartshorne has convincingly shown, is the very reason that creaturely freedom is genuine.

The flaw of traditional theism has been its inability to explain this genuineness *vis-à-vis* its conceptualization of God (as omniscient, omnipotent, immutable, impassible and so on). This flawed view has not only opened the door to a series of historical debates and controversies within the Church, most alarmingly those initiated by Luther, who denied free will completely, a position which gave further impetus to the modern world's ever-growing sceptical discontent with traditional theism. By implying in a complexity of scholastic argumentation that only a theological specialist could comprehend (and against its intention) that God's providential grace and sovereignty operates as a unilateral, predetermining power and in a foreknowledge of events which, as such, have been actualized in eternity 'before the foundations of the earth were laid', it is no mystery that such a view invited sceptical, atheistic challenges and criticisms from without and indeed from within Christianity as well.[41] The scholastic argumentation in support of traditional theism was not intended for the masses, of course, but the masses now include influential atheists and academics outside the Church who are not content to acquiesce to the paradoxical mysteries and incomprehensible complexities of the traditional arguments. They rightly seek clearer, more coherent arguments to explain God's role in human life and a much more cogent and conclusive presentation of the arguments for human freedom upon which the post-mediaeval, modern world has focused.

Please note that I am not arguing that traditional theism has valid arguments which, if presented with more care for a wider audience, would stem the atheistic protest against its conceptualization of God. This remains to be seen. What I am suggesting, rather, is that the traditional arguments have been unconvincing to Protestant reformers and to growing numbers of intellectuals outside the Church. I am suggesting also that process theologians have made impressive progress in amending some of the fundamental problems and contradictions in traditional theism, including those which are central to the issues of atheism and theodicy: the conception of God and the reconciliation of God's power with genuine human free will. The process God, for example, is relational; God is actively involved in the world; God is personal. The process radically modified conceptualization of God's attributes sees them no longer in terms of the 'monopolar' abstractions of traditional theism wherein God, for example, is conceptualized – against traditional theism's intention to account also for genuine human freedom – as the sole or primary cause of all acts and decisions. In the traditional conceptualization of God as monopolar, God alone was understood to be the sole exception to the 'law of polarity', the law Hartshorne has shown to be prevalent in all aspects of human life: God, for example, was defined by traditional theism solely as 'necessary', devoid of 'contingency', as wholly 'immutable', without 'mutable' aspects, as solely 'being', devoid of 'becoming', as solely 'absolute', devoid of 'relative' aspects, as 'independent' of the world in every respect, devoid of any need or knowledge of the world, and sole 'cause' of all things, without being 'affected' or 'influenced' by any other subject.

Unfortunately, there is no space here to explain in sufficient detail the arguments against the 'monopolar' God of traditional theism, or to detail the arguments in favour of a 'dipolar' conception of God.[42] We may note, however, one example of the process conception. Hartshorne and Reese have argued that a God 'who cannot in any sense change or have contingent properties is a being for whom whatever happens in the contingent world is literally a matter of indifference. Such a being is totally "impassible" toward all things, utterly insensitive and unresponsive.' This 'is the exact opposite of "God is love"... Strange that for so many centuries it was held legitimate to call such a deity a God of love ... What we really have is the idea of sheer power, sheer causation, by something wholly neutral as to what, if anything, may be its effects.'[43]

For God's interaction with the world to be conceptualized more adequately, there must be a real and mutual interdependence between God and creatures. God remains the supreme power, but not the only power. God remains the greatest conceivable being, the supreme object of worship, since perfection need not be understood – as it was by the Greeks and traditional theologians – as immutable and impassible and so on, but understood as the ability to surpass God's own self in responding in love, knowledge and justice to the acts of free, contingent beings. 'A new era in religion,' Hartshorne has insisted, 'may be predicted as soon as men grasp the idea that it is just as true to say that God is the supreme beneficiary or recipient of achievement ... as that [God] ... is the supreme benefactor or source of achievement.'[44]

The process theists' understanding of God is based on human experience, the only experience we know with any certainty and intimacy. What follows from this awareness is a generalization that all beings are sentient to some degree at least, depending on their level of complexity. This 'panpsychism' ('psychicalism' or 'panexperientialism') is in direct contradiction to modern scientific materialism and dualism, the latter implying a 'division of substances into those which do and do not possess a soul' (or mind), and the former positing 'the existence of atoms as discontinuous, discrete, independent bits of matter, devoid of feeling and life, isolated except for accidental external relations, timeless and unchanging with respect to internal constitution and hence without growth or evolution'.[45] The concept of 'mere matter' – the view that something can exist without having some aspect of genuine indeterminacy or creativity at the most fundamental level – has been shown to be superfluous by modern advances in physics and in the philosophical arguments of Leibniz, Bergson, Peirce, Whitehead and Hartshorne. Hartshorne writes:

> To have creatures without freedom would be to have creatures which are not creatures. Divinity is supreme freedom. The absolute negation of freedom is not creaturehood but nonentity. Creaturehood is precisely the status of freedom lacking the supreme qualities of divine freedom. Between divine freedom and zero freedom, there is plenty of room for all possible creatures. Those who think otherwise have a strange view of divine freedom! One or two steps down from it, they seem to suppose, lands one in no freedom. How illogical! Any number of steps down can still leave some freedom.[46]

In place of the traditional dualism that conceptualizes mind and matter as two distinct sorts of entities, process thought interprets mind and matter as 'two ways of describing a reality that has many levels of organization'.[47] The most fundamental aspects of all life are microscopic, momentary and processive instances of energy/matter, Whitehead's so-called 'actual entities'. These entities are 'dipolar', having both mental and physical characteristics. In entities that have not formed into complex patterns, the physical characteristics predominate; in more complex entities, creativity (freedom at the human level) have developed. As dipolar, human beings have minds and bodies, even though the latter is an abstraction of the former: all life is psychic, but the patterns formed by the basic units of life appear physical to sense experience (which in Whitehead's metaphysics is secondary to a basic, pre-sensuous experience). Basic reality is energy/matter in continual flux, forming various patterns which vary in complexity. The macroscopic objects of our senses are such patterns, constituted in fact by groupings ('societies' and 'nexus') of the basic units of reality constituted both by minds and bodies in a complex system of interaction, as Whitehead shows in his seminal work, *Process and Reality* (1929). As dipolar, God is the 'chief exemplification' of the metaphysical categories which define all life. God, as noted above and in contradistinction to traditional theism, is both 'immutable' in essence, but 'mutable', changeable in response to change in others; the supreme 'cause' of all, yet 'affected' by the causation of others; 'infinite' in the awareness of all possibilities, but 'finite' in the sense that God's knowledge is restricted by which specific possibilities have been actualized; 'necessary' in existence, but 'contingent' in response to the world's contingent acts, and so on.

Here is the basic vision of the God of process theism, one which stands as a clear and compelling alternative to the traditional understanding of God. Process metaphysics replaces traditional substance philosophy with a metaphysics of ever-processing energy/matter. God is no longer conceived as the unilateral cause of all events, since all reality has some fundamental aspect of creativity. Neither is God seen as the 'coercive' power of traditional theism, but as a 'persuasive' power by which creaturely minds are lured towards the best aesthetic values possible in every situation. This is a true 'metaphysics of freedom', wherein both God and creatures exert genuine creativity. God, of course, remains the greatest conceivable power, but not the sole power. There is 'a division of powers', and, thus, as Hartshorne writes, 'The justification of evil is ... that the creaturely freedom from which evils spring ... is also an essential aspect of all goods ... Risk of evil and opportunity for good are two aspects of just one thing, multiple freedom ... This is the sole but sufficient reason for evil as such as in general.'[48]

Multiple freedom is possible only if one understands God as persuasive and dipolar, dissolving the traditionally conceived problem of evil. (Theodicy is resolved also, as I have argued elsewhere, by the aesthetic theory in process thought.) God is no longer a threat to freedom, but the chief exemplification of the freedom (creativity) shared by creatures, for, without creativity as the ultimate and driving creative force in the universe, there could be no creatures, since creatures devoid of creativity cannot exist. The concept of vacuous being is meaningless; the world, moreover, would be a mass of chaotic primitive entities, lacking any organizing aim or purpose or focus without God's creative direction. In *Process and Reality*, Whitehead describes in detail how God sets before us (and in non-human creatures) the best aesthetic possibilities for actualization at each moment in our processive existence. Whitehead argues also that God organizes these possibilities into those ideals (Hartshorne sees this an an infinite continuum, rather than specific ideals) which are the most appropriate to be actualized in any situation.

Taking Process Thought Seriously

The fundamental flaw at the heart of modern Promethean atheism, then, is that it is based on a false view of God which has been influenced far too much by Hellenistic thought and this, in turn, has rendered the problems of suffering and atheism unavoidable and yet unnecessary. Unfortunately, the more coherent and religiously appealing understanding of God proposed by Whitehead (and then greatly expanded and defended by Hartshorne) remains largely unknown to the religious populace and to academics in all fields outside theological studies. It is largely unknown also to influential writers whose influence on the populace in films and mass market novels and stories is significant. The God of process theology seems to be virtually unknown, moreover, to the vast majority of atheistic scientists, including those (Carl Sagan, Isaac Asimov and a host of others) who write for the mass markets. Process theism is known to most theologians, of course, but it has not yet gained a solid foothold among the majority of traditional theologians and philosophers who continue to subject it to superficial critiques of its allegedly 'finite' and 'limited' God. I say 'superficial' critiques since process theists have answered these objections over and over again, largely without much success. It seems that traditional theologians remain content to espouse and defend the traditional, historical Christian paradigm, despite its apparent anomalies, contradictions and incoherencies. The continuing resistance to process theism by traditional theists seems based not only on the strong, almost overwhelming hold which any reigning paradigm would have on a society, but also on a misunderstanding of the alternative conception of God argued for in process theism, especially as it pertains to the denial of unilateral divine omnipotence and the radical revision of other traditional conceptions of fundamental divine attributes.

Hartshorne, for example, has argued that the traditional interpretation of divine power as unilaterally omnipotent, literally having 'all power', is a meaningless concept, for if this were the case, God would have nothing over which to exert such all-powerfulness.[49] It is, furthermore, not a 'limitation' on God's power to deny God this meaningless conception. Thus, in response to the complaint of traditional theologians that the process God demotes God to 'finiteness' and/or 'weakness', Hartshorne has replied that this complaint wrongly assumes without adequate argument that the traditional concept of God, as 'infinite' and implying a unilateral coerciveness, is meaningful. To deny God this meaningless power is not to weaken God or to reduce God to a finite power. Hartshorne has elaborated upon this as follows:

> Instead of saying that God's power is limited, suggesting that it is less than some conceivable power, we should rather say: his power is absolutely maximal, the greatest possible, but even the greatest possible power is still one power among others, is not the only power. God can do everything that a God can do, everything that could be done by a 'being with no possible superior'.[50]

To insist, as have classical theists, that 'divine omnipotence is the power to do anything that can be done' is to equivocate or talk nonsense. There *could not* be a power to 'do anything that could be done'. Some things could only be done by local powers; some only by cosmic power'.[51] 'We are what we are,' Hartshorne has argued,

> not simply because divine power has decided or done this or that, but because countless non-divine creatures (including our own past selves) have decided what they have decided. Not a single act of a single creatures has been or could have been simply decided by divine action. In the cosmic drama every actor, no matter how humble, contributes to the play something left undetermined by the playwright.[52]

Process thinkers, following Hartshorne's lead, have repeatedly rejected the claim of traditional theists that God must have coercive power (the God atheists likewise assume, and reject), since the 'merely' persuasive power of the process God would be unworthy of God as the supreme object of worship. To this, process theist David Griffin has responded that persuasive power not only is a far greater power than unilateral, coercive control, but it can be the sole means by which God interacts with creatures (since God, as Mind, implies that God interacts with creatures through our minds, rather than coercively controlling our bodies). It is because God has been conceived as coercive power that traditional theism has been faced with an unsolvable and intolerable problem of evil wherein God is indictable for evil as its cause or for allowing it when it could have been prevented.[53]

Philosophy and Theology

One final point needs to be addressed before concluding this chapter. All theodicies have been criticized for focusing far too much on rational defences of religious belief in God, that is, for engaging in intellectual debates with atheistic philosophers rather than seeking to give the discussions practical relevance for the masses of believers who have little time or ability for academic discussions, but who are in need of effective answers to help them cope with the stark reality of suffering. While it is true, unfortunately, that academic discussions on theodicy are often complex and intellectually demanding and, as such, inaccessible and seemingly irrelevant to the general populace, this gulf between academia and the populace is a problem for all academic disciplines: discussions by experts on music, art, literature, the physical and social sciences, medicine and philosophy likewise seem irrelevant to the populace (and even to academics in other fields).

Yet, beyond this obvious fact, I would argue that the criticism of academic discussions of theodicy confuses 'philosophical' with 'theological' discussions on evil. From the philosophical point of view the issues are discussed without the prior commitment to the theological doctrines and beliefs which are central to the theological discussions. Theologians seek to deepen and inform a faith which already exists by critically examining the rational evidence. Such is the theological mandate: a *fides quaerens intellectum* (a 'faith which seeks understanding'). The theological emphasis, accordingly, is not on philosophical debate with atheistic philosophers, but on seeking more understanding of what is already believed in faith – belief in

God and that God has a good reason for permitting evils – such that the faith of believers becomes more mature, more deeply and critically informed.

Philosophical discussions on theodicy, on the other hand, focus on the atheistic challenge that belief in God is contradictory to the preponderance of evil and suffering in the world. Atheistic philosophers claim to discuss the issues objectively, without the faith presuppositions of theologians, yet this claim is false. Atheistic philosophers, as is the case also for scientists, for example, who claim objectivity and neutrality in their scientific method – at least until the 1960s, when Thomas Kuhn, among other historians and philosophers of science, exposed the incredible array of subjectivity and bias in scientific investigation – are just as likely to bring their atheistic presuppositions to their arguments as theists bring theistic assumptions to their discussions.

Theological discussions, then, have a much different focus from philosophical discussions. The former are concerned primarily not to convert atheists, but to defend religious beliefs already held as truths based on biblical (and, for Catholics, also on Church) authority. The theological task is to enable believers in God to cope with suffering more effectively by providing a deeper understanding of the issues involved and to strengthen the faith of believers by sorting out bad answers from better ones. Christians should be mindful here that Jesus' command was to 'love the Lord your God with all your heart, and with all your soul, with all your mind, and with all your strength' (Mark 12:30). Loving God with the 'mind' refers not just to spiritual knowledge, I suggest, but to the rational and intellectual abilities God has given us. The commandment, then, refers to the whole nature of a human being, not just to our faith. Christians have an obligation to think about what we believe in in order to deepen our faith with understanding, rather than remain content with a faith which may be sincere, but without the necessary rational dimension, it can be a blind, untested, immature and uninformed faith. Theological discussions of theodicy, as such, are hardly intellectual contests with atheists, nor are they irrelevant to the masses of believers who are also subjected to suffering which wither, strengthen or weaken their faith. Theological discussions are, rather, the means by which the religious believers can deepen their faith and trust, and eliminate inadequate and dangerous speculations, based on irrationalism or uninformed biblical interpretations.

Conclusion

My purpose in this chapter has been to show, at least in a preliminary way, that the neglect of process theism by traditional theists has consequences. The main consequence is in traditional theism's inability to justify its central claims about God's attributes and God's relationship to human freedom and evil. Traditional theism's misrepresentation of God has influenced the growth of atheistic protest against its conception of God, fuelled by the perception that we are forced to choose between belief in God and human freedom, between the tyrant Zeus and the rebellious and free Prometheus. This 'either/or' option is one of the main forces behind modern atheism. Yet process theism endorses a 'both/and' position (both God and human freedom) and presents a cogent understanding of God based on the reality of human experience and creativity.

Modern Promethean atheism, which mistakenly thinks its only option is rebellion against and rejection of belief in God, is undercut by the process conception of God. The traditional conception of God has rightly been rejected by atheists, for its coercive and dispassionate Zeus-like deity with whom Prometheus had to contend does indeed threaten the genuineness of human freedom and dignity, thereby rendering the theodicy problem unsolvable: if God is the predetermining force, then how is human freedom responsible for a world saturated with evil, and why would God cause such evil; and so on? The process God of loving interaction and persuasive power, however, is compatible with human freedom, not its antithesis. Process theism is not hedged in esoteric scholasticism which renders it irrelevant to religion's cultured despisers. Indeed, the God of process theology is the very means by which freedom is made possible, for by setting limits to the chaos, presenting creatures with teleological aims and so on, God ensured that the world would be filled with creatures who are genuinely free. This, however, is not the creation 'out of nothing' of traditional theism, but creation from a pre-existing chaos which itself is co-eternal with God, and yet also an aspect of God's infinite potential which has been actualized. It is not an 'other' which was external to God or independent of God. God creates by persuasively luring a chaotic state of the universe into an orderly world, and within this world God lures creatures towards the actualization of the ideal aesthetic aims at each and every moment.

Griffin has argued convincingly, as did Hartshorne, that the traditional doctrine of creation by God 'out of nothing' implies unilateral divine power, since to hold that God could create 'out of nothing' implies that God would have sole and absolute power over that creation. This doctrine, then, has reinforced the traditional understanding of God's omnipotence. Hartshorne's contention, however, has been that God's creation is best understood not as *creatio ex nihilo*, but as everlasting and continuous creation. 'There is no presupposed "stuff" alien to God's creative work; but rather everything that influences God has already been influenced by him.' God 'is never confronted by a world whose coming to be antedates his own entire existence'. Every creature 'presupposes divine activity as antecedent condition of its coming to be'. The world is not to be understood as 'a second primordial and everlasting entity over against rather than created by God'.[54] Rather, it is internal to God, and *sine qua non* ('without which not'; that is, it would be non-existent without God as its cause). 'God is the self-identical individuality of the world somewhat as a man is the self-identical individuality of his ever-changing system of atoms.' As such, 'the only everlasting (and primordial) entity upon which God acts in creation is himself; all individuals, other than himself, which are influenced by his actions are less than everlasting, or at least less than primordial'. Thus it is 'not as if the given world [or its antecedent states] ... were simply imposed upon God from without as something alien'. Rather, all created realities arise 'out of potentialities, essences, of natures of all things, as embraced eternally in the divine essence'.[55]

God lures these potentialities into existence, directly influencing the indeterminate actions of creatures (formed by energy patterns of actual entities) at the lowest levels of life. This is not the coercive power of traditional theism, based on a cruel and powerful Zeus, or Aristotle's remote, immutable and unilaterally coercive God. The fact that the Zeus-like omnipotence of God has been synthesized into Christianity is, as Hartshorne points out, the most serious of 'theological mistakes' bordering on 'unconscious blasphemy, condemning God to a dead world, probably not distinguishable from no world at all' and responsible both for an unforgivable theodicy problem and the rise of modern atheistic protest. Process theism has undercut these problems and shown that the Promethean struggle against the tyrant Zeus is not the most coherent, cogent, viable and religiously appealing conception of the God–human relationship. God's power, rather, is the power of loving persuasion, as revealed in 'the Galilean origin of Christianity', and the source of creaturely freedom, not its negation or a threat to it or to human dignity.[56]

Notes

1. *Hesiod and Theognis*, translated by Dorothea Wender (London: Penguin Books, 1973). Also see James Morgan Pryse, *A New Presentation of Prometheus Bound of Aischylos Wherein is Set Forth the Hidden Meaning of the Myth* (Billings, MT: Kessinger Publishing Company, 1925).
2. Fragments of a second play, *Prometheus Unbound*, hint that Prometheus told his secret of Zeus's future to Zeus and was released. The lost third play and likely a satyr play are lost completely.
3. The theological term 'theodicy' was coined by Leibniz in his *Théodicée* (1710), a conflation of two Greek words: *theos* (God) and *dike* (justice). Thus the theodicy question asks: is God just in allowing evil in the world? See Barry L. Whitney, *Theodicy: An Annotated Bibliography on the Problem of Evil, 1960–1991* (Bowling Green, OH: Philosophy Documentation Center, 1998).
4. Aeschylus, *Prometheus Bound*, lines 520–24.
5. The 'esoteric layer of meaning' in the title of the Pryse book refers to the revelation by Aeschylus in *Prometheus Bound* of the Eleusinian mysteries: the characters represent various stages of the endless transmigration of the soul. Prometheus, further advanced in his cycle of reincarnation, cannot accept Zeus's authority since Zeus is far less advanced and a stumbling block which must be overcome. Io represents the reincarnating soul at the physical level of human life, while Oceanus represents the banality of traditional religious belief which pays homage to Zeus.
6. Aeschylus, *Prometheus Bound*, lines 240–43.
7. Aeschylus, *Prometheus Bound*, lines 436–506.
8. John Milton, *Paradise Lost and Paradise Regained*, edited by Christopher Ricks (New York: Penguin Books, 1982). Arguably, Milton's interpretation of the Genesis 'fall' of Adam and Eve is not consistent with traditional teaching, which holds that God had created Adam and Eve as good and free, as having no wants or needs, and sharing company with God. It was the 'fall' into disobedience, the 'original sin' of humanity – repeated generation after generation – the temptation to live independently of God, that caused evil and suffering in the world, and the banishment from the idyllic garden. Salvation from this 'fallen' state, however, has come with Christ's atoning sacrifice.
9. The paradox in the biblical story of the 'fall' is that, unlike the Promethean story of humanity benefiting from Prometheus's gifts, the 'fall' cast humanity out of a paradise, on the one hand, but awakened them to knowledge they otherwise could not have gained, on the other. To regard the latter as more beneficial than the created state of idyllic life would be erroneous, according to traditional theology. The 'fall' corrupted all of humanity and had to be redeemed by Jesus, who appeased the wrath of God, taking human sin upon himself.
10. Geoffrey Chaucer, *Canterbury Tales* (Pasadena, CA: World Library, 1995), line 523.

11. There has been an incredible amount of literature on the Book of Job, since Job is the most detailed Old Testament account of individual human suffering, raising the question as to why God has permitted it. Ironically, Job's three 'comforters' counsel him to repent, attributing his suffering to divine punishment for Job's sinfulness. The Book of Job's author, however, assures us of Job's innocence, thereby challenging the rather simplistic, though prevalent, view that all suffering and blessing came from God in direct proportion to what human beings deserve. Later, Jesus (Luke 13:1–5) would reject the divine punishment theory as an inadequate explanation for the specific instances of suffering and death brought to his attention. He does likewise in other passages, rejecting the view that the blind man he cured had been born blind as punishment for his own sins (in the womb) or his parents' sins (John 9:1–5). Despite the prevalence in biblical and post-biblical Christianity of the divine punishment view of suffering, there are clear indications that this theory is not valid, that the biblical God is not the punishing Zeus of Aeschylus' *Prometheus Bound*, but rather a loving God who permits suffering caused by the free choices of others, and who (as Jesus showed) has compassion for the sufferer and often, though not always, can effect a cure. For an excellent explanation of this view, see Gregory Boyd, *God at War: The Bible and Spiritual Conflict* (Downer's Grove, IL: InterVarsity Press, 1997). See also Barry Whitney, *Evil and the Process God* (New York: Edwin Mellen Press, 1985).
12. See Boyd, *God at War*. His interpretation seems one of the most plausible among a variety of interpretations, namely, that evil does not have its source in God. The story exemplifies that spiritual warfare is being conducted between God and free evil powers – both human and angelic – who wreak havoc on the world.
13. Milton, *Paradise Lost*, IV, lines 774–6; VIII, lines 172–7.
14. Dante Alighieri, *The Divine Comedy: Paradiso* (Pasadena, CA: World Library, 1995) XXI, lines 94–102.
15. These biblical passages tell how human pride built the Tower of Babel to reach, symbolically, into the domain of God, the heavens, in an attempt to glorify humanity, rather than God, resulting in God's punishment (Genesis 11:1–9); Exodus 33:20 tells us that 'no man can see God and live', this being forbidden; John 1:18 confirms that 'no one has seen God', but that God has been revealed in Jesus (John 1:18); The Deutero-Pauline letter to Timothy tells us that God is 'immortal, invisible' (1 Timothy 1:17) and that 'no man has seen or can see' God (1 Timothy 6:16).
16. Nicholas Rescher, *Forbidden Knowledge and Other Essays on the Philosophy of Cognition* (Dordrecht, Germany: Reidel Publishing, 1987), Chapter one.
17. I am indebted to Roger Shattuck's fine book, *Forbidden Knowledge: From Prometheus to Pornography* (New York: St Martin's Press, 1996).
18. See, for example, the discussion of Aristotle, traditional theism and numerous other understandings of God, in Charles Hartshorne and William L. Reese, *Philosophers Speak of God* (Chicago: University of Chicago Press, 1953). Also see Charles Hartshorne, *Omnipotence and Other Theological Mistakes* (Albany, NY: State University of New York Press, 1984), and Whitney, *Evil and the Process God*.
19. Aeschylus, *Prometheus Bound*, passim.
20. Ibid., lines 936–40.
21. See John Hick, *Evil and the God of Love* (London: Macmillan, 1977). Also see Stephen T. Davis, editor, *Encountering Evil: Live Options in Theodicy* (Atlanta: John Knox Press, 1981), especially 101–36.
22. While Hick conceived his solution to the problem of evil as an alternative to the unilaterally coercive God of traditional theology, process theists remain convinced that he has not gone far enough in his revision of traditional theism. In fact, Hick's conception of divine power can be defined as a *pseudo traditional theism* insofar as, while his God may

no longer be the sole cause of all events – since God has chosen to limit God's power to ensure creaturely freedom – this God nonetheless has the power to determine all events unilaterally. Process theists point out, accordingly, that Hick's God remains as responsible for evil and suffering as the traditional Augustinian–Thomistic–Lutheran–Calvinist God, since Hick's God has not eliminated the most horrendous of evils, including especially the gratuitous evils that seem not to lead to any greater good not otherwise attainable. Hick's God is as susceptible to lack of goodness as is the traditional God in permitting evils, especially those which appear gratuitous, when they could have been prevented. Hick's defence hangs on his reasons (see below) why his God will not intervene, reasons which are controversial at best. Passing judgment on Hick's model of God, David Ray Griffin has argued that if Hick's God is all-powerful, is able, that is, to eliminate the worst evils, then it would seem Hick's God is negligent in the use of divine power, for many evils occur in our world, with God allowing what God could otherwise have prevented. To this, Hick's response has been that God will not interfere with human acts and decisions, since this would thwart God's plan for us to choose freely to become spiritually perfected beings. There is, Hick claims, an infinity of time for this 'soul making' process to be completed, since life does not end with earthly life but continues in a spiritual realm until all are perfected. Moreover, while God could eliminate the worst of evils, Hick contends that God does not do so because this would become a 'slippery slope' problem: there would be no place to stop, since good and evil are relative to us, and no matter how much evil God eliminated or prevented, we would designate what is left as relatively good and relatively evil. To this rejoinder, Griffin replies that while we would not know where God should stop, God would know that the most horrendous and gratuitous evils should be eliminated. This, moreover, would not significantly affect our genuine freedom. So far, Hick has not replied to this critical point.

23. Timothy R. Wutrich, *Prometheus and Faust* (Westport, CT: Greenwood Press, 1995), 57–8. I am indebted to the author for his detailed documentation of the history of Promethean thought. Likewise, I am indebted to Joseph McLelland, *Prometheus Rebound: The Irony of Atheism* (Waterloo, ON: Wilfred Laurier University Press, 1988). While the author does not discuss process theism, I agree with his defining of the issue: 'Either Zeus or Prometheus, but not both: that is the root of the issue. As a reaction to Christian classical theism, Prometheanism represents "classical atheism"' (3). I am indebted also to Larry Kreitzer, *Prometheus and Adam: Enduring Symbols of the Human Situation* (Lanham, MD: University Press of America, 1995). See also Carl Kerényi, *Prometheus: Archetypal Image of Human Existence*, translated by Ralph Manheim (Princeton, NJ: Princeton University Press, 1963).

24. This view, in fact, is the basic premise behind the revised theism of process metaphysics. See Alfred North Whitehead, *Process and Reality: An Essay on Cosmology*, corrected edition, edited by David Ray Griffin and Donald W. Sherburne (New York: Free Press, 1978); Hartshorne, *Omnipotence and Other Theological Mistakes*; David Ray Griffin, *God, Power and Evil* (Philadelphia: Westminster Press, 1976) and Whitney, *Evil and the Process God*.

25. See *Basic Writings of St. Augustine*, edited by Whitney J. Oates (New York: Random House, 1953). See also Griffin, *God, Power and Evil*, Chapter six, for a critical discussion of Augustine's theodicy.

26. See Thomas Aquinas, *Summa Contra Gentiles*, translated by Charles O'Neill (Notre Dame: University of Notre Dame Press, 1975), III, I. See also Griffin, *God, Power and Evil*, Chapter seven, for a critical discussion of Aquinas's theodicy.

27. See the discussion on 'middle knowledge' in Whitney, *Theodicy: An Annotated Bibliography*, Chapter three. As long as both Molinists and Thomists assume the classical doctrine of God, demonstrating how this concept is coherent with human free will is

problematic. The Molinist view seems stronger to me than the Thomist – that God knows every free decision that every creature will make in every possible situation – but process theists undercut this view by proposing that genuine freedom is founded on a doctrine of God which does not attribute foreknowledge to God: God may know in almost complete detail what every creature is likely to do in free acts, but there is always the possibility that the creature will act otherwise. While our actions are influenced also completely by our character and environment, and also by God's lure, this is never a complete determination. Such is the view argued by Charles Hartshorne in his *Creative Synthesis and Philosophic Method* (London: SCM Press, 1970).

28. Charles Hartshorne, *The Divine Relativity: A Social Concept of God* (New Haven, CT: Yale University Press, 1948), 116–17, 135. Also see Whitney, *Evil and the Process God*, Chapter seven.
29. Cited in William A. Christian, *An Interpretation of Whitehead's Metaphysics* (New Haven, CT: Yale University Press, 1959), 388–90.
30. Whitehead, *Process and Reality*, 519–20.
31. John C. Robertson, Jr. 'Does God Change?', *Ecumenist* 10.1 (1971): 63.
32. Johann W. Goethe, 'Prometheus', in *Goethe: Selected Verse*, edited and translated by David Luke (Middlesex UK: Penguin Books, 1986), 17–19.
33. Lord Byron, *Complete Poetical Works*, edited by Jerome J. McGann (Oxford: Clarendon Press, 1980).
34. Percy B. Shelley, 'Prometheus Unbound', and 'Preface to 'Hellas', in *The Complete Poetical Works of Percy Bysshe Shelley,* edited by Neville Rogers (Oxford: Clarendon Press, 1972). Also see Percy B. Shelley, *Notes, Queen Mab*, in *The Complete Poetical Works of Percy Bysshe Shelley*. The problem of divine providence is that God's foreknowledge seems incompatible with human free decisions, an issue which has had a long and turbulent theological history. Shelley also rejected a personal God who was consciously behind this providential rule. He preferred, rather, the view of Nature's 'necessity'. At the same time, Shelley's wife, Mary, published the short, well-known novel, *Frankenstein*, appropriately subtitled, 'The Modern Prometheus', so named for the heroic qualities of the creative power of both Dr Frankenstein and Prometheus, at once fascinating and terrifying. See Mary Shelley, *Frankenstein, Or, The Modern Prometheus* (New York: Everyman's Library, 1992).
35. Karl Marx, in *Karl Marx, Friedrich Engels: Historisch-Kritische Geramtausgabe* (Berlin: Marx-Engels Verlag, 1932), I, 1–52. Also see Ludwig Feuerbach, *The Essence of Christianity*, translated by George Eliot (New York: Harper & Row, 1957). In addition, see Ludwig Feuerbach, *Thoughts on Death and Immortality*, translated by James A. Massey (Berkeley, CA: University of California Press, 1980).
36. See Friedrich Nietzsche, *Complete Works: The First Complete and Authorized English Translation*, translated and edited by Oscar Levy (New York: Russell and Russell, 1964).
37. See Jean-Paul Sartre, *Being and Nothingness: An Essay on Phenomenological Ontology*, translated by Hazel E. Barnes (New York: Philosophical Library, 1956). Also see Albert Camus, *The Myth of Sisyphus and Other Essays*, translated by Justin O'Brien (New York: Alfred A. Knopf, 1955).
38. Sigmund Freud, *The Future of an Illusion*, translated and edited by James Strachey (New York: Norton, 1975). Also see Hans Küng, *Freud and the Problem of God* (New Haven, CT: Yale University Press, 1979), 36. For an excellent study of Freud's writings on forbidden knowledge, with reference not only to Oedipus but also to Prometheus, see the collection of essays in Peter Rudnytsky and Ellen Handler Spitz, editors, *Freud and Forbidden Knowledge* (New York: New York University Press, 1994).
39. Carl G. Jung, *Answer to Job*, translated by R.F.C. Hull (London: Routledge, 1954).
40. Charles Hartshorne, 'A New Look at the Problem of Evil', in *Current Philosophical*

Issues: Essays in Honor of Curt John Ducasse, edited by F.C. Dommeyer (Springfield, IL: Charles C. Thomas, 1966), 202.
41. See Ephesians 1:11 for this predeterminist strain in New Testament theology.
42. See Whitney, *Evil and the Process God*, Chapter six.
43. Hartshorne and Reese, *Philosophers Speak of God*, 20.
44. Hartshorne, *The Divine Relativity*, 58.
45. Charles Hartshorne, 'Panpsychism', in *A History of Philosophical Systems*, edited by V. Ferm (New York: Philosophical Library, 1950), 442–53. Also see Charles Hartshorne, *Whitehead's Philosophy: Selected Essays, 1935–1970* (Lincoln, NE: University of Nebraska Press, 1972), 44. Also cited here is Andrew Reck's summary statement of Hartshorne's position, included in *The New American Philosophers* (Baton Rouge, LA: Louisiana State University Press, 1968). Finally, see Charles Hartshorne, *The Logic of Perfection and Other Essays in Neoclassical Metaphysics* (La Salle, IL.: Open Court, 1962), 191; and Charles Hartshorne, *The Philosophy and Psychology of Sensation* (Port Washington, NY: Kennikat Press, 1968), 11.
46. Hartshorne, 'A New Look at the Problem of Evil', 110.
47. Hartshorne, *The Logic of Perfection*, 217.
48. Charles Hartshorne, *Man's Vision of God and the Logic of Theism* (New Hamden, CT: Archon Books, 1964), 30. Also see Charles Hartshorne, *A Natural Theology for our Time* (La Salle, IL: Open Court, 1967), 81.
49. See Hartshorne, *The Divine Relativity*, 138. In addition, see Whitney, *Evil and the Process God*, 97–101.
50. Hartshorne, *The Divine Relativity*, 134.
51. Ibid., 138.
52. Hartshorne, *Creative Synthesis and Philosophic Method*, 239.
53. See David Ray Griffin, *Evil Revisited: Responses and Reconsiderations* (Albany, NY: State University of New York Press, 1991), Chapters six to eight.
54. Hartshorne, *The Divine Relativity*, 130.
55. Hartshorne, *Man's Vision of God*, 230–32.
56. On this central and controversial point, see Barry L. Whitney, 'Divine Persuasion and the Anthropic Principle', *The Personalist Forum* 14.2 (1998): 140–67; 'Process Theism: Does a Persuasive God Coerce?', *Southern Journal of Philosophy* 17.1 (1979): 133–43; 'Hartshorne's New Look at the Problem of Evil', *Studies in Religion* 8.3 (1979): 281–91; 'Hartshorne and Theodicy', in *Hartshorne, Process Philosophy and Theology*, edited by R. Kane and S. Phillips (Albany, NY: State University of New York Press, 1989), 55–71; 'Hartshorne and Natural Evil', *Sophia* 35 (1994): 33–46; 'An Aesthetic Solution to the Problem of Evil', *International Journal for Philosophy of Religion* 35 (1994): 21–3. Finally, the reader is advised to see Hartshorne, *Omnipotence and Other Theological Mistakes*, 18, and Whitehead, *Process and Reality*, 520.

Chapter 7

Sticky Evil:
Macbeth and the Karma of the Equivocal

William Desmond

Out, damned spot! Out, I say! One: two: why, then 'tis time to do't. Hell is murky. Fie, my lord, fie! A soldier and afeard? What need we fear who knows it, when none can call our pow'r to accompt? Yet who would have thought the old man to have had so much blood in him? (*Macbeth*, V, i, 38–43)

Sticky Evil

So cried Lady Macbeth and wandered in the disconsolate night. What does the outcry do? It redoes what she thought could be done, and then done with, done away with, without too much complication, or complicity. Her words recapitulate, they sleep-walk through, the night at the pitch kern of *Macbeth*. The plot of the play shows a doing and an undoing. And these words proclaim a karma in her deed, and now comes this karma unbidden, comes more and more to blazon itself, even beyond all knowing, even in sleep itself. The evil done is sticky, the karma a doom not to be undone in the relentless course of equivocal time. The karma of the equivocal is there in that damned spot of sticky evil. What is this sticky evil, what this karma of the equivocal?

The plot is familiar. The play opens as Macbeth fights the rebels on behalf of King Duncan. On his way back from victorious battle, he and Banquo meet on 'this blasted heath' the witches, the weird sisters. These sisters of fate (weird) offer prophecies intimating that Macbeth is the coming king of Scotland. The sisters have 'more than mortal knowledge', though their prophecies are deeply equivocal. They mix half-truth with half-lie; they tell the truth, but equivocally, and so do not tell the truth, for certain half-truths told equivocally hide the karma of their equivocity. Macbeth has presentiment of this: 'Two truths are told / As happy prologue to the swelling act of the imperial theme ... this supernatural soliciting / cannot be ill, cannot be good. If ill, / Why hath it given me earnest of success, / Commencing in a truth? ... if good, why do I yield to that suggestion / Whose horrid image doth unfix my hair...?' (I, iii, 127–35).

And now the prophecy seems fatefully to move within reach of realization, when Duncan invites himself to Macbeth's castle. If it is to be realized now, the prophecy of coming sovereignty must come through murder. Duncan comes in expectation of hospitality, but will never leave alive. Macbeth wavers with tormented misgiving; his wife sets him on; he commits the deed. His mind is in disarray, and he cries, 'Sleep no more'. Lady Macbeth is the one who now displays firmness of purpose. She seems to 'live up to the crime' (as Friedrich Nietzsche might say); she is determined not to be undone by being appalled at the deed. Later it will be Macbeth who is determined to 'live up to his crime', out of desperate insecurity about the succession. He is steadfast in evil, even as his wife encouraged, 'what's done is done'; 'what's done cannot be undone'. 'I am in blood / stepped in so far that, should I wade no more, / Returning were as tedious as go o'er' (III, v, 137–9). Stepped in blood, steeped in blood: the indelible evil brings forth a hyperbolic determination to drive right through to the end of darkness, and if so it will be, to go down into it.

The going down is already in train from the opening of the play. Lady Macbeth falters, the criminal who cannot stand (by) her deed, and the sleepless night of madness falls on her. 'Out, damned spot! Out, I say!' She re-echoes some of Macbeth's piteous cries when he stood appalled at the deed just done: 'What, will these hands ne'er be clean?' (V, i, 46), 'Will all great Neptune's ocean wash this blood / Clean from my hand? No; this my hand will rather / The multitudinous seas incarnadine, / Making the green one red' (II, ii, 59–62).[1] Macbeth will wade into the stickiness, seem as if to revel in it, where before he would wash, and wash, and wash, and not succeed. How bright were her expectations, how clean of complication, before the murderous deed itself. A simple matter: 'Th' attempt and not the deed confounds us' (II, ii, 10–11). 'A little water clears us of this deed: How easy is it then!' (II, iii, 66–7). A simple problem: Duncan stood between her ambition and the throne: her ambition for her husband you say, but her ambition through her husband was also for 'solely sovereign sway and masterdom' (I, v, 71). These lovers are surely partners in woe. Does their temptation mirror that of Eve and Adam? Not quite: temptation here is not in the cloudless beginning of vegetarian Eden; it is already in a carnivorous world enshrouded in darkening and warring. It is a kingdom of fallen time, where 'light thickens' and the crow, ominous black bird, 'makes wing to the rooky wood'. This world is already under assault from sinister powers and their spells. Evil already sticks to it: not the outright univocal 'thereness', but the insinuation, the taint, the shady suggestion that sticks. Even innocence seems besmirched. It is, so to say, a *smeared world*.[2]

Lady Macbeth discovers in her disarray that some stains resist being cleansed. 'Out, damned spot! Out, I say!' And 'none can call our pow'r to accompt'. So she thought. She is like Gyges, in Socrates' rendition of being beyond account (*Republic*), Gyges, successful dreamer of usurpation, graced with the ring of invisibility. It seems Macbeth and Lady Macbeth have not been seen, cannot be seen. Why then does their invisible horror become visible in the invisible blood that will not rinse off? The spot is damned. A strange spot, for it is not there. 'Something' that is, is as if it were 'nothing'. Or 'nothing' that is, is as if it were 'something'. Yet this 'nothing' is more tormentingly 'there' than the solidest things of the solid flesh. The spot is the apparition of the stain of the karma of the equivocal that, fatal temptation being acted on, brings on inner hell.

'Out! out!' We find the redoubled reiteration of this phrase, a phrase itself redolent with equivocal doubleness. This redoubled outcry recurs like a knell: *something will out*, like a fuller truth out of the half-truth. And this despite the fact that something will out in an opposed sense, in being snuffed out, or as a light is outed, an end being put to something. Bringing to light and striking out the light converge. Macbeth hears of his wife's suicide, but he has 'supped full of horrors. / Direness, familiar to my slaughterous thoughts, / Cannot once start me' (V, v, 13–15). And then Macbeth's great outcry, quickened at the last with the exhausted energy of despair: '…Out, out, brief candle! / Life's but a walking shadow, a poor player / That struts and frets his hour upon the stage / And then is heard no more. It is a tale / Told by an idiot, full of sound and fury / Signifying nothing' (V, v. 23–8). The darkness of the idiot is not merely invoked, it is called down upon life itself: the idiocy of being is nothing but the idiocy of the monstrous.[3]

Macbeth speaks as if he knew the truth of life, its light, which is 'nothing'. Life has become this for him, what he has made of it. The equivocal play between 'yes' and 'no', ever in tension in our fragile middle condition, is resolved to one side, and falls over into nothing. And the last 'no' turns on life itself as finally also the apparition of nothing: a tale told by an idiot, signifying nothing. Suppose this 'nothing' is enigmatically constitutive of the happening of life itself, in the equivocity of its chiaroscuro? But then, since this happening implicates us, how we live in this equivocity, live it, this too will shape the form the karma will assume. I mean we embody negation and our complicity in the karma will dominantly bring forth its nothingness: absolutize it, so to say. But what is this except perdition? The damnation of which the spot of 'nothing' is the sticky sign? 'Out, out, brief candle!': this is no enunciation of weary resignation, but the final, consumed pronouncement of *curse*.

I know there are few who would like to end it all just cursing. But blessing here? It seems that with Macbeth himself blessing cannot be named except as loss that is *irredeemable* – literally, without redemption. Any promise of redemption in being at a loss is here lost. This redoubling of loss is being given over to perdition. The curse, ending it, is the surfacing in utterance of a curse in process throughout the play as a whole. Had not Macbeth – recall – unequivocally announced his willingness to 'jump the life to come'? Are we given what we insist on? If we ask for heaven, heaven; for hell, hell?

Hyperbolic Evil

Evil solicits our rumination since it is one of the most intractable of perplexities. To ruminate on evil is hard, since thinking about evil is like trying to digest a stone. We speak of the problem of evil, but perhaps it is not a problem at all – certainly not in this sense: a problem is a determinate difficulty that, in principle, has an equally determinable solution. But something about evil suggests more an enigma or mystery that ever exceeds *any determinate solution* we might propose. Something exceeds *finite determination* in thus perplexing evil. The happening of evil is overdeterminate in that regard: it seems something *hyperbolic* relative to finite determinability. If so, there may be no solution to it. And were there a 'solving' to such a 'problem', perhaps it would be more like a 'salvation' or 'redemption'. But such considerations also seem just as hyperproblematic as evil. So too they are very difficult for our age to acknowledge in this form, with its problem-oriented mentality, and its obsession with the technical and instrumental determinability of being.

Thus, not surprisingly, Shakespeare's *Macbeth* is a difficult play for the modern reader. We have univocalized the world. We have stripped off all the qualitative values that immediately seem to show themselves to 'ordinary' perception. We pride ourselves on the superior truth of a *mathesis* of nature, bringing in its train all the benefits of calculation, computation and technology. Have we not washed clean the world with the solvent waters of scientific reason? But have we also washed off any suggestiveness that offers the shadow for a presentiment of evil, evil indeed as slyly enchanting? If the world is disenchanted, it is not only the ambiguous signs of the divine that are rinsed off, or to which we are proudly blind, but any lure of evil, any of its ambiguous glitter, also become unintelligible. How do we make sense of this enchantment? Suppose we seek a sense of being that is more deeply hospitable to the good. Must we not also then grant some more *intimate pervasiveness* of evil? Among its many fascinations, *Macbeth* offers us the feel of this intimate pervasiveness.

If we have a washed world, then we lack any basis for blessing or for curse, for the divine and the daimonic. Yes, yes, someone then is bound to say: This makes me very uncomfortable! Let us psychologize such 'qualities'! Very well: follow the pathway of early modern epistemology: objective – there you have the primary qualities; subjective – there you have the secondary qualities. Locate enchantments of the divine in the latter; subjectivize the enchantments; indeed even invoke René Descartes or earlier religious traditions: go the way of the inward self; and there also locate the glitter of the luring evil; the strife in enchantment is within the self. Go ahead: psychologize it all! But this is very hard to do, as *Macbeth*, I believe, will show. The stone will not be digested or easily sweated out. Here we are shown something neither subjective nor objective; neither primary nor secondary. What then? A hybrid? Or a monster? Ask it this way: suppose the primary and the secondary themselves derive from a more *equivocal matrix* which, once subjected to the process of being univocalized or mathematicized, seems to fall away into an uneasy forgetfulness. Is it surprising that then we are baffled when black powers suddenly surge up from beneath the surface of the univocalized earth? Maybe just what we need is attunement to this equivocal matrix?

If the truth is simply the scientific univocalization of nature, we cannot enter sympathetically into *Macbeth*. Since we do enter sympathetically, we need to suspend our scientific disbelief, that is, the belief that all the qualitative values of happenings, suggested by such things as blessing and curse, have no firm 'objective' grounding in the ontological situation. Of course, Samuel Taylor Coleridge claimed that aesthetically one always needs some 'willing suspension of disbelief'. But maybe even this is too 'psychologized', too much under the sway of the disenchanted world. Does it do justice to the *ontological situation* as equivocal matrix of being? What is the world we enter when the univocal world is 'suspended', when we meet happenings at the edge of our 'will', at the edge even of 'belief' and 'disbelief' in more determinate, even propositional senses? Do we need a little salutary 'superstition', so to say – a little alertness to the marvellous and to horror? Must we become again as children, indeed as terrified children? Is not this to approach the tragic and its terror? How do more scientific ways approach *phobos* (dread, horror and terror)? How do we get rid of phobias? Wash them away with scientific enlightenment? But what if this won't wash? And what of *eleos*, tragic pity or compassion? We too must come again to children and to pity.

And further: what if the world of *Macbeth* is a *bewitched world*?[4] What is a catharsis in a world of bewitchment? A purging. But what is a purging of evil? A washing away of it. But suppose the evil has a power that exceeds the will, do we not then need something more like an *exorcism*? But who can exorcise such a world? Perhaps we say: the world only *appears* to be under the sign of this equivocity; the univocalization work of science will do the washing of appearances? But this would be to deny the equivocity as beyond our will. Exorcism would have no final meaning. Should we psychologize that too? But what if the equivocity of evil has a more elusive ontological import, and the truer washing were an exorcism beyond psychologizing? Who or what within the world can perform the catharsis? Who or what is to redeem such a bewitched world?

Seeking redemption in bewitched equivocity brings us up against the limits of a univocal naturalism. Note in *Macbeth* the 'supernatural' forces of evil: the wicked sisters are in the world but not quite of it, though not as Jesus asked us to be: in and out, up and down, so they go about, defying nature, carried hither and thither, about must and about must go. How does all this fit in with a 'naturalistic' explanatory scheme such as process philosophy claims to offer us? One might speak of a *happening* of evil; but a happening need be neither objective nor subjective. I do not mean that evil simply happens to us, for we too are complicit in this happening; it is inside, and outside; more than us, and yet within our responsibility; beyond solving by us, and yet without our consent and cooperation there is no absolving.

Of course, evil allows of many approaches, some of which find their more systematic articulation and rejoinder in the diversity of traditional theodicies. Evil has been joined to absence, privation, joined to nothing; there is much in this approach, granted that we know how to talk about this 'nothing'. Of this, something has already been intimated. Evil has been blamed on free will; and surely it has to do with freedom; but there is something more equivocal prior to deliberate free will. Of this, more will come. Evil has been connected with virtue and becoming: 'the vale of soul-making' requires resistances that challenge us to become more perfect. But can we just will through ourselves the perfection? Can we even will through ourselves a pact with evil, were there not a prior tempting, an arising of evil solicitation from perplexing sources?

I want to suggest there is a more primordial apparition of evil, closer to the matrix out of which these more determinate articulations emerge. *Macbeth*, I think, shows us something of this matrix. This is closer to the predeterminate ethos of being, and this is, in some degree, pre-subjective and pre-objective. It is closer to the magic of the origin, or its transhuman power, and emergent for us when we are in attunement with the equivocity of being. This equivocity is not entirely negative. It intimates a positive saturation of the world with qualitative value. In this ethos there is an elemental sense of the hospitable or the hostile; calling out in us an elemental 'yes' or 'no': yes to the good of the 'to be' and no to the threat to the fragility of this good of the 'to be' in finite existents. The world may not *univocally* proclaim God's grandeur, but even the smeared world cannot quite entirely eclipse that grandeur.

I speak of a matrix of ontological value: this is not due to us, and yet it is matrix of our value. We live this equivocity of value in consent and refusal, blessing and curse. In living this consent and refusal, we become kinds of selves who incarnate consent or refusal, or mixture – mostly mixture. There is something indelible about this more original being in the matrix of the ethos. We think we free ourselves from its happening when we become more explicitly *willing* selves, deliberating and deciding for ourselves. But this is itself equivocal; for the inherent character of the matrix still works its original power in us. This is one reason I will speak below more of a *karma* of the equivocal. We are given to be in the original ethos or matrix; we grow to be in that matrix; we choose to be out of that matrix and thus, so to say, reconfigure that matrix and ourselves; and we may even think then we are free from it, and free in ourselves entirely to will as we choose, or to determine ourselves according to our own will. But this is misleading. These later, more self-mediating developments, are always rooted in that from which they seem to claim independence or freedom.[5]

This is very hard to communicate if one's sense of being is forged by the unrestrained ethos of human autonomy that shapes modernity, and which accompanies an often univocal devaluation of the ethos. If our freedoms are not only unintelligible without reference to the matrix or ethos, but ethically and ontologically precarious, what seems like the high ideal of autonomous being-for-self may be an artificial womb of monstrous corruptions. This is a knotted question, I grant.[6] I now just ask: how do we address this more primal, and equivocal, ethos? I say: *Macbeth* gives us a dramatic image of it, relative to such a strange kind of ethos: both a happening and yet something in which we are complicit. A great art work, a dramatic work with its saturated images (such as the damned spot of sticky evil) brings us closer to the predeterminate matrix of value in its overdeterminate character. It does so more than any more determinate proposition expressed in the prose of a thesis. It shows the happening. It offers the aesthetic appearance of what precedes the more objectivized phenomena of determinate discourse. We can have an image of the indeterminable, an image which makes it aesthetically determinate, without betraying what exceeds determination. This is an aspect of the metaphysical power of a great work of art.

The Bewitched between: beyond Univocity

The earth, one might say, is solid, univocally solid. Even Macbeth invokes a steady earth before doing the deed: 'Thou sure and firm set earth, hear not my steps...' (II, i, 56–7). Yet all things solid dissolve. The doubleness of equivocity comes again: 'double, double, toil and trouble; / Fire burn and cauldron bubble' (IV, i, 10–11). The earth seems as fluent as water, and as evanescent. 'The earth hath bubbles, as the water has, / And these are of them' (I, iii, 79–80). So says Banquo, as the witches vanish. One thinks of Heraclitus, that aristocrat of equivocal flux: everything runs or flows.[7] He also spoke of the logos that runs through all things. This relates to what I call 'the karma of the equivocal'. Generally, process philosophies seek to stay attuned to the passage and transience in the course of things. This does not obviate stabilities of being, yet they are relative. All things become in the universal impermanence. This impermanence points to a twofold character of being: it is, but is as becoming, and so it is not what it is fully. It both is and is not. The doubleness of becoming in the universal impermanence marks creation itself as a matrix of equivocal being. This can be taken in different directions. A more Parmenidean, or Platonic, response will tend to want to transcend it. A Nietzschean will want to celebrate it aesthetically. A process philosophy will want to articulate its categorial intelligibility. A dialectical philosophy will see in it the outlines of a teleological holism. What I call 'a metaxological metaphysics' will seek a different discerning mindfulness of the meaning of the doubleness, of what is communicated in and through the equivocal becoming of things.[8]

How should we see Macbeth's doubled world? It seems doomed under the shadow of time's own equivocity. Does anything stay? Sticky evil perhaps. What of the univocal earth, if there is one? Is there not rather a *bewitched* world? How think of this? A bewitched world cannot be described in the disenchanted language of univocal prose, or in terms of a neutral objectivism. Things and happenings within a bewitched world are charged with a riddling ambiguity. Potential portents, they are communications from powers that cannot be univocally objectivized. But if not objective, then subjective? You say: we project these ambiguities on the neutral screen and, owing to a subreption (with a bow to Immanuel Kant), we mistakenly think they are just there, even though *we* have put them there without self-consciously knowing it. Will this do? Doubtful. It is hard to interpret this bewitched world as just bearing the impress of a projecting subjectivity. But are there not occasions when Macbeth seems to project the fantasy of murder before him? 'Is this a dagger I see before me, the handle towards my hand...?' (II, i, 33–4). Macbeth is not even sure. Then there is the ghost of Banquo that Macbeth alone can see. But 'projection' seems too simple. Is this not already the retrospective superimposition of a disenchanted view, with the adornment of a compensating psychologizing added to the otherwise neutral milieu?

But a bewitched world is not so neutral. This world is a world of appearance: more correctly, of apparition. Things become apparent. And the apparition of things is inherently equivocal: 'Is this a dagger I see before me?' The apparition raises a question in us about its status, its truth. And its truth is not univocally firm or established: the apparition is resistant to reduction to univocal terms, be they subjective or objective. Even if we say 'subjective' – and perhaps we must say both 'subjective' and 'objective', to some degree, since we deal here with a *promiscuity* of selving and othering – then we must ask: what 'subject'? Even as we must ask about the dagger: what 'object'? For is it not so that the *projecting 'subject'* is also bewitched? What bewitches *that*, that putatively bewitching 'projector'?

I would say we have to bring the 'subject' back to the *idiocy of being*: the deepest intimacy of the soul where the monstrous and the demonic break forth. This is where the struggle between the powers is fought out. This is where the matrix of desire and temptation offers us alluring images of absolute being, and also the counterfeit doubles of absoluteness that cast their spell: the *fata morgana* of the idiocy of being. This too is consonant with the openness of apparition in a world that is one of time and becoming. The promise of the self, the promise of the world itself, both show an indeterminacy of being, an overdeterminacy in the sense of being in excess to univocal determination. To acknowledge this show of overdeterminacy helps us make sense of events such as temptation and betrayal, and happenings that incarnate the struggle between powers, within the human soul, but also, in another sense, transcending the 'subjectivity' of the individual.

If one dwells with some attunement to the equivocity of being, things are themselves, and yet not themselves: they are as they appear, and yet they are not what they immediately appear to be. They are double: themselves and more than themselves; themselves and less that what they are. In this doubled world everything takes on the character of a possible communication, or duplicity. Something is passing through the apparition; passing towards us; but also passing beyond us, and so passing always ambiguously. We must participate in discerning the signs of communication; and what we divine them to be is as much dependent on what we are as on what they are. Their very ambiguity brings to arousal our most secret ambiguities. The apparitions offer the occasions when the deepest desires, intimations, presentiments, mostly in motion below rational self-consciousness in the idiocy of being, take on a more determinate incarnate shape. A body is given to what otherwise seems nothing.

We are necessarily accomplices in the discerning of the communications. How we discern crystallizes possibilities that as much mirror us as the otherness being communicated in and through the intimation. Thus the sinister beyond us comes to a show in us, through our own sinister potency. But we cannot resolve the show into either subjective or objective terms. For there is something pre-subjective and pre-objective at work. This is the bewitched between. A later disenchanted view of the world will dismiss this as silly. But the dismissal is itself silly. The possibility of the bewitched between is always there as a potency of the equivocal matrix of being. As an illustration, think of Halloween. Grant me the conceit of becoming a terrified child again. Then we are the observers of the witching hour: the most potent time between the realms of life and death; when the two become most permeable to each other; when the powers of blessing and curse, saving and perdition are most intense and proximate, now in this time on the border of time, when we are exposed to the equivocal promiscuity of life and death.

But is this not also the world of *Macbeth*? How else but in this bewitched between could Banquo appear, reappear, though he is gone forever? The dead come back: he is there, and not there, in that undiscovered bourn between life and death. It is into this world that Macbeth has stepped, and he cannot extricate himself, even when he wills it, and boldly dares it to a contest that will resolve its duplicity. This is the in-between world that Lady Macbeth initially dismisses; but she has also stepped into it, and will also be swallowed up by it. She will kill herself in its nightmare, for she cannot step out of it into the daylight, as curse seems to strangle all blessing. And true to the equivocal, it is not that Shakespeare denies the blessing of apparition itself. So we feel the fresh breath of daylight, communicated in the 'innocent' description of Macbeth's castle, before the murder: 'This castle hath a pleasant seat; the air / Nimbly and sweetly recommends itself / Unto our gentle senses' (I, vi, 1–3). To be able to feel the sweet air thus would be to step out of the nightmare; to be saved from it; but we cannot be saved simply by acts of will alone. We can will it, be willing; but our willing alone is not enough; blessing powers must come to exorcise the curse.[9]

Once again the univocalizing of the world by science will not release us here. A great artist must have a living root of his being tapped into the enchanting between, pre-objective and pre-subjective. The magic of religion keeps alive that root. And in a way, the loss of the magic of the world is disastrous. Nor can this magic be captured in the language of univocity, either subjective or objective. Some believers in magic misinterpret it univocally as the unambiguous effect of power. Others who debunk it scientistically do the same from the point of claiming to unmask the mechanism of the duping, and bring this back to a devious play of instrumental power, rather than the apparition of the charisma of power. Neither does justice to the strange capacity of the effect of magic. That this is equivocal does not obviate the truth that something deeply real may be effected in this effect. Otherwise, you would also have to say, for instance, that the magic of love were also thus 'unreal'. And perhaps a loss of love is not unconnected with a betrayal of the poetry of being. For this too is tied to the equivocality of being, and a totalizing univocity kills it.

The sticky evil also shows this doubleness in the fluency of process which stays and dissolves, comes and goes, vanishes and yet remains persistent. See the images of blood and water. We say: 'Blood is thicker than water.' Images of thickening are recurrent in the play.[10] Water flows, but does it wash? Not here with the damned spot. We might say: water flows; blood circulates, streams or is spilt. Spilt blood stains and coagulates; it hardens into a sticky mess that seems thicker than the flow of process. (It is said about Macbeth: 'Now does he feel / His secret murders sticking on his hands' V, iii, 17–18.) In a way, does not blood show the stickiness of the equivocal matrix par excellence? What flows for the 'guilty river-god of the blood' (*schuldigen Fluss-Gott des Bluts*)?[11] What is blood but the carrier of life: the life-blood? Source of generation, the blood line is the carrier across time of the frail transience of human glory. In the blood of the women flows the cycle of renewal, the bloom of creation that renews itself in flowing away.

But blood is also violence and death. A man in rage: his blood was up: his anger towering, on the verge of violence. A crime of blood, the blood was in his eyes: something deep and urgent surges up. How do we start when blood is spilt? Wounded being: see Banquo with 'twenty trenched gashes on his head': destruction of the harmony of the whole. We speak of spilt blood: crime or horror or death that calls out for vengeance, or retribution or justice. The blood cries out on the stones. What cries out in spilt blood? In our disenchanted world, nothing much. Something elemental cries out in the bewitched world of Macbeth. The stickiness of the equivocal matrix retains its intimation of a stain or pollution beyond rationalistic cleansing. Heraclitus again gives us the double speak of the equivocal matrix: Dionysus is also Hades.

'Blood is thicker than water': Lady Macbeth knows this thickness from the side of life and the side of death. She who has abjured the tenderness of blood, involuntarily cannot but think about her own father in seeing the sleeping Duncan.[12] 'Had he not resembled my father as he slept, I had done't' (II, ii, 12–13). The blood of generation and its residual piety is not entirely dead. ('Yet who would have thought the old man to have had so much blood in him?') The spot of piety touches on a tender spot of pity. And she knows the thickness of blood later when water will not wash out the blood of her crime. This thickness often names the ties of generation that are fast and hold one fast ('thick as blood'). Fast here means slow: we are slowed by what we cannot entirely escape, run away from it as quickly as we might try. A blood tie catches up with us, though we flee it, because as we fly we bring it with us, for it is who we are. Blood lies deeper in our generation than self-consciousness can know lucidly, or will deliberately extirpate. Spilt blood will not let us run away from it, though in being spilt it seems to be poured out like water. But spilt blood congeals and stands in a way water does not. It cannot be poured away, washed away so easily. And then there are other even more seditious equivocities, as the surviving sons of Duncan know, before fleeing. Donalbain: 'Where we are / There's daggers in men's smiles; the near in blood, / the nearer bloody' (II, iii, 141–3).

Temptation and the Equivocity of the Ethos

Consider how *temptation* is at the heart of *Macbeth*. Temptation relates to a *presentiment* of evil, and in respect to the equivocal possibilities of the matrix. It does not quite fit into any simple difference of good and evil in terms of a fixed opposition. Nor does it entirely fit with our self-image as free to set options before us, to assess and judge them, and to choose and act on that basis. Temptation suggests something *prior* to this. To have deliberative power a prior, more confused situation must be mediated. The presentiment of evil arises, but does so with an intimated show of the good. The two seem poured together in an undifferentiated difference, not at all a univocal difference. This is a more primitive, baffling difference, less fixed than flickering in the chiaroscuro of the good, the evil. To be drawn to an undifferentiated difference is surely to be bewitched by a strange type of difference. In the chiaroscuro, we cannot easily set apart what is good from what is not, even though we are entirely energized with respect to this difference. The confused presentiment of equivocal difference in which evil passes into good and good into evil is correlative to the immanent indeterminacy of our desire.

Temptation beckons in an openness to possibility that enjoys its hovering in the confusion of opposites where the evil is tinctured by the good, the good by the evil. 'Fair is foul and foul is fair / Hover through the fog and filthy air'. Temptation is aroused by the lure in the murk. Initially one is indefinitely tempted but not definitely decided. A playing with possibility is savoured. Tempted by a beautiful woman, I do not decide to sleep with her. I am tempted by her, her beauty, by the luring possibility over which I linger. But I have not given myself over. Or rather I am given over to her but given over as not yet given over. I have my foot on the bank of the Rubicon but I do not feel the rush of water swirl round it yet. I *imagine* I have made the step but I have not. Temptation is an imagination of the equivocal good. If I am tempted I still play back and forth between the evil and the good. I want to do it; I do not want to do it. I tell myself, or am told by promptings, to do it; I tell myself, or am told by contrary promptings, not to do it. I am in the in-between of indefinite possibility that in being tempted is also in the process of yet becoming more and more definite, leading towards perhaps a fateful decision one way or the other. The decision may come to be more univocal, but until that point I swirl in the fog of possibility.

This in-between of confused possibility is reflected in the fact that Macbeth *toys* with an act. But he is also *being toyed with*. In *being tempted* the initiative is where one least suspects it to be. One can be the victim of temptation as much as the master. One can be both at once. One could not be tempted did one not acquiesce, yet to be tempted is not quite to acquiesce, yet. One could not be tempted if one were one's own complete master, and yet were one just simply the victim of an external impulse, one could not be tempted either – one would simply be put upon. One is 'responsible' for being tempted, and yet one does not simply choose to be tempted, and hence one is not 'responsible'. Temptation *happens* to me and yet temptation is something I *entertain*, and hence it does not happen, for I am complicit. I am complicit and not complicit in one act that itself is not an act but an active indefinition that entertains the possibility of a definite act. Hence the strange indeterminate in-between character of temptation. Only if the ethos is equivocal, as is our freedom, can we make sense of it.

More, temptation is a toying that experiences itself *already* as an indefinite guilty feeling. I did not go out of my way to be tempted, but I come across the occasion, but then I feel a guilt that seems disproportionate to my indefinite responsibility, responsibility that is profoundly mitigated since what happens to me is just what happens to me. Why then the indefinite guilt? It does not seem to be just due to something outside me. For there is nothing definite to correspond to it as its source or cause. It seems to spring up in me, as if the soil, at a pre-objective and pre-determinate level, were already prepared for a free possibility that properly brings us into the guiltiness of freedom. Embryo freedom is already guilty about itself, because it is the upsurge of open difference that, as it were, violates the stability and unity with self of a more total univocity of being. It is as if the entertainment of evil possibility itself contaminated one. To be tempted is already to be complicit or in the evil, though one has *done nothing* that brings one into the evil. Thus the witches do not simply tempt Macbeth, because *he starts* on hearing their prophecies. He is already in the temptation, before they utter the prophecies, and hence he falls into the temptation more turbulently, as if the utterance by these spectres made real what as yet was just a possibility. The temptation lets the power of a future possibility usurp the thoughts and deeds of the present, and it was so *as if* the consequences of the possible deed were already realized in the present. Temptation enacts a sinister assault on the present, although, since Macbeth himself is an accomplice of the temptation, he is assaulting his own soul in this temptation.

Why is this? Once again we have to say that there are secret recesses of innerness here, an uneasy idiocy at the most intimate ontological level, dormant and awaiting its awakening, as if from a most deep sleep, and we spring up on being awakened with almost a cry or a shout. As if in the sleep one cannot recall one was wrestling with monsters and angels, only to wake and unknowingly know that one has been closer to a source of happiness or horror in sleep. We cry out on coming to waking mindfulness. We cry out because we have come to the shore of articulation and what was compacted into the inarticulateness of innerness, the 'thought whose murder yet is but fantastical', now breaks forth with horror and a sweating helplessness.

Our *bent* for the *forbidden* emerges from equivocity, imposing a difference on the good and the evil. The forbidden seems to fix the difference, but here too fixed univocity breaks down. Why does the forbidden have such a double effect, bringing us to a halt and yet loosing us into a different longing? The forbidden fixes something, yet unfixes something else, makes definite and yet releases the seduction of the indefinite. We have equivocity again, and again we are found toying with the imagined, with what is other as imagined. What is, is released into an imagined otherness, and hence what is, as it is, may in truth be other than what it appears to be. *The appearance is redoubled in itself as a showing* by the release in it of imagined possibilities that peep out in being imagined but which yet keep themselves in reserve, since they remain possibilities. (Think again of the dagger.) This may sound very confusing. *It is confusion* because it is confusing. The expectation of univocity, again in an ironical way, only adds to the confusion.

The happening of temptation, in sum, points to a twilight in-between zone that constitutes the ethos more primally than any univocal fixation, and that outlives all univocal fixations. There is also a more affirmative side of the overdeterminacy of original freedom, divine freedom to do and be the good. Freedom ferments in the equivocal, but a secret love of the unconditional good may also be given a presentiment of its consummation in that ferment. In the seduction of the chiaroscuro, human desire is given also a taste of itself as infinite transcending that transcends itself towards the true infinite; and this like the equivocal ethos cannot be univocally determined or fixed. The truth of the temptation is not the temptation itself, but the release of freedom beyond freedom in the form of temptation. There is a freedom beyond entanglement in the ambiguity of the forbidden. The promise of this is in temptation itself.[13]

Temptation is still the close family relation of bewitchment. In the most intimate innerness, beyond determinate objectification, the monstrous and the divine are together in a confusing promiscuity close to the idiotic origin. Angels and devils mingle, for devils are fallen angels, and hence the fall and the source of divine freedom are promiscuously entwined each around the other. The idiocy of the divine is also the idiocy of the monstrous. Angels and devils are one and the same, for devils are rebel angels, and sometimes seem to twine themselves around each other in an embrace both blasphemous and holy. Blessing and curse come to be equivocal partners in the karma of the equivocal. The idiocy of the monstrous is a shadow cast by light from the idiocy of the divine.

This stirring of an indeterminate opening has the peculiar effect of freeing freedom, but also ensnaring it. For the indeterminacy, while free of determinacy, cannot escape being ensnared by determinacy. But this is not any kind of determinacy, not a neutral determinate thing, void of value, whether alluring or repulsive. Quite the opposite, the intertwining between the divine and monstrous *enchants the determinacy* with an inchoate halo of undefined ultimacy. Put differently, the stirring of our infinite desire is in excess of finite objects but cannot escape finite objects; and its being ensnared by the finite is really its own self-ensnarement. Hence the finite is *never* a neutral entity; it is embraced by the halo of equivocal freedom that wells up with the welling up of the indeterminate opening. The finite object is invested with the enchanting freedom of open desire, which, in being freed to openness, enchains itself to the object because it is chaining itself to itself in the object it can neither escape nor completely surpass. It is ensnared with itself in ensnaring itself in this or that determinate object.

Thus bewitchment is governed by the freedom and snare of the equivocal. Bewitchment is enthralment to an idol. The idol is protean; its name is legion. But in all bewitchments is shown the equivocal confusion of finite and infinite, relative and absolute: the finite infinitized, the relative absolutized, the infinite finitized, the absolute relativized. Bewitchment is the spell equivocal desire casts on itself through its secretion of false doubles of god, that is, of itself as that false double. Desire as equivocal freedom shows the duplicitous power: I finitize the infinite, infinitize the finite. Not that bewitchment is merely 'subjective'. The thing as good is equivocal; its finite goodness (say, political power) lends itself to being a dissembling of the ultimate good; it stands there because of the good, but it also can stand there in the way of the good. In that sense, nothing is absolutely innocent. And when we are freed towards the value of things, the possibilities of duplicity are doubled, redoubled again and again – infinitized. As within this redoubling process, we are bewitched. To be freed beyond this redoubling process is to be beyond bewitchment. Often we think we are thus freed, and who more so than us disenchanted moderns; but this thought, more often than not, is itself bewitched.

Nor is there bewitchment without *seduction*. But who or what seduces us into thinking we have been freed? Seduction too is hydra-headed. Some seductions are cold blooded, some warm enough to deceive even the seducer who feels he loves what he exploits. Seduction entails the *half-truth, the half-lie*. Macbeth learns too late: 'to doubt th' equivocation of the fiend / That lies like truth' (V, v, 44–5). 'And be these juggling fiends no more believed, / That palter with us in a double sense; / That keep the word of promise to our ear / And break it to our hope' (V, viii, 19–22).[14] Seduction is an exploitation of the equivocity of desire; it charms the chiaroscuro in desire itself that does not know what it desires, and yet has an indeterminate presentiment of what it desires. Seduction caresses the doubleness of desire. This doubleness fosters the strong power of the half-truth; for the half-truth speaks to the secret intimacy of the idiot self. The seducer must be a magician to cast his spells on that intimacy of being. The spell rouses a promiscuous amalgam, wherein the seduced does not know, does not want to know, which is which, and what is going on. To be a seducer you have to be extremely discerning; but the discernment is turned towards power over the equivocity of the heart. Seduction is deceit that works through truth, half-truth; is consideration that works through rousal of the vulnerable point in the other; is discernment of both the weakness of the heart in the other, and the mysterious place where a dangerous ardour takes fire. Macbeth, his ambition aflame, is as much seduced by himself as by the weird sisters, and his lady.

Ethical Dialectic and the Karma of the Equivocal

There are traces of an *ethical dialectic* evident in the karma of the equivocal. This is not a Hegelian dialectic. What is this karma? It has to do with being beyond dissolving relativism in the flux of process. It has to do with the fact that ethical potencies beyond our human power are let loose, and let loose through our use of power. Again this is not always easy to grasp for moderns who think of all value as the product of human power, and ethical value as inseparable from our determination and self-determination. There is something more than that, even though its course, and karma, works in and through the intimacies of human power.

And this play has so much to do with the karma of power and its abuse. Is this why the equivocal world of Macbeth reminds one of much in Nietzsche's feeling that being, at bottom, is something to fill the honest man with horror? This horror is especially evident in Nietzsche's *Birth of Tragedy*. I think it is never dispelled in his later work. Hence Nietzsche's need of salutary illusions: we need art to save us from truth, that is, save us from horror. Nietzsche had a feel for the equivocity of being as process of becoming. He might gesture beyond good and evil, but one doubts the hyperbolic claim about the innocence of becoming, unless horror and destruction are also innocent. Nietzsche would like the flux of process to wash being free from moralizing good and evil. What then of the sticky evil? (I will return to the theme of pity below.) Nietzsche will speak of fate. Is this the karma of the equivocal? Not quite. It is the amoral 'thus it must be'. It is not the enigmatic course in time of the good, and not the stickiness of evil, testament to the *incognito* accompaniment of the course of our doings by the good. Such a good forbears to let us keep what we claim for ourselves. Claim we evil for ourselves, the good forbears. The karma is an indirect communication of the forbearance. Nor can we wash the evil out through ourselves alone. We have to renounce it and repent; but that means to stand before another and grant we do not own our being, we cannot claim it. Nietzsche's contempt for the criminal who cannot live up to his deed precludes the possibility of repentance. To live up to the criminal deed is to confound confusion in shunning repentance. It is to lack divination of the forbearance. Repentance is just the recognition that there is something one cannot own, even in the course of our own deeds as owned up to by us: the incognito good that passes along in the karma of the equivocal. The karma of the equivocal is not the innocence of amoral becoming. It points to the offer of the redemption of moral becoming.

The world of *Macbeth* also puts us in mind of a certain kind of postmodernism, broadly in the Nietzschean coven. The all-pervasiveness of the will to power is emphasized. There is a karma of the equivocal here too: will to power devours its others and ends up cannibalizing itself. As Ulysses says in *Troilus and Cressida* (I, iii, 116-24): 'Force should be right; or rather right and wrong, / Should lose their names, and so should justice. / Then everything includes itself in power, / Power into will, will into appetite; / And appetite, an universal wolf, / So doubly seconded with will and power, / Must make perforce an universal prey, and last eat up himself'.[15] In such a world, there is everywhere the inner temptation to tyranny. What resources are there to resist that temptation? If the matrix of being is only, at bottom, will to power and nothing but will to power, there are finally no resources. Resisting the temptation is merely a more *feeble* form of will to power.

This is exactly the form of argument Lady Macbeth brings to Macbeth when he falters to express his will to sovereignty, in despite of his moral scruples. These scruples are 'weaknesses'. As the world of *Macbeth* is one of will to power, leading to tyranny, and marked by a karma which produces the self-evisceration of power, so too one wonders about the ethos of certain postmodernisms. At a certain extreme, relativism finally solicits a recoil against flux and gives birth to monstrous tyranny – itself a counterfeit form of stability in the flux, yet really only the apotheosis of relativism, when now all is relative to the one, the one will of the most devouring centre of wolfish will to power. This must be a simulacrum stability, since its inner core is unstable will to power, in whose instability the karma of the equivocal germinates its restorative seeds. To divine the equivocal need not be to succumb to postmodern relativism or tyranny. If there is a sinister equivocal, there is the restorative power of the matrix, the power of forgiving being that offers good anew. Nietzsche was not diviner enough of these differences.

Remember here also the mastering values that mark the *warrior king*. What would Nietzsche say to Macbeth? That Macbeth failed to be beyond good and evil? But then Macbeth did enact the will to be so beyond, but instead found himself floundering in a morass *between* good and evil. Shakespeare shows us enough to make us recoil from unexpurgated consequences of Nietzschean will to power. Some of the best values of the warrior Macbeth seems to embody when he is *not* king: courage, loyalty and endurance. Macbeth is a study in the equivocities of what I call *erotic sovereignty*.[16] We see him as, so to say, fighting his way to the top, showing some nobility prior to the usurpation, and most certainly strength of character. 'I dare do all that may become a man; / Who dares do more is none' (I, vii, 46-7). That we deal with the *agon* of erotic sovereignty only accentuates the sense of radical evil. *Corruptio optimi pessima:* it is on the heights that the evil is loosed. 'Angels are bright still, though the brightest fell: / Though all things would wear the brows of grace, / Yet grace must still look so' (IV, iii, 22–3): spoken by Malcolm, presented by Shakespeare as the honest, worthy embodiment of sovereignty to come. This very corruption of the best raises most acutely the problem of the *counterfeit doubles*: the original and the image look very alike, but one is evil and one is good, and the evil in its brightness mimics the good. This is policy for Lady Macbeth: 'To beguile the time, / Look like the time ... look th' innocent flower, / but be the serpent under 't' (I, v, 64–67). *Macbeth* is a deep sounding of the powers of doom, latent in the play of the counterfeit doubles.

Strength of character one might have, but perhaps not the final nobility. For this nobility one might have to forgo one's strength: not kill the king who has put himself in one's hospitality. There is a higher strength of forbearance wherein we find, so to say, abdication of the total will to power that tempts and too often bewitches the erotic sovereign. It is not quite that the sovereign abdicates, but that one abdicates from the temptation to seize sovereignty totally, since such total seizure is evil in essence. Lacking the forbearance, we find a turning against pity, as if pity were weak. In this case, it is will to power that is weak: it succumbs to the fatal temptation. Pity is strong, with the forbearance of strength that shows a higher nobility. Macbeth senses this, but he abdicates this higher nobility and takes the 'shorter way' to the summit of erotic sovereignty and so he corrupts this too.

Macbeth prophetically anticipates something of the karma from the outset: 'But in these cases / We still have judgment here; that we but teach / Bloody instructions, which, being taught, return / To plague th' inventor: this even-handed justice / Commends th' ingredients of our poisoned chalice / To our own lips' (I, vii, 7–12). The power of negation, seeming to leap beyond the measure of the ethical, comes back around to haunt the human being who would be the absolute self-mediating instance of power: again the tyrant. After all, Macbeth is a study of a certain tragic logic inherent in tyranny. It is noticeable how, in the later parts of the play, the many references to Macbeth speak again and again simply of 'the tyrant'. There is a metaphysical dimension to tyranny, in that it defines a fundamental comportment of seizure towards the good of being. Thus we find a usurpation of *time*, through a deed which forces the seeds of time to take form in accord with a sinister temptation: a temptation to evil that is an evil temptation, and one is in evil before one chooses to do the evil. There is a usurpation of time in the face of its equivocity ('nothing is but what is not'). One forces the 'not yet', forces the 'is' into accord with my own 'not'. 'That but this blow / Might be the be-all and end-all – here, / But here, upon this bank and shoal of time / We'd jump the life to come' (I, vii, 4–7). This is a usurpation of the process of happening itself. Such a usurpation is already a refusal of our participation in the powers of being beyond our power: ultimate power to be as gift, not as owned.

When Macbeth fails to secure his own security ('To be thus is nothing, but to be safely thus...') and insists on hearing the weird sisters again, his recourse to the powers of hell (as if under 'black Hecate's summons') is saturated with references to time, generation, 'nature's germens', Banquo's line of descendants stretching to the crack of doom and so on. He refuses to accept a 'barren sceptre'. All the ambiguous fructifying powers of nature are tied up with his desire to secure time. All this is concentrated in his will to secure the succession. This is to secure power over the child. This too is shot through with ambiguity, since *pity* is as deeply tied to the child as the line of time and lineal succession. Time does not seem a *pais paidon* to Macbeth. His seizure loses him this play. There is his defection from *patience*, and the patience of time, and this is his metaphysical treason. This brings with it the inversion into a different passivity. Time still is the medium of happening beyond one's will.

It is against the patience of time that Macbeth tries consistently to live up to his crime, and thus secure the future, and supreme power into the future: 'But yet I'll make assurance double sure, / And take a bond of fate ... and sleep in spite of thunder (IV, i, 83ff). Secured by usurpation, this power is inherently insecure; and hence its equivocity is in a state of dialectical dissolution right from the start. This is not the unity of opposites, but the now latent, not open, war, that these opposites create. The seizure continues the opposition and can be only continued through opposition and more seizure; which means Macbeth must again and again secure himself against the inherent insecurity of his position that reasserts itself against him again and again. On the terms of his seizure of the equivocal, the only outcome can be sovereignty in a kingdom of death. For the other as other will always be another opposite, hence a possible threat, and hence to be eliminated. Hence the struggle to the death, which marks the latter parts of the play.

On Macbeth's second visit to the weird sisters to secure time, the sisters deliver equivocal prophecies, which, just as equivocal, can be, and are, turned into the mirrors in which he will see only himself and what he wills. Time will show the pliable half-truth to have been a recessive half-lie, which, in time, will devour the half-truth, and show itself in the service of a more all-destroying falsity. He defies death at the end, but his defiance is really his own surrender to the kingdom of death; for if he must go down, then he will go down fighting and bring others with him also, for nothing has any value now for him.

It seems very hard to find any trace of exoneration or pretext for sympathy or forgiveness. We are shown a kingdom of war governed by a logic of war. The equivocal is dissolved into its warring opposites, set in motion by the will to power of those who would be supreme through the usurpation of governing authority. Certainly Shakespeare drops many hints about the divine source of governing power.[17] These hints serve to contrast the tyrant with the divinely anointed ruler: the ultimate source of power in the kingdom is not the human will to power. Of course, this notion is hard for the 'naturalistically' minded, as is the supernaturalism of the witches, and so forth. Nevertheless, there is an undoubted reference to ultimate sources of power beyond human power in which human power participates. These powers bless as well as curse. But blessing and curse are also a function of how we participate in their reign, how we seek to seize them and claim them as our own; or how we live as we should, namely, finding *ourselves in trust* to these powers, in the exercise of our own power. In the first case, we seek to own the power; in the second, even our own power is not our own. Blessing comes with owning to what is not ultimately our own. Curse comes from usurping as our own what cannot be owned at all, for it is in trust. Curse gives expression to the karma of the equivocal that follows when we cast ourselves out of the trust.

And remember Macbeth early on had a heightened sense of being in trust. 'He's here in double trust...' (I, vii, 12). The double trust is broken, indeed desecrated. The radical evil of the murder is accentuated by the trust of Duncan: 'There's no art to find the mind's construction in the face' (I, iv, 12–13) – pronounced as he faced his immediate saviour who will prove to be his future murderer; and faced him with thanks and the false feeling of security from threat. 'Away and mock the time with fairest show: / False face must hide what the false heart doth know' (I, vii, 81–2). And there is a false heart. All this is no matter of postmodern possibility whose diversity is to be celebrated. Evil is real and roots itself in the most intimate recesses of the false heart. This is the labyrinth of the equivocal at its most enigmatic and elusive. Macbeth's singular will congeals into the evil it has willed. This congealing is just the corrosion of distrust, distrust that cannot be put to sleep. Macbeth has murdered trust and therefore cannot sleep. And on this tormented rack of distrust an appalling Golgotha of destruction will be enacted: suspicion limitless, distrust unloosed, negation without the internal check of trust, and lurching towards its end and its exhaustion in the last death. And as perhaps happens often at the close of tyranny, the mixing bowl of weariness serves to stir one last audacity, limitless audacity in limitless murder that would drag all others with it into the pit.[18]

What of the human being's metaxological condition, our being in the between? Surely this is more than the sinister side of the equivocal ethos, where we can be crushed by excess of evil? Macbeth usurps the middle condition of time. He refuses to live in the *interim*, and will bend the future to his own deed. Implicit in all our deeds, in one sense, is some desire to shape time, or at least participate creatively in its process of unfolding. But with Macbeth the equivocity of the interim is resolved through the force of his will and deed; it is the refusal to let the interim be intermediated in terms of the course of time itself, in its own otherness as a course. I, the one, will be number one: the equivocal prophecy I will read in terms of my surrender to temptation; I will attend to one side of its double-sided message, and will not be patient to the double-speak of its prophecies: I charge it to speak to me, as if univocally. But then the doubleness, initially suppressed, returns to affirm *its justice*, just in its otherness to my will to be the one. The karma has to do with this irrepressible nature of the equivocal. It is not due to me or you or any of us. It is at work in the happening of the ethos or matrix, no matter how we reconfigure or deform that ethos.

Nor can it be fixed, or fixated or substantialized. We are dealing with dynamic potencies of the ethical, and the dynamic sources out of which the most extreme of the ethical potencies in us take shape. These potencies surge out of the deepest and most intimate: the idiocy of being. And they address the highest: here temptation is put to transcending at the level of the erotic sovereignty that will secure itself in an absolute and total way. So too, it corrupts the higher transcending of agapeic service; corrupts also the compassion and pity that go with the patience of time. Thus the karma of the equivocal prophetically hints at the transcendence of the will that wills itself, beyond the enchantment of the will with itself, its being rapt in itself in its seizure of supremacy.

Sticking at Amen

'Peace! The charm's wound up' (I, iii, 37). Is there any *release* from the sticky evil? What could a catharsis, or purgation here mean? Instead of purification, there seems more and more blood. Can we say that *Macbeth* does 'memorize another Golgotha'?

There is too much. 'But this place is too cold for hell. I'll devil-porter it no further': so says the jesting doorman, virtuoso of the sharp comedy of equivocation. Unwitting and with great wit, he stood guard at the gates of hell. But the knocking at the gate is too insistent, even for his wit, as something other demands to break into the claustrophobic closure of the sticky evil. The outside breaks in and reveals the pitiful condition of man, which is to say, its horror.

Aristotle, as we all know, spoke, perhaps too soberly, of pity (*eleos*) and horror/dread (*phobos*). This play, more than most, is *saturated* with horror. With Macbeth we 'have supped full with horrors'. And the pity? Do we pity Macbeth? There is no sympathy for the evil; quite to the contrary, the grisly nature of his crimes is underlined more and more. The murder of Macduff's wife and his children ('all my pretty chickens' – tender words) is perhaps the most searing. 'Did heaven look on, and would not take their part?' Is there some residual compassion for the human being? Perhaps to a degree for Lady Macbeth. Perhaps her breakdown makes her superior; her failure a truer revelation. Or is it that we feel superior to her because she has broken down and so we pity her? Pity is complex. But would we be superior, if we too had not broken down? Would we not then be one trying to live up to the crime? But would this be less a superiority, or more its counterfeit double? And is this what we find with Macbeth? He refuses to break down. 'I bear a charmed life...' Can we finally admire his resoluteness? Does there come a point where he is more to be pitied than hated? *We* may feel that; those under the tyrant do not feel pity. There is dread and the counter negation that would set at naught his power to threaten and destroy.

Nevertheless, pity recurs as a groundswell theme throughout the play. Initially, Lady Macbeth seems to lack pity. This seems more to mark her husband who is 'too full of the milk of human kindness'. What is the main image of pity? A baby. 'And pity, like a naked, newborn baby, / Striding the blast, or heaven's cherubin horsed / Upon the sightless couriers of the air, / Shall blow the horrid deed in every eye / That tears shall drown the wind' (I, vii, 21–5). Pity seems weak and helpless, like a baby, but it is also, paradoxically, elemental and powerful, 'striding the blast'. This second elemental power is hidden to those who would be hard. Do not ask how many children Lady Macbeth had. No matter how many, pity did not transfer from her babies to the king, and indeed to the pitiful condition of Macbeth himself before and after the deed. 'Bring forth men children only; / For thy undaunted mettle should compose / Nothing but males' (I, vii, 73–5). She must kill pity in herself, to pluck the baby from her nipple and dash the brains out, in favour of the deed. In this respect, her will seems initially the stronger will than Macbeth's. Without her will, he could not have willed the deed; though again, his willing has the feeling of a kind of hypnosis, or indeed a kind of sleep-waking: he was not completely in his own waking will, but followed a doom, as a sleep-walker strays from the restfulness of night into its nightmares. Only after the deed does he wake up. Her being awake, and her willing to stifle pity, make it possible for her to screw her courage to the sticking place. 'And we'll not fail,' she says. The karma of the equivocal is in her very success: a disastrous failure is set in motion and she will be the beneficiary of her success in going under into sleep-walking, that will perhaps spare her the agony of wakeful consciousness. The night-time torture of the evil comes over her, and she must sleep walk, as if wandering in an infernal labyrinth.

Note this: Lady Macbeth talks to Macbeth as Nietzsche often talked to *himself* (as also later Macbeth did to the prospective murderers of Banquo): kill pity, become hard, screw your courage to the sticking-place. And what was Nietzsche's great temptation, as he confesses himself? *Pity*. This showed the so-called effeminate will-less will of the Christian altruist who lacked the robust will to power of the superior creators. Nothing was to stand in the way of the higher purpose of these superiors. Pity was the last temptation to be overcome, else such superiors would not be up to the great and perhaps dark deeds they are fated to perform. To be beyond pity would be supposedly to be beyond good and evil. But suppose rather we are always *between* good and evil; tested and agonized no doubt by the equivocal face of the good, and the evil, there; yet called upon to discern the good in the equivocity; and to do it, though the consequences are themselves enigmatically equivocal to us. Least of all can we absolutely secure ourselves in that equivocity. The will to secure ourselves flowers in the most dangerous of ambitions: supreme will to power as our masterdom over the equivocity of the ethos. There are wicked sisters egging us on to this outcome. Nietzsche conjured up his own wicked sisters: they were some of his own legion names. Macbeth and Lady Macbeth in one? And he too went mad. Do not put it down to mere melodramatic gesture when he spoke of the need to descend more and more into evil in order to be creative, to be a superior creator. In one sense he is right: we must descend into the terrifying maelstrom of the equivocal; and this is not unlike the sinister heath, where hideous powers materialize, as if from nothing, and bar one's way. But when we couple this descent with the killing of pity, we surely have a recipe for complicity with the dark powers. Demonic creativity beyond good and evil, evil creativity beyond good and evil, this is the sinister mimicry of the divine. This is the counterfeit double that issues in a 'false creation'.[19]

One may smirk at the Mephistopholean bargain: how Gothic! How Gothic indeed. But look up there and see the gargoyle faces leer out, leer out and from *very high up*. Those gargoyles are *outside* the consecrated temple. But what if I am that temple? (Duncan is 'the Lord's anointed temple'.) I am the ape of God in my most intimate gargoyle soul. To murder the anointed soul would be for the gargoyle self to kill pity in oneself. Without pity we become monsters. Without pity we are devilish.[20] Is this not part of the deep insight in the image of pity as the baby. This is something most elemental. To cease to have pity for the suffering other, we have to stifle it. Nietzsche: become hard! Among other things, pity entails a feeling with, a compassion for, the vulnerable and powerless and helpless other. The baby is the image of this defencelessness. We must care for them, they cannot take care of themselves. So also with those who are old, old like Duncan, or Lady Macbeth's father. Macbeth will not become old: 'My way of life is fall'n into the sear, the yellow leaf, and that which should accompany old age, as honour, love, obedience, troops of friends, I must not look to have.' Pity is inseparable from a form of *restraint*. It reveals an inner measure. Have pity on me! The appeal means: do not exercise your power on me; forbear; hold off. Macbeth did not hold off. And so too he must plot to kill the babies, the children of those who threaten his security on the throne, into the future. Hence the rising panic in trying to kill the son of Banquo. And again this most sickening of murder: the innocent children of Macduff. As Macduff says: 'He has no children. All my pretty ones? / Did you say all? O hell kite! All? / What all my pretty chickens and their dam / At one fell swoop?' (IV, iii, 216–19). Lady Macbeth says: 'The Thane of Fife had a wife. Where is she now? What will these hands ne'er be clean?' (V, i, 45–6).

What Nietzsche says about pity masks evil. It was as if he was never a baby, and would never become old. He was old before his time (the little Pastor) and never aged, frozen in the madness that one fears was the karma of his descent into the equivocal. Nietzsche was afraid: he feared the stickiness of love: feared being limed in vulnerability. Pity before the vulnerable other asks one also to become vulnerable. One becomes a baby again, one becomes old: young before the will that wills itself; old beyond the will that wills itself. Another regal sovereign, old Lear, learns pity, after madness. 'Expose thyself to feel what wretches feel.' Compassion is younger than a child again, older than age. 'In boy, go first. You houseless poverty ... O, I have ta'en too little care of this!' (*King Lear*, III, iv, 25ff).

Images of sleep and peace are here revealing. Macbeth sleeps in the 'affliction of these terrible dreams that nightly shake us'. Better be with the dead, than on 'the torture of the mind to lie in restless ecstasy'; better be with Duncan – 'after life's fitful fever, he sleeps well' (III, ii, 18ff). By contrast, a child secure in love sleeps peacefully. For this there is irrepressible longing. Sleep is an important image connected with rightness of order in the individual and the kingdom.[21] Sleep, 'the season of all natures', has healing power, sleep that 'knits up the ravelled sleeve of care'. Neither the single individual nor the community can sleep when the powers of usurpation are loose. When evil sleeps not, neither does the good, for life is condemned to suspicion and threat. Sleep is also an image of the idiocy of being: it is like the baby or the aged person, or the face of death itself. So also it is a metaphor for the predeterminate and the overdeterminate. It is presubjective, pre-objective: a threshold happening, and yet we are involved. On the threshold dreams appear. These can be apparitions out of the inhuman night: 'subjectivity' is not in control and yet there is here nothing of neutral objectivism. An intimate and idiotic openness appears – a pocket of openness at the dark roots of the soul. It is there too where the predeterminate struggle between powers takes shape. Ways of interpreting dreams are ways of discerning the truth of the idiocy of being. Sleep is also *more* than the determinate. Wiser age, cleansed of bitterness, can be overdeterminate. It rests in peace. Sleep is death, or its double ('shake off this downy sleep, death's counterfeit and look on death itself!'). This too, of course, is equivocal.[22] There is the peace of the good: the sleep of the just. The face of a sleeping man: either the just man composed, or a man dead; or an infant, innocent as a breathing flower. The infant is the peace of innocence before evil; the aged person, who has sought to be good, is the peace of justice not betrayed.

The matter is not just moral good or evil. It has to do with curse and blessing. These are on the boundary between the ethical and the religious.[23] Curse and sleeplessness are connected: 'Sleep shall neither night nor day / Hang upon his penthouse lid; / He shall live a man forbid' (I, iii, 19–21). Curse and blessing, they go together with the death of sleep or the life. In *Macbeth* everything of this is condensed in prophetic form in the immediate deed of murder itself. When it is done, it cannot be undone, and already what is not, is as if it were unfolded. The meaning of patience to the equivocal matrix, and the release that comes with patience, have everything to do with being able to accept blessing and to bless: being able to say *Amen*. Usurpation is the counter-movement to saying Amen. (One fears that Nietzsche was here one of the most confused: mixing up the counter-movement with the saying of Amen, the great yes.) Macbeth is *overcome* by this karma, immediately after doing the deed, and before he has time to harden his will to usurpation. Blood is on his hands, and he is lost in perplexity. He knows he has most need of blessing, but is at a loss as to why he cannot say Amen. Being overcome is superior to being hardened; but being hardened has already happened in the immediate congealing of the evil, shown forth in perplexity at this sticking at the Amen. Something has been decided and its irrevocable nature secretes horror.

He has screwed his courage to the sticking-place, and now the Amen sticks in his throat: 'One cried "God bless us!" and "Amen" the other, / As they had seen me with these hangman's hands: Listening to their fear, I could not say "Amen", / When they did say "God bless us!"' Lady Macbeth: 'Consider it not so deeply'. Macbeth: 'But wherefore could I not pronounce "Amen?" / I had most need of blessing, and "Amen", / Stuck in my throat'. Lady Macbeth: 'These deeds must not be thought / After these ways; so, it will make us mad.' And it is then, still between asking for release of the Amen, and the hardening that will come, that Macbeth cries out in agony about the death of sleep: 'Sleep no more! Macbeth does murder sleep' – the innocent sleep (II, ii, 26ff). To all of this, the matter-of-fact Lady Macbeth can only say: '...The sleeping and the dead / Are but as pictures. 'Tis the eye of childhood / That fears a painted devil'. Yes, but the eye of the child is also more intimate with wonder, and pity and undisguised horror. The dead are not just pictures, and certainly not the murdered. Macbeth is still in touch with the archaic terror of the child, closer yes to the monstrous, but also closer to the divine.

Sticky evil for Macbeth is not a damned spot on his hands, as it will be with Lady Macbeth, but is in the sticking in his throat of the 'Amen'. What can be done when the 'Amen' sticks? Patience we certainly need. But Macbeth lacks the patience to wait. It cannot dissolve, this sticking evil, if he does not repent. But repentance is also giving up his power, the abdication of illicit sovereignty. This he cannot and will not do. So he wills himself forward, and in the flush of warlike activity deadens himself to the paralysis that sticks the 'Amen' in his throat. But here there is, as it were, a hook of consequence that cannot be either swallowed or spat out. And the more one pulls away, the more it sticks and one is torn. The hardened will tries to ride over every resistance that brings to appearance the karma of the equivocal, but the will only enmeshes itself more stickily in that karma by refusing it. For the release of the 'Amen', one has to be willing, but willing itself has to undergo a *metanoia*. None of this happens in the play. Do we end with any promise? Yes, after all, there will be a new king, and the renewed charisma of power. Perhaps we should say: not quite a promise, only perhaps the promise of a promise. For new kings too can betray old promises, and they too await the test of the equivocal, both its charm and its karma. For the hurly burly's never done, and the battle's always to be lost and won.

Notes

1. Lady Macbeth on trying to wash her hands: 'Here's the smell of blood still. All the perfumes of Arabia will not sweeten this little hand. Oh, oh, oh!' The gentlewoman says: 'Heaven knows what she has known' (V, i, 52–5).
2. 'Go get some water and wash this filthy witness from your hand ... go carry them [daggers], and smear / the sleepy grooms with blood' (II, ii, 45–9). 'Smear' is a word of

coagulating, and sticking, and thickening; see below, note 10. Think of the Dutch word for a bribe, '*smeergeld*': such tainted money buys complicity in evil. We say: his reputation was smeared; he was a victim of a smear campaign. Think of what Gerard Manley Hopkins says of the world in his poem 'God's Grandeur': 'bleared, smeared with toil; / and wears man's smudge and shares man's smell'.
3. On the idiocy of being, see William Desmond, *Perplexity and Ultimacy* (Albany, NY: State University of New York Press, 1995), Chapter three; on the idiocy of the monstrous, see William Desmond, *Beyond Hegel and Dialectic* (Albany, NY: State University of New York Press, 1992), Chapter four.
4. By the way, and between ourselves, I too have been visited by the hex of that Scottish play. I had written in pen a very detailed outline of this current paper, and had put it aside until the dread day of deadline, and final submission. That day coming, I sought my text, and astonishingly it had vanished! It was nowhere to be found. My desk had bubbles, even as the air, and into them my paper had vanished. What had I said in *that* piece to merit this curse? I will not contemplate what I bring on my head with *this* paper. And that lost paper was all written by hand and in ink – *red* ink!
5. In *Ethics and the Between* (Albany, NY: State University of New York Press, 2001), I develop more fully the meaning of ethos, as well as the different potencies of the ethical, including, especially relative to the present reflection, the meaning of what I call *the transcending potency of the ethical* (our self-surpassing towards the ultimate) and *the transcendent* (the good that cannot be surpassed). Caught between these two, Macbeth chooses his own sovereignity, as if it were the ultimate, with the result of a grisly corruption of the transcending potency.
6. See William Desmond, 'Autonomia Turranos: On Some Dialectical Equivocities of Self-Determination', *Ethical Perspectives* 5.4 (1998): 233–52.
7. Heraclitus: Zeus is satiety and longing, full and empty: to be spoken and not to be spoken. On being and the equivocal, see William Desmond, *Being and the Between* (Albany, NY: State University of New York Press, 1995), Chapter three.
8. Ibid., Chapter seven.
9. One gets the impression from some descriptions of societies under certain tyrannies that they were bewitched worlds. We find a widespread being in thrall to the spell of, say, Stalin, or Hitler, and also a sinister equivocity that breeds its more and more destructive karma. The more the evil of the charm, the more the charisma of the demonic works its effect. It is very hard to escape the charm, to escape the spell. One thinks of Albert Speer still under the spell of Hitler, even when he knew that what Hitler had made was evil. Martin Heidegger fell under the spell of the charisma of power.
10. Lady Macbeth asks the infernal powers to 'make thick my blood, stop up th'access and passage to remorse'. Her invocation: 'Some thick night...' We feel the thickness in phrases such as 'gouts of blood', 'badged with blood', 'Blood-boltered Banquo', 'Light thickens...' Lady Macbeth becomes 'troubled with thick-coming fancies...' The spell thickens; evil coagulates; one is caught in the stickiness, the more one struggles to free oneself from it. Time, as seeming to be an equivocal process, makes this evident. Blood congeals in the thickness of an evil concrescence.
11. This is Rainer Marie Rilke's phrase in his Third Duino Elegy, where he celebrates the work of the dead in the living.
12. 'Come to my woman's breasts, and take my milk for gall...'; later, 'I have given suck, and know / How tender 'tis to love the babe that milks me: / I would, while it was smiling in my face, / Have plucked my nipple from his boneless gums, / And dashed the brains out, had I so sworn as you / Have done to this' (I, vii, 54ff).
13. That this in-between zone is unavoidable all the way up, as well as down, is suggested by the fact that even Christ was tempted. On these temptations, also with reference to

Nietzsche, see William Desmond, 'Caesar with the Soul of Christ: Nietzsche's Highest Impossibility', in *Tijdschrift voor Filosofie* 61 (1999): 27–61.
14. Very early on Banquo had been startled: 'What, can the devil speak true?' (I, iii, 108). And there is also the foreboding: 'But 'tis strange: / And oftentimes, to win us to our harm, / The instruments of darkness tell us truths, / Win us with honest trifles, to betray's / In deepest consequence' (I, iii, 123–7).
15. See the many images of things unnatural in Act II, scene iv; for instance, Duncan's horses eating each other – unnatural as a king killed by his sons: ''Gainst nature still. / Thriftless ambition, that will ravin up / Thine own life's means' (II, iv, 27–9).
16. See Desmond, *Being and the Between*, Chapter eleven; also Desmond, 'Caesar with the Soul of Christ: Nietzsche's Highest Impossibility'. The theme is most fully developed in Desmond, *Ethics and the Between*, with respect to the potencies of the ethical.
17. See especially the discussion of kingship throughout Act IV, scene iii.
18. How penetrating is Shakespeare in relation to the karma of tyranny. We read of Hitler, when defeats began to mount, blaming his generals, or the people, and others, for failing him. They have failed him, let them go under him, everything must go under.
19. The phrase occurs when Macbeth is rapt before the dagger, and wonders if it is 'a dagger of the mind, a false creation' (II, i, 38).
20. The Nazi lacked pity; many Germans, even Himmler, *must have had to convince themselves* to have no pity: become hard. So elemental is pity that the first visceral reaction, even of Himmler, to the horrific suffering of others is to become sick: this sickness is deeply healthy, but, 'becoming hard', we have to overcome this with a sick health that is evil.
21. See the speeches of the Lord and Lennox in III, vi: freeing the feasts from blood, giving 'sleep to our nights ... all of which we live for now' are coupled with the return of 'swift blessing' to 'our suffering country under a hand accursed'. On sleep, see also my paper, 'Murdering Sleep: Shestov and *Macbeth*', in a volume of papers delivered at the Shestov-Fondane conference on Philosophy and Tragedy, Paris, October 2000.
22. See the double-play with 'peace', when the death of his wife and children is being told to Macduff (IV, iii, 176ff).
23. Seeing and overhearing her sleepwalk, the doctor says of Lady Macbeth: 'More needs she the divine than the physician. / God, God forgive us all; Look after her' (V, i, 78–9).

Chapter 8

Graham Greene's Teilhardian Vision

Darren Middleton

Introduction

A most prolific author, and this despite the fact that he wrote just five hundred words a day, the English Roman Catholic novelist Graham Greene (1904–91) was an elusive, engaging, multifarious man-of-letters who was always trying to navigate the murky borderlands between belief and unbelief.[1] Understanding how and why he was fascinated with this metaphysical territory, an imaginary yet indisputably real landscape that some scholars call 'Greeneland', is virtually impossible. For one thing, in both his life and writings, Greene frequently sent out conflicting signals. Indeed, he would often go out of his way to force his reader-critics to make interpretative decisions on the basis of confusing messages. Unlike some of these commentators, however, I do not presume to offer a detailed map to an understanding of Greeneland. Rather, I propose to examine the way in which a version of *Catholic process theology* makes an appearance in *The Honorary Consul* in the person and work of Father Léon Rivas, the dissident priest of a little port city by the Paraná river in Argentina.

In the sections that follow I outline Father Rivas's allegedly scandalous belief that God is not unchanging and beyond the world, but active in the here and now, and in the process of evolving, with our help, from God's 'night side' to God's 'day side'.[2] Also, I address Father Leopoldo Durán's claim that this 'new theology' – as Greene once called it – is perfectly compatible with the Catholic doctrine of the Mystical Body of Christ.[3] Lastly, while I concede that it is possible to study and enjoy *The Honorary Consul* on its own, without reference to any other text, I suggest that Father Rivas's controversial figuration of God owes a great debt to Greene's private reading of the writings of the Jesuit scientist Father Pierre Teilhard de Chardin (1881–1955), whose Catholic version of process theology was regarded as suspect by his ecclesiastical superiors and only published after his death.[4]

Father Léon Rivas: Priest of the Revolution

Most of Graham Greene's novels have been set in the poverty and the misery of the Third World: *The Power and the Glory* (1940) in Mexico; *The Heart of the Matter* (1948) in Sierra Leone; *The Quiet American* (1955) in Saigon; *Our Man in Havana* (1958) in Cuba; *A Burnt-Out Case* (1961) in the French Congo; *The Comedians*

(1966) in Haiti; and *The Honorary Consul* (1973) in Argentina.[5] For my purposes, the two outside dates in this list are important. Indeed, between 1940 and 1973, many Latin American countries experienced massive social and political change. Several left-wing dictatorships toppled and, over time, the vast majority of Latin American women, men and children became trapped in privation and torture, oppressed by societies ruled by wealthy and powerful elites. Over almost forty years, a number of right-wing regimes emerged and flourished. Furthermore, those few people at the top became determined to keep their power at all costs, even if it meant torture, assassination and 'death squads' for the hapless individuals who dared to oppose them.[6] Speaking to the journalist Michael Menshaw in 1977, Greene comments on the connection between *The Power and the Glory* and *The Honorary Consul* in light of these dramatic changes and brutal realities:

> In a sense, *The Honorary Consul* can be seen as a companion piece to *The Power and the Glory*, a gauge of the political and philosophical distance the world has traveled in the last four decades. Whereas the priest in *The Power and the Glory* overcomes his cowardice and preserves his faith despite the religious persecution of a left-wing military dictatorship, the priest in *The Honorary Consul* becomes a revolutionary and abandons the Church which has allied itself with a right-wing military dictatorship.[7]

During the mid-to-late 1960s, opposition to right-wing governments grew, especially within certain sections of the Catholic Church.[8] Many priests and nuns, inspired by *liberation theology*, spoke out against poverty, exploitation and lack of human rights.[9] A Colombian Catholic priest, Father Camilo Torres (1929–66), summarized his own understanding of this sociopolitical development within Christianity when he confessed:

> I chose Christianity because I believed it to be the purest way of serving my neighbor. I was chosen by Christ to be a priest for all eternity, and I was urged on by the desire to dedicate myself twenty-four hours a day to the love of my fellow-man. As a sociologist I have tried to make that love genuinely efficacious by means of scientific research and technical advances. Analyzing Colombian society I have come to realize that the country needs a revolution in order to feed the hungry, give drink to the thirsty, clothe the naked and provide well-being for the majority of our people. I believe that the revolutionary struggle is a Christian struggle, and a priestly one. Indeed, in the present specific conditions of Colombia, participation in that struggle is the only way men can show love for their neighbor as they should.[10]

Sensing that the Colombian government would annihilate any peaceful protest, Father Torres became a guerrilla. He advocated revolutionary violence to alter the Colombian social system. In 1966 he was shot and killed by government troops in a skirmish. Because he admired Father Torres, Graham Greene 'immortalized' him in the character of Father Rivas; indeed, according to Father Leopoldo Durán, 'there are many biographical details of the guerrilla priest incorporated into his portrait of Rivas'.[11]

One of several moving and convincing characters in *The Honorary Consul*, Father Léon Rivas identifies himself with the poor as Father Torres did. In one scene he addresses Charley Fortnum, the honorary consul of the novel's title, and he describes his frustration towards the Catholic Church, especially his superiors, for failing to address institutionalized violence against the underclass.[12] Extremely reluctant to represent the Church in the *barrio* while the diocesan archbishop enjoys the fat army general's hospitality, Father Rivas eventually leaves the priesthood. He then marries a young woman named Marta, becomes a fearless *abogado*, and begins to stress the need for the people of his community to be given 'liberation'. In doing little to alleviate injustice, Father Rivas declares, the Church has failed to nurture and protect its people. And so, motivated by a compelling obligation to fight against poverty and oppression, Father Rivas abandons the Church, and he sets off in search of a way to create a fairer, peaceful and more just society.

Paradoxically, he attempts to fashion this new social order by engaging in an act of revolutionary violence. Working with a group of dissidents who take orders from a mysterious man known only as El Tigre, Father Rivas sets out to kidnap the American Ambassador in Buenos Aires and to demand certain political prisoners as ransom. Unfortunately, he runs into difficulty when he kidnaps the wrong man – he grabs Charley Fortnum, by mistake – and, as the rest of the novel unfolds, we watch as the local police close in on Father Rivas and the other guerrillas. Although Father Rivas tries to make up for his inefficiency by enlisting the help of Dr Eduardo Plarr, a local physician, Colonel Perez, the remarkably efficient chief of police, eventually catches up with and kills the nonconformist priest. In effect, then, Father Rivas goes the way of Father Torres, the way for all those who dare to oppose unjust authorities.

Before he dies, however, Father Rivas outlines his Catholic process understanding of God and divine action in the world. This *theistic evolutionism* makes an appearance in part five of Greene's novel, when Father Rivas explains his decision to use revolutionary violence to change the social system, and it is to this segment of *The Honorary Consul* that I now turn.[13]

Theistic Evolutionism in Catholic Perspective

Most Christian theologians acknowledge that our opinion of God and the question of what we think about life relate to our sense of the problem of evil and suffering. In part five of *The Honorary Consul* Dr Eduardo Plarr, the physician to the disease-ridden *barrio*, refuses to look at the senseless suffering of the poor and think of God in any other way than as 'the horror up there'. Overwhelmed by the pain and sickness he finds in the slums, traumatized by the incurable conditions that his medical science cannot heal, and now puzzled by the revolutionary actions of his friend, the dissident priest, Dr Plarr rejects a belief in a good God, and he questions the meaning and reason for human existence. As part of his initial response to Dr Plarr, Father Rivas declares 'I am no theologian, I was bottom in most of my classes, but I have always wanted to understand what you [Dr Plarr] call the horror and why I cannot stop loving it.'[14] In my view, there are four important points to Father Rivas's understanding of 'the horror'.

First, Father Rivas appears to believe that some answers to the important questions about life and meaning and God are much too formulaic to be worthy of acceptance. Reflecting on his preparation for the ordained ministry, he turns to Dr Plarr and announces:

> In the seminary... there were lots of books in which I could read all about the love of God, but they were of no help to me. Not one of the Fathers was of any use to me. Because they never touched on the horror – you are quite right to call it that. They saw no problem. They sat comfortably down in the presence of the horror like the old Archbishop at the General's table and they talked about man's responsibility and Free Will. Free Will was the excuse for everything. It was God's alibi. They had never read Freud. Evil was made by man or Satan. It was simple that way. But I could never believe in Satan. It was much easier to believe that God was evil.[15]

Now, Father Rivas's last remark would appear to place him *outside* the permissible bounds of Christian theological speculation. Very few Christians, Catholic or otherwise, would feel comfortable or at ease with his seemingly outlandish suggestion that evil lurks in the heart of God. In their view, the New Testament witness does not support a knavish or sinister deity; rather, the Galilean origin of Christianity shows God to be tender and merciful. However, a close reading of the Bible reveals a scriptural precedent for Father Rivas's theology. The Hebrew Bible scholar David Penchansky claims that there is evidence for a 'theology of negative deity' in the Tanakh. Indeed, he sees an insecure God in Genesis 3; an irrational God in 2 Samuel 6; a vindictive God in 2 Samuel 24; a dangerous God in Leviticus 10; a malevolent God in Exodus 4:24–6; and, finally, an abusive God in 2 Kings 2:23–5. According to Penchansky, 'God in these passages is rough, violent, unpredictable, liable to break out against even his most faithful believers without warning.'[16] In his view, these six narratives 'are genuine expressions of an Israelite sensibility, an Israelite theology, and not primitive holdovers of an earlier, less monotheistic faith'.[17] Assuming that there is continuity between the God of the New Testament and the God of the Tanakh, and assuming that God *evolves* within the pages of the Bible, and in the religious imagination of women and men responsible for composing the Bible in different eras, Father Rivas's theological ruminations do not appear to be all that scandalous after all. They seem to be a part of a legitimate, if admittedly unsettling, biblical faith still in the making. Interestingly, in the briefest of references, Penchansky connects Greene's *The Honorary Consul* to the Yahwist's 'seditious formulation of deity' in Genesis 3.[18]

In any event, Father Rivas's concept of an evil (or an ironic) God scandalizes Dr Plarr, at least in the first instance, and so Father Rivas develops his idea by addressing the concept of divine goodness. In his view, and this is the second point to Father Rivas's theological understanding, good and evil are vital and necessary concomitants within the divine character. Put another way, at any one moment in the divine becoming, God coagulates numerous contradictions within Godself:

> 'I believe in the evil of God,' Father Rivas said, 'but I believe in His goodness too. He made us in His image – that is the old legend. Eduardo, you know well how many truths in medicine lay in old legends. It was not a modern laboratory which first discovered the use of a snake's venom. And old women used the mould on over-ripe oranges long before penicillin. So, I too believe in an old legend which is almost forgotten. He made us in His image – and so our evil is His evil too. How could I love God if He were not like me? Divided like me. Tempted like me. If I love a dog it is only because I can see something human in a dog.'[19]

Concerned to cultivate a theology from and for the grassroots of his small and largely destitute town on the Paraná river, Father Rivas claims that good and evil impulses conflict within God's character. While he believes that the divine is holy, just, loving and good, he also believes that God is volatile, sinister, prone to dark and inscrutable actions. Disturbingly protean, this God fuses good and evil in one and the same divine character. Although it is fairly easy to see how this theology presents the traditional Christian believer with a real problem, Father Rivas insists that belief in an ironic God is the only way to explain the history of social distress in his corner of Latin America. 'I can see no other way to believe in God,' he protests, 'the God I believe in must be responsible for all the evil as well as for all the saints.'[20]

Even so, and this is the third point to his theological understanding, *Father Rivas believes in theistic evolutionism*, which is to say, he believes that a dynamic God interacts with and grounds the complex process of the universe. The idea here is that God is not an eternal, unchanging, unmoved mover; according to Father Rivas, God is the circumambient matrix within which all created actualities live, move and have their becoming. God is the energetic mechanism that propels the creative advance. Because of this belief in theistic evolutionism, Father Rivas entertains and articulates his own version of Catholic process eschatology – a hope that God will one day evolve to the point where it is no longer necessary for God to embody *both* good *and* evil qualities. Confident that the divine is making *progress* in the midst of *process*, Father Rivas announces:

> 'The God I believe in must be responsible for all the evil as well as for all the saints. He has to be a God made in our image with a night-side as well as a day-side. When you speak of the horror, Eduardo, you are speaking of the night-side of God. I believe the time will come when the night-side will wither away... and we shall see only the simple daylight of the good God. You believe in evolution, Eduardo, even though sometimes whole generations of men slip backwards to the beasts. It is a long struggle and a long suffering, evolution, and I believe God is suffering the same evolution that we are, but perhaps with more pain.'[21]

Unconvinced by this seemingly audacious theology, Dr Plarr questions Father Rivas's belief that God proceeds towards perfection, and he ruminates that history itself provides the strongest support for his own supposition that the night-side of God has engulfed the day-side completely.

In response to such forthright scepticism, Father Rivas plays his trump-card, namely, *he grounds his theistic evolutionism in a poetic vision of the Cosmic Christ evolving throughout history*. This is the fourth and final point to his theological understanding. According to Father Rivas, with each valiant act of women and men to mount a step higher in the evolutionary growth of the Spirit, history inches towards the Omega Point, which is the Christic consummation of life's creative advance:

> 'But I believe in Christ,' Father Rivas said, 'I believe in the Cross and the Redemption. The Redemption of God as well as Man. I believe that the day-side of God, in one moment of happy creation, produced perfect goodness, as a man might paint one perfect picture. God's good intention for once was completely fulfilled so that the night-side can never win more than a little victory here and there. With our help. Because the evolution of God depends on our evolution. Every evil act of ours strengthens His night-side, and every good

one helps His day-side. We belong to Him and He belongs to us. But now at least we can be sure where evolution will end one day – it will end in a goodness like Christ's. It is a terrible process all the same and the God I believe in suffers as we suffer while He struggles against Himself – against His evil side.'[22]

Father Rivas is optimistic, and the ultimate aim of his Catholic process theology is human meaning and authenticity. He feels that we have a role to play in God's character development, a contribution to make to the enrichment and enhancement of the divine (as well as temporal) life. Evil actions, such as human conflicts, inequality and social oppression thwart the forward movement of God and the world; by contrast, good and noble actions, such as working for a higher standard of living, for a humane, free, equal society, accelerate the creative process. Hence, we face a challenge; according to Father Rivas, we can live inauthentically, which involves becoming cut off from others, blind to the conditions of their existence, or we can live authentically, which involves working to make life better for the good of all, including God. For Father Rivas, then, *genuine Christian spirituality leads to the salvation of God as well as the transformation of women and men.*

Having made his case for an evolving God, whose experience of the world is incremental, and who remains dependent upon us to assist the forward movement of the divine life, Father Rivas realizes that one important question remains: how is his current revolutionary behaviour, his kidnap of Charley Fortnum, his willingness to murder Britain's honorary consul to Asunción, going to help the evolution of God and the world? His tentative answer, part of a conversation with Dr Plarr, makes full use of the Apostle Paul's theological anthropology, especially Paul's belief that we display both good and evil traits (Romans 7). While Father Rivas admits that carrying and using a gun impedes God's evolution, he insists that an evil God demands evil things. This scandalous theodicy is an interim conviction, however, for Father Rivas believes God will one day emerge victorious, having sloughed off his evil side in favour of the good:

> 'But one day with our help He will be able to tear His evil mask off forever. How often the saints have worn an evil mask for a time, even Paul. God is joined to us in a sort of blood transfusion. His good blood is in our veins, and our tainted blood runs through His. Oh, I know I may be sick or mad. But it is the only way I can believe in the goodness of God.'[23]

The world, Father Rivas believes, will get better, not worse, but only with our and God's help, and so he declares that we are travelling forward, inching ahead, straining every nerve to reach the climax point that will be actualized in Christ.

While there can be no doubt that much of Father Rivas's theistic evolutionism is insightful and challenging, it is not morally precise. The problem with his version of Catholic process theology is that it does not give us a clear sense of how we accelerate human and divine evolution. What if my sense of what it takes to enhance God's development conflicts with another's? This important theological and spiritual question notwithstanding, I now move to consider two extraliterary comments regarding Father Rivas's theology of evolution. In my view, these remarks help to explain what Greene is up to in part five of his novel.

Some Extraliterary Comments

What did Graham Greene hope to achieve with the 1973 publication of *The Honorary Consul*, which eventually became his favourite novel, and what did he want us to see in Father Rivas's theistic evolutionism? The 'intentional fallacy' notwithstanding, I have found answers to these two questions in sources outside the novel itself. For example, in her 1978 *Rolling Stone* interview with Greene, the journalist Gloria Emerson tells us that at one time Greene was quite worried about Father Rivas's apparently scandalous theology:

> Mr. Greene said that he had asked his friend, a Spanish priest who teaches English literature, if he had not found the character of Father Rivas 'a little bit off the rails'.
> 'But he [the Spanish priest] said, "Not a bit of it, not a bit of it – perfectly Catholic, perfectly acceptable"', Mr. Greene said. 'You know, Father What's-His-Name in *The Honorary Consul* had the idea of a night side of God and a day side of God, you know – God's evolution and God as evil. God and the devil are the same person. I invented this for him because he's got to have his theology, as it were, as he had left the church and married. Well, I thought it would probably not be acceptable to the Catholic Church.'[24]

Significantly, Father Leopoldo Durán is the Spanish priest mentioned in the Emerson interview. And according to Father Durán, *The Honorary Consul* is not theologically scandalous; rather, it is 'the doctrine of the Mystical Body of Christ, although expressed in a literary and poetic form'.[25]

Drawing on ideas first mentioned in Pauline and Deutero-Pauline texts, the Catholic Church teaches the cosmic ubiquitousness of the Resurrected Christ (Ephesians 1:10, 22–3; 4:10; Colossians 1:16; 2:9–10; Galatians 4:4; 1 Corinthians 8:6; Hebrews 1:2, 10). And it proclaims Christ as the beginning, the middle and the end of God's desire for our evolving, multidimensional and fragmented world. In Durán's view, we hear an echo of this teaching in *The Honorary Consul*. Here is his thesis in full:

> Graham did not study any systematic theology, but he was an intuitive theologian. In *The Honorary Consul*, Father Rivas speaks of the 'night-side of God' and the 'day-side of God.' According to Greene's priest, there is a continual evolution within God himself, so that 'with our help' the light side of God or Christ overcomes the darkness. In this way, the evil in the world will come to an end. And God or Christ will be total light. This is a brief synthesis of Father Rivas' reasoning.
> Is there a better way of expressing the doctrine of Christ's mystical body? This was what I told Graham and he was very surprised.
> Later, he said in *The Other Man*: 'Well, listen: in *The Honorary Consul* I did suggest this idea, through the guerilla priest, that God and the devil were actually one and the same person – God had a day-time and a night-time face, but that He evolved as Christ tended to prove, towards His day-time face – absolute goodness – thanks to each positive act of men. I thought I had invented a new theology for my dissident priest, so I was a little disappointed when my friend Father Durán told me that this was perfectly compatible with Catholic doctrine.' Graham Greene is so orthodox that he wishes to invent a 'slightly' heretical doctrine for his guerrilla priest, and he doesn't succeed![26]

Father Durán's attempt to connect Greene's fictional priest to a wider, Catholic ecclesial imagination makes sense. In the *Catechism of the Catholic Church* we are told that 'the Church is both visible and spiritual, a hierarchical society and the Mystical Body of Christ. She is one, yet formed of two components, human and divine. That is her mystery, which only faith can accept'.[27] Catholic doctrine teaches that it is in and through the Church that Christ manifests His own mystery as God's desire to reconcile all things back to Godself. Jesus Christ mysteriously and mystically forms His body, his ecclesial field of force, out of those women and men who freely come to Him in response to the good news of the Gospel. Here the Jesuit theologian Karl Rahner links the mysterious, mystical communion of the Church to its primal source, a mysterious God:

> God is present in the church as mystery. God's approach does not dissolve the mystery which God is, but makes the mystery even more inescapably and sharply apparent. As the church realizes itself and becomes more and more what it should be, God, Christ, and the church become more mysterious... Faith and preaching are an ever more ineluctable confrontation with God's mystery, a command to enter into believing and loving communication, a grace-given personal meeting with and transcendence of the formula, sign, or institution. Ultimately the church is not the representative of God's honor and gift of salvation for the affairs of our world. Our very God becomes present for us as mystery.[28]

Women and men participate in the paschal mystery of Christ when the love made manifest in Christ's cross and resurrection finds its way into their lives, into the lives of those whom they serve and into the development of natural creation. In short, the aim of all things is to serve the becoming of God-in-Christ.

When taken together, the Emerson and Durán sources suggest that *The Honorary Consul* is a narrativized form of Catholic doctrine regarding this mystery of humanity's union with God through the crucified and resurrected Christ. In other terms, *The Honorary Consul* is a fictional meditation on Christ *kata pneuma*, the Christ of Spirit, who instantiates the new humanity, the convocation of God, who enacts *le milieu divin*, and who calls us forward to meet Him at the end point of history, transfigured and perfect in His radiant goodness.

While I do not oppose Durán's avowedly Catholic reading of *The Honorary Consul*, I want to conclude this section by registering one important *caveat lector*. While I think it is true to say that Catholic themes pervade Greene's literary fiction, and while I believe it is accurate to say that *The Honorary Consul* is informed by the spirit of Catholic ecclesiology, I also consider it important to recognize that Greene affirms the self-sufficiency of fiction. This is to say, Greene believes that a novel should not be seen as an artfully contrived theological tract, at least not in the first instance, for this would evacuate it of its fictionality. For Greene, novels should be read and appreciated on their own terms. 'What is there in common between writing a novel and writing apologetics?' he asked Marcel Moré in 1949, 'These are two entirely different occupations.' And 'that's what most of the [literary] critics forget,' he remarked to Robert Osterman in 1950, 'they're enthusiastic about the faith but they mix jobs too easily.'[29]

While I have no desire to 'mix jobs', as Greene puts it, I do wish to affirm and build upon Father Durán's observations. To this specific end, I want to suggest that *The Honorary Consul* works, if it works at all, not just because it is aesthetically satisfying, and not just because it trades in *Catholic* ideas, but because it serves as a narrativization of Catholic *process* theology, especially the version of Catholic process theology associated with Father Pierre Teilhard de Chardin, whom Greene read and admired.[30]

Father Teilhard de Chardin's Process Theology

'Talking as a Catholic,' Graham Greene remarked to Israel Shenker in 1971, 'I would argue that Christ was a kind of overpowering expression of the day side [of God] – which was a guarantee that the day side could never be swamped.'[31] Evil will not prevail in history, Greene believes, for the love of God in Christ will work in us, luring us to contribute to the evolution of God and the world. Now, when Father Rivas articulates his brand of theistic evolutionism, I think we are reminded in part of Catholic teaching regarding the Mystical Body of Christ and in part of Father Pierre Teilhard de Chardin's process theology. This is because Father Teilhard de Chardin, like Father Rivas, believes that women and men are the dynamic bearers of an adventurous faith in an unfinished God and an unfinished universe:

> It is through the collaboration which he [God] stimulates in us that Christ, starting from *all* created things, is consummated and attains his plenitude. St. Paul himself tells us so. We may, perhaps, imagine that the creation was finished long ago. But that would be quite wrong. It continues still more magnificently, and at the highest levels of the world. *Omnis creatura adhuc ingemiscit et parturit*. And we serve to complete it, even by the humblest work of our hands. That is, ultimately, the meaning and value of our acts. Owing to the interrelation between matter, soul and Christ, we bring part of the being which he desires back to God *in whatever we do*. With each one of our *works*, we labour – in individual separation, but no less really – to build the Pleroma; that is to say, we bring to Christ a little fulfilment.[32]

A passionate reader of the process philosopher and Nobel prize-winning author Henri Bergson (1859–1941), Father Teilhard de Chardin used his training in science and theology to yoke basic Christian beliefs to central claims within evolutionary thought. His most celebrated texts are *The Phenomenon of Man*, *Le Milieu Divin* and *The Future of Man*, which appeared in his native France from 1955 to 1959. According to Father Teilhard de Chardin, God is One who never stops being born in a world of endless change. To quote from *Hymn of the Universe*:

> Where human holiness offers itself as a means to his ends, God is not content to send forth in greater intensity his creative influence, the child of his power: he himself comes down into his work to consolidate its unification. He told us this, he and no other. The more the soul's desires are concentrated on him, the more he will flood into them, penetrate their depths and draw them into his own irresistible simplicity. Between those who love one another with true charity he appears – he is, as it were, *born* – as a substantial bond of their love.[33]

Father Teilhard de Chardin's Catholic process theology rests on four basic ideas. First, he views and describes life as a complex evolutionary process. Drawn by an enigmatic energy, a pulsating power that serves to fructify the heart of (the) matter, life inexorably moves on. 'Those who look reality in the face,' he insists in *The Future of Man*, 'cannot fail to perceive this progressive genesis of the Universe.'[34] Responding, as did Bergson, to ideas of evolution and progress prevalent at the onset of the twentieth century, Father Teilhard de Chardin asserts that *becoming*, not *being*, is at the base of all things. The world has been, always will be, malleable.[35]

A second Teilhardian idea focuses on God as the vivifying force and ground of the ceaseless processes of cosmic and terrestrial becoming. Father Teilhard de Chardin claims: 'It is in fact God, God alone, who through his Spirit stirs up into a ferment the mass of the universe.'[36] In his view, the unfolding cosmos is the field of divine activity; indeed, the universe is the total environment in which everything is grounded in an energetic God, and where God confers worth upon everything in the overall temporal development. In this quotation from *Hymn of the Universe*, Father Teilhard de Chardin gives powerful and poetic expression to his belief in *God's transcendence-within-immanence*:

> God, at his most vitally active and most incarnate, is not remote from us, wholly apart from the sphere of the tangible; on the contrary, at every moment he awaits us in the activity, the work to be done, which every moment brings. He is, in a sense, at the point of my pen, my pick, my paint-brush, my needle – and my heart and my thought. It is by carrying to its natural completion the stroke, the line, the stitch I am working on that I shall lay hold on that ultimate end towards which my will at its deepest levels tends. Like those formidable physical forces which man has so disciplined that they can be made to carry out operations of amazing delicacy, so the enormous might of God's magnetism is brought to bear on our frail desires, our tiny objectives, without ever breaking their point.[37]

The third feature of Father Teilhard de Chardin's world-view follows from his belief in God and life's dynamic and organic character. Very generally, he believes that evil accompanies all changes and experiences, that our world-in-the-making is, by nature, partially disorganized, replete with physical and moral faults, and that these failures are instrumental in ensuring that evolution proceeds. God stands at the centre of this expanding universe, sharing in its pain and joy, inexhaustibly at work in a struggle against evil:

> In virtue of his perfections, God cannot ordain that the elements of a world in the course of growth – or at least of a fallen world in the process of rising again – should avoid shocks and diminishments, even moral ones: *necessarium est ut scandala eveniant*. But God will make it good – he will take his revenge, if one may use the expression – by making evil itself serve a higher good of his faithful, the very evil which the present state of creation does not allow him to suppress immediately.[38]

Assuredly, Graham Greene shares this Teilhardian emphasis on the messy verities of creaturely becoming. 'I have always been preoccupied with the mystery of sin,' he revealed to Marcel Moré in 1949, 'it is always the foundation of my books.'[39] A novelist who sought to 'illuminate God's mercy' by making use of 'indirect lighting', Greene believes that God grants grace, and thus hope eternal, 'to the most degraded of human beings'.[40] Furthermore, addressing Christopher Burstall in 1968, Greene proclaims that life is a process, a vale of soul-making, and that moral development ought to continue after bodily death. 'I can't believe in a Heaven which is just passive bliss,' he ruminates, 'if there's such a thing as Heaven, it will contain movement and change.'[41]

A fourth and final aspect of Father Teilhard de Chardin's theological imagination is his belief that the 'cosmic Christ' complements and completes the 'historical Jesus'. An intentional and energetic urge, which grounds and cherishes the creative advance, the cosmic Christ beckons nature, history and humanity into an open, stochastic future. Christ the Evolver sanctifies each and every tiny droplet of experience that marks the processes of reality; and, as its culmination, its Omega Point, Christ ensures the final enrichment of the cosmic environment as a whole:

> Since Jesus was born, and grew to his full stature, and died, everything has continued to move forward *because Christ is not yet fully formed*: he has not yet gathered about him the last folds of his robe of flesh and of love which is made up of his faithful followers. The mystical Christ has not yet attained to his full growth; and therefore the same is true of the cosmic Christ. Both of these are simultaneously in the state of being and becoming; and it is from the prolongation of this process of becoming that all created activity ultimately springs. Christ is the end-point of evolution, even the *natural* evolution, of all beings; and therefore evolution is holy.[42]

In Teilhardian Catholic process theology, the cosmic Christ is the basic source of unrest in the evolutionary process. Christ the Evolver is the ground of the dissatisfaction which women and men feel as they evaluate their previous accomplishments, as they become aware of novel, intrinsically good possibilities, and as they strive to actualize them. Christ-Omega is at work in our relational, ongoing world:

> It is God himself who rises up in the heart of this simplified world. And the organic form of the universe thus divinized is Christ Jesus, who, through the magnetism of his love and the effective power of his Eucharist, gradually gathers into himself all the unitive energy scattered throughout his creation... Christ *binds* us and *reveals* us to one another.[43]

Writing in his *Jesuits: A Multibiography*, the journalist and author Jean Lacouture suggests that Father Teilhard de Chardin's evocative reflections on God-in-Christ are 'likelier to fascinate poets ... than the old gents of the Roman Curia'.[44] Assuredly, Greene is one of many poets, or creative writers, who champion Father Teilhard de Chardin's notion of the Omega Point. Indeed, Greene's autobiography, the widely-acclaimed *A Sort of Life*, confirms his fascination for this French Jesuit's belief that Christ pervades all things.[45] And of course, it scarcely needs remarking how closely the four aforementioned ideas – especially the last one about the cosmic Christ – stand in relation to Father Rivas's Catholic process theological vision. Like Father Teilhard de Chardin before him, Father Rivas believes that God in Christ is a part of the genesis, the growth and the consummation of the cosmos, is its Shepherd and Animator, and is actively involved in the world and affected by events in it, sometimes to the point of suffering its many evils and numerous imperfections.

For Father Teilhard de Chardin, as for Father Rivas, God is bound up with the cosmos and cannot be isolated from it. In their view, God voyages with us in the temporal world, which implies that the future is the future for God, not only for us. But what of this indeterminate future? Where will it all end? Here Father Rivas and

Father Teilhard de Chardin appear to be of one accord, namely, they believe that Christ's mystical body irresistibly pervades and evolves within our world; therefore salvation, for God as for humanity, is gradual and not one exclusive feat. In the words of Father Teilhard de Chardin:

> Christ – for whom and in whom we are formed, each with his own individuality and his own vocation – Christ reveals himself in each reality around us, and shines like an ultimate determinant, like a centre, one might almost say like a universal element. As our humanity assimilates the material world, and as the Host assimilates our humanity, the eucharistic transformation goes beyond and completes the transubstantiation of the bread on the altar. Step by step it irresistibly invades the universe. It is the fire that sweeps over the heath; the stroke that vibrates through the bronze... *In Christo vivimus, movemur et sumus*.[46]

Similarly, Father Rivas declares:

> I think sometimes the memory of that man, that carpenter, can lift a few people out of the temporary Church of these terrible years, when the Archbishop sits down to dinner with the General, into the great Church beyond our time and place, and then ... those lucky ones ... they have no words to describe the beauty of that Church ... But now at least we can be sure where evolution will end one day – it will end in a goodness like Christ's.[47]

So, for both figures, one historical and one fictional, Christ reveals Himself gradually, minute by painful minute, instantiating Himself in the cosmos, and especially in our lives, fructifying us with a mood and a desire for that which is enrichingly novel, namely, empowering love, and all the time completing Himself in the sum of our creative endeavours. All our noble actions are like prayers to an evolving God, to the day-time deity, to the goodness of the divine.[48] Whereas Greene's Father Rivas uses the phrase 'God's day-time face' to refer to the Christic consecration of creation, Father Teilhard de Chardin speaks of the 'Omega point'.

Concluding Remarks

While I concede that it is possible to read and enjoy *The Honorary Consul* on its own terms, without reference to any other text, I nonetheless believe there are significant grounds for treating Graham Greene's novel as a literary meditation on Teilhardian Catholic process theology. With a little help from Father Leopoldo Durán, I have demonstrated that Father Rivas is a model Catholic because he asserts that Christ works to incorporate sinful humanity into His Mystical Body. More importantly, perhaps, I have made my own contribution to the history of criticism surrounding Greene's novel by suggesting that Father Rivas is a process theologian, even a Teilhardian process theologian, because he asserts that the world is in the process of evolution, and Christ is completing himself within it: *En pasi panta Theos* (1 Corinthians 15:26–8).

Notes

1. The Harry Ransom Humanities Research Center, The University of Texas at Austin, Texas, USA, houses many drafts of *The Honorary Consul*, beginning with handwritten notes and an autograph manuscript (1970). They also have the first to fifth typescripts (1970–72), the final typescript (1972), and galley and page proofs (1973). The proofs and drafts contain autograph corrections. They also own at least thirty copies of the novel, most of them being translations. I travelled to Austin to consult these many drafts during the Fall of 1999. Here I wish to thank Steve Lawson, Intern, Office of the Research Librarian (HRHRC), for his invaluable assistance.
2. Graham Greene, *The Honorary Consul* (Beccles, UK: Book Club Associates, 1973), 284–7. The provocative theology at the heart of this novel may be traced to one of Greene's dreams. See Graham Greene, *A World of My Own: A Dream Diary* (New York: Viking Penguin, 1994), 59–60.
3. Leopoldo Durán, *Graham Greene: An Intimate Portrait by His Closest Friend and Confidant* (San Francisco, CA: HarperSanFrancisco, 1994), 94–116.
4. For an excellent biography of Father Pierre Teilhard de Chardin, see Ursula King, *Spirit of Fire: The Life and Vision of Teilhard de Chardin* (Maryknoll, NY: Orbis Books, 1996).
5. For commentary on the international aspect of Greene's fiction, see Maria Couto, *Graham Greene: On the Frontier. Politics and Religion in the Novels* (New York: St Martin's Press, 1988), 111–44.
6. Eduardo Galeano documents the recent (and past) history of this part of the world. See Galeano, *Open Veins of Latin America: Five Centuries of the Pillage of a Continent* (New York: Monthly Review Press, 1973). Also see Martha K. Huggins, editor, *Vigilantism and the State in Modern Latin America: Essays on Extralegal Violence* (New York: Praeger Press, 1991). Finally, see Carlos H. Waisman, *Reversal of Development in Argentina: Postwar Counterrevolutionary Policies and Their Structural Consequences* (Princeton, NJ: Princeton University Press, 1987).
7. Henry J. Donaghy, editor, *Conversations with Graham Greene* (Jackson, MS: The University Press of Mississippi, 1992), 99.
8. The 1968 conference of Latin American bishops (Medellín, Colombia) is the most famous example of churchly resistance during this period. Alarmed by institutionalized violence, by structural sin, the bishops emphasized the urgent need for the people to be granted social and political emancipation ('liberation').
9. Liberation theology became enormously popular in the months and years following the 1968 Medellín conference of bishops. A largely Catholic movement, liberation theology emphasizes the biblical call to fight injustice and oppression. Drawing on the proclamations of the eighth-century Hebrew prophets as well as the life and message of Jesus of Nazareth, liberation theologians seek to alleviate poverty, to call for change and to stress the need for freedom from military dictatorships and wealthy power elites. While there are many books on the origins, nature and scope of liberation theology, I recommend Christopher Rowland, editor, *The Cambridge Companion to Liberation Theology* (Cambridge: Cambridge University Press, 1999). Interestingly, in a 1988 interview with Maria Couto, Greene feigns ignorance of liberation theology. 'I am not a theologian,' he declares, 'but if it [liberation theology] means that the priests are allowed to play their part in politics in defense of the poor then I'm all for it.' See Couto, *Graham Greene: On the Frontier*, 213.
10. Cited in Walter J. Broderick, *Camilo Torres: A Biography of the Priest-Guerrillo* (Garden City, NY: Doubleday and Company, 1975), 254.
11. Durán, *Graham Greene: An Intimate Portrait*, 74. It is worth noting that Father Durán

writes this in spite of Greene's second thoughts, expressed in Greene's 1988 interview with Maria Couto. See Couto, *Graham Greene: On the Frontier*, 214–15.
12. Greene, *The Honorary Consul*, 143–4.
13. I am indebted to the work of David Griffin for the term 'theistic evolutionism'. See his *God and Religion in the Postmodern World: Essays in Postmodern Theology* (Albany, NY: State University of New York Press, 1989), 80–82. Here Griffin uses 'theistic evolutionism' to describe his own theological position, which is informed by Whiteheadian and Hartshornean process metaphysics, and yet I am using it to extend its meaning; as will I hope, become clear, I believe 'theistic evolutionism' summarizes a position that links Father Rivas and Father Pierre Teilhard de Chardin.
14. Greene, *The Honorary Consul*, 283.
15. Ibid., 284. An early typescript of this novel has Father Rivas complain that his seminary professors talked of the 'Beatific vision' only. On page 274 of the novel's third typescript, Greene instructs his secretary to omit this reference.
16. David Penchansky, *What Rough Beast?: Images of God in the Hebrew Bible* (Louisville, KY: Westminster John Knox Press, 1999), 1–2.
17. Ibid., 1. Interestingly, Penchansky's observations may be compared with the work of the Pulitzer prize-winning author Jack Miles. His *God: A Biography* (New York: Random House, 1996) offers a literary reading of the Tanakh, treating God as an evolving character in a complex narrative, and Miles concludes that God is a kind of cosmic Hamlet: tormented, divided and dangerously unpredictable (408).
18. Penchansky, *What Rough Beast*, 19. It is worth adding that Greene's characterization of an ironic God appears throughout his so-called 'Catholic novels'. For instance, the nameless Catholic priest in *Brighton Rock* declares – to Rose, Pinkie's girlfriend – that no one can conceive 'the appalling strangeness of the mercy of God'. See Graham Greene, *Brighton Rock* (New York: Alfred A. Knopf, 1993), 297. Furthermore, God appears to use underhand tactics to secure Sarah Miles's love in Greene's *The End of the Affair*. See Graham Greene, *The End of the Affair* (London: Penguin Books, 1951), 67; 70–73. Finally, I have addressed this provocative figuration of God elsewhere. See Darren Middleton, 'Graham Greene's *The End of the Affair*: Toward an Ironic God', *Notes on Contemporary Literature* 29.3 (1999): 8–10.
19. Greene, *The Honorary Consul*, 284. The sentences 'divided like me' and 'tempted like me' do not appear in early drafts of the novel; Greene inserts them in the third typescript. Assuredly, these sentences point up Greene's awareness of the anthropological conditioning of theological understanding.
20. Ibid., 285.
21. Ibid.
22. Ibid., 285–6. The arresting phrase 'the Redemption of God' is not added until the second typescript. In addition, I view the early drafts of *The Honorary Consul* as decidedly more Christological than the final version. On page 271 of the second typescript, for example, Father Rivas declares that Christ is 'someone of perfect goodness', and that Christ's Incarnation, the point at which eternity touched time, caused the day-side of God to become 'invulnerable'. On page 276 of the third typescript, Greene instructs his secretary to remove these remarks. Returning to the second typescript, page 271, Father Rivas says that 'the degree of Christ's goodness was so great, his intention was so perfect, that the night-side now can never win more than a temporary victory here and there'. Finally, Father Rivas declares that 'at least we can be sure now where evolution ends – it ends in Christ'. In the fourth typescript, page 276, Greene alters the last sentence to read '… it will end in a goodness like Christ's'. This is a small but not insignificant difference.
23. Greene, *The Honorary Consul*, 286–7.
24. Cited in Donaghy, *Conversations with Graham Greene*, 129.

25. Durán, *Graham Greene: An Intimate Portrait*, 239.
26. Ibid., 111.
27. *Catechism of the Catholic Church* (New York: Doubleday, 1994), 223–4.
28. Cited in Geffrey B. Kelly, editor, *Karl Rahner: Theologian of the Graced Search for Meaning* (Minneapolis, MN: Fortress Press, 1992), 264.
29. Donaghy, *Conversations with Graham Greene*, 26, 32.
30. See A.F. Cassis, editor, *Graham Greene: Man of Paradox* (Chicago: Loyola University Press, 1994), 425.
31. Ibid., 215–16.
32. Pierre Teilhard de Chardin, *Le Milieu Divin: An Essay on the Interior Life* (London: Collins, 1960), 62.
33. Pierre Teilhard de Chardin, *Hymn of the Universe* (New York: Harper and Row, 1965), 119.
34. Pierre Teilhard de Chardin, *The Future of Man* (New York: Collins, 1964), 13.
35. Ibid., 12–13.
36. Pierre Teilhard de Chardin, *Hymn of the Universe*, 79.
37. Ibid., 84.
38. Pierre Teilhard de Chardin, *Le Milieu Divin*, 86.
39. Donaghy, *Conversations with Graham Greene*, 17.
40. Ibid., 18.
41. Ibid., 62.
42. Pierre Teilhard de Chardin, *Hymn of the Universe*, 133.
43. Ibid., 119.
44. Jean Lacouture, *Jesuits: A Multibiography* (Washington, DC: Counterpoint, 1995), 427.
45. Graham Greene, *A Sort of Life* (Harmondsworth, UK: Penguin Books, 1971), 120.
46. Pierre Teilhard de Chardin, *Le Milieu Divin*, 125–6.
47. Greene, *The Honorary Consul*, 276, 286.
48. Father Rivas expresses this idea on page 299 of the third typescript for *The Honorary Consul*. He asserts that 'prayer is a part of our evolution'. Curiously, Greene omits this evocative notion from later drafts of his novel.

Chapter 9

Nikos Kazantzakis, Bergson and God

Daniel A. Dombrowski

Introduction

At least since the seventeenth century with Spinoza's critique, the traditional conception of God in the Abrahamic religions (Judaism, Christianity and Islam) has been in retreat. Despite the turbulent relations among Jews, Christians and Muslims, religious believers in these traditions have generally had the same concept of God in mind when they declared their beliefs. God in the Abrahamic faiths has generally been seen as an immutable being outside of time who is omniscient, omnipotent and omnibenevolent, and hence, as a consequence of these exalted attributes, was only with difficulty, if at all, amenable to accurate description by human beings. Further, it was held, God created the world through a free act of will: the world needs God but God could have done just as well without the world.

There are two problems in particular with this traditional concept of God, problems that have contributed to the attenuated place of spiritual concerns in modern life, in contrast, say, to the place of such concerns in the lives of people in the Middle Ages. It is significant that Nikos Kazantzakis struggled with these problems throughout his life and that he developed a view of God that he thought was superior to the traditional one, a view of God that, at the very least, deals with these two problems better than the traditional view of God deals with them.

The first problem concerns theodicy, the difficulty of reconciling belief in the existence of God with the obvious evil that exists in the world. Put simply, if God is all-powerful, God *could* eliminate all of the evil in the world; if God is all-good, God *would* eliminate all of the evil; and if God is all-knowing, God would *know how* to eliminate all of the evil. But evil exists, as Kazantzakis well knew, hence, to his way of thinking, either there is no God, or, if there is a God, this being is quite different in some respects from the being identified as God in the traditional view of the Abrahamic religions. Kazantzakis's antipathy to the traditional view of God in the Abrahamic religions often leads him to give the impression that he does not believe in God, but a more defensible view is that Kazantzakis *does* believe in God, but what he means by 'God' is something that is very often heterodox from the traditional point of view.

However, the heterodox nature of Kazantzakis's theism can be, and often has been, exaggerated. His Christology *is* heterodox from the perspective of traditional Christianity, as the uproar created by the film version of *The Last Temptation of Christ* indicates. But his view of *God* is a peculiar combination of heterodox, or partially heterodox, views that grow out of solidly orthodox concerns and sources.

The second problem is that regarding human freedom. Specifically, the problem is the following: if God is omniscient, God knows everything that will occur in the future with absolute assurance and in minute detail; but if God has such knowledge, it is difficult, if not impossible, to see how human beings could be free, for if God has such knowledge, then human beings *must* do what God knows they will do, and hence they would not be free. Even if God does not physically compel human beings, if God is omniscient in the aforementioned strong sense, they are nonetheless logically compelled to do what God knows they will do. Even if a human being decides to fool God, the omniscient mind of God would know beforehand that the human being would try to do this.

But human freedom is a non-negotiable item in Kazantzakis's view of ultimate reality and meaning. Hence God for him could not have the properties traditionally found in the Abrahamic religions. That is, Kazantzakis's God does not have all three attributes – omnipotence, omniscience and omnibenevolence – because a God with all three of these attributes, as Kazantzakis sees things, would be at odds with the presence of evil in the world and with the presence of human freedom. It is omnipotence that is especially criticized by Kazantzakis. And it should be noted that only a partial solution, at best, to these problems is offered if one accounts for the existence of suffering in terms of a misuse of human freedom in that only a fraction of suffering is due to moral evil; and to say that God *wants* us to suffer is to turn God into a sadist. The fact that Kazantzakis's God is not a sadist perhaps indicates that in *some* sense his God is omnibenevolent. If a being does not have all three of the aforementioned attributes, however, 'How can it be God, the greatest conceivable being?', it will be asked. It will be one of the aims of this chapter to respond to this question.[1]

Life and Major Writings

Kazantzakis was born on 18 February 1883 in Iraklion, Crete, then still part of the Ottoman Empire. His stern father became the model for Kapetan Mihalis in the novel, *Freedom or Death*. During a rebellion against the Turks, young Nikos was sent to safety to the island of Naxos, where he attended a French school run by Franciscans. In 1902 he went to Athens to study law, but even before he received his law degree he published the essay, 'The Sickness of the Age' and the novel, *Serpent and Lily*. And his play 'Day Is Breaking' stirred a controversy in Athens that made Kazantzakis instantaneously (in)famous. He would remain controversial among Greek political leaders and Greek Orthodox religious leaders for the rest of his life.

In 1908 a decisive moment in Kazantzakis's life occurred when he went to Paris to attend lectures by the man who was at that time the most important philosopher in Europe, the process thinker Henri Bergson – a Jew who eventually converted to Catholicism. While in Paris, Kazantzakis worked as a journalist and he continued to read Friedrich Nietzsche, from whom he learned to be sceptical of traditional religion. But it was Bergson who provided Kazantzakis with clues as to how to develop a positive view of God that responded to his questions regarding ultimate reality and meaning and that enabled him to reconcile his spiritual concerns with Darwinian dynamism. In fact, in 1914 he spent forty days at the Holy Mountain, Athos, where he dreamed of actually founding a new religion.

In 1917 Kazantzakis linked up with a workman named George Zorbas; this experience provided the material for the novel *Zorba the Greek*, which was written over a quarter-century later. After World War I, Kazantzakis was named director of a mission to repatriate 150 000 Greeks who were being persecuted by the Bolsheviks in the Caucasus, an experience that provided the material for his later novel *The Greek Passion* (in Britain, *Christ Recrucified*).

Kazantzakis abandoned nationalism in the 1920s, however, after Greece's defeat by the Turks in the 'Asia Minor disaster'. But he became very much interested in Russian communism and later in Italian and Spanish fascism. (His political views are detailed and analysed in Peter A. Bien's magisterial book, *Kazantzakis: Politics of the Spirit*.) Also in this decade Kazantzakis travelled to Austria, Germany, Italy (where he continued a lifelong discipleship to St Francis), Egypt, the Sinai, Czechoslovakia, Spain (where he wrote movingly about St Teresa of Avila) and the Soviet Union. It is not surprising, given these travels, that he also started work on his monumental poem *The Odyssey: A Modern Sequel*.

Much of Kazantzakis's literary output came in the form of travel books (for example, *Spain*, *England*, *Russia*, *Japan–China*, *Journey to the Morea* and *Journeying*) and translations that dealt with the places where he lived and the languages spoken there; most of his life was spent outside Greece. For example, his *The Saviors of God: Spiritual Exercises* was written in German-speaking lands. The title to this religious programme is interesting because it captures both the 'neo' and the 'classical' dimensions of his neoclassical, process theism; he clearly has St Ignatius of Loyola in mind in this title as well as his own belief that human beings help to keep the divine struggle alive. And as a literary exile he could not help but notice his similarity to the previous Greek exile, El Greco; in fact, Kazantzakis's own autobiography is titled *Report to Greco*.

Throughout the 1930s and 1940s Kazantzakis continued to work on many writing projects and to intermittently re-enter politics; by 1945 he was interested in uniting all of the splinter groups of the Greek, non-communist left. Also in that year he married Helen Samiou, whom he had known since the 1920s and who became a cherished partner for the rest of his years. (A first marriage in 1911 was not so happy.) His work became well enough known for him to be nominated (several times) for the Nobel Prize in Literature, although he never won the prize.

Kazantzakis died on 26 October 1957, at the age of 74. But it was not until the last decade of his life that his most famous works, his novels, were either published for the first time or translated into languages other than Greek. Hence much of what Kazantzakis is known for today is due to this last period in his life, which he largely spent in Antibes in France. These works include *Saint Francis*, *The Last Temptation of Christ*, *Zorba the Greek*, *The Greek Passion*, *The Fratricides*, *Freedom or Death* and *Report to Greco*. The spiritual intensity of these works led Albert Schweitzer to say that no author affected him so profoundly as Kazantzakis.

However, the Pope and Greek Orthodox leaders were not as impressed with his work, which they condemned. His death was caused by an epidemic of Asian flu; he became a victim of this epidemic while travelling in China. (He was also a lifelong admirer of the Buddha.) The Greek Orthodox Church refused to allow his body to lie in state. He is buried in Iraklion, however, with the following words inscribed on his tomb: '*Den elpizo tipota. Den fovumai tipota. Eimai eleftheros*'. (I hope for nothing. I fear nothing. I am free.)

The Bergsonian Background

Kazantzakis learned from Bergson that the intellect deals with the world by means of discrete units, as though reality were fundamentally static and immobile. The intellect does this because it apprehends the world externally as a collection of things in space. Living beings, however, exist durationally, they become. Life's flow is asymmetrical and irreversible in that the past is settled, whereas at each moment one is always straining towards a future that is at least partially indeterminate, and often largely so.

Bergson, like Kazantzakis, wavers between saying that the intellect, because of this defect, is helpful but needs to be supplemented by intuition or instinct, on the one hand, and suggesting that intellect is necessarily dissembling and should be thwarted, on the other. The former, I think, is the more plausible interpretation to take regarding these two writers. In any event, Kazantzakis follows Bergson in the belief that reality, including divine reality, is better known intuitively or instinctively rather than discursively. For example, Aristotle's view of the gods as *unmoved* movers, a view that very much influenced traditional theism in the Abrahamic religions, is defective precisely because it is overly intellectual.

Bergson is most famous for his view that there is an *élan vital* driving life, including divine life, to ever higher levels of organization. Intellect translates the *élan vital* into mechanical terms. Or better, to use an image from Bergson quoted by Kazantzakis: the vital impulse is like a jet of steam spurting continually into the air, condensing into myriad drops that fall back to the source. The drops represent the purely material aspect of the universe against which the *élan vital* wages the continual warfare apotheosized by Kazantzakis. It is the summit of the jet with which Kazantzakis is often concerned and which he also divinizes. Matter, by way of contrast, is seen as devitalized life. That is, if God is not omnipotent – and this on the evidence of there being evil in the world – then there is no reason to believe that there was a creation of matter *ex nihilo,* nor is there reason to believe that there will be an apocalypse: continual (Odysseus-like) struggle is the rule! Suffering disproves the existence of an *omnipotent* God even if it does not disprove the existence of *God*, for Kazantzakis. Among the following three prayers, Kazantzakis's favourite was the third: 'Lord, bend me, or else I shall rot. Lord, do not bend me too much, for I shall break. Lord, bend me too much.'[2]

Both Bergson and Kazantzakis were exhaustively bothered by the immobility of the traditional God, a product of analysis rather than of religious experience or of biblical exegesis, and they were both animated by divine mobility. Divine immobility is the extreme limit of slowing down the movement of God as one would a motion picture so as to be left with a single, static frame. Kazantzakis repeatedly attempts to speed up the frames so that the divine process would be restored. What is called eternity is not the substratum for change so much as it is an abstraction away from living process. Eternity is movement stripped precisely of its mobility; it is death.

A divine *life* without end is perhaps better termed an everlasting or sempiternal life, rather than an eternal one.

The saints of Christianity, the sages of Greece, the prophets of Israel, the bodhisatvas of Buddhism are those who allow human beings to carried beyond mechanism; they appeal to us precisely because of their perfect aspiration, if not their perfect morality and spirituality. Bergson reinforced Kazantzakis's belief both that much of what existed, and had for some time existed, in organized religion was, for lack of a better word, bunk, *and* that the very topic of God was a significant one – the most significant one! – that needed contemporary rethinking. Organized religions are important, but primarily to the extent that they preserve the classics in the history of religious experience that make this rethinking possible and to the extent that they provide the spark for one of its members to be touched by the inwardness of the tradition. The word 're-form', after all, presupposes form.

It should be noted that at the heart of the Abrahamic religions lies an Eastern restlessness, a Jewish battle to upset ceaselessly the balance that is the goal of those who have inherited from the Greeks the tendency to harmonize opposite forces. In this regard Kazantzakis's theism very much resembles Christianity in general: a peculiar combination of this Hebraic restlessness with a Greek sense of harmony. This is his 'Cretan Glance' wherein one eye is on Asia and one on Europe. From the very start Christianity has exhibited this peculiar mixture. Kazantzakis's thoroughly Bergsonian way of describing the tension here is as follows:

> I could clearly feel the two great torrents struggling within me: the one pushes toward harmony, patience and gentleness. It functions with ease, without effort, following only the natural order of things. You throw a stone up high and for a second you force it against its will; but quickly it joyfully falls again. You toss a thought in the air but the thought quickly tires, it becomes impatient in the empty air and falls back to earth and settles with the soil. The other force is, it would seem, contrary to nature. An unbelievable absurdity. It wants to conquer weight, abolish sleep, and, with the lash, prod the Universe upward.[3]

That is, immortality, for Kazantzakis (and here he partially departs from Bergson), does not consist in the soul leaping up to heaven without the body, but rather it consists in making the most out of the single instant at our disposal. Here Kazantzakis relies on intellect rather than on instinct. He is no more opposed to intellect (or the West) than Bergson; rather he is interested in putting it in its proper place. What bothers both of them is a hegemonic intellect that crowds out (eastern) mysticism: 'We can deny neither East nor West.'[4] Indeed, one of the familiar criticisms of Kazantzakis by literary critics is that he is *too* philosophical (that is, too western).

The Cry Passage

Kazantzakis's Bergsonian opposition to reification of the spiritual life, and his opposition to reification of God, means that at times we should be shaken – forcefully shaken – out of our complacency when reification begins, when the divine film starts slowing down to the point where we can imagine it a snapshot. The 'Cry' of God serves as a call forward to new possibilities, some of which may in fact strike us as terrifying. For example, in order to show 'forgetfulness' of self we might be asked to kiss a leper, as was St Francis. Each of us, at least some of the time, and perhaps most of the time, wants to continue essentially as we are, and it is this security that is shattered by the Cry. But our response to the Cry is for the sake of some things that are good for us: life *in extremis*, heightened consciousness, expanded freedom and, in some cases, more extensive and sensitive love. As John Cobb has emphasized, however, the way to these often lies through the valley of the shadow of death. Bergson's God of love and Kazantzakis's dark divinity do not contradict each other; rather, they are mutually reinforcing correlatives. This passage from *Report to Greco* is worth quoting at some length:

> Christ's every moment is a conflict and a victory. He conquered the invincible enchantment of simple human pleasures; He conquered every temptation, continually transubstantiated flesh into spirit, and ascended. Every obstacle in His journey became an occasion for further triumph, and then a landmark of that triumph. We have a model in front of us now, a model who opens the way for us and gives us strength.
>
> Blowing through heaven and earth, and in our hearts and the heart of every living thing, is a gigantic breath – a great Cry – which we call God. Plant life wished to continue its motionless sleep next to stagnant waters, but the Cry leaped up within it and violently shook its roots: 'Away, let go of the earth, walk!'... It shouted in this way for thousands of eons; and lo! as a result of desire and struggle, life escaped the motionless tree and was liberated.
>
> Animals appeared – worms – making themselves at home in water and mud. 'We're just fine here,' they said. 'We have peace and security; we're not budging!'
>
> But the terrible Cry hammered itself pitilessly into their loins. 'Leave the mud, stand up, give birth to your betters!'... And lo! after thousands of eons, man emerged, trembling on his still unsolid legs.
>
> The human being is a centaur; his equine hoofs are planted in the ground, but his body from breast to head is worked on and tormented by the merciless Cry. He has been fighting, again for thousands of eons, to draw himself, like a sword, out of his animalistic scabbard. He is also fighting – this is his new struggle – to draw himself out of his human scabbard. Man calls in despair, 'Where can I go? I have reached the pinnacle, beyond is the abyss.' And the Cry answers, 'I am beyond. Stand up!' All things are centaurs. If this were not the case, the world would rot into inertness and sterility.[5]

This divine Cry is much like Whitehead's 'primordial nature of God', the *eros* of the universe, the appetitive urge to realize, to as great an extent as possible, the possibilities for us and for our world.

Transubstantiation

The above transubstantiation from plant life to animals, from animals to human beings, and from human beings to God, should clearly indicate three things: (a) Kazantzakis presents transubstantiation as a natural *process* rather than as an instantaneous act of 'hocus pocus'; (b) he nonetheless indicates the *real presence* of God in the process of transubstantiation, hence allying himself with Catholicism and Orthodoxy rather than with Protestantism regarding transubstantiation; and (c) transubstantiation (*metousiosis* or *metabole* and their cognates) is the *key to his writing* in that the sublimity of the transubstantiation that occurs in the Eucharist is spread across the whole of human life, indeed across the whole *cosmos*. There is no other modern writer concerning whom one could make this last claim.

The transubstantiation of matter into spirit is explicitly treated in theoretical terms many times in Kazantzakis's writings, but in addition it has a strong symbolic mode of ingression in most of his works, novels as well as travel books and plays. The easiest passages to identify are those where Kazantzakis uses communion metaphors or describes the distribution of communion. But transubstantiation is not a mere theme among other themes in Kazantzakis's writing, but a dominant theme around which cluster the notes of subordinate themes that run counterpoint to it. Bread and wine, for Kazantzakis, are transubstantiated into the body and blood of communion, and communion is transubstantiated into penitence, rest, salvation, peace, paradise and God. In fact, eating *any* food makes transubstantiation possible. In one of Kazantzakis's most imaginative passages, he has Zorba say to his boss:

> Tell me what you do with the food you eat, and I'll tell you who you are. Some turn their food into fat and manure, some into work and good humour, and others, I'm told, into God. So there must be three sorts of men. I'm not one of the worst, boss, nor yet one of the best. I'm somewhere between the two. What I eat I turn into work and good humour. That's not too bad, after all!... As for you, boss... I think you do your level best to turn what you eat into God, but you can't quite manage it, and that torments you.[6]

The boss learns from Zorba that eating is a spiritual function and that bread and wine are the raw materials from which mind is made. Each person has an element of the divine whirlwind that allows the transubstantiation of bread into thought and action. Bread is the necessary if not sufficient condition for spiritual perfection, even if it is true that Kazantzakis himself, unlike Zorba, was not a voracious eater but an ascetic.

Kazantzakis's asceticism recalls the ancient meaning of *askesis* as healthy bodily training as if for an athletic event; on this view, asceticism is equivalent to bodily discipline. What human beings can do self-consciously (discipline themselves so as to transubstantiate matter into spirit) is done unconsciously by the rest of nature: silkworms (a favourite metaphor in Kazantzakis, perhaps derived from St Teresa of Avila), trees and so on. But because human beings are, or can be, self-conscious of themselves as disciplined, transubstantiating agents it is in *human* history that the process of transubstantiation achieves its greatest intensity. Regarding the first human beings, Kazantzakis says:

> Now, for the first time since the world was made, man has been enabled to enter God's workshop and labor with Him. The more flesh he transubstantiates into love, valor, and freedom, the more truly he becomes Son of God...This ancestor is the bulky, unwrought beast given to me to transubstantiate into man – and to raise even higher than man if I can manage in the time allotted me. What a fearful ascent from monkey to man, from man to God![7]

It would be a mistake, however, to see Kazantzakian transubstantiation exclusively in cosmic or historical terms, in that Kazantzakis is also a very personal writer. One's personal life is also the locus for transubstantiation:

There is much darkness in me, much of my father. All my life I have fought desperately to transubstantiate this darkness and turn it into light, one little drop of light. It has been a harsh struggle without pity or respite... Virtue, for me, is not the fruit of my nature, it is the fruit of my struggles. God did not give it to me, I have had to labor in order to conquer it by the sword. For me, virtue's flower is a pile of transubstantiated dung.[8]

Within Christianity, this transubstantiation of one's personal life is focused on Christ: 'There is no other way to reach God but this. Following Christ's bloody tracks, we must fight to transubstantiate the man inside of us into spirit, so that we may merge with God.'[9] Here it is clear that God, for Kazantzakis, is not merely humanity spoken of in a loud voice, even if our best clue as to the nature of ultimate reality and meaning comes through the God–man, Christ: 'He conquered every temptation, continually transubstantiated flesh into spirit, and ascended. Every obstacle in His journey became an occasion for further triumph.'[10] Or again: 'My deepest joy is to see how the mysterious force seizes hold of man and shakes him like a lover, an epileptic, or a creator. Because, as you know, what interests me is not man himself, but the being that I so imperfectly designate as "God".'[11]

The New Middle Ages

It is a commonplace in the writings of Kazantzakis that we are passing through a new Middle Ages, a transitional period that will last a very long time, perhaps two hundred years. His theory of history, heavily reliant on Bergson, goes something like this: in the twentieth century we have lost the primitive, spontaneous, pristine appreciation of the beauty of the world. We are far too sophisticated for this attitude, which is preserved by more atavistic peoples. But we have also lost the spontaneous, unquestioned faith in the traditional God of the Abrahamic religions. In short, we cannot be pagans because Christianity has civilized us; and we cannot be Christians *in the traditional sense*, primarily because of the inability of traditional religious theories to deal adequately with the problems of theodicy and reconciling the existence of God with the existence of human freedom.

The barbarians had penetrated to the core of modern western civilization at least by the time of the Spanish Civil War, if not before, a penetration that made Kazantzakis pessimistic regarding the near future. Wars, shadows, pograms, selfish individualism and bureaucratic management are the tangible results of our age, results that tend to overpower the efforts of the few magnificent, fiery hearts left in the world, those who reject, in a way, the ancient dictum. 'Nothing in excess', by proclaiming in a Zorbatic way, 'Everything in excess!' In the desert of contemporary culture, one's duty is to remain faithful to the flame. This 'flame' refers to authentic human life between two black voids: we come from a dark abyss and we end in one as well; life is a transition from one abyss to the other. This life of the *élan vital*, symbolized by the flame, consists in a spiritual energy that tries to separate itself from matter, just as a flame consumes the wax in a candle. Human beings are lumps of matter infused with the possibility of living vibrantly, with Zorba-like zest, wherein it is possible to burn up one's material substance in the effort to transform it into spiritual light.

If one imagines Kazantzakis writing in mid-winter 1938 in Germany, one can easily understand his pessimism, his fear that a tiny lighted candle could easily be blown out by the winds of change, hence his belief that the best we could do is to daydream, plan and work for the coming civilization. Our epoch is the end of the modern period, which has reached its senility and is in the process of decomposition, and the beginning of a new Middle Ages. We have passed from an era of light to an era of darkness, but night is not less wonderful than day. In fact, night may well be closer than day to divinity. That is, Kazantzakis's view of history is affected not only by Oswald Spengler, but also by St John of the Cross and St Teresa of Avila in their 'dark night of the soul'. The common use of the phrase 'mediaeval darkness' misses the deeper, ontological sense that Nicholas Berdyaev (who influenced Kazantzakis here) and Kazantzakis have in mind when they refer to the new Middle Ages.

At the time of the fall of the ancient world it was reactionary to defend the principles of civilization, in that such a defence could easily be interpreted as an *apologia* for late Roman decadence. Likewise, contemporary defenders of 'progress' are more reactionary than the true progressives in our culture, those who welcome the new Middle Ages, its interiority and its possibilities for spiritual growth. Kazantzakis does not have in mind a resurrection of the temporary and accidental in mediaeval culture. Rather, the new Middle Ages is a figure of speech, hence there is no need to idealize the real Middle Ages of the past, as in pre-Raphaelite painting. Serfdom, ignorance of nature, and fear of hell are, in fact, as the moderns have claimed, examples of primitivism. To 'return' to the new Middle Ages is to hope for a better religious type without dogmatism, it is to find religious liberty in the spiritual quest itself. What Kazantzakis thought we needed in the twentieth century was a combination of chaotic, barbaric forces (so as to destroy the remnants of the modern world) and a new, secular asceticism. The 'blond barbarians' from the north have actually exacted their constructive destruction three times in Europe: the prehistoric Dorian invasion of Greece, Knossos and Egypt – the basis for the barbarian invasion treated in Kazantzakis's *The Odyssey*; the second horde at the fall of Rome; and the third through modern Russia.

If Kazantzakis is a postmodern thinker and writer, however, it should be emphasized that he is a constructive rather than a deconstructive one. He admires figures like Odysseus, the Buddha, Jesus and St Francis because God for them, in his interpretation, is an unquenchable flame, indeed a fire, that burns in them day and night. Human life for Kazantzakis is not an ironic joke, nor is it filled with existential despair, as it appears to be for many deconstructionist postmodernists. For the Kazantzakian 'mediaeval' religious believer, there is no such thing as quotidian pain unaccompanied by exultation, and no everyday life without miracles.

Dipolar Theism

In *The Saviors of God: Spiritual Exercises* and elsewhere, Kazantzakis makes it clear that the greatest conceivable being, God, would have to be both active *and* passive. Kazantzakis frequently refers to God as eternal or as undying in the sense that God *always* exists throughout time; God has no beginning or end; God is immutably mutable, the being who always becomes, hence God's struggling activity is forever evident. But it is one thing to say that God exists everlastingly, it is quite another to say *how* God exists. That is, there is a (Charles Hartshorne-like) distinction in Kazantzakis between God's bare existence (which is independent of us) and God's mode of existence, which depends on us to be saved, as Kazantzakis constantly reminds us. God's greatness does not just allow God to change, it *requires* God to change so as to respond to new instances of suffering and to new decisions on the part of free creatures. This does not mean that God's earlier existence was inferior, because it was at that particular time the greatest existence.

A human being is constantly changing yet retains an identity throughout these changes, and this largely through a Bergsonian memory that a human being possesses; but a human being will die, hence a human being is not dipolar in a supreme way. God *always changes* (both terms are needed) and yet always maintains a stable identity through these changes as 'God'. To be an everlasting agent *and* recipient (in Kazantzakis's terms, a being who needs to be 'saved') is in truth incomparably better than being either alone. Insufficiently subtle or defective receptivity is called wooden inflexibility, mulish stubbornness, inadaptability, unresponsiveness and the like. But there is also a good receptivity that should not be denied of divinity: sensitivity, responsiveness, adaptability, sympathy or, as Kazantzakis puts it, God's dependence on us to be saved. To altogether deny God the ability to change does avoid fickleness, but at the expense of the ability to react lovingly to the sufferings of others, albeit the Kazantzakian tough love depicted above in the 'Cry' passage.

All of this is in contrast to the traditional, monopolar view of God in the Abrahamic religions (a view that seems to be at odds with biblical theism) wherein God is seen as a pure actuality that does not change, indeed that is sometimes described as an *unmoved* mover who is outside temporal passage altogether. But for Kazantzakis the greatness of God not only allows God to change, but *requires* God to change. New moments bring with them new possibilities for Zorba-like or Franciscan heroism, new possibilities for enriching the divine life (that is, for 'saving' God). The future is not here yet to be known in detail, hence God is still the greatest conceivable knower even if God is not omniscient with respect to the future. The greatest knower would know all past actualities as already actualized and all present events in their presentness. But no being, not even a divine one, could know with absolute assurance and in minute detail what will happen in the future if the future is not here yet to be known: in fact, to claim to know future possibilities as already actualized is to misunderstand what the concept of futurity is all about.

The greatest sin of all for Kazantzakis is satisfaction, so we should not be tempted to give up the struggle to understand God too early, say by resting content with the monopolar view that God is being but not becoming, or eternal fixity rather than becoming. God is *both* being and becoming, just as God is *both* supreme activity as well as supreme receptivity, for Kazantzakis. It is true that for Kazantzakis God is the liberating struggle itself, whereby God is gradually liberated from animality in Centaur-like or Minotaur-like fashion (favourite metaphors of his). But God is also to be identified with that spiritual being that is already (that is, everlastingly) liberated. We toil for the sake of 'Someone Else' or the 'Great Ecstatic', not just for the sake of our own creaturely efforts; we struggle for the sake of a deathless God that is behind phenomena. In each of the contrasting pairs treated in this section of the chapter (being–becoming, activity–passivity) Kazantzakis wisely tried to preserve the best in each individual element and eliminate the worst. For all the daring in his *neo*classical theism, he is still, in a way, neo*classical*.

Mysticism

From the above it makes sense to suspect that, if Kazantzakis claimed to have direct (that is, mystical) experience of God, it would come in two forms: immediate experience of an immanent God in transubstantiating activity (mysticism-1) and immediate experience of a transcendent God as ineffable or paradoxical or awful precisely because of a permanent God's dematerialized condition (mysticism-2). It would be odd if God, as an omnipresent being-in-becoming, could only be known or affirmed indirectly. Most of us are more like unreflective, mechanical and dull-witted human beings than we usually admit. The most readily detectable data are those that are sometimes present, sometimes not, as in redness or pain. What is always given tends to escape notice. Mysticism-1 consists in the transubstantiating *activity* of putting oneself in a position to be *receptive* to the divine or the spiritual as ubiquitous. That is, some human beings intuitively prehend (as opposed to intellectually apprehend) or grasp implicitly that there is *some* sort of meaning in the world; they *feel* as an inchoate object of experience that they are parts of a meaningful whole, that there is a concrete fact of relatedness between themselves and a personal force at work in the *universe*. Consider the following lines by Zorba's boss from *Zorba the Greek*:

> Zorba sees everything every day as if for the first time ... As I listened to Zorba ... the world was recovering its pristine freshness. All the dulled daily things regained the brightness they had in the beginning, when we came out of the hands of God. Water, women, the stars, bread, returned to their mysterious, primitive origin and the divine whirlwind burst once more upon the air ... The universe for Zorba, as for the first men on earth, was a weighty, intense vision; the stars glided over him, the sea broke against his temples. He lived the earth, water, the animals and God ... God changes his appearance every second. Blessed is the man who can recognize him in all his disguises. At one moment he is a glass of fresh water, the next your son bouncing on your knees or an enchanting woman, or perhaps merely a morning walk.[12]

There is a tension here. Kazantzakian blessedness consists in recognizing God, on the one hand, and in 'saving' God, on the other. Or again, those, like Zorba, who recognize God are like innocent children or primitive people, on the one hand, whereas the religious hero in his or her struggles 'saves' God, on the other. The tension can perhaps be resolved in the following way: in this Zorba-like seeing God is, in a way, saved', that is, the real presence of God is confirmed once again.

The eclecticism of Kazantzakis's religiosity can perhaps better be termed his belief in the transubstantiation of matter into spirit as ubiquitous but seldom noticed, the mystics being the exceptions to the rule. But the ubiquity of deity is not the same as omnipotence:

> My God is not Almighty. He struggles, for he is in peril every moment; he trembles and stumbles in every living thing, and he cries out. He is defeated incessantly, but rises again, full of blood and earth, to throw himself into battle once more.[13]

As before, Kazantzakis's fear is that an *omni*potent God would make it logically impossible for creatures to have any power, not even the power to decide freely for themselves. Freedom is a species of the general spiritual power which is *'the sole method* followed by all organic beings in order to deliver themselves from inertia, tranquility, and prosperity, and to throw themselves into danger, adventure, and unexpected success'.[14] Kazantzakis himself alerts us to the fact that his Bergsonian dynamism is connected to his religious concerns, as when he says that 'The major and almost the only theme of all my work is the struggle of man with ' "God".'[15] But those who feel that the view of Jesus in *The Last Temptation of Christ* is too anthropocentric should consider the following remark from Kazantzakis. He says explicitly that 'I do not want him', with 'him' referring to a god who looks too much like a human being.[16]

The dialectical tension between the human and the divine is a commonplace in mystic literature. The intimacy of mystical union is in tension with the terrifying darkness of God's essence. In *Report to Greco*, Kazantzakis says the following about this tension:

> Every man is half God, half man; he is both spirit and flesh. That is why the mystery of Christ is not simply a mystery for a particular creed; it is universal. The struggle between God and man breaks out in everyone, together with the longing for reconciliation ... [but] God does not love weak souls and flabby flesh ... the supreme purpose of the struggle – union with God.[17]

Kazantzakis was very clear about the fact that he thought there was some 'mystic law' at work in the universe, a mystic law that indicates to us that the very idea of limits brings into existence the possibility of transcending them. It is precisely this 'More', this 'Something Else', that mysticism-2 is all about.

Two fundamental elements constitute the essence of Christian *and* Kazantzakian sanctity: a disciplined life or asceticism, on the one hand, and union with God, to the extent that this is possible, on the other. And, it should be noted, these two are connected. It is only through a disciplined, transubstantiating life that one can be in a position to achieve union with God when conceived as pure spirit. Human knowing (*gnosis*) – 'You and I are one, Lord' – is necessarily followed by unknowing (*agnosis*) – 'even this one does not exist'. The former element is reminiscent of the kataphatic tradition of Christian mysticism, otherwise known as the *via positiva*. But the latter element does not necessarily lead to nihilism in that it is part of traditional apophatic theology or the *via negativa*. This negativity is not absolute, but rather is indicative of a psychic renewal; silence as part of the *via negativa* can abrogate the differentiation implicit in words so as to tease into consciousness the wholeness of God.

The modesty of negative theology is somewhat suspect because it puts a human veto on the wealth of the divine life. Kazantzakis is, in fact, influenced by negative theology, but not exclusively so: he *does* say many things about God. We can speak literally about the fact that God is relative, that is, related to creatures. But we cannot speak literally about what it is like to *be* God. Here we must be silent or speak metaphorically.

Method

The following twelve points can be safely claimed about the method at work in Kazantzakis's effort to explore ultimate reality and meaning. (a) There is a tension in Kazantzakis between western (specifically, Greek) moderation and eastern (that is, Asian – whether Near Eastern or Far Eastern) restlessness. (b) There is a tension in Kazantzakis between the desire to harmonize opposites and the desire to break all harmonizing boundaries in the effort to progress by conquering the weight of the status quo in religion. (c) We can deny neither the western harmony of opposites tendency nor the eastern tendency to shatter this harmony, but it is clear that for Kazantzakis the former rests on the latter. (d) Thus, in a sense, it is fair to say that all that is worthwhile in the human–divine relationship is ultimately eastern. (e) Nonetheless there is a symbiotic relationship between western rationalism and eastern mysticism such that there is more matter in spirit than many eastern believers think and more spirit in matter than many western thinkers imagine. (f) The reason for the derivative status of reason in Kazantzakis is that divinity itself is a whirlwind (as in the book of Job) who breaks every harmony.

(g) This transcendence of rational harmony leads to what Kazantzakis refers to as an abyss or to a transubstantiation of matter into spirit or pure air or nothingness. (h) But this abyss or nothingness is not sheer non-being (whatever this might be: to think about *it* is to turn it into a somethingness, as Parmenides realized); rather, it is one moment in the systole and diastole of the religious life: knowing (*gnosis*) shattered by creative unknowing or silence (*agnosis)* leading to an attempt to reach a higher sort of knowing and so on. (i) That is, in both Buddhism and Christianity there is an attempt to extol the virtues of the ascetical life so as to achieve union with the Unborn and Uncreated; in both of these religions that affected Kazantzakis so profoundly there is a place for silence and for the claim that 'even this one does not exist'. (j) As Bien emphasizes, the apophatic way or the *via negativa* is needed to provide rest or psychic renewal so as to abrogate the differentiation implicit in words (in the kataphatic efforts of the *via positiva*), a differentiation that prevents the union mentioned above at (i). (k) God is, as the Hesychasts with their somatic techniques realized, at least partially knowable, contra those who would assert (strange as this sounds) the hegemony of the apophatic. And (l), there is a dialectical tension in Kazantzakis between Bergsonian tendencies and Buddhist ones, but the tension can perhaps best be understood in terms of the inclusion of the latter in the former; once again, silence and the experience of nothingness are but moments in the ongoing and apparently never ending process of the universe. There is no contradiction between (l) and (d) because Bergson, although French, nonetheless defended a view that relies heavily on eastern tendencies, as we have seen.

Kazanzakis's method, lying as it does between west and east, can be referred to, as Bien suggests, as the perennial Greek predicament. There is something *both* knowable and unknowable about *both* God's being and God's becoming. The process theism that Kazantzakis represents can also, as we have seen, be called a dipolar theism: God necessarily exists and remains steadfastly good *in the midst of* all of the divine and creaturely changes. Hence there is no necessary conflict between this view and a qualified, Olympian polytheism or cult of the saints, which is often used by Kazantzakis as a device to criticize the traditional view of God as an unmoved mover.

To take polytheism seriously, rather than to take it too seriously, is to refuse to see any huge gap between it and the perennial Greek predicament. The gods (half-glimpsed visions or absent-minded absorptions in memory or fable, which constitute a sort of divine immanence) may be evoked by music, poetry and Zorbatic dance; and to disprove their existence one needs to do more than dredge Loch Ness. The world we live in, for Kazantzakis, is a weird *mix* of matter and spirit.

In the preparation for an improved religious belief Kazantzakis makes it explicit that Russia plays a role in bringing 'the fine Asiatic madness under the control of the rigorous logic of the West'.[18] Russia is very much like Greece in symbolizing the problem that Kazantzakis's method is meant to solve. In the following remarkable quotation we can see that: (i) even in his works about Russia Kazantzakis is primarily interested in spiritual concerns; (ii) his 'materialism' can perhaps better be termed an incarnational theology; and (iii) even in his works on Russia Kazantzakis is very much concerned with his method of reconciling east and west:

> Every man is an ephemeral Son who contains the eternal Father within himself. The purpose of art is to discover the invisible spirit of the Father and to express it through the visible body of the Son. If man can grasp and express nothing but the Son, he creates a merely superficial work of art; if he expresses nothing but abstract ideas, nothing but the Father, he produces not art but metaphysics. The Effort to find the Word able to capture the immortal essence alive in us; this is magic. That's why art is a mysterious science, a veritable theurgy. Words attract and imprison the invisible spirit, force it to become incarnated and to exhibit itself to man. *Sitka*, meaning Utterance, the Word, in Georgian means also seizure and sexual intercourse. The Word must seize, subjugate and fecundate matter. Just as Adam knew woman, so must the Word know matter ... The consciousness of the West ... is dominated by appreciation of the individual; that of the East by a profound sense of union with the Universe. The Westerner has been liberated from the great Whole; the umbilical cord binding him to the Universe has been cut ... turned him into a monad ... The Oriental on the other hand is a hybrid...The Father predominates in the Oriental, the Son in the Westerner. But holy wedlock has already been announced between Asia with her abandonment to the Whole and Europe with its individualistic logicality.[19]

This wedlock was taking place, he thought, in Russia, Greece and, more slowly, throughout the western and eastern worlds. Kazantzakis thought himself saddled with the 'thankless' task of defending Russia despite the fact that it, like all institutions at the end of a civilization, stood for the view that materialism is the key to all mysteries.

There can be no doubt that in the short run Kazantzakis favoured the eastern constituent of the perennial Greek (and Russian) predicament, but whether he did so in the long run is a debatable question. While in Russia he even complained about the 'excessively silent and incomprehensible' Asians he met there.[20] Also:

> if we allow ourselves to be too much enchanted by Greek harmony, we are in danger of missing the first step of Creation – destruction and Chaos – and we run the risk of moving on prematurely toward our second duty: the establishment of a balance, which is certainly not the mission of our generation on this earth ... For art and beauty, I often have the same feeling of hatred that the primitive Christians used to have. The first adherents of a faith always have a similar hatred for the lovely balanced form of the universe they are called on to destroy. For in truth this beauty is the great temptation; it gives the mystical enchantment to the idols – those 'false' manifestations of God.[21]

Panexperientialism and Death

Kazantzakis was obviously not a reductionistic materialist, indeed he often argues against this position. In fact, there is much evidence in his texts that he was a dualist who saw an everlasting battle between two irreducible forces: matter and spirit. But a more accurate view, I think, would be to claim that he was a panpsychist or a panexperientialist who saw spirit ubiquitously infused in matter, and this on several pieces of evidence: (a) Kazantzakis saw God as an explosive power who broke out in the smallest particle of matter;[22] (b) even bats and manure had the potential to be transubstantiated, that is, deified;[23] (c) the transubstantiation of mud into sap and then into the blossoms of a tree was made possible by the presence of God in lightning and rain;[24] (d) that is, God, for Kazantzakis, was not suspended in mid-air, but was rooted in earth, water, stone and fire.[25]

Nonetheless (e), the omnipresent character of deity in Kazantzakis did not preclude an intensification of the process of transubstantiation in human beings, say when he suggested that God was in the guts of a potent man on his wedding night. But (f) despite Kazantzakis's clarity regarding the point that divinity as found in human beings was at a higher level of dematerialization than that found in the remainder of nature, he was equally clear that the divine struggled in every cell of flesh and was striving for light.[26] Or again (g), God, for Kazantzakis, was like Plato's or Origen's deity in being the soul for the body of the world, forever in self-motion; transubstantiation was a cosmic process that was as refreshing as cool water or an enchanting woman, he thought.[27] And (h), it was especially the mystics who heard God breathing everywhere,[28] although, presumably, most human beings could perceive God if their lives were appropriately disciplined.

This Kazantzakian emphasis on *psyche* driving even microscopic cells, this emphasis on the Bergsonian (or Teilhardian, although Kazantzakis was not influenced by Teilhard de Chardin) *élan vital* in nature obviously makes death an obstacle for Kazantzakis. There are elements of life which make it better, and some which make it worse. But what is left when these are bracketed out of consideration is not merely neutral: life is emphatically positive! That is, life is worth living even when the bad elements of experience are abundant. It is be-ing alive and do-ing certain things that are good. In effect, it is not the static state of death that is evil, but the loss of the process of living. This is why Zorba thought he should live a thousand years and why Kazantzakis indicates in *Freedom or Death* that some great human beings should never die.[29]

Some might object that the inevitability of death should make it tolerable, otherwise we simply fail to understand ourselves as biological animals. But suppose we were all going to die in *agony*. Would inevitability make *that* prospect tolerable to us? If our normal life-span were a thousand years, death at eighty would be a tragedy. As things are, however, it is, on Kazantzakian grounds, just a more widespread tragedy. The Kazantzakian trick is to compete in the game of life strenuously (in that we only have one life to live) while retaining a sense of humour and a sense of lightheartedness, however difficult these may be. Consider the following anecdote by Kazantzakis:

> The young professor of sociology at the Communist University of Moscow analyzes in a

clear and confident manner all the economic factors present in ancient Greek society and proves that the smile of the caryatids on the Acropolis of Athens has its origins in economic causes. The audience, orthodox Marxists, accepts this wise explanation without hesitation and bursts into applause. I smile, and the young professor unnerved, turns to me: 'Why are you smiling?' 'I assure you, comrade Professor,' I reply, 'my smile is not the result of economic causes.'[30]

It is this serious–lightheartedness that characterizes Kazantzakis's entire corpus and that enables him to hold that attainment of spiritual perfection is inferior to the Odysseus-like struggle for it.

Kazantzakis is in earnest when he says that some people should not die, and he at least flirts with the idea of immortality of the soul, say when the old grandfather in *Freedom or Death* washes his blood off from war, goes to church for communion, then feels his body to be a lightly flying cloud. At death the same grandfather had a similar experience that was supplemented by a magical voice, perhaps from God, that came from beyond life. At the moment of death his body lightened as it was softly transubstantiated into a cloud. But this cloudlike body does not completely evaporate or fly off into the heights; rather it condenses and falls as rain to the ground so as to nourish the young shoots. In the final analysis, it is in *this* world that we must find God and, hence, find meaning in our lives. In a peculiar way it makes sense to say that for Kazantzakis transubstantiation is from spirit into flesh; our project is to redeem the bodies we have. For example, despite all of his accomplishments in life, Zorba did not think on his deathbed that he had done enough, hence his claim that men like him ought to live a thousand years.

Further, the 'Cry passage' from *Report to Greco*, quoted above, captures many of the features of Kazantzakis's thought as they bear on both panexperientialism and death. In this passage Kazantzakis makes it clear that he thinks of Jesus not as a disembodied cogito or as an overly Apollonian character, but as a model of the *élan vital*, transubstantiation and ascension. Like Jesus and the rest of creation – wood, rocks, birds, everything – we struggle to liberate a God who is incessantly defeated only to rise again, full of blood and earth, so as to be thrown into the battle once more. Blowing through all things is a great Cry that prevents plants and animals from stagnating, and that acts as a lure for centaur-like humanity, which has been struggling for thousands of years to draw itself out of its human scabbard. When the locus of this struggle is the human confrontation with death, human beings are often tempted to despair. The Cry answers, 'I am beyond. Stand up!'

The meaning of our lives is obviously not found, for Kazantzakis, in any sort of personal or subjective immortality, as the words on his tombstone indicate. We and everyone we know will, in fact, die, but in addition to the intrinsic value of our transubstantiating struggles we have the solace that comes from knowing that our efforts will be taken up into the divine life. Some of us do not wish for more than this solace: we die, but God is everlasting.

Notes

1. This essay was previously published in Daniel A. Dombrowski, 'Ultimate Reality and Meaning in Nikos Kazantzakis', *Ultimate Reality and Meaning* 21.3 (1998): 177–94. Also see Daniel A. Dombrowski, *Kazantzakis and God* (Albany, NY: State University of New York Press, 1997).
2. Nikos Kazantzakis, *Saint Francis*, translated by Peter A. Bien (New York: Simon and Schuster, 1962), 178.
3. Nikos Kazantzakis, *Journeying*, translated by Themi Vasils and Theodora Vasils (San Francisco, CA: Creative Arts, 1984), 186.
4. Nikos Kazantzakis, *Journey to the Morea*, translated by F.A. Reed (New York: Simon and Schuster, 1965), 171.
5. Nikos Kazantzakis, *Report to Greco*, translated by Peter A. Bien (New York: Simon and Schuster, 1965), 291–2.
6. Nikos Kazantzakis, *Zorba the Greek*, translated by Carl Wildman (New York: Simon and Schuster, 1952), 66–7.
7. Kazantzakis, *Report to Greco*, 24–5.
8. Ibid., 476.
9. Ibid., 289.
10. Ibid., 291.
11. Helen Kazantzakis, *Nikos Kazantzakis: A Biography Based on His Letters*, translated by Amy Mims (New York: Simon and Schuster, 1968), 189.
12. Kazantzakis, *Zorba the Greek*, 51.
13. Nikos Kazantzakis, *The Saviors of God: Spiritual Exercises*, translated and with an introduction by Kimon Friar (New York: Simon and Schuster, 1960), 103.
14. Peter A. Bien, *Kazantzakis: Politics of the Spirit* (Princeton, NJ: Princeton University Press, 1989), 95.
15. Helen Kazantzakis, *Nikos Kazantzakis: A Biography Based on His Letters*, 507.
16. Nikos Kazantzakis, *The Suffering God: Selected Letters to Galatea and Papastephanou*, translated by Philip Ramp and Katerina Anghelaki Rooke (New Rochelle, NY: Caratzas, 1979), 37.
17. Kazantzakis, *Report to Greco*, 290.
18. Nikos Kazantzakis, *Toda Raba*, translated by Amy Mims (New York: Simon and Schuster, 1964), 64.
19. Ibid., 90–91.
20. Nikos Kazantzakis, *Russia*, translated by Michael Antonakes and Thanasis Maskaleris (Berkeley, CA: Creative Arts, 1989), 237.
21. Kazantzakis, *Toda Raba*, 207–8.
22. Kazantzakis, *Journeying*, 92.
23. Kazantzakis, *Report to Greco*, 477.
24. Nikos Kazantzakis, *Symposium*, translated by Theodora Vasils and Themi Vasils (New York: Minerva Press, 1974), 54.
25. Nikos Kazantzakis, *The Odyssey: A Modern Sequel*, translated by Kimon Friar (New York: Simon and Schuster, 1958), the Prologue.
26. Kazantzakis, *The Saviors of God*, 91.
27. Kazantzakis, *Zorba the Greek*, 51, 136, 208.
28. Kazantzakis, *The Odyssey*, XIV, 8.
29. Nikos Kazantzakis, *Freedom or Death*, translated by Jonathan Griffin (New York: Simon and Schuster, 1955), 325.
30. Kazantzakis, *Russia*, 209.

Chapter 10

Jacob Boehme and the Romantic Roots of Process Thought

Lewis Owens

There is nothing in nature where there is not good and evil, everything moves and lives in this double impulse, working or operating, be it what it will. (Jacob Boehme)[1]

Introduction

Although process thought has found its most systematic form in the relatively recent philosophy of Alfred North Whitehead, it is clear that its roots have a much deeper and distinguished history. The aim of this chapter is to provide a historical perspective that highlights process thought's rich theological, philosophical and literary inheritance. By necessity, therefore, this chapter will be somewhat general, seeking to present a broad overview of similar concepts and ideas. Our starting point will be the thought of the German mystic Jacob Boehme who is justifiably seen by Charles Hartshorne as the founder of a dipolar theology.[2] Indeed, I wish to show that the core tenets of process thought (creativity, becoming, time) had their genesis largely in the notion of the deity espoused by Boehme. Boehme's thought also greatly influenced the later thought of Freidrich Schelling whose ideas in turn nourished the soil from which grew the religious philosophy of Henri Bergson and Nicholas Berdyaev, two further thinkers belonging to the distinguished family of process philosophers, according to Hartshorne.[3] Furthermore, Boehme's influence also permeates into Romantic poetic literature, of which William Blake, William Wordsworth and Samuel Taylor Coleridge are prime representatives. However, before beginning this historical journey, it will be necessary to set the scene by looking briefly at the thought of Whitehead.

Alfred North Whitehead and the Roots of Process Thought

Like any seminal philosophy, Whitehead's thought is both reactionary and revolutionary: he is reacting against the static, mechanical Newtonian world and proclaiming notions of becoming, creativity and novelty as central cosmological principles. This overarching principle of creativity is intimately linked to the becoming of each novel situation. God, for Whitehead, is the source of this novelty, the lure towards creativity, 'the eternal urge of desire'.[4] Whitehead is attempting to formulate a notion of God that is commensurate with an evolutionary world-view. To achieve this, he posits a dipolar God, constituted by an eternal, abstract, unconscious primordial actuality that is ontologically independent from the world, and an incomplete and conscious consequent nature that, complementing the former, concerns a temporal and mutable side to God, one that is affected by the world's creative advance. For Whitehead, therefore, God is 'an actual entity immanent in the actual world, but transcending any finite cosmic epoch – a being at once actual, eternal, immanent and transcendent'.[5] God's teleological aim is the fulfilment of God's being by assimilating God's primordial and consequent natures into one Whole; God and the world feed off of each other, hence Whitehead's famous reference to God as a poet who cares tenderly for the temporal world. God requires the world's assistance to advance into the future and is in Godself an integral part of the world's formation and novelty.

This notion of a dipolar God has become an increasingly attractive alternative to the Thomistic notion of God as *actus purus*. It is justifiably argued that a God who is immutable, omnipotent, passionless and hence immune from human suffering is of little religious significance, as such a concept of God fails to account sufficiently for the problems of theodicy and human freedom, and remains spiritually unapproachable. In Whitehead's process thought, God and the world are inextricably related, to the extent that the actions of creatures have a direct influence on the Divine Life: God is thus liable to suffer and change.

However, the notion of a polarity within the Godhead that is employed by process theology may be seen to have its genesis in the thought of Boehme, who asserts an intimate relationship between God and the world, constituted by the eternal reciprocity of the three persons of the Trinity. Hartshorne acknowledges that Boehme 'goes a good way to defining a dipolar theology'[6] and, mediated largely through Schelling, influences the thought of Berdyaev, that 'thoroughgoing dipolarist',[7] who moves away from the Scholastic doctrine of God as immutable and the impassive Supreme Being. With the Boehme–Schelling influence behind Berdyaev, Hartshorne believes, 'Here at last is an out-and-out dipolar theology. Berdyaev speaks frankly of a divine history, a divine becoming, divine need, and above all, divine suffering.'[8] 'Indeed I hold with Berdyaev and Whitehead', Hartshorne writes elsewhere, '... that God sympathises with and in that sense *shares* the suffering.'[9] Schelling's belief in a suffering God is inextricably linked to a notion of the progression of history, the goal of which is the complete reintegration of the universe with the Absolute. He writes:

> Pain is something universal and necessary and in all life, the inevitable point of transition to freedom ... Suffering is generally the way to glory, not only with regard to man, but also with respect to the creator. God leads human nature through no other course than that through which his own nature must pass. Participation in everything blind, dark, and suffering of God's nature is necessary in order to raise him to highest consciousness. Each being must learn to know its depths; this is impossible without suffering. Pain comes only from being.[10]

Drawing on the analogy between the macro- and microcosm, Schelling asserts there to be an intimate link between the freedom of God and that of created humanity.

Hence the exercise of human freedom to overcome darkness and evil is a continuation of the Divine conflict in which God eternally overcomes the dark ground within Godself. As a result of God's self-manifestation, this Divine conflict is manifested into the historical spatiotemporal realm, and humanity is required to aid God's struggle and suffering.[11] Like Schelling, Berdyaev also wishes to see the human drama intimately linked with the evolving inner Divine life. For Berdyaev, freedom is the primordial, meontic, uncreated reality (Boehme's *Ungrund*) out of which God the Creator creates. As the image of God, humanity also partakes of this freedom and hence of the Divine life itself when creative, new acts are performed out of the freedom of non-being. We can see already that the key ideas of process thought stretch back much further than Whitehead. Having set the scene, let us look more closely at Boehme.

Jacob Boehme

Boehme is an opaque but nevertheless momentous thinker.[12] He is justifiably seen as foreshadowing the dialectical process advocated by George Hegel, where history is interpreted as the temporal unfolding of *Geist* in its desire for self-consciousness and self-knowledge, a feat achieved in the consciousness and speculative thought of human rationality. The basis of all reality, Boehme argues, is the *Ungrund*, the groundlessness, the eternal rest, God as God is in Godself, where all is One and no differentiation occurs. He writes of the *Ungrund* as follows:

> For it cannot be said of God that he is this or that, evil or good, or that he has distinctions in himself... He is in himself the ungrounded ... He is the nothing and the all, and is a single will in which the world and the whole creation lies ... He is neither light nor darkness, neither love nor wrath, but the eternal One.[13]

All contradictions are reconciled in the *Ungrund*, hence Boehme refers to an androgynous God, a unification of active (male) and passive (female) principles. From within this *Ungrund*, however, there emerges a primordial imaginative craving for self-revelation. As a result, opposing forces emerge within the Godhead itself. Only this desired projection of the Divine Will to be something truly characterizes God, according to Boehme. Without such manifestation, God would remain in the silence of the *Ungrund* without essence or Being. God, willing to manifest and become conscious of Godself, subsequently splits into two centres of darkness and light. This polarity within God emerges from the *Ungrund* and is the result of the conflict between will and desire. Will is pure freedom, whilst desire is characterized as a fire furiously searching for an object to consume in order for God to have an essence. The will breaks free from desire and establishes a centre of light as opposed to the latter's centre of darkness. These two poles constitute God's essence. The dark centre contains potentially destructive powers of non-being situated within Godself. The other pole within God, God's light centre, seeks to overcome the dark potential for non-being. Therefore God's being is characterized by a dynamic synthesis of the opposing principles in both the dark and light centres.

Boehme's emphasis is on the whole of created reality as a manifestation of the Divine Will – a self-evolution and self-realization of the consciousness and personality of God. Creation is constituted by the unfolding of the triune God's self-revelation and actualization which, as a microcosm, acts as a medium through which the essence of God may be reflected back to Godself, enabling God to become consciously aware of God's existence and glory. God therefore wills creation into life, and although it is not divine in itself, it is the result of God's free self-objectification and self-manifestation. Boehme claims:

> The hidden God has brought himself into nature and dwelleth in it. Had he not with his will brought forth himself out of himself, how then would the hidden will of God, which is in itself and is but one, be manifested and revealed to himself? How can there be in One who is only Will a knowledge or apprehension of itself?[14]

Creation reflects the same structure and process as God, although it is manifested into the temporal realm and hence not eternal, as in God, but constituted by change and duration.[15] All created beings are characterized by structural polarities and an inner 'quality' which strives for self-realization: 'For from its twofold source, everything has its great mobility, running, springing, driving and growing. For meekness in nature is a still *rest*, but the fierceness in every power makes all things moveable, running and generative'.[16]

Boehme thus has a central place for novel creativity and becoming within the Godhead, emerging from the pre-ontological freedom of the *Ungrund*. Paul Tillich notes: 'Through Boehme, Lutheran mysticism influenced Schelling and German Idealism, and through Schelling it in turn influenced the philosophies of irrationalism and vitalism that emerged in the nineteenth and twentieth centuries.'[17] Boehme focused on the idea of 'chaos', strife and polarity, as well as the emotions of will and desire, within the Godhead. We shall see later that similar conceptions emerge in the thought of Bergson, a further family member of process thought. For Bergson there is a primal, indeterminate, inexhaustible source to all life out of which emerges an original urge for life and need for creation. It is from this will to life that creation begins; supra-(Divine) consciousness is thus the primary ground of all being. However, before looking at Bergson in greater detail, let us first look at Boehme's influence on Schelling, as this helped to nourish the soil from which Bergsonian philosophy grew.

Jacob Boehme and Friedrich Schelling

Boehme's stress on the psychology of the Godhead, emphasizing the will or desire of God for self-manifestation and consciousness, provides the tension necessary for the unification of opposites in the *Ungrund* to become dynamically and creatively opposed. Boehme came to exert a marked influence upon the middle and later philosophy of Schelling.[18] Indeed Boehme, according to Schelling, 'was a miraculous phenomenon in the history of mankind ... As popular mythologies and theogonies preceded science, so J. Boehme, in the birth of God, as he describes it for us, precedes all the scientific systems of modern philosophy'.[19] After his introduction to the thoughts of Boehme, Schelling shifted his thought to a mystical theosophy that he believed accounted for problems inherent in his early *Naturphilosophie*. His later thought was therefore dominated by an insistence that history is an epic composed within the eternal Trinity, with the second Person, the Logos, as the paradigm for the sensible world.

It was largely from Boehme that Schelling developed a theory of evolution as a self-manifestation of God in history and nature, fulfilling the scriptural passage of 1 Corinthians 15:28: 'in order that God may be all in all'. It was a theory of evolution prior to Darwin in which the Abyss of God, 'the nursing mother of the whole visible world', was revealed in corporeal and visible forms.[20] God's self-manifestation is seen in terms of a spiritual corporeality that is necessary for perfection. This completion of God's unfolding existence is what Schelling referred to as 'theogony': the manifestation of the eternal God into time and space. Indeed, Schelling refers to the universe as the 'heartbeat' of God.[21]

Schelling therefore offers a theogony of the Christian Trinity which is aligned with a cosmology. Creation presupposes a contraction and concentration (a 'heartbeat') of the two wills that constitute God, ideas that have clear affinities with Boehme. The first is a supra-existent will that wills no object; the second is a divine will, which wills to exist. Commenting on Schelling, Edward Booth writes: 'And from this "heart-beat" of God between supra-existence and existence, the alternation of negating systole and affirming diastole, comes the like of God, and the natural cosmos, which corresponds to it.'[22]

Drawing on the notion of the deity largely expressed by Boehme, both Schelling and Hegel agree that God is an '*ens manifestativum sui*': a self-manifesting Being. However, whereas Hegel's emphasis was on a more necessary, precise law of historical progression that was determined by the dynamic power of negation within a triadic formula of thesis–antithesis–synthesis, Schelling was more concerned to highlight the free will and liberty of God in God's self-revelation. Thus, although Hegel and Schelling agree that God was a self-manifesting Being, arriving at knowledge of Godself through God's self-unfolding in the Trinity and creation, they differed as to how this manifestation was to be conceived. Schelling wrote, with Hegel in mind:

> It is now a very common idea to see in the whole history of the world a progressive revelation of God. But how has the divinity arrived there, how has it begun to reveal itself? The response: God is by nature and necessity a being who reveals himself (*ens manifestativum sui*) is correct *but not exact*.[23]

Schelling's mature thought was strongly characterized by an emphasis on history and eschatology; the latter being the culmination of the former and the means by which the self-revelation of God is manifested:

> Taken as a whole, history is a continual and progressive revelation of the absolute. We are never able, then, to determine the precise point in the course of history where the stamp of Providence or God himself becomes visible, so to speak. For God never is, if he is called to be that which manifests itself in the objective world; if he was, we would not be; but he does not cease to reveal himself.[24]

This idea of God in a process of realizing Godself through finite nature enables the possibility of creaturely, existential freedom. The human mind, made in the image of God and a microcosm of the whole, is embroiled in the struggle to overcome darkness, and in so doing gives external form to the inner conflict of God. It is the duty of humankind, and indeed the goal of history, to move from darkness to light and awaken the 'slumbering spirit' that will lead humanity back to the true Source of its being. Schelling drew heavily on classical mythology as the supreme expression of Divine transcendence and self-consciousness:

> History is an epic composed in the mind of God. Its two main parts are: first, that which depicts the departure of humanity from its centre up to its furthest point of alienation from this centre, and, secondly, that which depicts the return. The first part is the *Iliad*, the second the *Odyssey* of history.[25]

Schelling was the most important contemporary influence upon the thought of Coleridge. In his poetry, Coleridge wishes to defend the priority of the divine will and the desire for divine self-consciousness achieved through the evolution of nature. This romantic interest in the drama and evolution of self-consciousness also surfaces in the philosophy of Bergson. Indeed, Gabriel Marcel, who was a student and a keen admirer of Bergson, wrote a dissertation while in Paris (1909) on 'The Metaphysical Ideas of Coleridge Considered in their Relation to Schelling', which was later published in 1971 under the title *Coleridge et Schelling*. This dissertation suggests that Marcel saw in Coleridge and Schelling an idealism conducive to the Bergsonian philosophy. Jack Haeger writes of such an affinity: 'He [Coleridge] stands as a prominent representative of the reservoir of philosophic precedent that had formed a century before Bergson would draw from it, and his own struggles with idealist and vitalist conceptions help to place the formulations in historical context.'[26] Bergson, Haeger continues, provided an 'idealist version of the principle of evolution'.[27] The emphasis of the generative creative power of divine self-consciousness prominent in Coleridge (to whom we shall return below), as well as Bergson's concept of the *élan vital*, resonate with ideas which may be found in Schelling but which, as we have seen, largely go back to the work of Boehme. Let us now look at some key process ideas of Bergson.

Henri Bergson

Bergson claims that any attempt to understand the human self by using static concepts will fail to reveal the dynamic and changing character of the self. Owing to unceasing thoughts, feelings and passions, there is constant change and creativity within our inner selves that cannot be adequately described by the static axioms of the intellect. This is because the intellect can only grasp things through the static concepts defined by itself. Although the intellect is closely related to individual consciousness, and is able to formulate general truths, it is unable to grasp the inner nature of things because of its necessity to freeze reality into digestible and analysable concepts: 'It [the intellect] imagines, therefore, a formless ego, indifferent and unchangeable, on which it threads the psychic states which it has set up as independent entities.'[28]

Put another way, 'The most living thought becomes frigid in the formula that expresses it.'[29]

To account for the dynamics of change within the self, as well as the emergence of the intellect, Bergson turns to an examination of biological phenomena and the evolution of living things. He rejects the mechanistic and materialistic accounts of evolution (for example, the Lamarckian and Darwinian), as they fail to account sufficiently for the evident dynamic process of life. Instead, Bergson claims there to be life-force (*élan vital*) which shows itself in all living things. This *élan vital* desires life to free itself from the constrictions of matter and to achieve self-consciousness; it therefore accounts for creative evolution and the emergence of instinct and intellect in living things.

The *élan vital* begins as a dim spark that willed to become alive; therefore, it distinguishes living things from those that are dead. Thrusting up through diverging branches of the evolutionary tree and differing species of nature (vegetable, animal), it seeks the best route to achieving self-consciousness from various differing species of nature. The *élan* has progressed through plant and animal evolution before locating the channel of human consciousness: 'The animals, however distant they may be from our species, however hostile to it, have nonetheless been useful travelling companions, on whom consciousness has unloaded whatever encumbrances it was dragging along, and who have enabled it to rise, in man, to heights from which it sees an unlimited horizon open before it.'[30] However, although the self is essentially spiritual, dynamic and creative, it serves to weigh down the *élan* in periods of stagnation and sterility. Bergson uses his famous metaphor of a jet of steam that surges upwards before its loss of energy forces it to descend. The upward stream signifies the ascent of the *élan*, whilst its descent represents congealed spirit – materiality – which prevents its continuing upward spurt: 'Life in general is mobility itself.'[31] The *élan vital* and matter are not two independent entities; matter is congealed spirit that has lost the energy to continue its surge upwards towards self-consciousness; it is thus devoid of life. Perpetually creative life therefore attempts to 'unmake itself' in the sense of freeing itself from the matter into which it has congealed. Life attempts to surge upwards, matter serves to weigh it down and the faculty of the intellect is specifically related to this restriction of the *élan*: 'The intellect is characterised by a natural inability to comprehend life.'[32] The processes of matter and the related faculty of the intellect are inverse to that of life. The *élan vital* has a need and desire for creation and thus attempts to insert as much indeterminacy into matter as possible in order to overcome its fatigue:

> The impetus of life, of which we are speaking, consists in a need of creation. It cannot create absolutely, because it is confronted with matter. That is to say with the movement that is the inverse of its own. But it seizes upon this matter, which is necessity itself, and strives to introduce into it the largest possible amount of indetermination and liberty.[33]

As well as the faculty of intellect, humanity also shares with the animal world the capacity for instinctual behaviour. However, although instinct is able to act spontaneously and grasp the fluidity of life freed from the distorting constrictions of the intellect, it is not conscious of itself. Hence both the intellectual and instinctual faculties within humanity are unable to account sufficiently for the dynamic principle in life. Both the intellect and instinct serve in manipulating matter and hence weigh life's *élan* down. Bergson, therefore, proceeds to invoke a third faculty that the *élan vital* has been working to produce, a faculty that will combine the advantages of the intellect and instinct in its ultimate transcendence of both: intuition. Intuition, Bergson claims, consists of instinct becoming self-conscious; life becomes conscious of itself directly and immediately, not through the static concepts of the intellect. Intuition empathizes with all beings and manifests itself in situations of intense human experience, action, joy and sadness.

Bergson, therefore, prioritizes intuition as the channel from which life's vital impulse can continue its ascent; only intuition can fully enable the vital impulse in life to ascend to higher levels of consciousness. Nevertheless, despite the attempt of the *élan vital* to produce beings who can maintain this intuitive empathy with life, even if this requires the surpassing of what is regarded as 'human', intuition remains at present only a weak light in the darkness of the intellect.

Only intuition, therefore, is able to experience and perceive life's vital impulse, which Bergson equates with God: 'Distinct from God, who is this energy itself, [beings] could not emerge except in a universe, and that is why the universe has emerged.'[34] For Bergson, God is not a 'thing' or specific object, but the source of the vital impulse in life: 'Everything is obscure in the idea of creation if we think of things which are created and a thing which creates, as we habitually do, as the understanding cannot help doing.'[35] Again he asserts:

> I simply express this probable similitude when I speak of a center from which worlds shoot out like rockets in a fire-work display – provided, however, that I do not present this center as a thing, but as a continuity of shooting out: God, thus defined, has nothing of the ready made; He is unceasing life, action, freedom.[36]

Despite a lack of a clearly defined teleology within the philosophy of Bergson, we can nevertheless see a clear line of ideological continuity from Boehme through Schelling and Coleridge to Bergson. Boehme's emphasis on a creative God who evolves through history and time en route to self-consciousness makes him a pivotal figure in any discussion concerning the evolutionary process of the world. He may justifiably be termed the father of process thought. As we now turn to the work of Blake, Wordsworth and Coleridge, we also see key elements of Boehme's thought mediated through the channel of poetry, which attempts to capture an intuitive and visionary experience of the Divine.

William Blake, Samuel Taylor Coleridge and William Wordsworth

The influence of Boehme on Blake, particularly within *The Marriage of Heaven and Hell*, has already been documented. John Beer notes: 'There can be no doubt of the paramount influence on Blake of Jacob Boehme.'[37] Bryan Aubrey asserts that 'the direct influence of Boehme's work, including works other than *Aurora*, on *The Marriage* is incontestable'.[38] Moreover, 'The prophetic careers of Blake and Boehme reveal an unmistakable parallelism, and *The Marriage of Heaven and Hell* was Blake's *Aurora*.'[39] Likewise, Kathleen Raine asserts that *The Marriage* 'marks the strongest influence of Boehme on Blake'.[40] Indeed, Blake's *The Marriage* is a testament to the dynamism and energy of life, which result from the creative conflict of opposing forces: 'Without Contraries is no progression. Attraction and Repulsion, Reason and Energy, Love and Hate, are necessary to Human existence / From these contraries spring what the religious call Good and Evil.'[41] As with Boehme, there is the suggestion of a dark side to God, implying the necessity of a dialectical tension between light and darkness, good and evil. After descending into a fiery infinite Abyss that clearly resembles Boehme's *Ungrund*, the Angel embraces the flame of fire and becomes a Devil: both good and evil emerge from abyssal depths of God.

Boehme's thought also resurfaces in the poetry of Coleridge and Wordsworth.[42] For Coleridge, sublime poetry is able to capture and convey something of the enigmatic perception of the Godhead in religious experience. In developing his emphasis on the growth of self-consciousness, Coleridge asserts the primary human imagination to be a 'repetition in the finite mind of the eternal act of creation in the infinite I AM'.[43] In his poem *Kubla Khan*, a poem described by John Beer as an 'expressive obeisance to absolute energy',[44] he draws upon the image of the walled garden, which symbolizes the transcendent *numinous* reality that the soul strives for:

> So twice five miles of fertile ground
> With walls and towers girdled round:
> And here were gardens bright with sinuous rills
> Where blossomed many an incense-bearing tree.[45]

This imagery of the walled garden is seen most clearly in the mystical thought of Nicholas of Cusa, who refers in his *De Visione Dei* to a vision of the Divine 'beyond' the 'walls' of rational discursive thought. Nevertheless, in *Kubla Khan* Coleridge also employs clear Boehmist imagery. For Boehme, fire and ice represent the principles of expansion and contraction inherent in all phenomena. Ice is therefore the necessary polar opposite of fire. In *Kubla Khan* this necessary polar dynamic tension is portrayed: 'the miracle of rare device/A sunny pleasure dome with caves of ice'.[46] For Coleridge, as for Boehme, all emergent novelty or 'creativity' is a generative conflict-in-attraction of polar forces that constitute the dynamic expansion and contraction of the world.

Although Wordsworth's poetry lacks the transcendental idealism that characterizes much of Coleridge's work (Wordsworth claimed to have 'never read a word of German metaphysics, thank Heaven!') there remains a dynamic portrayal of Nature that certainly deserves to be credited as a forerunner to process thought. Indeed, Hartshorne asserts that Wordsworth rescued both him and Whitehead from materialism and dualism.[47] Although Whitehead did not borrow the term 'organism' from Wordsworth, Hartshone claims, 'he certainly was influenced by Wordsworth's attribution of feeling to the active agents in nature'.[48] Furthermore, Alexander Cappon's work on Wordsworth and Whitehead develops the relation between the two in some depth.[49] Newton P. Stallknecht asserts that 'one source of Wordsworth's transcendentalist concepts seems to be Jakob Boehme'.[50] Like Boehme, Wordsworth emphasizes the creative power of the mind and prioritizes the imagination as the active mental faculty which serves to create 'a new world'.[51]

It is primarily in *The Prelude* that we may see ideas similar to Boehme's.[52]

Humanity, Wordsworth asserts at the very beginning of the work, has been 'foster'd' by Nature.[53] Nature, however, is not a simple harmony, but rather like the workings of Boehme's theosophy, constituted by a dynamic conflict of difference and opposition. It is the role of the creative imagination, symbolized by childlike innocence,[54] to organize, unify, arrange and interpret Nature's 'Severer interventions'.[55] Nature is therefore constituted by a dynamic interplay of opposing forces; like humanity, nature abounds 'with passion and with life'.[56] Wordsworth's emphasis on the unconscious, represented by the innocence of childhood that has been lost, leads him to assert the necessity of poetic imagination to re-present a lost totality. In *The Prelude* this desire for a lost unity is portrayed as a journey back to a true abode or 'home'. Wordsworth's famous 'spots of time', which enable the past to live on and shape the present and future, provide continuity between the 'lost' self and the present self that seek to journey 'home'.[57] 'Home' constitutes a union between the self and something greater: 'Our destiny, our nature, and our home / Is with infinitude, and only there.'[58] The success of this journey, for Wordsworth, is intimately linked to the role of the creative imagination. Poetic creativity is humanity's highest activity and analogous to the creative process of God:

> Such minds are truly from the Deity,
> For they are Powers; and hence the highest bliss
> That can be known is theirs, the consciousness
> Of whom they are habitually infused
> Through every image, and through every thought...[59]

Poetic imagination thus constitutes a dialogue with Nature, the 'breath of God', the mental, creative process behind nature:

> Wisdom and Spirit of the Universe!
> Thou Soul that art the Eternity of Thought!
> And giv'st to forms and images a breath
> And everlasting motion![60]

Conclusion

Process thought clearly has a long and distinguished history. This chapter has argued that the chief tenets of process thought had their genesis in the thought of Jacob Boehme. Boehme's somewhat opaque but nonetheless highly influential thought permeated through the philosophical speculative thought of German Romanticism and into the vitalism of Bergson and Berdyaev, whom Hartshorne justifiably sees as past process thinkers. We highlighted how Boehme's focuses on the notion of time and history, which result from the inner dialectics of the Divine Mind. Furthermore, this emergence of the world's temporal evolution is a result of God's *imaginative* desire for self-realization and self-manifestation. It is this aspect of Divine creativity that appeals so much to thinkers with process tendencies, particularly Berdyaev. Humanity, in the image of this creative, imaginative God, is also essentially creative, and is called to produce *new*, novel ideas rather than actualizing eternal ideas. It is the human imagination that shapes the material forms. Boehme writes: 'For the Soul comprehends the *highest* sense, it beholds what God its Father acts or makes, also it co-operates in the heavenly Imaging or Framing: And therefore it makes a Description, Draught, Platform or Model for the Nature-Spirits, showing how a Thing ought to be imaged or framed.'[61] Moreover, God *needs* humanity to be creative in order to enhance the Divine theogony. God and the world are therefore by no means opposed but, on the contrary, intimately and inextricably linked. We saw earlier how Schelling employs ideas from Boehme to suggest a temporal, suffering God who requires human assistance. Likewise Berdyaev, admitting that the notion that God has need of humanity is 'extraordinarily daring', stresses God's need for human creativity: 'God awaits man's creative act, which is the response to the creative act of God.'[62] Moreover, 'The very personality of man, the disclosure within him of the image of God, is the product of a creative act, of free creative action.'[63]

We also saw how the priority of imaginative self-consciousness is central to the Romantic literature epitomized by Blake, Coleridge and Wordsworth, for whom poetry was the most authentic channel for expressing religious experiences and perceptions. Indeed, Blake, in his tract *All Religions are One*, asserts that Poetic Genius is 'the true faculty of knowing'.[64] For Wordsworth, as we saw, the pure, transformative imaginative faculty is symbolized by childhood in a manner strikingly similar to Boehme, who refers to the unfallen angels as 'little children'.[65] We can see similar ideas on the pristine, creative nature of childhood imagination in the thought of Nikos Kazantzakis, whose close affinity with process thought has already been documented.[66] He writes:

> Truly, nothing more resembles God's eyes than the eyes of a child; they see the world for the first time, and create it. Before this, the world is chaos. All creatures – animals, trees, men, stones; everything: forms, colors, voices, smells, lightning flashes – flow unexplained in front of the child's eyes (no, not in front of them, inside them), and he cannot fasten them down, cannot establish order. The child's world is made not of clay, to last, but of clouds. A cool breeze blows across his temples and the world condenses, attenuates, vanishes. Chaos must have passed in front of God's eyes in just this way before the Creation.
> ... When I wish to speak of the sea, woman, or God in my writing, I gaze down into my breast and listen carefully to what the child within me says.[67]

Kazantzakis, like Wordsworth and Schelling, speaks of the quest for the restoration of the creative imagination in terms of an 'Odyssey', a search for a lost 'home', a return to a state of 'childlike' existence prior to the distorting analytical distinctions of reason and epistemology.[68] This authentic experience also has thought-provoking parallels with the vision and experience of the *numinous* that Coleridge attempted to portray in *Kubla Khan*[69] – an intuitive vision of the Unity of God which may only be experienced by going 'beyond' the guarding, flaming sword of reason and glimpsing into the walled garden of paradise. It is an intuitive vision that is unable to be captured by discursive rational thought, but only in a form of sublime poetry which employs imagery from religious mythology to symbolize experiences and perceptions of the Divine. We saw earlier how Bergson claims that only an intuitive mode of perception can grasp the true dynamic essence of life. This form of intuitive mysticism is indeed rare, as Bergson points out:

In defining mysticism by its relation to the vital impetus, we have implicitly admitted that true mysticism is rare... Let us confine ourselves for the moment to noting that it lies... at a point which the spiritual current, in its passage through matter, probably desired to reach but could not. For it makes light of obstacles with which nature has had to come to terms, and on the other hand, we can only understand the evolution of life, setting aside any bypaths it has been compelled to follow, if we view it as seeking something beyond its reach, something to which the great mystic attains.[70]

Nevertheless, although true intuitive mysticism is rare, 'when it does call, there is in the innermost being of most men the whisper of an echo'.[71] In attempting to convey this mystical perception symbolically, poetry remains a most authentic and dynamic literary mode of expression for process thought.

Notes

1. Jacob Boehme, *The Aurora*, translated by John Sparrow (London: John M. Watkins, 1914) ch. 2: 7, 51. I would like to express my thanks to Dr Sally Bushell for always being willing to share her extensive knowledge of Wordsworth with me.
2. Charles Hartshorne and William L. Reese, *Philosophers Speak of God* (Chicago: University of Chicago Press, 1953), 164.
3. Lewis S. Ford, editor, *Two Process Philosophers. Hartshorne's Encounter with Whitehead*, American Academy of Religion Studies in Religion 5 (Tallahasse, FL: American Academy of Religion Series, 1973), 100.
4. Alfred North Whitehead, *Process and Reality: An Essay in Cosmology*, corrected edition, edited by David Ray Griffin and Donald W. Sherburne (New York: The Free Press, 1978), 344.
5. Ibid., 93.
6. Hartshorne and Reese, *Philosophers Speak of God*, 164. Hartshorne and Reese claim their reason for omitting a detailed analysis of Boehme in this work was 'because of the obscurity of its language and because Schelling and Berdyaev seem to us to have appropriated what is of value in the earlier author. For example, Boehme in one passage speaks of God as changing or in time, and in another he seems to deny this. Berdyaev's doctrine of disintegrated or creaturely and integrated or divine time seems superior' (164).
7. Ibid., 286.
8. ibid., 285–6.
9. Lewis Edwin Hahn, editor, *The Philosophy of Charles Hartshorne* (La Salle, IL: Open Court, 1991), 594.
10. Friedrich Schelling, *The Ages of the World* (New York: Columbia University Press, 1942), 225.
11. Schelling elsewhere claims: 'Without the concept of a humanly suffering God... history remains altogether incomprehensible.' See Friedrich Schelling, *Of Human Freedom* (Chicago: University of Chicago Press, 1936) 84.
12. For a fuller elucidation of Jacob Boehme's thought in English, see David Walsh, *The Mysticism of Inner Worldly Fulfilment: A Study of Jacob Boehme* (Gainsville, FL: University Presses of Florida, 1983) and Andrew Weeks, *Boehme: An Intellectual Biography of the Seventeenth-Century Philosopher* (Albany, NY: State University of New York Press, 1989).
13. Cited in Robert Brown, *The Later Philosophy of Schelling: The Influence of Boehme on the Works 1809–1815* (Lewisburg, VA: Bucknell University Press, 1977) 55, note 7.

14. Cited in E.S Haldane, 'Jacob Boehme and his relation to Hegel', *The Philosophical Review* 6.1 (1897): 156.
15. Robert Brown succinctly describes Boehme's theogony as follows: 'The world is the finite image in space and time of all of the qualities of the divine nature. The dark centre of God is operative in the creation as well as the light centre. The creation consists of the same opposing forces that in God have a relationship of eternal harmony and order, now expressed in a process that involves temporal change and spatial extension.' See Brown, *The Later Philosophy of Schelling*, 68.
16. Boehme, *The Aurora*, ch. 2: 4, 51.
17. Paul Tillich, *On the Boundary* (London: Collins, 1967), 75.
18. Roughly, we can distinguish Schelling into three periods: (a) 1794–1800: 'Ich' related philosophy and *Naturphilosophie*; (b) 1800–1806: *Identitätsphilosophie*; (c) 1807 onwards (the so-called 'middle and later philosophy of Schelling'): it is primarily in this third period that we see Boehme's influence.
19. Cited in Meyer Howard Abrams, *Natural Supernaturalism: Tradition and Revolution in Romantic Literature* (Oxford: Oxford University Press, 1971), 170.
20. Cited in Ernst Benz, *The Mystical Sources of German Romanticism*, translated by Blair R. Reynolds and Eunice M. Paul (Allison Park, PA: Pickwick Publications, 1983), 54. Benz writes: 'The evolution of the universe through the different kingdoms of inorganic matter, plants, animals and man belongs as much to this theogonic process as to soteriology, which forms a kind of prolongation or continuation of creative evolution in the kingdom of history' (48).
21. Schelling claims: 'The entire universe, stretched out and unfolded in space, is nothing more than the palpitating heart of the divinity which, held by invisible powers, continues to beat in an endless pulsation, in a rhythmic expansion and contraction.' (Cited in Benz, *The Mystical Sources*, 55.)
22. Edward Booth, 'Τὸ υπερειναι (of Pseudo-Dionysus and Schelling)', *Studia Patristica* 23 (1989): 220.
23. Cited by Benz, *The Mystical Sources*, 41 (emphasis added).
24. Ibid., 28.
25. Schelling, *The Ages of the World*, 84–5.
26. Jack Haeger, 'Samuel Taylor Coleridge and the Romantic Background to Bergson', in Frederiick Burwick and Paul Douglas, editors, *The Crisis in Modernism: Bergson and the Vitalist Controversy* (Cambridge: Cambridge University Press, 1992), 98.
27. Ibid., 100.
28. Henri Bergson, *Creative Evolution*, authorized translation by Arthur Mitchell (New York: Henry Holt and Company, 1911), 3.
29. Ibid., 134.
30. Ibid., 281.
31. Ibid., 134.
32. Ibid., 174.
33. Ibid., 265.
34. Cited in K.M. Jamil, *Nietzsche and Bergson: In the Domain of Evolutionary and Moral Philosophies* (Rajshahi, East Pakistan: Md. Majed Ali Miah, 1959), 41.
35. Bergson, *Creative Evolution*, 261.
36. Ibid., 262.
37. John Beer, *Blake's Visionary Universe* (Manchester, UK: Manchester University Press, 1969), 25. For the influence of Boehme on Blake's 'The Tree of the Soul', see 25–30.
38. Bryan Aubrey, *Watchmen of Eternity: Blake's Debt to Jacob Boehme* (London: University Press of America, 1986), 381.
39. Ibid., 37.

40. Cited in Aubrey, ibid., 38.
41. William Blake, *The Marriage of Heaven and Hell* (New York: Dover Publications, 1994), 29.
42. Coleridge was transcribing phrases from Boehme around 1796 and later claimed in a letter from 1817 that he had 'conjured over' *The Aurora* of Boehme while in hospital. See John Beer, *Coleridge's Poetic Intelligence* (London: Macmillan 1977), 23. In his *Biographia Literaria*, Coleridge acknowledges his 'debt of gratitude' to Boehme. See James Engell and W. Jackson Bade, editors, *The Collected Works of Samuel Taylor Coleridge* (London: Routledge and Kegan Paul, 1983), 161. Elsewhere he refers to the German mystic as possessing what Wordsworth called 'The Vision and the faculty divine'. See *Marginalia I: Abbt to Byfield* in *The Collected Works of Samuel Taylor Coleridge*, edited by George Whalley (Routledge and Kegan Paul, 1980), 558 and, especially, 553–696. Duncan Wu has suggested that Wordsworth may have been reading Boehme's work around the years 1797–8. See Wu, *Wordsworth's Reading 1770–1799* (Cambridge: Cambridge University Press, 1993), 17. Wordsworth's library contained Boehme's 'De Signatura Rerum' and Edward Taylor's Commentary on Boehme.
43. Coleridge, *Biographia Literaria*, 304.
44. John Beer, *Coleridge's Poetic Intelligence*, 202.
45. Samuel Taylor Coleridge, *Kubla Khan*, lines 6–9, in Samuel Taylor Coleridge, *Poems*, edited by John Beer (London: J.M. Dent, 1963), 205.
46. Coleridge, *Kubla Khan*, lines 35–6, in *Poems*, 206.
47. Hahn, *The Philosophy of Charles Hartshorne*, 13.
48. Ibid., 694.
49. Alexander P. Cappon, *Aspects of Wordsworth and Whitehead: Philosophy and Certain Continuing Life-Problems* (New York: Philosophical Library, 1983); as well as *Action, Organism and Philosophy in Wordsworth and Whitehead* (New York: Philosophical Library, 1985).
50. Newton P. Stallknecht, *Strange Seas of Thought: Studies in William Wordsworth's Philosophy of Man and Nature* (Bloomington, IN: Indiana University Press, 1962), 73.
51. Wordsworth, *The Prelude*, edited and with an introduction by Harold Bloom (New York: Chelsea House, 1986), XII: 368–79.
52. However, we may see similar ideas in Wordsworth's earlier poem 'Tintern Abbey'. See William Wordsworth, *The Pedlar, Tintern Abbey, and the Two-Part Prelude*, edited and with a critical introduction and notes by Jonathan Wordsworth (Cambridge: Cambridge University Press, 1985):

> ...And I have felt
> A presence that disturbs me with the joy
> Of elevated thoughts, a sense sublime
> Of something far more deeply interfused,
> Whose dwelling is the light of the setting suns,
> And the round ocean, and the living air,
> And the blue sky, and in the mind of man –
> A motion and a spirit that impels
> All thinking things, all objects, all thought,
> And rolls through all things. (Lines 94–103)

53. Wordsworth, *The Prelude*, I: 306.
54. Ibid., IV: 531–3.

> ...our childhood sits,
> Our simple childhood sits upon a throne
> That hath more power than all the elements.

55. Ibid., 1: 371.
56. Ibid., XI: 147.
57. Ibid., XII: 258–68.

> There are in our existence spots of time,
> Which with distinct preeminence retain
> A renovating Virtue, whence, depress'd
> By false opinion and contentious thought,
> Or aught of heavier or more deadly weight
> In trivial occupations, and the round
> Of ordinary intercourse, our minds
> Are nourish'd, and invisibly repair'd,
> A virtue by which pleasure is enhanced
> That penetrates, enables us to mount
> When high, more high, and lifts us up when fallen.

58. Ibid., 538–9.
59. Ibid., XIII: 106–10.
60. Ibid., I: 429–32.
61. Boehme, *The Aurora*, ch. 15: 51.
62. Nicholas Berdyaev, *Dream and Reality: An Essay in Autobiography*, translated by Katherine Lampert (London: G. Bles Ltd., 1950), 208, 209.
63. Nicholas Berdyaev, *Truth and Revelation*, translated by R.M. French (London: G. Bles Ltd., 1953), 73.
64. William Blake, *All Religions are One* (London: Frederick Hollyer, 1926), 'The Argument'.
65. Boehme, *The Aurora*, ch. 12: 45–7.
66. See Daniel A. Dombrowski's essay in the present collection. See also Darren Middleton's *Novel Theology: Nikos Kazantzakis's Encounter with Whiteheadian Process Theism* (Macon, GA: Mercer University Press, 2000).
67. Nikos Kazantzakis, *Report to Greco*, translated by Peter A. Bien (New York: Simon and Schuster, 1965), 45, 49.
68. See Abrams, *Natural Supernaturalism*, 256–78 (Blake and Coleridge); and 278–92 on Wordsworth's 'long journey home'.
69. Rudolf Otto, in his *The Idea of the Holy*, refers to Coleridge's 'savage place' in Kubla Khan as an example of the 'Numinose'. See Rudolf Otto, *The Idea of the Holy*, translated by John W. Harvey (Oxford: Oxford University Press, 1928), 222. Furthermore, C.S. Lewis refers to the 'opening lines of Kubla Khan' when discussing the longing for the 'unnameable something' that dominates Romanticism. See C.S. Lewis, *The Pilgrim's Regress: An Allegorical Defence for Christianity, Reason and Romanticism* (London, G. Bles Ltd., 1943), 9. See Douglas Hedley's 'Coleridge's Intellectual Intuition, the Vision of God, and the Walled Garden of "Kubla Khan"', *Journal of the History of Ideas* 59.1 (1998): 115. Coleridge, *Kubla Khan*, lines 53–4, in *Poems*, 206.
70. Henri Bergson, *The Two Sources of Morality and Religion*, translated by R. Ashley Audra, Cloudesley Brereton, and W. Horsfall Carter (Notre Dame, IN: University of Notre Dame Press, 1977), 182.
71. Ibid., 182.

Chapter 11

Denise Levertov's Poetics of Process

Bobby Caudle Rogers

Images are more demanding than ideas. (Gaston Bachelard)[1]

With memory we are, in truth, in the domain of spirit. (Henri Bergson)[2]

Introduction

As with all lyric poetry, the lines in Denise Levertov's poems seek to raise themselves from the page in a struggle towards transcendence. By the time of her 1984 book *Oblique Prayers*, this struggle becomes unself-consciously theological. 'God's in the dust / not sifted / out from confusion,' she writes, offering an apologetics for her more confident essays into 'religious poetry' and putting forth a justification for her famously small and quotidian imagery like that of her High Modernist mentor and model, William Carlos Williams.[3] Hers is a poetry of moments, a poetry of the small, luminous surprise; and hers is a poetry that becomes more comfortably and evidently religious as her career progresses. 'I now define myself as a Christian, but not a very orthodox one,' she said in a 1986 interview, 'and I think there is a way of looking at Christian faith as involving the cooperation of man.'[4] Even her politically directed writings during the decades of the 1960s and 1970s, when political engagement, rather than taking energy from religious commitment, often seemed to render such commitment irrelevant, showed a concern with spiritual matters, a concern for what could outlive its physical moment. Poems such as the title poem of her 1964 book *O Taste and See*, which has become one of her most anthologized works, show her propensity, even at this early stage, to search for the transcendent in the earthly, the lyrical in the material. She finds transcendence in the non-transcendent world, or in this case, underworld – a subway train. The phrase from the 34th Psalm which makes up the title is an *objet trouvé*, a found piece of text 'the subway Bible poster said'.[5] She asserts that 'The world is / not with us enough', reversing William Wordsworth's contention that we are too much in and of the material world. In Levertov's poem, 'The Lord', religious abstractions such as 'grief, mercy' become as tactile, as tangible, as tasteable as 'plum, quince', as real as 'crossing the street'.

Henri Bergson's process thought, his notions of time and persistent change, his ideas of God, form a useful means to approach this rich body of work. In the final sentence of *The Two Sources of Morality and Religion*, Bergson makes the claim that 'The universe ... is a machine for the making of God.'[6] Bergson's own considerable gift for metaphor seems but a preparation for the more poetic explorations of Levertov. It is in the quotidiana of the world, Levertov realizes, that one may find God. As we shall see, some contemporary critics find Levertov's approach trivial, reductive, overly 'domestic' and sentimental. But in the context of Bergson's thought, a concern with the small, accessible image is no less than essential. The measurement of individual moments is a hallmark of process philosophy: 'Each moment is not only something new,' Bergson writes in *Creative Evolution*, 'but something unforeseeable; ... change is far more radical than we suppose'.[7] Bergson's philosophy has always been an aesthetic one, highly amenable to literature, and generally it has been appreciated as being literature in its own right. Indeed, Bergson's Nobel Prize award in 1928 was in literature. Shiv Kumar's 1963 treatment of the stream of consciousness novel finds Bergson's thought much more useful than psychology for understanding the highly psychological modernist fictions of James Joyce and Virginia Woolf. Kumar writes, 'Bergson's presentation of the human situation in terms of durational continuity, *l'émotion créatrice* and intuition, brings his philosophy closer to contemporary writers and artists than to psychologists and metaphysicians.'[8]

Bergson, the High Modernists and Levertov

Levertov's art may be more profoundly read if we consider it as an embodiment of Bergson's philosophy. There seems to be a low-grade Bergsonism running throughout the twentieth century, and it certainly may be felt in the work of the High Modernists, and particularly in the experimental poetics of William Carlos Williams, Levertov's single most significant source. Paul Douglass writes of a dialogue with the evolutionary ideas of Bergson which included the voices of most American Modernists of note:

> But there is, as it turns out, a genuine consistency of approach, argumentation, and vocabulary among major American writers between the wars; and that vocabulary emerges from a dialogue in which Bergson was the most important single voice. That is why one can speak of such different writers as Miller, Eliot, Faulkner, Williams, Frost, and Stein as sharing a Bergsonian impulse, for they were writing about his issue – about the possibility of reasserting freedom for the human spirit...[9]

Levertov, through her early study and emulation and career-long refinement and extension of Williams's poetics, has obviously internalized the terms of this debate. Her work gains from an application of process thought, and Bergson's ideas are more solidly rendered than even his own gift for metaphor could accomplish. Bergson held that 'for a conscious being, to exist is to change, to change is to mature, to mature is to go on creating one's self endlessly'.[10] Levertov's is a world of continuous utterance and refinement. Consciousness extends to even the smallest particulate of matter. Her poems preach the significance of the small thing; they are beatitudes of dust, wrought in the belief that 'the world, a word / intricately incarnate, offers ... / what hunger craves ...'.[11]

Levertov's work has embodied process thought from early on, and in a way this has prepared the ground for her later theological explorations. In fact, her more openly religious poems have served to clarify the process impulse that has been evident in her work in all its phases, early and late. The final lines of the title poem to her 1958 book *Overland to the Islands*, ' – every step an / arrival', is a miniature of this philosophy. She admits to having taken this last line from Rilke, but it serves as an illuminating emblem of her poetics in which every moment bears its own significance: there is no ultimate arrival that negates the need for or diminishes any next step.[12]

Levertov's much discussed conception of organic form and organic poetry seems drawn from process thought:

> A partial definition, then, of organic poetry might be that it is a method of apperception, i.e., of recognizing what we perceive, and is based on an intuition of an order, a form beyond forms, in which forms partake, and of which man's creative works are analogies, resemblances, natural allegories. Such poetry is exploratory.[13]

This approach harmonizes with the intuitive method that Bergson brings to his engagement with philosophical problems, a method that could justly be described as poetical: '*Intuition* is the method of Bergsonism', writes Gilles Deleuze in his study of Bergson's thought.[14] (Deleuze's own philosophy has been referred to as a 'New Bergsonism.'[15]) *The Princeton Encyclopedia of Poetry and Poetics* refers to Bergson's enterprise as no less than an attempt at the 'poeticization of human experience'.[16] The entry on 'Twentieth Century Poetics' written by Paul de Man and Claudia Brodsky Lacour speaks of Bergson as being 'concerned with the imagining process as the unifying activity of human consciousness'.[17] As Deleuze explains it, 'the brain is an "image" among other images' and is, thus, not involved in the 'manufacture [of] representations, but only complicates the relationship between a received movement (excitation) and an executed movement (response)'.[18] In Levertov's work, the poetic consciousness resides amongst the images, as changeful as the world in which it is immersed. She would agree that 'we perceive things where they are, perception puts us at once into matter, is impersonal, and coincides with the perceived object'.[19] Bergson states it most directly himself in the first chapter of *Matter and Memory*: 'Perception, in its pure state, is, then, in very truth, a part of things.'[20]

Bergson's conception of the past is also useful to us in realizing the more complex issues Levertov's seemingly simple poems pose to the attentive reader. For Bergson, the past endures and intrudes into the present; nothing is ever fully lost: 'Doubtless we think with only a small part of our past; but it is with our entire past ... that we desire, will, and act.'[21] The past is never left behind. We are surrounded by it; our sensations are a compendium of present and past sensations. Indeed, what we believe to be the immediacy of the world is shaped by our past, and without experience we have no capability of touching the present. As Bergson so compellingly argues in *Matter and Memory*, 'our senses require education'.[22] This is the role that memory plays, to continually shape the stream of data from our sensory apparatuses, to give each moment coherence and form. The present cannot be isolated from the background noise of the past. 'We assert at the outset,' argues Bergson,

> that if there be memory, that is, the survival of past images, these images must constantly mingle with our perception of the present and may even take its place. For if they have survived it is with a view to utility; at every moment they complete our present experience,

enriching it with experience already acquired, and, as the latter is ever increasing, it must end by covering up and submerging the former. It is indisputable that the basis of real, and so to speak instantaneous, intuition, on which our perception of the external world is developed, is a small matter compared with all that memory adds to it.[23]

'A Time Past'

For Levertov, the process of decay wrought by time is only a movement towards transcendence. In the 1975 poem 'A Time Past', the disappearance of a run of wooden steps on which the speaker was sitting during the time alluded to in the title seems to pose little threat to the memory. The abstraction may still emerge whole even though granite steps, 'hard, gray, and handsome', have supplanted the steps she remembers:

> A Time Past
>
> The old wooden steps to the front door
> where I was sitting that fall morning
> when you came downstairs, just awake,
> and my joy at sight of you (emerging
> into golden day –
>   the dew almost frost)
> pulled me to my feet to tell you
> how much I loved you:
>
> those wooden steps
> are gone now, decayed,
> replaced with granite,
> hard, gray, and handsome.
> The old steps live
> only in me:
> my feet and thighs
> remember them, and my hands
> still feel their splinters.
>
> Everything else about and around that house
> brings memories of others – of marriage,
> of my son. And the steps do too: I recall
> sitting there with my friend and her little son who died,
> or was it the second one who lives and thrives?
> And sitting there 'in my life,' often, alone or with my husband.
> Yet that one instant,
> your cheerful, unafraid, youthful, 'I love you too,'
> the quiet broken by no bird, no cricket, gold leaves
> spinning in silence down without
> any breeze to blow them,
>   is what twines itself
> in my head and body across those slabs of wood
> that were warm, ancient, and now
> wait somewhere to be burnt.[24]

The steps recalled from the past contain greater power than these seemingly more durable stone replacements, a power which continues to accrue as the poem extends towards its final image. 'The old steps live / only in me,' she writes. They have become the kind of tactile memory that Bergson liked to write about and struggled to explain. '[M]y feet and thighs / remember them,' the poem tells us, 'and my hands / still feel their splinters.' In memory the steps were 'warm, ancient' but in the subsequent line, the line which ends the poem, they 'wait somewhere to be burnt', ready to break into a life fiercer and more sensuous than the material steps from which the voiced consciousness ruminates in the 'present'.[25] That somewhere very well may be the memory, where images reside and may be recalled to explain or enrich our perceptions. This past moment, the perception of the wooden stairs, may illuminate a present or future moment. Bergson found it impossible to separate the past from the present. 'Perception,' he wrote, 'is never a mere contact of the mind with the object present; it is impregnated with memory-images which complete it as they interpret it.'[26] The present is never fully free of the past:

> What is, for me, the present moment? The essence of time is that it goes by; time already gone by is the past, and we call the present the instant in which it goes by. But there can be no question here of a mathematical instant. No doubt there is an ideal present – a pure conception, the indivisible limit which separates past from future. But the real, concrete, live present – that of which I speak when I speak of my present perception – that present necessarily occupies a duration. Where then is this duration placed? Is it on the nearer or on the further side of the mathematical point which I determine ideally when I think of the present instant? Quite evidently, it is both on this side and on that, and what I call 'my present' has one foot in my past and another in my future.[27]

According to Deleuze, 'the Bergsonian revolution is clear: We do not move from the present to the past, from perception to recollection, but from the past to the present, from recollection to perception'.[28] Deleuze has in mind the Summary and Conclusion of *Matter and Memory* in which Bergson speaks of the past as 'that which acts no longer but which might act, and will act by inserting itself into a present sensation from which it borrows the vitality. It is true that, from the moment when the recollection actualizes itself in this manner, it ceases to be a recollection and becomes once more a perception'.[29] We see this happening with the stairs in this poem. The wooden stairs which have been demolished and replaced maintain presence and a vitality the extant stone steps cannot claim.

Even though the focal point of this poem – the stairs – is an inanimate object, a static image, Levertov does not present it as her Imagist forebears might. The Imagists, T.E. Hulme in particular, often viewed the poem as *sculptural*. When speaking of the Modernist verse emerging at the beginning of the twentieth century, Hulme certainly makes a helpful observation, if not an ultimately true one, when he states that 'This new verse resembles sculpture rather than music; it appeals to the eye rather than to the ear.'[30] In some ways the poetry that was to have a formative influence on Levertov's prosody (though not her subject matter) was a static, sculptural poetry. Williams's 'Between Walls' is an example:

> Between Walls
>
> the back wings
> of the
>
> hospital where
> nothing
>
> will grow lie
> cinders
>
> in which shine
> the broken
>
> pieces of a green
> bottle[31]

Levertov has learned a great deal from this type of poem making, this Imagist–Objectivist approach employed by Williams. Her seeing is just as precise; she strives for the same spareness of composition. In his study of modern prosody, Harvey Gross writes that 'The objectivist poem achieves its vividness by stopping time; the poem sits on the page in its unmoving "thingness" ... Rhythmic structure moves in time, but the Objectivist poem does not move; ... it sit[s] motionless, pinned down by typography and visual form.'[32] Levertov's poems are hardly ever so stopped. As in 'A Time Past', her images never become disembedded from time. Her poems are more amenable to Pound's well-known musical metaphor, his admonition that practitioners of the new poetry should 'compose in sequence of the musical phrase, not in sequence of the metronome'.[33]

The idea, emerging from a physical stimulus in the past, has intensified. The past 'is what twines itself / in my head and body...'.[34] The passage of time has clarified the event. It is no longer dependent on the context for its life. The past, the physical detail itself, is made to release its energy as wood does by burning.

Poetic Vocation

Levertov's evolution as a poet of Christian concerns has been about as gradual as one life-time allows. By the time her *New & Selected Essays* appeared in 1992, when the poet was almost 70, she was able to open the book with the following statement:

> In the fall of 1990, I realized that my own preferred reading in current poetry as the last decade of the century began was of two kinds: a certain kind of poem about the world of nature written predominantly by poets of the Pacific Northwest, and poems of various provenance that were concerned more or less with matters of religious faith.[35]

There is still a palpable ambivalence about declaring herself as a poet drawn to issues of faith. She even broaches the subject indirectly through a consideration of her reading tastes. The poet seems surprised that she can now read and take something from the work of T.S. Eliot, the arch-rival and in some ways antithesis of her mentor William Carlos Williams (though the two were not so antithetical as Williams would have liked to believe, or as critics often claim). More accurately, one can sense her unease at how this statement will be received by her readership, what the statement will mean for the relatively narrow and specialized audience who have read it and will read it in the future. No poet of Levertov's stature wishes to be called a Christian poet. In the community of poets, such a positioning, conventional wisdom tells us, is unpopular, limiting, even deadly. Christian poetry is synonymous with bad poetry; Christian thinking is narrow thinking. Even Donald Davie in his introduction to *The New Oxford Book of Christian Verse* holds the term in some contempt:

> As soon as we set up 'Christian verse' as a category on a par with, say, 'political verse' or 'comic verse', we are making a distinction that the truly devout and thinking Christian is obliged to repudiate ... We may as well admit, that the very concept, 'Christian verse', is one that won't stand up to close scrutiny.[36]

Davie observes that poets in prior times did not separate their religious lives from their other selves in a way that seems to be necessary in our own secularized age. The term 'Christian poet', once a redundancy, has retained the meaning 'Christian' but, for most, rarely means poet.

In this essay on her evolving reading tastes, Levertov graphs her maturing appetites and needs as a poet and, indeed, her development as a poet, for we tend to read acquisitively and jealously, seeing mostly our own ambitions in what other poets have attempted, the effects they achieve and the means. She speaks highly of poets whom we would never classify as overtly Christian, but yet who pursue spiritual ends, who thirst after God. She mentions Charles Wright's *China Trace*,[37] and perhaps has in mind a poem such as 'Snow', whose first tercet postulates that 'If we, as we are, are dust, and dust, as it will, rises, / Then we will rise, and recongregate / In the wind, in the cloud, and be their issue...'.[38] Wright's insistence on a world beyond this one, his constant pursuit of realizing that other world in the minute, apprehensible beauties of this broken one, separates him from the crowd of contemporary poets who have no interest in any world other than this material one. Later in the book Wright tells us, 'I write poems to untie myself, to do penance and disappear / Through the upper right-hand corner of things, to say grace.'[39]

More and more, Levertov's enterprise as a poet has come to be a similar pursuit. She and Wright are both after what Paul Tillich has called the 'ultimate concern'. 'What modern art tries to do,' Tillich writes, 'is to move away from the surface which had nothing to say anymore to men of the twentieth century, and to move to the *Urelemente*, the original elements of reality which in the physical realm are cubes, planes, colors, lines and shadows.'[40] Speaking of the plastic arts, Tillich asserts that there are four 'levels' of relation between art and religion. (Tillich later abandoned the term 'levels' in favour of the less hierarchical 'dimensions'.) These are: (1) Non-Religious Style, Non-Religious Content; (2) Religious Style, Non-Religious Content; (3) Non-Religious Style, Religious Content; (4) Religious Style, Religious Content. Tillich's parsing of the relationship between art and religion, his championing of 'Religious Style' in seemingly non-religious pieces such Giorgio de Chirico's *The Mystery and Melancholy of a Street* or Mark Rothko's *Orange and Tan*, is by now well known. Tillich defends these works as employing a religious style – or, to use his rich if somewhat enigmatic term, they are in pursuit of 'ultimate concern' – even though their content is bereft of religious iconography or allusion. He places them in the second dimension, 'Religious Style, Non-Religious Content', which is clearly Tillich's favourite. This dimension allows for a more profound reading of the work of the Abstract Expressionists coming to the fore at mid-twentieth-century, people such as Jackson Pollock and Rothko. It is the final level – he never suggests that it is the highest level – that Tillich doubts is possible in the context of

> the disrupted style which modern art has created. In this context I put a question which I cannot answer: Is it possible to have this fourth level today? Is it possible to use these elements of expressionist visual art in dealing with the traditional symbols of Christianity? Sometimes ... I am willing to say that it is possible. Sometimes I am not willing to say so.[41]

Poets such as Denise Levertov and Charles Wright seem poised between these two dimensions, seeking to escape somehow this corporeal world and effect transcendence, no matter how short-lived. Levertov's poetry shows some tentative interest in moving from the second to the fourth level. Her later poems are more determined and more explicit in exploring a 'religious content'. We can see this in her movement from being primarily interested in formal structure to an interest in 'content or concern'.[42] The movement can be summed up as a shift from matter to spirit, though for any poet, and especially this one, matter and spirit are never far apart.

Pilgrimage

An element of what Tillich might consider 'religious style' which may be traced through the entirety of Levertov's work is that ancient mode of expressed devotion, the pilgrimage. Pilgrimage – in its essential denotation: a physical journeying towards a spiritual destination – is a concept that is present early on in Levertov's work and which remains important in her later poems. In a talk she gave in 1967 to a conference of theologians and poets sponsored by the Church Society for College Work, she goes back to her very first pre-literate attempts at poetry, a poem she dictated to her sister when she was five years old, analysing the poem for her audience in order to throw light on her mature work: 'in an infantile way it introduced the theme of a journey that would lead one from one state of being to another that later I find defined in many poems as the sense of *life as a pilgrimage*' (original emphasis).[43] (As one might expect, the interpretation she brings to this piece of juvenilia is more illuminating than the poem itself.) Later, in her Paul Zweig Memorial Lecture given in 1991 at the Poets' House in New York City, she spoke of seeking a poetry that

> is itself 'on pilgrimage,' as it were, in search of significance underneath and beyond the succession of temporal events: a poetry which attests to the 'deep spiritual longing' that Jorie Graham, in her very interesting essay of introduction to *The Best American Poetry, 1990* says is increasingly manifest in recent American verse.[44]

This movement towards a spiritual destination would be recognizable to Bergson and is characteristic of process thought in general. A pilgrimage is by definition a process, a becoming; in process thought only processes are fully actual. What is static is an abstraction, an excision from a process, and therefore less real.

Misreading Levertov

Philosophical underpinnings – such as the Bergsonian conception of process – are routinely overlooked in Levertov's work and her accomplishment is viewed as wholly derivative of male stylistic influences such as Robert Creeley and Robert Duncan and, most profoundly, William Carlos Williams. Certainly, her work was influenced by the poets she respected and with whom she was in close communication. Her fortuitous encounter with the writers that would become her influences has been well documented. Meeting in a Swiss hostel and later marrying the American writer Mitchell Goodman, who had been Robert Creeley's roommate at Harvard, she soon came to know Robert Duncan and William Carlos Williams, and found herself under the spell of Williams's credo, 'no ideas but in things'. But Levertov's poetry has been linked too easily to the poetics of these important forebears, and read too often through the reductive lens of William Carlos Williams's brand of modernism. The misreading commonly brought to her work posits a poetry that is surface obsessed, devoid of ideas, adroit but not profound. This is to miss the point of her poetics. Certainly, her poems employ the diction of Williams and reject the scholasticism of Eliot: there are few Latinates; the grammar is often broken and simplified, simpler even than the grammar of prose, her statements punctuated by space and line breaks more so than by syntax and traditional markings. But to read this lack of adornment as a lack of substance is to fail to invest adequately in the poems – scant returns should be expected. Her poems are about the surfaces of the seen world, the dust and detritus of the matter we push against in our daily lives, but this is just a means through which she can speak about the world's depth and wonder, the incarnation of the world's great mystery.

Robert Bly has written about Levertov along these lines, finding in her poems only a surface accomplishment, considering them to be five-finger exercises of negligible complexity or heft. His chapter on Levertov in his 1990 book, *American Poetry: Wildness and Domesticity*, puts forth most of the readings I have set out in this essay to dispel. 'One weakness her poems always have had and still have,' Bly offers, 'is that there are no real *ideas* in them, as there are ideas in Rilke's work or Yeats's. As a substitute for ideas, there are liberal *attitudes*, mostly taken from William Carlos Williams.'[45] This mischaracterization of her work arises from a narrow notion of what constitutes an idea and how one may be stated. Certainly, the very form of a William Carlos Williams poem constitutes an idea – and at the historical moment of its composition, it presented a very provocative and discomfiting idea for many. And it should go without saying that ideas alone do not make for poetry, and sometimes great poetry occurs in spite of its ideas rather than because of them. Rilke and Yeats may be two of the best examples of this; their ideas range from the profound and epic to the laughable and perverse. Yeats's notions of history, say, are often inscrutable and in the best of circumstances difficult to defend and must be read around at times to get to the genius and beauty of his work. The ideas of process that so mark Levertov's work are embodied in her poems, they are not hobbyhorses or lecture topics the poet descants on in verse. The ideas expressed in Levertov's work are expressed as much in the poem's structure as they are in the 'prose sense' content of the poem. Her ideas may often be read in the movement from one poem to the next. Certainly, there are ideas to be found if one is willing to interpret images. Rarely are her interests stated prosaically as in some position paper: as in all good poetry, her ideas are integral to the poem.

In *American Poetry: Wildness and Domesticity*, Bly speaks mostly of her earlier work, dismissing her later poems as sentimental. He does recognize 'one of her greatest qualities: the marvelously crisp sound' of her lines.[46] The compliment is back-handed at best, delivered almost as an afterthought at the end of his essay, and it is doubtful Bly truly considers it a compliment at all, suggesting, rather, that she should leave the realm of ideas to more muscular intellects and continue her five-finger exercises to the delight of those who appreciate such minor things.

Bly also has a simplified notion of free verse that offers no illumination of Levertov's carefully built lines. 'In good free verse,' he writes:

> all the supposed requirements of meter, of parallelism, of syllable count, of repeatable stanza, are shunned, so that the poetic conventions will be replaced by the poet's voice. It is a matter of taking the voice and distributing it among the words. Once the voice is on the page, the words are made to arrange themselves in such a shape that they can carry it. It is like making fifty mules arrange themselves in a barnyard so they can carry some weirdly shaped object that has ten or twenty arms on a body with a dozen right angles.[47]

It is hard to imagine a serious maker of free verse accepting (or even understanding) this strange model of free verse composition. Certainly, freedom and spontaneity are at the core of decision making when establishing a free verse line – Levertov contends that 'There's very little strictly deliberate about anything I do'[48] – but all technical understanding of traditional prosody is not scrapped. Bly uses 'voice' to suggest some quasi-supernatural, non-rational utterance that is merely captured onto a page by a naive scribe with no knowledge or control of the effects that the language will have on the reader/listener. Free verse is not so mystical as all that. It would truly be an *idiot savant* who would not be attuned to the satisfying power of a spondee at the end of a free verse line or the surprise of a trochee at its beginning or to any number of metrical effects in the interior of a line that chooses to measure itself by a logic more subtle and complex than a count to ten.

Bly also dismisses Levertov's poems as being domestic, and too feminine for his taste: 'A holy man becomes a holy man only by incredible physical sacrifice. Denise Levertov wants to have a prosaic housewifely life and find that her kitchen stepladder is Jacob's Ladder. It won't work.'[49] Levertov obviously has a different notion of holiness. For her, connection with the eternal is the product of reflection and quietude, of faith, rather than some prize earned through Olympic-calibre self-denial and abnegation. Even weakness, a failure of faith, an unheroic act, can lead to a closing of the breach between the earthbound and what endures. In the poem 'Poetics of Faith', Levertov begins with a paraphrase of Dickinson's 'tell it slant':

> 'Straight to the point'
>   can ricochet,
>   unconvincing.
> Circumlocution, analogy,
>   parable's ambiguities, provide
>   context, stepping-stones.[50]

Her poetics are not the heroic poetics that Bly longs for. The subject of 'Poetics of Faith' is the 'impetuous Peter' trying to imitate Christ's miracle of walking on the water. It is a failure on Peter's part: he plunges beneath the waves and has to be supported by Christ. The pay-off in this poem is small and of less than heroic proportions: 'years later, / his toes and insteps, just before sleep, / would remember their passage'. The smallness of this image, to Bly, would hardly seem worth the trouble, yet this small progression towards what is holy is where the power of the poem resides. A long-remembered display of weakness becomes a source of strength.

Bly believes Levertov's acolyte-like adherence to the poetics of Creeley and Duncan has stunted her growth,[51] and perhaps there is some value in this. She has admitted to being too much in thrall to Williams early in her career (in her essay on Williams and Eliot,[52] among other places). She relates that 'It's only in recent years that I've been able to appreciate Eliot again',[53] which suggests how tenacious her loyalty to Williams has been. But the ideas in her poetry which are under consideration in this essay have evolved independent of the orthodoxy of the Black Mountain 'school' – especially her ideas of faith and spirituality.

Ezra Pound's early poem, 'An Object', elegantly poses the central project of Levertov's work, albeit through a satire of the kind of soulless cerebration her work opposes. The poem – an epigram, really – reads in its entirety:

> This thing, that hath a code and not a core,
> Hath set acquaintance where might be affections,
> And nothing now
>   Disturbeth his reflections.[54]

Levertov is certainly after *affection* – a profound and almost occult connecting with the meaning and significance of the world – rather than mere *acquaintance*. She seeks not theory or 'code' but what is at the *core*, the heart of the matter. Jonathan Culler, in his critique of Georges Mounin's *Introduction à la sémiologie*, recognizes that listeners interpret sentences rather than decode them.[55] The figure in the Pound poem is eternally decoding, lost within a travail of pure abstraction that peels away a layer at a time and never reveals the 'object''s nucleus, which is absent. Levertov pursues a kind of knowing beyond knowledge, or, as Gaston Bachelard says in the introduction of his *Poetics of Space*, 'Forces are manifested in poems that do not pass through the circuits of knowledge.'[56] She is not mesmerized like the philosopher satirized by Pound, in thrall to a code that obscures essence; rather, she engages with the world, constantly pursuing and seeking to tell the meaning which resides below its lovely and unlovely surfaces, a world which continually arises to disturb reflections.

As we have seen, Levertov will isolate and break open an image to release its stored up power. It is a trick that she learned from Pound and Williams. Bergson's claim is that images become more than virtual through a process of isolation: 'To transform [an image's] existence into representation, it would be enough to suppress what follows it, what precedes it, and also all that fills it, and to retain only its external crust, its superficial skin.'[57] Levertov's pared down style, as though she were a pointillist with only half a dozen points' worth of paint to apply to the canvas, seems embedded in this theory. Bergson writes:

> To obtain this conversion from the virtual to the actual, it would be necessary, not to throw more light on the object, but, on the contrary, to obscure some of its aspects, to diminish it by the greater part of itself, so that the remainder, instead of being encased in its surroundings as a *thing*, should detach itself from them as a *picture*.[58]

Any poem is a simplifying of the world, a framing of a piece of its infinitude so that it may be comprehended, a few notes sifted from the background noise. Levertov goes about this selecting with a sure hand, making the simplest of images come alive with significance, following Bergson's prescription that 'the reality of things is no more constructed or reconstructed, but touched, penetrated, lived...'.[59]

Levertov's Later Work

Levertov's later book, *Sands of the Well*, contains some of her most powerful and controlled work, and is where her ideas of process reach their highest expression in her poems' embodiment of movement and becoming. The brief poem, 'Rage and Relenting', is one of the stronger examples:

> Rage and Relenting
>
> Hail, ricocheting off stone and cement, angrily
> sprinkling its rock-salt among fallen
> blossoms on earth's
> half-awakened darkness,
>   Enters
> the folds of sturdy camellias
> as if to seek
> refuge in those phyllo-layers of immaculate soft red,
> a place in which
>   to come to rest,
>   to melt.[60]

The poem begins simply enough with an image of hail fiercely striking the earth in a dawn hailstorm, 'ricocheting off stone and cement, angrily'. There are no gentle hailstorms. The hail is transformed into rock salt, certainly an accurate visual rendering of these particulates of frozen precipitation, and it calls up images of 'the salt of the earth', emphasizing in its compounding of the words 'rock' plus 'salt' and, in the simplicity of the phrasing of the poem itself, a simplicity that is to be desired. The image suggests the unhardening of a heart: ultimately the hailstone melts, changes its form. The petals are described as 'those phyllo-layers', the lightest of pastries, the phyllo dough having risen to an airy lightness. Phyllo-layers is an accurate rendering of these flowers, risen delicately and lightly as pastry dough. The word *immaculate* obviously carries connotations of perfection and Christ, and the camellia blossom itself takes on an other-worldly perfection, as anyone who has seen the architectural perfection of a *Camellia japonica* blossom will attest. These blossoms have a symmetry and perfection that is unlike the other, less-structured blossoms in the garden. Ultimately, the hailstones will change their state of matter, the frozen hardness transforming into liquid, a product which will nourish the camellia.

All is process in this poem, all is realizing rather than realized. The dawn, the briefest division of the day, is divided, somehow cleaved into a half-dawn. The sunrise, looked at with a microscopic rigour, is only halfway arrived, 'half-awakened'. This partial state is somehow to be desired. Perhaps it is all that is possible. The hailstone, not yet dissolved, is merely seeking 'a place in which / to come to rest'. Its transformation has not occurred by the ending of this momentary poem. It is in this movement from hardness to fluidity that the poem finds its beauty. Its transcendence is in the moving towards transcendence. Levertov is attempting what artists such as Eliot and Beethoven have attempted before her, to write beyond poetry, to write beyond music, to transcend the limitations of their medium and capture a rumour of the eternal in the crude net that earthbound meanings and sounds afford us. Both Eliot and Beethoven were writing late in their careers; Eliot's *Four Quartets* and Beethoven's final essays in the string quartet form seem to care little for the expectations that attended poetry or chamber music at the times of their making. They were seeking what was most elemental, moving beyond earlier considerations of form into a realm of pure content that might best be labelled *truth*.

In *Sands of the Well*, 'Rage and Relenting' is followed by a series of four poems that ruminate upon the image of Mount Rainier. A mountain may at first seem to be a stable and unchangeable object, the most resistant to processes geological and otherwise, but in Levertov's sequence Mt Rainier becomes an unstable and illusive image. The movement of the series of short lyrics provides an excellent illumination for a metaphor Bergson employs to begin his argument in *Creative Evolution*:

> Let us take the most stable of internal states, the visual perception of a motionless external object. The object may remain the same, I may look at it from the same side, at the same angle, in the same light; nevertheless the vision I now have of it differs from that which I have just had, even if only because the one is an instant older than the other. My memory is there, which conveys something of the past into the present. My mental state, as it advances on the road of time, is continually swelling with the duration which it accumulates: it goes on increasing – rolling upon itself, as a snowball on the snow.[61]

The Mt Rainier poems could not be a better embodiment of the phenomenon Bergson is describing. The first poem of the sequence, 'The 6:30 Bus, Late May', is careful to establish the exact circumstances of the sighting and contemplation of the mountain, the precise season, the particular bus, the locus of the image in the subject.

> The 6:30 Bus, Late May
>
> The mountain
> a moonflower in late
> blue afternoon.
>
> The bus
> grinds and growls.
> At each stop
>
> someone gets off,
> the workday over,
> heads for home.
>
> Trees in their first
> abundance of green
> hold their breath,
>
> the sky is
> so quiet, cloudless.
> The mountain
>
> mutely
> by arcane power
> summons the moon.[62]

The initial metaphor could not be more transient: 'The mountain / a moonflower in late / blue afternoon.' The trope pushes metaphor to its ultimate limits, straining the literary strategy until it almost becomes comedic. A mountain, the ultimate emblem of permanence, is made into a flower, a conveyor of fleeting beauty. This mountain is fragile and momentary, however; it is as changeful and volatile as a radioactive isotope already decaying, the whole of creation poised in a moment soon lost. The vegetal world itself is between breaths: 'Trees in their first / abundance of green / hold their breath'.

The forms of the poems evolve as the sequence evolves, moving from this six-tercet arrangement to a more organic tercet / six-line-stanza / tercet / tercet composition, to a ten-line lyric with no stanza breaks, ending with a poem fashioned in a version of William Carlos Williams's famous triadic line. These poems share a common object but little structural affinity. It is as though each poem is a new essay, a new form of the same subject, as though the unceasing revision in form is necessitated by the changefulness of the subject. Perception in these poems is never definitive. Perception is a continuous stream that is undergoing constant revision. In Bergson's chapter 'Of the Selection of Images' in *Matter and Memory*, he writes:

> in fact, there is for us nothing that is instantaneous. In all that goes by that name there is already some work of our memory, and consequently, of our consciousness, which prolongs into each other, so as to grasp them in one relatively simple intuition, an endless number of moments of an endlessly divisible time.[63]

The only knowing possible to us is this mode of gradual penetration of the world, as though our understanding must be a slow rain if it is to enter the land and not become muddy run-off.

The second Mt Rainier poem, 'Midsummer Eve', comes the closest to making a definitive statement of perception: 'All day the mountain boldly / displayed its white splendor, / disavowing all ambiguity.'[64] The poem avoids the seduction of uttering something definitive, though, realizing that ambiguity is more worth considering. The fourth line begins 'but now' – signalling a certain reversal into the richer terrain of uncertainty – and the mountain is in motion once again; it 'retreats from so much pomp, / such flagrant and superficial pride, / and drifts above the horizon, / ghostly, irresolute…'. This irresoluteness, this changeful and inchoate nature, is beautiful to the poet. The mountain here, under its snow pack, becomes a 'frail white moth' and recedes with the lightness and fragility of these short-lived insects.

The third poem in the sequence, 'The Mountain Assailed', speaks of the mountain as an 'Animal mountain' – these two words constituting the opening line. As the snow melts, the face of the mountain changes; it matures and ages: 'dark streaks reveal / your clefts, your secret creases'. The mountain, though we may mistake it for a permanent structure, is actually in geological time, a malleable feature, rising and falling subject to geological forces. It has a life span that in its own way is brief. The mountain; it suffers in the sun:

> I feel your breath
> over the distance,
> you are panting, the sun
> gives you no respite.[65]

Personification is a risky strategy, tending always towards the sentimental, but the mountain is personified in a way that underscores its temporality and changefulness rather than simply its pathos.

The last poem of the sequence presents a fourth prosodic approach, Williams's triadic line.

> Pentimento
>
> To be discerned
>   only by those
>   alert to likelihood –
> the mountain's form
>   beneath the milky radiance
>   which revokes it.
> It lingers –
>   a draft
>   the artist may return to.[66]

As Bergson says in the opening sections of *Creative Evolution*, this is an instance of 'transition' or becoming. The form of the mountain is presented then revoked to be reconsidered and revised. These transitions have substance and merit; the becoming has weight and is ultimately more significant than the object itself. *Pentimento* is a painting term derived from the Italian *penti(re)*, literally 'to repent'. Pentimento is the existence of previous images, lines, brush strokes, that have been painted over and altered. It is a kind of memory, an image of revision, as the poem makes clear. The apparition-like presence of pentimenti necessarily affects our reading of the topmost image. Bergson asserts that 'any memory-image that is capable of interpreting our actual perception inserts itself so thoroughly into it that we are no longer able to discern what is perception and what is memory'[67] – a kind of confusion, brushstrokes from different times merging into one composition. Every experience comes with its buried pentimenti. Even a mountain's form is changeful, revocable. It is another 'draft / the artist may return to'. What is mysterious, what may be apprehended only by consciousnesses 'alert to likelihood', the buried brush strokes which teasingly emerge from the rewrought palimpsest of the writer's world – this is what moves Levertov.

Perhaps poets are best positioned to understand and express process, the exhausting daily return to the same problem, the same line, the same image, working and reworking until the words become acceptable and perhaps even, for a moment, transcendent. How all this happens is a mystery, as distant and mysterious as the face of God. Levertov seems to be comfortable with this distance. Of her poems about Mt Rainier, she says, 'I've taken a vow not to desecrate it [the mountain] by going up there. People should stop trampling all over it, leaving their garbage behind, and necessitating the placing of comfort stations around so-called wilderness. They should let wilderness revert to being wilderness.'[68] The parsing of an image until no mystery remains, no 'wilderness', leaves no image at all. There must be some distance and uncertainty for anything to exist. Always there must be some room for movement and growth.

Conclusion

Levertov's entire career is best understood as a movement towards and refinement of these ideas of process. Even her early writings express a clear preference for process over any kind of absolutism. In her 1967 essay 'The Poet in the World' she writes:

> the understanding of a result is incomplete if there is ignorance of its process. The literary critic or the teacher of literature is merely scratching a section of surface if he does not live out in his own life some experience of the multitudinous interactions in time, space, memory, dream, and instinct that at every word tremble into synthesis in the work of a poet, or if he keeps his reading separate from his actions in a box labeled 'aesthetic experiences.' The interaction of life on art and of art on life is continuous. Poetry is necessary to a whole man, and that poetry be not divided from the rest of life is necessary to *it*. Both life and poetry fade, wilt, shrink, when they are divorced.[69]

Poetry must be alive, and to be alive is to be in a dynamic, transitional state, which seems consistent with later views on the nature of poetry. The following is from a response to a questionnaire circulated by the journal *Religion & Intellectual Life* in the Summer of 1984:

I must also emphasize that the subject of our inquiry appears to me to be a process, not a fixed quantity. For myself, at least, I feel I am focusing on an artificially isolated moment in a slow and continuing personal evolution. What I might write five years from now could be as different from what I say now as that is from what I might have written five years ago, although the direction of my development has, I believe, been consistent.[70]

She is in dialogue with a world that is continually being remade. The past echoes and informs the present. She cites the prayer of St Anselm which asserts, 'I do not seek to understand so that I may believe, but I believe so that I may understand; and what is more, I believe that unless I do believe I shall not understand.'[71] Belief for Levertov is always a gradual, ever-changing attainment:

But no: if the work truly has the living complexity I term 'numinous,' it is rather that by one's own development, by moving along the road of one's own life, one becomes able to see a new aspect of the book. The newly seen aspect, facet, layer, was there all the time; it is our recognition of it that is new.[72]

Notes

1. Gaston Bachelard, *The Poetics of Space*, translated by Maria Jolas (Boston: Beacon Books, 1994), 79.
2. Henri Bergson, *Matter and Memory*, translated by N.M. Paul and W.S. Palmer (New York: Zone Books, 1991), 240.
3. Denise Levertov, *Oblique Prayers* (New York: New Directions, 1984), 80.
4. Lorrie Smith, 'An Interview With Denise Levertov', *Michigan Quarterly Review* 24.4 (Fall 1985): 596–604.
5. Denise Levertov, *Poems 1960–1967* (New York: New Directions, 1983), 125.
6. Henri Bergson, *The Two Sources of Morality and Religion*, translated by R. Ashley Audra, Cloudesley Brereton and W. Horsfall Carter (Notre Dame, IN: University of Notre Dame Press, 1977), 317.
7. Henri Bergson, *Creative Evolution*, authorized translation by Arthur Mitchell (New York: Henry Holt and Company, 1911), 3.
8. Shiv K. Kumar, *Bergson and the Stream of Consciousness Novel* (New York: New York University Press, 1963), 3–4, 18.
9. Paul Douglass, *Bergson, Eliot, and American Literature* (Lexington, KY: The University Press of Kentucky, 1986), 175.
10. Bergson, *Creative Evolution*, 10.
11. Levertov, *Obilique Prayers*, 81.
12. Denise Levertov, *The Poet in the World* (New York: New Directions, 1973), 69.
13. Ibid., 7.
14. Gilles Deleuze, *Bergsonism*, translated by Hugh Tomlinson and Barbara Habberjam (New York: Zone Books, 1991), 13.
15. Ibid., 9.
16. Alex Preminger and T.V.F. Brogan, editors, *The New Princeton Encyclopedia of Poetry and Poetics* (Princeton, NJ.: Princeton University Press, 1993), 1320.
17. Ibid., 1320.
18. Deleuze, *Bergsonism*, 24.
19. Ibid., 25.
20. Bergson, *Matter and Memory*, 64.

21. Bergson, *Creative Evolution*, 8.
22. Bergson, *Matter and Memory*, 48.
23. Ibid., 65-6.
24. Denise Levertov, *The Freeing of the Dust* (New York: New Directions, 1975), 15.
25. Ibid., 15.
26. Bergson, *Matter and Memory*, 133.
27. Ibid., 137-8.
28. Deleuze, *Bergsonism*, 63.
29. Bergson, *Matter and Memory*, 240.
30. Harvey Gross, *Sound and Form in Modern Poetry* (Ann Arbor, MI: The University of Michigan Press, 1964), 101, quoting T.E. Hulme, 'A Lecture on Modern Poetry', reprinted in Michael Roberts, *T.E. Hulme* (London, 1938), 269-70.
31. William Carlos Williams, *Selected Poems* (New York: New Directions, 1969), 84.
32. Gross, *Sound and Form in Modern Poetry*, 120-21.
33. Gross, *Sound and Form in Modern Poetry*, 101, quoting Ezra Pound, *Literary Essays of Ezra Pound*, edited by T.S. Eliot (London, 1954), 3.
34. Levertov, *The Freeing of the Dust*, 15.
35. Denise Levertov, *New & Selected Essays* (New York: New Directions, 1992), 1.
36. Donald Davie, introduction to *The New Oxford Book of Christian Verse* (New York: Oxford University Press, 1981), xvii-xviii.
37. Levertov, *New & Selected Essays*, 11.
38. Charles Wright, *Country Music: Selected Early Poems* (Middleton, CT: Wesleyan University Press, 1982), 112.
39. Ibid., 141.
40. Paul Tillich, *On Art and Architecture*, edited by John Dillenberger and Jane Dillenberger (New York: Crossroad, 1987), 96.
41. Ibid., 99.
42. Levertov, *New & Selected Essays*, 1.
43. Levertov, *The Poet in the World*, 63.
44. Levertov, *New & Selected Essays*, 4.
45. Robert Bly, *American Poetry: Wildness and Domesticity* (New York: Harper & Row, 1990), 113.
46. Ibid., 114.
47. Ibid., 116.
48. Nicholas O'Connell, 'A Poet's Valediction', *Poets & Writers* 26.3 (May/June 1998): 20-25.
49. Bly, *Wildness and Domesticity*, 118.
50. Denise Levertov, *Sands of the Well* (New York: New Directions, 1996), 110.
51. Bly, *Wildness and Domesticity*, 124.
52. Levertov, *New & Selected Essays*, 60.
53. O'Connell, 'A Poet's Valediction', 22.
54. Ezra Pound, *Selected Poems of Ezra Pound* (New York: New Directions, 1957), 18.
55. Jonathan Culler, *Structuralist Poetics: Structuralism, Linguistics, and the Study of Literature* (Ithaca, NY: Cornell University Press, 1975), 19.
56. Gaston Bachelard, *The Poetics of Space*, xxi.
57. Bergson, *Matter and Memory*, 36.
58. Ibid., 36.
59. Ibid., 69.
60. Levertov, *Sands of the Well*, 26.
61. Bergson, *Creative Evolution*, 4.
62. Levertov, *Sands of the Well*, 27.

63. Bergson, *Matter and Memory*, 69–70.
64. Levertov, *Sands of the Well*, 28.
65. Ibid., 29.
66. Ibid., 30.
67. Bergson, *Matter and Memory*, 103.
68. O'Connell, 'A Poet's Valediction', 22.
69. Levertov, *New & Selected Essays*, 134.
70. Ibid., 239–40.
71. Ibid., 17.
72. Ibid., 105.

III
PROCESS POESIS

Chapter 12

A Place and a Moment: One Poem about Becoming

Christina K. Hutchins

Introduction

This poem attempts to integrate various experiences of my own human becomings with some of the intellectual conversation partners of my adult life, in particular with the Alfred North Whitehead of *Process and Reality*. I am interested in processes that open human beings, both individually and communally, to quickenings of ethical social transformations, broadening the relational possibilities of and for the future. Such transformations seem to move simultaneously towards the development of individual identities through events such as coming publicly to voice *and* into affirmation and expansion of the complexity and plurality of relations between humans, between humans and that which surrounds us, and between humans and the Spirit of God, creativity's impulse or, as Whitehead says, the Poet of the World. Some aspects of experience that play a role in opening humans to such motion are deliberate attention or permeability to the breadth of the past in the present moment; death and grief; creative participation; beauty; intimacy, pain, humour and play; and community and processes of voices coming into conversations of integrity together. These aspects become the six parts of the poem: (i) a place and a moment, (ii) perishing, (iii) creativity, (iv) beauty, (v) intimacy, pain and humour (saying *yes*), and (vi) motions of voice. Together the six parts form a study of the dynamic of becoming, exploring the felt tracings of a moment or 'drop of experience'.

Three primary images emerge and develop themselves throughout the poem. The first image, in a sense containing or embodying the poem, is a wide front porch, a gathering porch on which various thinkers whose work resides with me are sitting, drinking lemonade or iced tea, and sharing in conversation with each other. As the poet, I am both a *participant* in the conversation and the *place* of the conversation, both someone sitting on the porch and the gathering porch itself. The poem proceeds by the extensive use of quotations from the various participants in the conversation. The second major image is a drop of water: a drop perhaps dribbling down the side of one of the lemonade glasses, a drop collecting itself as it moves, until swollen to capacity and full of infinite reflections, it falls onto and *into* the dusty dry boards of the porch floor. The swelling, the fall, and the absorption and evaporation of the drop convey the motion of both the poem itself, coming into being and being read, *and* each Whiteheadian atomic 'drop of experience'. The developing experience gathers, swells, and in its fullness 'concresces', releasing itself and perishing, the *moment* of the poem, and a moment of the poet and of the reader or hearer. In the final section, the image of the drop grows into a whole river of drops joined and joining, 'a river guided by no banks ... gushing forth', each drop both carrying and carried by the process of becoming. Along the way, the image of the drop has gathered into itself other images and affects: light, absence, presence, remanation, pain, love, laughter and voice. The final major image of the poem, a hand 'unfolding and spreading open', is at least a partial response to the poem's initial, urgent question, 'Is there a falling into openness that transforms death into life's motion?'

A few personal notes: this poem was composed in a time of loss and grief in my own life. Owing to the HIV/AIDS epidemic, I knew my first experiences of the deaths of close peers. In addition, I had recently left a thriving parish ministry to return to graduate school, leaving behind a beloved community, a regular salary, professional role, and a familiar vocational identity. Finally, the previous year my former husband and I had divorced, I had come out as a lesbian, and the resultant loss of heterosexual privilege and altered friendships and family relationships had become unexpectedly pervasive and sharp realities. Like May Sarton, I was rich with loss that 'made everything sharp',[1] loss inseparably intertwined with a nascent freedom and joy.

As a composition of the contrasting griefs and joys that layer particular moments of my own becoming, the poem also became a means of conjoining other, more academic, felt contrasts, and a deliberate attempt to broaden my integrity as a human being and as a scholar. As I have moved further into academic life and into my own work of thinking, feeling and conversing, I have found myself increasingly troubled by the firm partition between poetry and philosophy or metaphysics. Distressingly vast potential richnesses of critical insight, adventure and awe are lost or obscured by the separation of dynamically interrelated motions of meaning into methodologically bounded disciplines. With some notable exceptions, since Plato poetry and philosophy have functioned in different dialogical realms, engaging different conversation partners, and carrying different epistemological assumptions and warrants for moving on to further knowledge, further unfolding. This division continues even though the two discursive fields share a whole set of questions: *How are we related to each other, to the universe, to time, to eternity? What are the characteristics of, the meanings of: death, life, love, nature, change, stasis, beauty, hope, culture, the subject? How do we move (are we moved) from what we know/feel in this moment to what we know/feel in the next?* As Bernard Meland writes, 'The poet and the metaphysician often trespass on one another's ground.'[2]

The ever-shifting ground of common questions may be a site of mutual trespass, but poetry and philosophy or metaphysics have maintained their separation through differing methodological approaches. Philosophy has built itself through logical reasoning, with clarity defined as internal consistency, while poetry has crafted itself to move by affective and imagistic leaps, by rhythms and precise tastings of the motions of language. In the majority of my own writing, following the inherited separation, either the poet or the philosopher takes priority for a particular project. In this poem, however, I tried to do and be both together, mingling methodological and epistemological tendencies, conjoining not only poetry and philosophy, but aesthetics and ethics, two additional discursive fields deemed separate by current social habit and by academic convention.

I also tried to compose the poem in a way that displays or performs the inseparable conjunction between theory and experience. Even as experiential reality exceeds theoretical categories and formulations, it also informs, inspires and directs theory; even as abstract theories describe and critique human experience, theory also constructs and extends that experience. Yet I have struggled to find patterns of language and genre adequate for work that seeks to be both experientially concrete and conscientiously reflective. This poem attempts to integrate various facets of my own processes of scholarly critical reflection and of being/becoming human, and, at the same time, to retain the felt densities and layers of meaning of those processes.

A final note: I wrote this poem in 1996. Since that time, I have been immersed in and irrevocably affected by the work of other thinkers, notably postmodern and poststructuralist feminist and queer theorists such as Judith Butler, and by the work of various modern poets. Were I to compose this poem today it would not be the same poem. However, rather than revise it into another poem altogether, I decided to let it basically remain as originally completed. For, if as Whitehead claims, '*how* an actual entity *becomes* constitutes *what* that entity *is*',[3] the poem as it stands appropriately performs the moment of its composition, including the particular complexities and limitations engendered by the specific opportunities and decisions that shape a singular entity into the event that it is.

i. a moment and a place

In me, Alfred North Whitehead talks with John Updike and Pablo Neruda
and with Audre Lorde dying of breast cancer,
with Kimberly Whitney my friend alive and talkative and my lover Sally,
and in the silent presence, too, of those I grieve   who died too young –
– Gene and singing Bill of AIDS, and Clayton, whom I never even met,   of a leap
from the fortyfourth floor of the New York City Marriot hotel,
landing in the atrium below.
I looked up atrium
in my dictionary. It comes from a root meaning   an opening.   Clayton,
lover of words, you knew what you were doing –   you died literally trying to fall
into openness.

Is there a falling into openness that transforms
death into life's motion   suffering into splashing joy
disappearance into spaces of becoming,
mute despair into speech that is heard?
How do we open to our lives   how do we open
to each other?   Can many become one and remain many
plus one more?

Here, too, gathered into this moment,   are
my two old professors, the historian David Hall and the beauty-lover Dick Niebuhr,
Chung Hyun Kyung and Beethoven and Theodore Roethke,
T.S. Eliot, Adrienne Rich and Mary Oliver,
Denise Levertov and Niebuhr's uncle Reinhold and the Sandinista
Arturo Zamora of *La Barricada*.   John Adams
the composer, and Jonathan Edwards the Puritan,   and you,
Joseph, a preacher and Clayton's father and my friend:

In me you all talk together,   and I am both conversation partner
and the *place* of the conversation,   a porch in summer shade
glasses of tea and lemonade,
ice clinking, tall glasses slick
with beads clinging sliding lightly   down
dropping falling   water
disappearing into the floorboards' old wood –   becoming
splinters' blood
and humidity of air breathed in –

I am place of condensation and release.

ii. perishing

Audre Lorde, in the last poem before her death says,
*"I can't just sit here
staring death in her face
blinking and asking for a new name
by which to greet her*

*I am not afraid to say
unembellished
I am dying
but I do not want to do it
looking the other way"*[4]

And Updike: "The great thing about the dead,
they make space."[5]   And this is not a cruel thing
not cruel words to Audre Lorde.

Pablo's slapping sea riddle voice begins to sing:
"And now I'm going behind
this page, but not disappearing.
I'll dive into clear air

like a swimmer in the sky,
and then get back to growing
till one day I'm so small
that the wind will take me away
and I won't know my own name
and I won't be there when I wake.

Then I will sing in the silence."[6]

What is this space,   not a disappearance but a space of appearing,   a silence opened by singing?

Whitehead's quiet voice runs the porch rail and leaps:
"This ... is the whole notion ...
when you feel that
what we are is of infinite importance,
because *as we perish we are immortal.*"[7]

There is a refusal that relation speaks to mortality.
Audre Lorde, dying and loving the dead, understands this refusal,
this heritage of love: "I can't believe you are gone
out of my life

So you are not."⁸

And Pablo again,
"I don't want my heritage of joy to die."
But,   "Don't call up my person.   I am absent.
Live in my absence as if in a house.
Absence is a house so vast
that inside you will pass through its walls
and hang pictures on the air...

"Survive me with such sheer force
that you waken the furies of the pallid and the cold
... from sun to sun dream through your singing mouth."⁹

What is this absence,   this space of remembering,   surviving,   awakening through the singing of our mouths?   What this heritage of joy,   this immortality that comes through perishing?

iii. creativity

These questions are not abstract. I am the place of this conversation.
History lives in me.　　　In my body and mind,　my love and rage,
in truth-telling of becoming,　of waking
into spaces left behind,　　　　　my own voice calling forward.

In 1988 I visited a Nicaragua dragging through eight years of U.S. Embargo and
Contra War.　　I met Arturo Zamora, editor of the Sandinista paper
La Barricada. He said, "We are coming into the twenty-first century,
but our minds are in the past."[10] We need
the past in our minds
but not our minds in the past.　　Zamora was intense,　intent, leaning forward,
virility falling from him　fountain water from a laughing child　his words *earnest*,
flicker in his eyes carrying　passion　through the air,　　and I heard him.

The historian of popular religion David D. Hall crosses his legs, leans back,
says "It is crucial that we not romanticize the people."
He says the New England Puritans were "unsettled from within by their very own
tradition".[11]　　That is what I mean when I say we carry the past within us,
when I say we carry the past
in our own becoming.　　I mean we are unsettled.　We
ought to be unsettled.

I mean we carry this:
U.S. backed Contra soldiers attacking villagers
attacking villagers gathered round a single well of fresh water gushing
killing villagers because *they dug that well together.*

I mean we are responsible:
How we incorporate the past,　history,　　the joy of the dead and the dying
and their pain,　　　　matters.　　How we fill space with our own becoming
matters –　the process of our becoming　　　　shimmers the empty future:
　　　light passing through water and emerging
　sounds of waves that crash once　everlastingly echo on the rocks.

I will live in your body,　in the shape of your voice
under the leafy tree,　　in your beginning,　finally, to sing.

We will all live in the gatherings of whoever is alive: humans, the rocks and the fish,
bolt of lightning,　rage of starlight　calm with distance,　flesh, leaves: *how* we
become　　will live in their becomings.　　　This happens moment by moment.

Richard R. Niebuhr sucks at his pipe. He blinks and nods.　His voice
so quiet I bend near to hear. "Construed as creative action,

knowing is participatory... It engages the whole human intellect: perception, feeling, will, imagination, understanding and reflection...   authentic knowledge arises not from acquaintance with life
but from participation in the conscious extension of life."[12]

Create is a *verb*,   the verb of participatory transformation,   a spiral
turning in and turning out: galaxy,   swirl of nautilus,   whirlpool,   twister
pulling dead leaves drifted forgotten in the corner where two walls meet   into flight,
freeing them.   This happens here.

Theodore Roethke's voice shakes and steadies: "if the wind means me
I'm here.
Here."[13]

T.S. Eliot whispers, "The hint half guessed, the gift half understood, is Incarnation."[14]
Creativity,   restless uneasy twirl of joy,   of God incarnate in the making,
you collect and natal spin
unsettle from within.   "I had seen birth and death,
But had thought they were different; this Birth was
Hard and bitter agony for us, like Death, our death.
We returned to our places, these Kingdoms,
But no longer at ease here, in the old dispensation,
With an alien people clutching their gods."[15]

It's like that bumper sticker I saw last autumn in Berkeley: "Your karma just ran over my dogma."
   It was a windy day and clear.
Walking beside a church building,   I heard
a child crying   and saw   a tree   thriving in narrow dirt
between sidewalk and street: branches dancing
with wind,   whipping round and round,   each leaf shouting its color,
   and underground
those restless reaching roots   seeking water,   seeking and
finding water,   a whole underground river,   the flexing joy
of those roots   lifting sidewalk, guttercurb, street,   even the church steps,
cracking the concrete foundations
of a civilization.   I had to look down to keep from tripping.

Creativity's motion runs over, under old dispensations,   cracks open
sacred traditions, inviolate creeds –   – whatever insists
we live in the past rather than the other way around.

We have to watch our step.

Whitehead clears his throat and begins: "'Creativity' is the ultimate of ultimates ... the principle of *novelty*..."[16]   Kimberly Whitney shyly suggests

A Place and a Moment: One Poem about Becoming   237

"Would hell, then, be a lack of novelty?"   Whitehead cannot hear her, but I do.
"The 'production of novel togetherness' is the ultimate notion
embodied in the term 'concrescence'....   'Together'
presupposes the notions 'creativity,' 'many', 'one', 'identity' and 'diversity'.
The ultimate metaphysical principle is the advance from disjunction to conjunction,
creating a novel entity...   The novel
entity is at once the togetherness of the 'many' which it finds,
and also it is one among the distinctive 'many' which it leaves ...
The many become one, and are increased by one."[17]

Is this what it means to fill the space of becoming?   To inherit
the legacy of joy and destruction: each pliant or brittle leaf,
each molten star and cracking of rock,
each human voice distinctly singing?

"An actual entity... is self-creative; and in its process of creation
transforms its diversity of roles into one coherent role. Thus 'becoming' is
the transformation of incoherence into coherence, and in each particular instance
ceases with this attainment."[18]

Remember this is not an abstraction.   I am also a place –
this gathering porch –   and a time –   this
moment –   condensation and release.   This is death and life,

and there is a verb by which they are inseparable –
– Yes, Pablo shouts – the verb!
"... the verb is the source
and vivid life – it is blood,
blood which expresses its substance
and so ordains its own unwinding..."

Whitehead, quickly, almost apologetic, adds, "'God' is 'the poet of the world'" –
– and this is a poem creating itself.

Both natality's longing, "the lure for feeling, the eternal urge
of desire"   – lovers love by longing –   and everlasting memory,
"combining creative advance with the retention of mutual intimacy...
the growth of God's nature is best conceived as that of a tender care
that nothing be lost".[19]

And this is a poem creating itself.

Niebuhr nods,   taps his pipe on a porch rail   shining with wear,
lathe-turned wood throwing back   light
smooth with the touch of human hands,
"I learned this from Coleridge: Poets are makers,
and in making poems they make themselves ...   we are all poets in this sense:

we make ourselves,   we create ourselves
by the attitudes and responses we cultivate
toward the social and natural worlds surrounding us."
We have to "attend to our responsibilities as poets ...
to become open or generous requires of us that   we practice
our poetic abilities".[20]

Mary Oliver, surprising and stern: "poetry is a life-cherishing force".[21]

Adrienne Rich gathers in a long silence and speaks in her voice that feeds the night:
"Freedom.   It isn't once, to walk out
under the Milky Way, feeling the rivers
of light, the fields of dark –
freedom is daily, prose-bound, routine
remembering.   Putting together, inch by inch
the starry worlds.   From all the lost collections."[22]

And so poems labor,   gather in and spin out,   begin to fall open,
increase the intensity,   expand
the diversity of the universe,   human life and atomic joy.
These are the routine remembrances of novel becoming
that widen faith   widen the day   tap moving sources   loosen
the world and fling it free.   Joe, preaching with a voice I can hear, says,   "Belief

comes from the experiential appropriation of the reality of being transformed.
Insofar as we participate in a transforming power,
we are generators of a kind of intensity which radiates
itself in the vitality of our lives."[23]

Jonathan Edwards admits – at least to the present company –
"Here is both an *emanation* and *remanation*.   The refulgence
shines upon and into the creature and is reflected back
to the luminary.   The beams of glory come from God,
and are something of God,
and are refunded back again to their original."[24]

This is quite something for a Puritan.
Remanation is not mere reflection, but refraction: absorbing, shaping and layering,
creating the return.   High in the Sierra Nevada
I once watched   craggy, stratified granite
throw alpenglow at dusk,   return not just the glory that was given
but more.

This is a responsibility,   the heritage of joy.

iv. beauty

I think beauty happens like this: When the sun
each moment creates its furnace heat, and the dust this moment deftly swirls
and this poem emerges; when the drop   swollen and stretched,   pauses,   lets go
and falls.   Each drop,   each poem,   each breath and dust mote whirl
each leaf and atom's leap.

And perceiving this matters.   *If* I pay attention, and *if* I prehend –
incorporate into my own becoming all that I can hold with value – this leaf, this drop,
creak of porch step,   this grin,   this table by leaps of faith holding together
beneath my spilling pen,
then this moment, place –   *the here and now* –   expands, deepens   broadens
the space   for future becomings.

"What is beauty?" I ask Chung Hyun Kyung   directly.
(I think *she* is beautiful.)

"Beauty is like whatever makes your whole being   open and receptive."[25]
This is not the beauty of perfection, of something finished, but of the finishing.
It is the beauty of the woman bent with age who sweeps leaves
from her porch stairs.   She hasn't any teeth.
There is room in this beauty for pain.
It is the beauty of the train whistle long and low late at night –
the 12:54 and the one oh one
and the shaking of the earth   rattling of the cars –   it wakes the sleepers
carries its load of lumber and petroleum and vegetables and people,
leaves its diesel smoke in the dark.
This beauty can hold ugliness.

Jonathan Edwards cries at beauty, his tears a rain we need: "Particular
disproportions
sometimes greatly add to the general beauty..."[26]
suggest relations beyond themselves.

Chung Hyun Kyung, beautiful woman who cares about women, cares, I say,
tells a story she learned by heart.   It is her own story.
"In order to get to this beauty we have to get naked.
Have to uncover layers of oppression.
If you bring out the genuine beauty of a person,
that is their salvation, in the community, in the world...
Eventually beauty will save us – genuine beauty."[27]

Beethoven knows this: all that waterfall music crashing over,
after yearning,   yearning toward an edge –
deep pools clear to the bottom,   swirling water
gathering again and again,   uncovering itself,
uncovering its yearning.
John Adams knows this[28] in layers of sound pressed out: the drilling density
of the city,   beauty of sirens and screams and blunt machines unfolding
themselves,   unfolding,
growing naked as cello strings,   becoming something new.

v. intimacy   pain   humour   (saying *yes*)

"You can be vulnerable here," my lover Sally invites and I rest
my tired head on the heartbone between her breasts.   I cry here, now –   wet tears
uncover muted layers of pain.

Some things have no beauty:
uniformity, tyranny, totalitarianism, violent force –
some things open   no life-cherishing course.   Beauty cannot conform
so it disappears.

Pablo mourns sometimes:
"Our wretched contribution to the world is a narrower world."[29]   But

we can share suffering   somewhat,   can unfold ourselves beside each other,
widen
       this narrowed world again
and again.   This,   a place, a time without clarity,   a place where words cannot
be written,   a time when language fails   but humans sometimes do not.

Adrienne Rich, at the edge of her voice, stretching,   "You who think I find words
for everything
this is enough for now

cut it short   cut loose from my words
"You for whom I write this
in the night hours when the wrecked cartilage
sifts round the mystical juncture of the bones . . .
remember: the body's pain and the pain on the streets
are not the same   but you can learn
from the edges that blur   O you who love clear edges
more than anything   watch the edges that blur."[30]

Understanding begins in watching the edges that blur.   So does love,
love for the beloved   and from her   and for
reality itself, begins here, too,   and if we continue,   the blurring
becomes clarity and affirmation,
becomes *yes* to the self and to the other.

And this intimacy, this saying yes, is also laughing together,   singing mouth to mouth,
believing.   It is the play of balls   arching through air,   wild ocean
wetting my pantlegs, my ankles,   shuffling pebbles over and over,   play of balls
and waves,   the dark sea of imagination.

Pablo laughs.   He seems to crave my laugh and yours   bells ringing up and down
the air: "Your laugh: it reminds me of a tree
fissured by a lightning streak ...
slash your laughter through the shadows..."[31]

This is filling space lightly, falling lightly into openness.   What it means
to not take ourselves
too seriously.   I've really never heard myself laugh,
but I know Sally's quiet chuckle and siren screech.
I know Joe's low crackling drawn out long for my pleasure –
Not too serious, but it leaves its mark, keeps us alive.   Like beauty –   but not –
humour   opens and receives,   receives and opens.

The whole porch spasms with laughter,   a sudden living river
of faces, mouths pouring out joy   running
through fingers and hair.

I cannot catch it all, but it goes on and on,   enough.
Pablo stops laughing: "What I owe you
is like a well in the wilderness."[32]
I haven't the faintest idea who he's talking to.   But in this place
where I have no word but yes, I borrow his.   I look at Sally and at Joe.
They catch my laugh
and let it go.

vi. motions of voice

The voice is a voice becoming
mine and yours   unfolding   a silence opened
by singing.

Denise Levertov whispers, "Transformed.
A silence
of waking at night into speech."[33]

This silence is in the midst of the people.

And the clarity of a voice
calling in the wilderness   into spaces left behind   is born in the midst of the people.
Joy inherits itself by singing.

Audre Lorde, quiet awhile,   now tells,   "the erotic is not a question only
of what we do: it is a question of how
acutely and fully we feel in the doing".[34]

Waking in the night wakes the night and day: heritage of joy   and struggle
authenticity of finding voice, transforming mute despair.

Nothing at all becomes something whole and round,   a measure
of truth.   This is momentary.   It ceases
when it gains itself.

I learned this while playing the piano,   playing with words,   the sea,
my father, brothers,   with my mother's voice,   reading,   with lovers
and sisters by choice.   I learned it while dancing,   running,
holding and being held.   I was awakened through the singing
of my own mouth.

My voice in motion, tasting words
and letting them go   watching faces   the play of the sea
of a ball thrown out and back again and again   every time a different
ball   a different drop swelling and falling,   conversation
shuffling the stones,
I have heard my voice stretch and fall and know it is caught and   held and
                                                                                                        released.

I learned to speak among some who loved and some   who hated.   I said myself
anyway.   The saying freed something in me and something in them
when they spoke too.   And my listening grew free.
Sometimes I hear the voices of   rock   cracking.

Community swirls out with speaking and listening.   Spiral voicings of children
old women and men,   the tellings of distinct footfalls winding on wood and stone –
disagreement and singing –   telling is a vocation.
Denise Levertov again: "Testimonies of lived life ...
is what writers have vocation to give, and readers have a need to receive ...
That *evocative* sense of *how things are*."[35]
We are all writers and readers.   The texts our lives.
We evoke one another.

I want to hear *you*.   Want you here with me on the porch
you whom I have not met
whose life spinning forward whose voice round with space well filling and letting go
beckons.   We have so much to say to one another.

Someone must begin.   Over and over someone needs to risk breaking open
our silence.   I do not mean
humming polite words that bury death, suffering, birth,   not a cunning hiding
of the absence we live in,   this terrifying space of becoming –
but language that reveals and shapes the air,   a voice *alive*   in the midst
of routine remembering,   hands unfolding and spreading open.

Pablo knows how to begin: "I have come out of that landscape, that mud,
that silence, to roam, to go singing through the world..."[36]

What is the risk of beginning, of coming to voice in the world, of roaming
singing through a world
that can kill?   I have been threatened, cajoled, stalked
by more than one man (older straighter heavier stronger wealthier than I)
who would have me say nothing at all,
who would not have me be
in the world we share,
a world we create together.

To come to voice this way is to risk death
and to risk *our lives*,   necessary, because
"... for human beings, not to speak is to die".[37]

Dick's uncle Reinhold – quiet all this time! – booms out now,   "I am convinced
that the simplest way to get liberty is to take it.   The liberty to speak
on all vital questions of the day   without qualifying the message
in a half-dozen ways."[38]

And Audre again, tired and wise, "There are *so* many ways in which I'm vulnerable
and cannot help but be vulnerable,   I'm not going to be more vulnerable

by putting weapons of silence
in my enemies' hands."[39]

The motions of our own voices bring us home.
No hatred no danger is greater than this emerging from mute despair, this motion
into our home in the world.
When I speak I get tired, yes, but I get *energized* too. I grow
strong and unafraid, freely, *inevitably* moving home. I swell and stretch and pause
and let go.

This is condensation and release: water falling
dropping lightly down, not disappearing but appearing
in floorboards' old wood –
splash of splinters' blood clear, new
humidity of air breathed in
and breathed out
a voice of appearing creating itself.

And sooner or later, our voices discover one another appearing.
We become a river of voices.

Audre Lorde, her voice a ringing bell dying away, dares give
a stage direction: "*(All)*" she croaks,
"'*We cannot live
without our lives.*'"[40]

Suddenly we are singing, clear and joined together an odd, surging hymn: "We
cannot live without our lives." We sing, each
from hollow spaces rounded by our flesh. In absence
that is a place of appearing,
we form the sounds of our lives, push them out, create
something harmonious and strange
and joining together, inner conversations moving out
into the world, becoming
something new a chorus of survival
the flooding heritage of joy.

Each life unconforming itself letting go the rush of our differences
your skin her hands my loves no longer suppressed – not lack
but a richness unsettling the gravel – a heard music. This is not destiny
but adventure, possibility, novelty, episodic eye of the storm
galaxy, nautilus spinning out, the unloosing of our voices
stirring the mud swirling
carrying without confining.

The rhythms of these conversations   propel us   a river guided by no banks
bursting,   gushing forth,   each drop
carried and carrying   the space of appearing   to a different place.
This river of voices   flooding   spreading open   soaking in
flourishes mud   blooms we will never smell
wild laughters we will never hear
   but someone   will.

We are a throaty people and for a moment,   *here, now* –
rush of river over rock and underground,   we are we,   iridescent as silk
and setting free –   the many becoming one and
remaining many   plus one more.

And so this porch   this moment,
this drop falling   soaking into dry wood,
soaking in
and evaporating   expresses itself
as river breath,

perishes.

We cannot live   without
our lives: drops of reality   falling
spilling color,   carrying everything and nothing,
eaves
   trees
             dripping,   the motion of hands   unfolding

spreading open.

Notes

1. May Sarton, *Journal of a Solitude* (New York: W.W. Norton, 1973), 32.
2. Bernard Meland, *The Seeds of Redemption* (New York: Macmillan, 1947), 155.
3. Alfred North Whitehead, *Process and Reality: An Essay in Cosmology*, corrected edition, edited by David Ray Griffin and Donald W. Sherburne (New York: The Free Press, 1978), 23.
4. Audre Lorde 'Today is not the day' in *The Marvelous Arithmetics of Distance* (New York: W.W. Norton, 1993), 57.
5. John Updike, *Rabbit is Rich* (New York: Fawcett Crest, 1981), 3.
6. Pablo Neruda, *Absence and Presence*, edited by Luis Poirot (New. York: W.W. Norton, 1990), 90, 184, 14.
7. Alfred North Whitehead, *Essays in Science and Philosophy* (New York: Philosophical Library, 1947), 117.
8. Audre Lorde, 'Lunar Eclipse', *Marvelous Arithmetics*, 55.
9. Neruda, *Absence and Presence*, 14.
10. Comment by Arturo Zamora, editor of *La Barricada*, made during a meeting in Managua, Nicaragua, July 1988.
11. David D. Hall, *Worlds of Wonder, Days of Judgment: Popular Religious Belief in Early New England* (New York: Alfred A. Knopf, 1989), 19, 14.
12. Richard R. Niebuhr, *Streams of Grace: Studies of Jonathan Edwards, Samuel Taylor Coleridge and William James* (Kyoto, Japan: Doshisha University Press, 1983), 4.
13. Theodore Roethke, 'I'm Here', in *The Collected Poems* (New York: Doubleday, 1966), 158.
14. T.S. Eliot, 'Four Quartets', in *The Complete Poems and Plays* (New York: Harcourt, Brace and World, 1971), 136.
15. T.S. Eliot, 'Journey of the Magi', *Complete Poems*, 69.
16. Alfred North Whitehead, *Process and Reality*, 21.
17. Ibid., 25.
18. Ibid., 25.
19. Ibid., 344, 346.
20. Richard R. Niebuhr, *Streams of Grace*, 9.
21. Mary Oliver, *A Poetry Handbook* (New York: Harcourt Brace, 1994), 122.
22. Adrienne Rich, 'For Memory', in *A Wild Patience Has Taken Me This Far: Poems 1978–1981* (New York: W.W. Norton, 1981), 22.
23. Joseph C. Williamson in an address to the Annual Meeting of the Washington/North Idaho Conference of the United Church of Christ, 1 May 1988.
24. Jonathan Edwards, 'The End for Which God Created the World', *The Works of Jonathan Edwards, Volume 8: Ethical Writings*, edited by Paul Ramsey (New Haven, CT: Yale University Press, 1989), 531.
25. Chung Hyun Kyung, conversation after Earl Lectures, Berkeley California, January 1995.
26. Jonathan Edwards, 'The Mind., No. 1', *The Works of Jonathan Edwards, Volume. 6: Scientific and Philosophical Writings*, edited by Wallace E. Anderson (New Haven, CT: Yale University Press, 1980), 334.
27. Chung Hyun Kyung, conversation after Earl Lectures, Berkeley California, January 1995.
28. The brief portraits of music by Ludwig Von Beethoven and John Adams were evoked by the last movement of Beethoven's *Seventh Symphony* and the first half of Part I of Adams's 1985 *Harmonielehre*.
29. Pablo Neruda, 'The Sea', in *The House at Isla Negra*, translated by Dennis Maloney and Clark Zlotchew (Fredonia, NY: White Pine Press, 1988), 24.

30. Adrienne Rich, 'Contradictions: Tracking Poems', in *From Your Native Land, Your Life: Poems* (New York: W.W. Norton, 1986), 111.
31. Pablo Neruda, *100 Love Sonnets*, translated by Stephen Tapscott (Austin, TX: University of Texas Press, 1989), 109.
32. Ibid., 137.
33. Denise Levertov, *Poems 1960–1967* (New York: New Directions Press, 1983), 95.
34. Audre Lorde, 'Uses of the Erotic: The Erotic as Power', in *Sister Outsider: Essays and Speeches* (Freedom, CA: Crossing Press, 1984), 57.
35. Denise Levertov, *New and Selected Essays* (New York: New Directions, 1992), 3.
36. Pablo Neruda, *Memoirs*, translated by Hardie St. Martin (New York: Farrar, Straus and Giroux, 1977), 6.
37. Pablo Neruda 'The Word', in *Fully Empowered* (New York: Farrar, Straus and Giroux, 1977), 7.
38. Reinhold Niebuhr, *Leaves from the Notebook of a Tamed Cynic* (San Francisco, CA: Harper and Row, 1980), 28.
39. Audre Lorde, 'An Interview: Audre Lorde and Adrienne Rich', in *Sister Outsider*, 99.
40. Audre Lorde, *Undersong: Chosen Poems Old and New: Revised* (New York: W.W. Norton, 1992), 206.

Bibliography

Abrams, Meyer Howard (1971), *Natural Supernaturalism: Tradition and Revolution in Romantic Literature*, Oxford: Oxford University Press.
Aristotle (1984), *The Complete Works of Aristotle*, Jonathan Barnes (ed.), Bollingen Series LXXI-2, 2 vols, Princeton: Princeton University Press.
Aubrey, Bryan (1986), *Watchmen of Eternity: Blake's Debt to Jacob Boehme*, London: University Press of America.
Bachelard, Gaston (1944), *The Poetics of Space*, Maria Jolas (trans.), Boston: Beacon Press.
Basinger, David and Randall (1994), 'The Problem with the "Problem of Evil"', *Religious Studies*, 1(30), 89–97.
Beardslee, William (1997), 'Review of *The Fountain Arethuse*', *Creative Transformation*, 1(7), 23.
Beer, John (1969), *Blake's Visionary Universe*, Manchester, UK: Manchester University Press.
—— (1977), *Coleridge's Poetic Intelligence*, London: Macmillan.
Benz, Ernst (1983), *The Mystical Sources of German Romanticism*, Blair R. Reynolds and Eunice M. Paul (trans.), Allison Park, PA: Pickwick Publications.
Berdyaev, Nicholas (1950), *Dream and Reality: An Essay in Autobiography*, Katherine Lampert (trans.), London: G. Bles Ltd.
—— (1953), *Truth and Revelation*, R.M. French (trans.), London: G. Bles Ltd.
Bergson, Henri (1910), *Time and Free Will*, F.L. Pogson (trans.), New York: Macmillan.
—— (1935), *Creative Evolution*, Arthur Mitchell (trans.), New York: Henry Holt and Company.
—— (1935), *The Two Sources of Morality and Religion*, R. Ashley Audra and Cloudesley Brereton (trans.), London: Macmillan.
—— (1991), *Matter and Memory*, N.M. Paul and W.S. Palmer (trans.), New York: Zone Books.
Bien, Peter (1989), *Kazantzakis: Politics of the Spirit*, Princeton, NJ: Princeton University Press.
Blake, William (1926), *All Religions are One*, London: Frederick Hollyer.
—— (1994), *The Marriage of Heaven and Hell*, New York: Dover Publications.
Bly, Robert (1990), *American Poetry: Wildness and Domesticity*, New York: Harper & Row.
Boardman, Gwenn R. (1971), *Graham Greene: The Aesthetics of Exploration*, Gainesville, FL: University of Florida Press.
Boehme, Jacob (1914), *The Aurora*, John Sparrow (trans.), London: John M. Watkins.

Booth, Edward (1989), 'Τὸ ὑπερεῖναι (of Psuedo-Dionysus and Schelling)', *Studia Patristica*, 1(23), 215–25.
Broderick, Walter J. (1975), *Camilo Torres: A Biography of the Priest-Guerillo*, Garden City, NY: Doubleday and Company.
Brown, Robert (1977), *The Later Philosophy of Schelling: The Influence of Boehme on the Works 1809–1815*, Lewisburg, VA: Bucknell University Press.
Bruns, Gerald L. (1992), *Hermeneutics Ancient and Modern*, New Haven: Yale University Press.
Cappon, Alexander P. (1983), *Action, Organism and Philosophy in Wordsworth and Whitehead*, New York: Philosophical Library.
—— (1985), *Aspects of Wordsworth and Whitehead: Philosophy and Certain Continuing Life-Problems*, New York: Philosophical Library.
Cassis, A.F. (1980), *Graham Greene: An Annotated Bibliography of Criticism*, London: Scarecrow Press.
Cassis, A.F., (ed.) (1994), *Graham Greene: Man of Paradox*, Chicago, IL: Loyola University Press.
Caston, George M.A. (1984), *The Pursuit of Salvation: A Critical Guide to the Novels of Graham Greene*, Troy, NY: Whitston Publishing Company.
de Chardin, Pierre Teilhard (1960), *Le Milieu Divin: An Essay on the Interior Life*, B. Wall (trans.), London: Collins.
—— (1964), *The Future of Man*, N. Denny (trans.), New York: Collins.
—— (1965), *Hymn of the Universe*, S. Bartholomew (trans.), New York: Harper and Row.
Cobb Jr., John, B. and David Ray Griffin (1976), *Process Theology: An Introductory Exposition*, Philadelphia: The Westminster Press.
Cocking, J.M. (1991), *Imagination: a Study in the History of Ideas*, London: Routledge.
Coleridge, Samuel Taylor (1963), *Poems*, John Beer (ed.), London: J.M. Dent.
—— (1980), *The Collected Works of S.T. Coleridge: Marginalia I, Abbt to Byfield*, G. Whalley (ed.), London: Routledge and Kegan Paul.
Couto, Mario (1988), *Graham Greene: On the Frontier: Politics and Religion in the Novels*, New York: St Martin's Press.
Culler, Jonathan (1975), *Structuralist Poetics: Structuralism, Linguistics, and the Study of Literature*, Ithaca, NY: Cornell University Press.
Dannhauer, Johann Conrad (1654), *Hermeneutica sacra sive methodus exponendarum sacrarum literarum*, Strassbourg.
Darwin, Charles (1971), *The Origin of Species*, L. Harrison Matthews (ed.), London: Everyman.
Davie, Donald (1981), 'Introduction', *The New Oxford Book of Christian Verse*, New York: Oxford University Press.
Deleuze, Gilles (1991), *Bergsonism*, Hugh Tomlinson and Barbara Habberjam (trans.), New York: Zone Books.
Derrida, Jacques (1976), *Of Grammatology*, Gayatri Spivak (trans.), Baltimore, MD: The Johns Hopkins University Press.
—— (1978), *Writing and Difference*, Alan Bass (trans.), Chicago: University of Chicago Press.
—— (1981), *Positions*, Alan Bass (trans.), Chicago: University of Chicago Press.

—— (1981), *Dissemination*, Barbara Johnson (trans.), Chicago: University of Chicago Press.
—— (1982), *Margins of Philosophy*, Alan Bass (trans.), Chicago: University of Chicago Press.
—— (1984), 'Two Words for Joyce', in Attridge, Derek and Daniel Ferrer (eds), *Post-Structuralist Joyce: Essays from the French*, Cambridge: Cambridge University Press, pp. 145–59.
—— (1987), *The Post Card: From Socrates to Freud and Beyond*, Alan Bass (trans.), Chicago: University of Chicago Press.
—— (1988), *The Ear of the Other: Otobiography, Transference, Translation: Texts and Discussions with Jacques Derrida*, P. Kamuf and A. Ronell (trans.), Lincoln, NE: University of Nebraska Press.
—— (1988), *Limited Inc*, Jeffrey Mehlmann and Samuel Weber (trans.), Gerald Graff (ed.), Evanston, IL: Northwestern University Press.
Desmond, William (1987), *Desire, Dialectic and Otherness: An Essay on Origins*, New Haven, CT: Yale University Press.
—— (1992), *Beyond Hegel and Dialectic*, Albany, NY: State University of New York Press.
—— (1995), *Perplexity and Ultimacy*, Albany, NY: State University of New York Press.
—— (1995), *Being and the Between*, Albany, NY: State University of New York Press.
—— (1998), 'Autonomia Turranos: On Some Dialectical Equivocities of Self-Determination', *Ethical Perspectives*, 4(5), 233–52.
—— (1999), 'Caesar with the Soul of Christ: Nietzsche's Highest Impossibility', *Tijdschrift voor Filosofie*, (61), 27–61.
—— (2001), *Ethics and the Between*, Albany, NY: State University of New York Press.
Dillard, Annie (1999), *For the Time Being*, New York: Alfred A. Knopf.
Dillon, John M. and Brendan O Hehir (1977), *A Classical Lexicon for Finnegans Wake*, Berkeley: University of California Press.
Dilthey, Wilhelm (1968), *Gesammelte Schriften*, vol. 5 and 7, Stuttgart and Göttingen: Verlag Teubner/Vandenhoeck & Ruprecht.
Donaghy, Henry J., (ed.) (1992), *Conversations with Graham Greene*, Jackson, MS: University Press of Mississippi.
Douglass, Paul (1986), *Bergson, Eliot, and American Literature*, Lexington, KY: The University Press of Kentucky.
Durán, Leopoldo (1994), *Graham Greene: An Intimate Portrait by His Closest Friend and Confidant*, San Francisco, CA: HarperSanFrancisco.
Eckhart, Meister (1994), *Selected Writings*, Oliver Davies (ed.) (trans.), London: Penguin.
Eco, Umberto (1990), *Limits of Interpretation*, Bloomington: Indiana University Press.
Edwards, Jonathan (1980), *The Works of Jonathan Edwards, Vol. 6: Scientific and Philosophical Writings*, Wallace E. Anderson (ed.), New Haven: Yale University Press.
—— (1989), *The Works of Jonathan Edwards, Vol. 8: Ethical Writings*, Paul Ramsey (ed.), New Haven: Yale University Press.

Eliot, T.S. (1971), *The Complete Poems and Plays*, New York: Harcourt, Brace and World.
Evans, R.O. (ed.) (1963), *Graham Greene: Some Critical Considerations*, Lexington, KY: University of Kentucky Press.
Ford, Lewis S. (1987), 'Creativity in a New Key', in Neville, Robert (ed.), *New Essays in Metaphysics*, Albany, NY: State University of New York Press.
—— (1994), 'The Creation of "Eternal Objects"', *The Modern Schoolman*, 3(71), 191–222.
Ford, Lewis S. (ed.) (1973), *Two Process Philosophers. Hartshorne's Encounter with Whitehead*, American Academy of Religion Studies in Religion 5, Tallahasse, FL: American Academy of Religion.
Frankenberry, Nancy (1983), 'The Power of the Past', *Process Studies*, 2(13), 132–42.
Galeano, Eduardo (1973), *Open Veins of Latin America: Five Centuries of the Pillage of a Continent*, New York: Monthly Review Press.
Goodall, Jane (1986), *The Chimpanzees of Gombe*, Cambridge: Harvard University Press.
Greene, Graham (1951), *The End of the Affair*, London: Penguin.
—— (1962), *A Burnt-Out Case*, New York: Bantam Books, Inc.
—— (1971), *A Sort of Life*, Harmondsworth UK: Penguin Books.
—— (1973), *The Honorary Consul*, Beccles, England: Book Club Associates.
—— (1993), *Brighton Rock*, New York: Knopf.
—— (1994), *A World of My Own: A Dream Diary*, New York: Viking Penguin.
Griffin, David Ray (1976), *God, Power, and Evil: A Process Theodicy*, Philadelphia: Westminster Press.
—— (1991), *Evil Revisited: Responses and Reconsiderations*, Albany, NY: State University of New York Press.
—— (1993), *Founders of Constructive Postmodern Philosophy: Peirce, James, Bergson, Whitehead, and Hartshorne*, Albany, NY: State of University of New York Press.
Griffin, David Ray (ed.) (1988), *The Reenchantment of Science: Postmodern Proposals*, Albany, NY: State University of New York Press.
Gross, Harvey (1964), *Sound and Form in Modern Poetry*, Ann Arbor, MI: The University of Michigan Press.
Gutiérrez, Gustavo (1973), *A Theology of Liberation*, Sister Caridad Inda and Eagleson (trans.), New York: Orbis Books.
Haeger, Jack (1992), 'Samuel Taylor Coleridge and The Romantic Background to Bergson', in Burwick, Frederick and Paul Douglass (eds), *The Crisis in Modernism: Bergson and the Vitalist Controversy*, Cambridge: Cambridge University Press, pp. 98–107.
Hahn, Lewis Edwin (ed.) (1991), *The Philosophy of Charles Hartshorne*, La Salle, IL: Open Court.
Haim, Gordon (1997), *Fighting Evil: Unsung Heroes in the Novels of Graham Greene*, Westport, CT: Greenwood Press.
Haldane, E.S. (1897), 'Jacob Boehme and his relation to Hegel', *The Philosophical Review*, 6(1), 146–61.
Hall, David D. (1989), *Worlds of Wonder, Days of Judgment: Popular Religious Belief in Early New England*, New York: Alfred A. Knopf.

Harkness, Georgia (1935), *Holy Flame*, New York: Bruce Humphries, Inc.
Hartshorne, Charles (1966), 'A New Look at the Problem of Evil', in Dommeyer, F.C. (ed.), *Current Philosophical Issues: Essays in Honor of Curt John Ducasse*, Springfield, IL: Charles C. Thomas, pp. 201–12.
—— (1970), *Creative Synthesis and Philosophic Method*, London: SCM Press Ltd.
—— (1978), 'Can We Understand God?', *Louvain (Leuven) Studies*, 2(7), 75–84.
—— (1984), *Omnipotence and Other Theological Mistakes*, Albany, NY: State University of New York Press.
—— (1987), 'Some Theological Mistakes and Their Effects on Modern Literature', *Journal of Speculative Philosophy*, 1(1), 55–72.
Hartshorne, Charles and William L. Rees (1953), *Philosopher's Speak of God*, Chicago: Chicago University Press.
Heidegger, Martin (1962), *Being and Time*, John Macquarrie and Edward Robinson (trans.), Oxford: Basil Blackwell.
—— (1971), *On the Way to Language*, Peter D. Hertz (trans.), New York: Harper and Row.
—— (1971), *Poetry, Language, Thought*, Albert Hofstadter (trans.), New York: Harper and Row.
—— (1986), *Sein und Zeit*, Tübingen: Max Niemeyer Verlag.
Hoskins, Robert (1991), *Graham Greene: A Character Index and Guide*, New York: Garland Publishing.
Huggins, Martha K. (ed.) (1991), *Vigilantism and the State in Modern Latin America: Essays on Extralegal Violence*, New York: Praeger Press.
Iser, Wolfgang (1971), 'Indeterminacy and the Reader's Response in Prose Fiction', in Miller, J. Hillis (ed.), *Aspects of Narrative*, New York: Columbia University Press, pp. 1–45.
—— (1987), 'The Play of the Text', in Budick, Sanford and Wolgang Iser (eds), *Languages of the Unsayable*, Stanford: Stanford University Press, pp. 325–39.
James, William (1985), *The Varieties of Religious Experience: A Study in Human Nature*, New York: Penguin Books.
Jamil, K.M. (1959), *Nietzsche and Bergson: In the Domain of Evolutionary and Moral Philosophies*, Rajshahi, East Pakistan: Md. Majed Ali Miah.
Johnson, Christopher (1993), *System and Writing in the Philosophy of Jacques Derrida*, Cambridge: Cambridge University Press.
Johnson, A.H. (1983), 'Some Conversations with Whitehead Concerning God and Creativity', in Ford, Lewis S. and George L. Kline (eds), *Explorations in Whitehead's Philosophy*, New York: Fordham University Press, pp. 3–13.
Joyce, James (1992), *Finnegans Wake*, London: Penguin.
Kazantzakis, Helen (1968), *Nikos Kazantzakis: A Biography Based on His Letters*, Amy Mims (trans.), New York: Simon and Schuster.
Kazantzakis, Nikos (1952), *Zorba the Greek*, Carl Wildman (trans.), New York: Simon and Schuster.
—— (1955), *Freedom or Death*, Jonathan Griffin (trans.), New York: Simon and Schuster.
—— (1958), *The Odyssey: A Modern Sequel*, Kimon Friar (trans.), New York: Simon and Schuster.

—— (1960), *The Saviors of God: Spiritual Exercises*, Kimon Friar (trans.), New York: Simon and Schuster.
—— (1962), *Saint Francis*, Peter Bien (trans.), New York: Simon and Schuster.
—— (1964), *Toda Raba*, Amy Mims (trans.), New York: Simon and Schuster.
—— (1965), *Journey to the Morea*, F.A. Reed (trans.), New York: Simon and Schuster.
—— (1965), *Report to Greco*, Peter Bien (trans.), New York: Simon and Schuster.
—— (1974), *Symposium*, Thema Vasils and Theodora Vasils (trans.), New York: Minerva Press.
—— (1979), *The Suffering God: Selected Letters to Galatea and Papastephanou*, Philip Ramp and Katerina Anghelaki-Rooke (trans.), New Rochelle, NY: Caratzas.
—— (1984), *Journeying*, Thema Vasils and Theodora Vasils (trans.), Berkeley: Creative Arts.
—— (1989), *Russia*, Michael Antonakes and Thanasis Maskaleris (trans.), Berkeley: Creative Arts.
Kelly, Geffrey B. (ed.) (1992), *Karl Rahner: Theologian of the Graced Search for Meaning*, Minneapolis, MN: Fortress Press.
Kelly, Richard (1984), *Graham Greene*, New York: Frederick Ungar.
Kinast, Robert L. (1999), *Process Catholicism: An Exercise in Ecclesial Imagination*, Lanham, MD: University Press of America.
King, Ursula (1996), *Spirit of Fire: The Life and Vision of Teilhard de Chardin*, Maryknoll, NY: Orbis Books.
—— (1997), *Christ in All Things: Exploring Spirituality with Teilhard de Chardin*, Maryknoll, NY: Orbis Books.
Kumar, Shiv K. (1963), *Bergson and the Stream of Consciousness Novel*, New York: New York University Press.
Kunkel, F.L. (1959), *The Labyrinthine Ways of Graham Greene*, New York: Sheed and Ward.
Lacouture, Jean (1995), *Jesuits: A Multibiography*, Washington, DC: Counterpoint.
Lao Tzu (1961), *Tao Te Ching*, John C.H. Wu and Paul K.T. Sih (ed.) (trans.), New York: St John's University Press.
Lawrence, D.H. (1990), *Lady Chatterley's Lover*, London: Penguin Books
Levertov, Denise (1973), *The Poet in the World*, New York: New Directions.
—— (1975), *The Freeing of the Dust*, New York: New Directions.
—— (1983), *Poems 1960–1967*, New York: New Directions.
—— (1984), *Oblique Prayers*, New York: New Directions.
—— (1992), *New & Selected Essays*, New York: New Directions.
—— (1996), *Sands of the Well*, New York: New Directions.
Lewis, R.W.B. (1959), *The Picaresque Saint: Representative Figures in Contemporary Fiction*, New York: Barnes and Noble.
Lodge, David (1991), *Paradise News*, London: Secker and Warburg.
Lorde, Audre (1984), 'Uses of the Erotic: The Erotic as Power', in *Sister Outsider: Essays and Speeches*, Freedom, CA: Crossing Press, pp. 53–9.
—— (1992), *Undersong: Chosen Poems Old and New: Revised*, New York: W.W. Norton.
—— (1993), 'Today is not the day', in *The Marvelous Arithmetics of Distance*, New York: W.W. Norton, p. 57.

McEwan, Neil (1988), *Graham Greene*, London: Macmillan.
Meland, Benard (1947), *The Seeds of Redemption*, New York: Macmillan.
Middleton, Darren (1999), 'Graham Greene's *The End of the Affair*: Toward an Ironic God', *Notes on Contemporary Literature*, 3(29), 8–10.
—— (2000), *Novel Theology: Nikos Kazantzakis's Encounter with Whiteheadian Process Theism*, Macon, GA: Mercer University Press.
Miles, Jack (1996), *God: A Biography*, New York: Random House.
Murdoch, Iris (1997), *Existentialists and Mystics: Writings on Philosophy and Literature*, London: Chatto and Windus.
Neruda, Pablo (1977), *Memoirs*, Hardie St. Martin (trans.), New York: Farrar, Straus and Giroux.
—— (1977), 'The Word', in *Fully Empowered*, Alastair Reid (trans.), New York: Farrar, Straus and Giroux, pp. 5–9.
—— (1988), 'The Sea', in *The House at Isla Negra: Prose Poems*, Dennis Maloney and Clark Zlotchew (trans.), Fredonia, NY: White Pine Press, n.p.n.
—— (1989), *100 Love Sonnets*, Stephen Tapscott (trans.), Austin, TX: University of Texas Press.
—— (1990), *Absence and Presence*, Luis Poirot (trans.), New York: W.W. Norton.
Niebuhr, Reinhold (1980), *Leaves from the Notebook of a Tamed Cynic*, San Francisco, CA: Harper and Row.
Niebuhr, Richard R. (1983), *Streams of Grace: Studies of Jonathan Edwards, Samuel Taylor Coleridge and William James*, Kyoto, Japan: Doshisha University Press.
Nietzsche, Friedrich (1973), *Nietzsche Werke. Kritische Gesamtausgabe*, vol. V2, Berlin and New York: Walter de Gruyter.
O'Connell, Nicholas (1998), 'A Poet's Valediction', *Poets & Writers*, 3(26), May/June, 20–25.
O'Prey, Paul (1988), *A Reader's Guide to Graham Greene*, London: Thames and Hudson.
Oliver, Mary (1994), *A Poetry Handbook*, New York: Harcourt Brace.
Otto, Rudolf (1928), *The Idea of the Holy*, John W. Harvey (trans.), Oxford: Oxford University Press.
Penchansky, David, (1999), *What Rough Beast?: Images of God in the Hebrew Bible*, Louisville, KY: Westminster John Knox Press.
Plantinga, Alvin (1981), 'Reply to the Basingers on Divine Omnipotence', *Process Studies* 1(11), 25–9.
Pound, Ezra (1957), *Selected Poems of Ezra Pound*, New York: New Directions.
Preminger, Alex and T.V.F. Brogan (eds) (1993), *The New Princeton Encyclopedia of Poetry and Poetics*, Princeton, NJ: Princeton University Press.
Pryce-Jones, David (1963), *Graham Greene*, Edinburgh: Oliver and Boyd.
Rich, Adrienne (1981), 'For Memory', in *A Wild Patience Has Taken Me This Far: Poems 1978–1981*, New York: W.W. Norton, pp. 21–2.
—— (1986), 'Contradictions: Tracking Poems', in *Your Native Land, Your Life: Poems*, New York: W.W. Norton, pp. 83–111.
Roethke, Theodore (1966), 'I'm Here', in *The Collected Poems*, New York: Doubleday, p. 58.
Rowland, Christopher (ed.) (1999), *The Cambridge Companion to Liberation Theology*, Cambridge, England: Cambridge University Press.

Salvatore, Anne (1988), *Greene and Kierkegaard: The Discourse of Belief*, Tuscaloosa, AL: University of Alabama Press.
Sarton, May (1973), *Journal of a Solitude*, New York: W.W. Norton.
Schelling, Friedrich (1936), *The Ages of the World*, New York: Columbia University Press.
—— (1942), *Of Human Freedom*, Chicago: Chicago University Press.
Selden, Raman (1988), *The Theory of Criticism*, New York: Longman.
Shakespeare, William (1939), *Macbeth*, Bernard Groom (ed.), Oxford: Clarendon Press.
Shaw, Bernard (1987), *Man and Superman: A Comedy and a Philosophy*, London: Penguin Books.
Sherburne, Donald (1971), 'Whitehead without God', in Brown, D., R.E. James, Jr. and G. Reeves (eds), *Process Philosophy and Christian Thought*, Indianapolis, IN: Bobbs-Merrill, pp. 305–28.
Sia, M.F. and S. Sia (1994), *From Suffering to God: Exploring Our Images of God in the Light of Suffering*, New York: Macmillan/St Martin's Press.
Sia, M.S. (1997), *The Fountain Arethuse: A novel set in the university town of Leuven*, Lewes UK: The Book Guild Ltd.
Sia, Santiago (1990), 'Process Thought as Conceptual Framework', *Process Studies*, 4(19), 248–55.
Smith, Lorrie (1985), 'An Interview With Denise Levertov', *Michigan Quarterly Review*, 4(24), Fall, 596–604.
Spurling, John (1983), *Graham Greene*, London: Methuen.
Stallknecht, Newton P. (1962), *Strange Seas of Thought: Studies in William Wordsworth's Philosophy of Man and Nature*, Bloomington, IN: Indiana University Press.
Staten, Henry (1984), *Wittgenstein and Derrida*, Lincoln, NE: University of Nebraska Press.
Stratford, Philip (1964), *Faith and Fiction: Creative Process in Greene and Mauriac*, South Bend, IN: University of Notre Dame Press.
Thiselton, Anthony C. (1992), *New Horizons in Hermeneutics*, Grand Rapids: Zondervan.
Thomas, Brian (1988), *An Underground Fate: The Idiom of Romance in the Later Novels of Graham Greene*, Athens, GA: University of Georgia Press.
Tillich, Paul (1967), *On the Boundary*, London: Collins.
—— (1987), *On Art and Architecture*, John and Jane Dillenberger (eds), New York: Crossroad.
Updike, John (1981), *Rabbit is Rich*, New York: Fawcett Crest.
Vann, J. Don (1970), *Graham Greene: A Checklist of Criticism*, Kent, OH: Kent State University Press.
Van der Veken, Jan (1990), 'Process Thought from a European Perspective', *Process Studies*, 4(19), 240–47.
de Waal, Frans (1989), *Peacemaking Among Primates*, Cambridge, MA: Harvard Univerity Press.
Waisman, Carlos H. (1987), *Reversal of Development in Argentina: Postwar Counterrevolutionary Policies and Their Structural Consequences*, Princeton, NJ: Princeton University Press.

Walker, Theodore (1999), 'Review of *The Fountain Arethuse* and *From Suffering to God*', *Process Studies*, 1–2(28), 148–9.
Walsh, David (1983), *The Mysticism of Inner Worldly Fulfilment: A Study of Jacob Boehme*, Gainsville, FL: University Presses of Florida.
Watson, Lyall (1995), *Dark Nature: A Natural History of Evil*, London: Hodder & Stoughton.
Weeks, Andrew (1989), *Boehme: An Intellectual Biography of the Seventeenth-Century Philosopher*, Albany, NY: State University of New York Press.
Whitehead, Alfred North (1926), *Science in the Modern World*, Cambridge: Cambridge University Press.
—— (1929), *Symbolism: Its Meaning and Effect*, Cambridge: Cambridge University Press.
—— (1947), *Essays in Science and Philosophy*, New York: Philosophical Library.
—— (1958), *The Function of Reason*, Boston: Beacon Press.
—— (1967), *Adventures of Ideas*, New York: The Free Press.
—— (1968), *Modes of Thought*, New York: The Free Press.
—— (1974), *Religion in the Making*, New York: Meridian.
—— (1978), *Process and Reality: An Essay in Cosmology*, David Ray Griffin and Donald W. Sherburne (eds), New York: The Free Press.
Whitney, Barry L. (1985), *Evil and the Process God*, Toronto Studies in Theology, vol. 19, New York: The Edwin Mellen Press.
Williams, William Carlos (1969), *Selected Poems*, New York: New Directions.
Wordsworth, William (1985), *The Pedlar, Tintern Abbey, and the Two-Part Prelude*, Jonathon Wordsworth (ed.), Cambridge: Cambridge University Press.
Wright, Charles (1982), *Country Music: Selected Early Poems*, Middletown, CY: Wesleyan University Press.
Wyndham, Francis (1955), *Graham Greene*, Longmans Green.

Index

Aeschylus, *Prometheus Bound* 7, 103, 109
Aristotle
   on metaphor 72–3
   on propositions 72
   Rhetoric 72
art, Paul Tillich on 213–14
atheism
   and freedom 115
   and the Promethean myth 113, 123, 126
   and The Enlightenment 112

Bachelard, Gaston, *Poetics of Space* 217
becoming
   poem about 232–46
     composition 229–31
   and process thought 138–9, 166
   and reading 15
Being, *see Dasein*
Berdyaev, Nicholas 191, 192, 193
Bergson, Henri
   Denise Levertov, influence on 208–12
   influence 3, 165
   on the intellect 196–7
   on intuition 198
   on life 2, 197–8
   on memory 209–10
   Nikos Kazantzakis, influence on 8, 174–5, 176–7
   on the past 209
   on perception 209, 211
   Shiv Kumar on 208
   works
     Creative Evolution 208, 219, 221
     Matter and Memory 209, 211, 220
     The Two Sources of Morality and Religion 207
Bertalanffy, Ludwig von, and systems theory 37
Bible, The, as text in process 26
Bien, Peter A., *Kazantzakis: Politics of the Spirit* 175
Blake, William

All Religions are One 201
   Jacob Boehme, influence of 198–9
   The Marriage of Heaven and Hell 198–9
blood, images of, in *Macbeth* 141
Bly, Robert
   American Poetry: Wildness and Domesticity 215, 216
   on Denise Levertov 215–17
Boehme, Jacob 8
   Friedrich Schelling, influence on 194–6
   on God 193–4, 200–1
   influence 191, 194, 201–2
   Samuel Taylor Coleridge, influence on 199
   and the *Ungrund* 193
   William Blake, influence on 198–9
   William Wordsworth, influence on 199–200

Camus, Albert, on God 119
causation, Whitehead on 51
Center for Process Studies 1
Centre, The, Derrida on 34–8
Chardin, Pierre Teilhard de 3, 4
   Graham Greene, influence on 7–8, 157, 167–8
   process theology of 165–8
   works
     Hymn of the Universe 165, 166
     Le Milieu Divin 165
     The Future of Man 165, 166
     The Phenomenon of Man 165
Coleridge, Samuel Taylor 136
   Friedrich Schelling, influence of 196
   Jacob Boehme, influence of 199
   Kubla Khan 199, 201
creativity
   Charles Hartshorne on 84
   nature of 85
Culler, Jonathan 217
Cusa, Nicholas of, *De Visione Dei* 199

Dannhauser, Johann Conrad, *Hermeneutica sacra* 63
Dante, *Divine Comedy* 107
Dasein, Heidegger on 17–18, 65, 66
Davie, Donald, *The New Oxford Book of Christian Verse* 213
death, Nikos Kazantzakis on 187–8
Deleuze, Gilles 209, 211
Derrida, Jacques 5
   on the Centre 34–8
   on *différence* 35–6, 38
   on language 35
   on text 44 n.35
determinism
   Charles Hartshorne on 4
   see also freedom
Dichtung, Heidegger on 19
différence, Derrida on 35–6, 38
Dillard, Annie, *For the Time Being* 4
Dilthey, Wilhelm
   Aufbau der geschichtlichen Welt 63–4
   on hermeneutics 63
   on natural and human sciences 63–4
   on nature 64, 66
   and Whitehead, compared 68
   Whitehead on 67
Durán, Leopoldo, Father 163–4

Enlightenment, The, and atheism 112
entities, Whitehead on 41–2, 67, 122
equivocity, and *Macbeth* 139–40, 151
essentialism, Whitehead on 30–3
evil
   Charles Hartshorne on 122
   evidence for 79
   and good 160–1
   Graham Greene on 165
   and *Macbeth* 136–8, 153
   Nietzsche on 145–6
   problem of 7, 79, 110–11, 135
   roots of 84
   and temptation 142
   and theodicy 110–11, 173
experience
   and literature 53
   Whitehead on 50–1, 52, 69
expression, Whitehead on 69

Faustian myth 112
Feuerbach, Ludwig
   The Essence of Christianity 118
   Thoughts on Death and Immortality 118
Finnegans Wake 5
   reader-response 24
   and reading 20–6
free verse 216
freedom
   and atheism 115
   and God 114–15, 117, 122–3, 174
   and Prometheus 112
   Sartre on 119
   see also determinism
Freud, Sigmund
   on God 119
   Hans Küng on 119
   on Prometheus 119

Gadamer, Hans-Georg
   on hermeneutics 68
   Literature and Philosophy in Dialogue 49
'Gaia' hypothesis 97
Genesis, and Prometheus 105–6
God
   in Abrahamic religions 173
   Camus on 119
   Charles Hartshorne on 79–80, 85
   and freedom 114–15, 117, 122–3, 174
   Freud on 119
   Friedrich Schelling on 195–6
   in Greek thought 7
   human defiance of 106
   images of 81, 97, 108–9, 113–14, 118, 120, 160
   Jacob Boehme on 193–4, 200–1
   Jung on 119
   as the Muse 73
   nature of 40, 85, 111
   Nikos Kazantzakis on 181–4
   in the Old Testament 106
   persuasive power of 88–90, 97, 102 n.56 123–4, 126–7
   in process theology 119–23, 125–7, 157, 161–2
   revelations of 107
   and suffering 85, 94–6, 98–9
   and theology 115–17
   Whitehead on 116
Goethe, Johann Wolfgang von
   on poetry 53
   'Prometheus' 117
good, and evil 160–1

Greeks, the, and the Promethean myth 111
Greene, Graham 158
  on evil 165
  on the novel 164
  Teilhard de Chardin, influence of 7–8, 157, 167–8
  works
    A Burnt-Out Case 3–4
    A Sort of Life 167
    The Honorary Consul 7, 157, 159–62
Gross, Harvey 212

Harkness, Georgia, 'God Suffers' 2
Hartshorne, Charles
  on creativity 84
  on determinism 4
  on divine power 123–4
  on evil 122
  on God 79–80, 85
  on the soul 98
Heidegger, Martin 5
  on *Dasein* 17–18, 65, 66
  on *Dichtung* 19
  on hermeneutics 65–6
  on language 18–19, 49
  on poets 48–9
  Sein und Zeit 18, 49, 65
  on truth 65, 71
hermeneutics
  Hans-Georg Gadamer on 68
  Heidegger on 65–6
  meaning 63
  Nietzsche on 65
  Whitehead on 67, 68–71, 73
  Wilhelm Dilthey on 63
Hesiod
  Theogony 103, 104
  Works and Days 103
history, Nikos Kazantzakis on 180–1
horror, and *Macbeth* 150
Hulme, T.E. 211

intellect, Henri Bergson on 196–7
intuition, Henri Bergson on 198
Iser, Wolfgang 5
  on reading 14, 16–17, 24

James, William, on surrender 87
Job, suffering 106–7, 109–10
Johnson, A.H. 39, 40
Johnson, Christopher 36, 37

Joyce, James, *Finnegans Wake* 5, 20–6
Jung, Carl
  Answer to Job 119
  on God 119

Kant, Immanuel, *Critique of Pure Reason* 63
Kazantzakis, Nikos
  beliefs 185–8
  on death 187–8
  on God 181–4
  Henri Bergson, influence of 8, 174–5, 176–7
  on history 180–1
  life 174–5
  and mysticism 183–4
  and transubstantiation 179–80
  works
    Freedom or Death 174, 187, 188
    Report to Greco 175, 178, 184, 188
    Saint Francis 175
    Serpent and Lily 174
    The Fratricides 175
    The Greek Passion 175
    The Last Temptation of Christ 173–4, 184
    The Odyssey: A Modern Sequel 175, 181
    The Saviors of God: Spiritual Exercises 3, 175, 181
    Zorba the Greek 175, 183
knowledge
  empirical 113
  forbidden
    and Adam 107
    biblical sources 107–8
    and Dante 107
    and Job 106–7
    and Prometheus 105
  scientific
    as forbidden knowledge 108
    Nicholas Rescher on 108
Kumar, Shiv, on Henri Bergson 208
Küng, Hans, on Freud 119

Lacouture, Jean, *Jesuits: A Multibiography* 167
language
  Derrida on 35
  Heidegger on 18–19
  and regeneration 25
Lao Tzu, on surrender 88

Latin America, social change 158
Lawrence, D.H., *Lady Chatterley's Lover* 2
Levertov, Denise
  Henri Bergson, influence of 208–12
  influences 213, 215
  on pilgrimage 214–15
  poems
    'A Time Past', analysis 210–12
    'Midsummer Eve' 221
    'Pentimento' 221–2
    'Poetics of Faith' 216–17
    'Rage and Relenting' 218–19
    'The 6:30 Bus, Late May' 219–20
    'The Mountain Assailed' 221
  poetic development 212–14
  poetics 215–18
  and process thought 208–9, 222–3
  Robert Bly on 215–17
  William Carlos Williams, influence of 207, 208, 213, 217
  works
    New & Selected Essays 212
    O Taste and See 207
    Oblique Prayers 8, 207
    Overland to the Islands 209
    Sands of the Well 218
liberation theology
  Father Camilo Torres on 158
  meaning 169 n.9
life
  Bergson on 2, 197–8
  nature of 97–8
literature
  and experience 53
  and philosophy 55
  and process thought 56–7, 191
  Whitehead on 52–3, 56
Lodge, David, *Paradise News* 1

Macbeth (Shakespeare) 7
  blood images in 141
  and equivocity 139–40, 151
  and evil 136–8, 153
  and horror 150
  and pity 150–2
  and power 146–7
  and sleep 152
  and temptation 134, 142–5
  and time 148–9
Marx, Karl, on Prometheus 118
meaning, and text 13–14

memory, Henri Bergson on 209–10
metaphor, Aristotle on 72–3
Milton, John, *Paradise Lost* 106, 107
mind and matter, and process thought 122
Murdoch, Iris, on literature and experience 53
Muse, The, God as 73
mysticism, and Nikos Kazantzakis 183–4

nature, Wilhelm Dilthey on 64, 66
Nietzsche, Friedrich
  on evil 145–6
  on hermeneutics 65
  on Prometheus 118–19
  works
    Beyond good and Evil 118
    The AntiChrist 118
    The Birth of Tragedy 118, 145
    The Gay Science 65, 118
    Twilight of the Gods 118
non-doing *see* surrender
novel, the, Graham Greene on 164

Old Testament, The, God in 106

Pandora's box 104
panentheism, meaning 98
Paradise Lost (Milton) 107
  and Prometheus 106
past, the, Henri Bergson on 209
perception, Henri Bergson on 209, 211
phenomenology, and reading 14
philosophy
  and literature 55
  and poetry 48–9
  and suffering 92–3
  and theology, comparison 124–5
  Whitehead on 55–6
pilgrimage, Denise Levertov on 214–15
pity, and *Macbeth* 150–2
Plantinga, Alvin 94
Plato
  on poets 48, 49
  Whitehead on 30
poetics, of Denise Levertov 215–18
poetry
  Goethe on 53
  and philosophy 48–9
poets
  Heidegger on 48–9
  Plato on 48, 49

postmodernism
  constructive 80
  deconstructive 80
  and reading 13, 15
Pound, Ezra, 'An Object' 217
power, and *Macbeth* 146–7
praemotio, meaning 73, 75 n.64
praxis
  application 95–6
  meaning 95
problem-solving, methodology 91–2
process, reading as 14–15, 16
process theology
  and God 119–23, 125–7, 157, 161–2
  and Pierre Teilhard de Chardin 165–8
  and *The Honorary Consul* 157, 159–65
  and transubstantiation 178–80
process thought
  application 93–4
  and becoming 138–9, 166
  and Denise Levertov 208–9, 222–3
  and literature 56–7, 191
  methodology 56
  and mind and matter 122
  poem demonstrating 231–56
  and reality 48
  value 8–9, 47
  and Whitehead 16, 191–3
Prometheus
  as creator 104
  and forbidden knowledge 105
  and freedom 112
  Freud on 119
  and Genesis 105–6
  in literature 117–18
  Marx on 118
  myth of
    and atheism 113, 123, 126
    and the Greeks 111
    influence 103–4
    and the Romans 111
  Nietzsche on 118–19
  and *Paradise Lost* 106
  treatment by Zeus 109
propositions
  Aristotle on 72
  Whitehead on 72

reader, and text 17, 19
reader-response
  and *Finnegans Wake* 24
  meaning 5
  and reading 14–15
reading
  and becoming 15
  and *Finnegans Wake* 20–6
  phenomenology of 14
  and postmodernism 13, 15
  as process 14–15, 16
  and reader-response 14–15
  theory of 20
  Wolfgang Iser on 14, 16–17, 24
reality, and process thought 48
reason
  distrust of 80
  recovery of 80–1
  Whitehead on 54
regeneration, and language 25
Rescher, Nicholas, on scientific knowledge 108
Romans, The, and the Promethean myth 111

Sartre, Jean-Paul, on freedom 119
Schelling, Friedrich 192–3
  on God 195–6
  Jacob Boehme, influence of 194–6
  Samuel Taylor Coleridge, influence on 196
sciences, natural and human
  Whitehead on 66
  Wilhelm Dilthey on 63–4
sensationalism, Whitehead on 69
Shaw, Bernard, *Man and Superman* 3
Shelley, Percy Bysshe
  Prometheus Unbound 118
  Queen Mab 118
Sherburne, Donald 39, 40
Sia, M.S.
  From Suffering to God... 6, 79, 81–2, 95
    analysis 90–4
  The Fountain Arethuse 6, 79, 95
    analysis 82–90
sleep, and *Macbeth* 152
societies, Whitehead on 39–40
soul, the, Charles Hartshorne on 98
Staten, Henry 34, 37
suffering
  and God 85, 94–6, 98–9
  and philosophy 92–3
surrender
  Lao Tzu on 88
  meaning 87–9, 101 n.34

in Taoism 88
   William James on 87
symbolic reference, Whitehead on 51–2
systems theory 36–7
   and Ludwig von Bertalanffy 37

Taoism, and surrender 88
temptation
   and evil 142
   and *Macbeth* 134, 142–5
text
   Derrida on 44 n.35
   and meaning 13–14
   meaning 27 n.19
   and reader 17, 19
   Whitehead on 69–70
The Honorary Consul, process theology in 157, 159–65
theodicy
   and evil 110–11, 173
   meaning 94, 97, 127 n.3
theology
   and God 115–17
   and philosophy, comparison 124–5
thinking, Whitehead on 50
Thiselton, Anthony 14
Tillich, Paul 194
   on art 213–14
time, and *Macbeth* 148–9
Torres, Camilo, Father, on liberation theology 158
transubstantiation
   and Nikos Kazantzakis 179–80
   and process theology 178–80
truth
   Heidegger on 65, 71
   Whitehead on 71

Ungrund, Jacob Boehme on 193

Voltaire, *Pandore* 112–13
Vorgriff 18
Vorhabe 18
Vorsicht 18

Whitehead, Alfred North 2, 5, 6
   on causation 51
   on entities 41–2, 67, 122
   on essentialism 30–3
   on experience 50–1, 52, 69
   on expression 69
   on God 116
   on hermeneutics 67, 68–71, 73
   on human and natural sciences 66
   on literature 52–3, 56
   on philosophy 55–6
   on philosophy and poetry 48
   on Plato 30
   and process thought 16, 191–3
   propositions, theory of 72
   on reason 54
   on sensationalism 69
   on societies 39–40
   on symbolic reference 51–2
   on text 69–70
   on thinking 50
   on truth 71
   on Wilhelm Dilthey 67
   and Wilhelm Dilthey, compared 68
   on Wordsworth 53
   works
      Adventures of Ideas 41, 48, 69
      Modes of Thought 48, 68
      Process and Reality 15–17, 31, 41, 67, 122, 229
Williams, William Carlos 8
   'Between Walls' 212
   Denise Levertov, influence on 207, 208, 213, 217
Wordsworth, William
   Jacob Boehme, influence of 199–200
   The Prelude 199–200
   Whitehead on 53
Wright, Charles 214
   China Trace 213

Yeats, W.B. 54

Zeus, Prometheus, treatment of 109

For Product Safety Concerns and Information please contact our EU representative GPSR@taylorandfrancis.com
Taylor & Francis Verlag GmbH, Kaufingerstraße 24, 80331 München, Germany

www.ingramcontent.com/pod-product-compliance
Lightning Source LLC
Chambersburg PA
CBHW071814300426
44116CB00009B/1307